Praise for *How We Missed the Story*

"Roy Gutman, a tireless reporter, has written a deeply researched and fascinating account of the various U.S. foreign policy failures that helped account for the rise of the Taliban and al Qaeda in Afghanistan before the 9/11 attacks. Gutman also explains how so many institutions in the United States, from the media to the national security establishment, largely missed what would turn out to be one of the most important stories of our time."

—Peter Bergen, author of *Holy War, Inc.* and *The Osama bin Laden I Know*

"In a detailed account and analysis of Afghanistan events after the Soviet military left in 1989, Roy Gutman shows how the world's abandonment of interest in the country led not only to horrors there but also to the spread of terrorism worldwide. His book provides graphic and valuable background to today's problems— and a warning of tomorrow's dangers from ignoring such troubled areas."

—Henry Bradsher, award-winning journalist and author of *Afghanistan and the Soviet Union* and *Afghan Communism and Soviet Intervention*

"This well-written, on-the-mark book is an informative and entertaining read. No other study that examines the events leading up to 9/11 is as persuasive in placing the blame where it belongs—on the failure of three successive U.S. presidents to provide the foreign policy leadership and direction needed to address the politics, philosophy, and disposition to violence of Islamist extremism."

—Thomas E. Gouttierre, Dean, International Studies and Programs, University of Nebraska, Omaha

"In the early 1990s, the United States turned a blind eye to the civil strife in Afghanistan. In How We Missed the Story, *Roy Gutman traces U.S. inaction amid civil war, the Taliban's ascension, and Osama bin Laden's rise in riveting detail. To truly understand and combat the threat we face, Gutman's exploration of missed opportunities and lessons learned is essential reading."*

—Lee H. Hamilton, president and director, Woodrow Wilson International Center for Scholars, cochair of the Iraq Study Group, and vice-chair of the 9/11 Commission

"Roy Gutman has succeeded admirably in exposing the missed opportunities and serious errors of U.S. policymakers that led them to misjudge the threat that became all too real on September 11, 2001. Writing in a highly informative and readable style, he explores many of the intelligence failures and policy predispositions that are not so clearly or so thoroughly examined elsewhere. Additionally, his extensive and well-chosen interviews offer new insights and convey scholarly objectivity."

—Marvin Weinbaum, Middle East Institute

How We Missed the Story

How We Missed the Story

Osama bin Laden, the Taliban,
and the Hijacking of Afghanistan

Roy Gutman

UNITED STATES INSTITUTE OF PEACE
Washington, D.C.

UNITED STATES INSTITUTE OF PEACE
1200 17th Street NW, Suite 200
Washington, DC 20036-3011
www.usip.org

First published 2008

Printed in the United States of America

The paper used in this publication meets the minimum requirements of American National Standards for Information Science—Permanence of Paper for Printed Library Materials, ANSI Z39.48-1984.

Library of Congress Cataloging-in-Publication Data

Gutman, Roy.
    How we missed the story : Osama bin Laden, the Taliban, and the hijacking
of Afghanistan / Roy Gutman. — 1st ed.
        p. cm.
    Includes bibliographical references and index.
    ISBN 978-1-60127-024-5 (hardcover : alk. paper)
    1. United States—Foreign relations—Afghanistan. 2. Afghanistan—
Foreign relations—United States. 3. United States—Foreign relations—1989-
4. Afghanistan—History—1989-2001. 5. Masoud, Ahmadshoh, 1953-2001.
6. Bin Laden, Osama, 1957- 7. Taliban. 8. September 11 Terrorist Attacks,
2001. 9. Terrorism—Government policy—United States. I. Title.
    E183.8.A3G88 2008
    327.730581—dc22
                                                                2007032944

To the memory of Prince Sadruddin Aga Khan,
who spoke up for those who had no voice:
the refugees, the displaced,
and the victims of war and war crimes

Contents

Foreword

Journalism, as former *Washington Post* editor Phil Graham famously put it, is best considered "a first rough draft of history." That is, despite journalism's noble ideals, even the best journalism tells only part of any given story. The true scope, scale, and significance of even a major event can only be understood with a certain distance provided by time and context. But as we are learning about the origins and impact of the surprise attacks of September 11, 2001, sometimes a story of profound import has neither been gotten first nor gotten right: sometimes the story simply has not been gotten.

How We Missed the Story: Osama bin Laden, the Taliban, and the Hijacking of Afghanistan represents one veteran journalist's attempt to ensure that the fundamental story behind 9/11 is not only told but is told right. Winner of the Pulitzer Prize for his reporting on Serb atrocities in Bosnia-Herzegovina, Roy Gutman—a senior fellow at the Institute in 2003-04—focuses here principally on events in Afghanistan in the 1990s. Drawing on field research and numerous interviews with key individuals both in the United States and abroad, he advances a narrative that reveals the inner workings of U.S. foreign policymaking, the internal debates among key actors in and around Afghanistan during the 1990s, and the media's lapses in coverage of Afghanistan during that period that might have put that situation higher up on our foreign policy agenda. His analysis highlights key strategic mistakes made by the West: first in allowing the Taliban to fill the power vacuum left in the wake of the Soviet withdrawal in 1989; and then, with the emergence of Osama bin Laden, in leaving strategic policies in the hands of counterterrorism experts rather than political and diplomatic officials.

It is essential that this history be closely examined for insights that can guide both U.S. policy and media planning in the present and future. Today, more than six years after the Taliban was forcibly removed from power, Afghanistan yet again is in danger of becoming a "hijacked" state. As the U.S. government and the UN Security Council have recently warned, the country's fragile institutions of governance face threats not only from a booming illicit drug trade but also from a resurgent al-Qaeda–influenced Taliban. The Taliban continues to receive support from al-Qaeda and also from supporters in Pakistan and from wealthy Arab financiers. Equally troubling, the Taliban and other antidemocratic forces in Afghanistan are finding sanctuary in those regions of the country, and in Pakistan's tribal areas, that lie beyond central government control. They are adopting brutal tactics honed by their insurgent brethren in Iraq, as evidenced by the dramatic number of suicide and improvised-explosive-device attacks within the country in the past two years; and they are waging a successful media campaign to build support for their cause.

To forestall a repeat of the 1990s and stave off a reinvigorated Taliban, the United States and other Western nations must renew efforts to build Afghan governance capacity at both the central government and local levels, devote much-needed resources for reconstruction and the provision of public services, and help stabilize areas of the country currently outside central government control. Collectively, such efforts can help the government in Kabul establish the legitimacy it vitally needs to gain public support.

While in a previous era distant conflicts may have been so far from American shores that they posed little threat to the United States, post-9/11 Afghanistan teaches us that in the current era of global interdependence and advanced technologies of communication, transport, and warfare, ostensibly local conflicts can harbor lethal threats to America's security. As Gutman states, "Obscure, faraway conflicts have given rise to the evils of this era."

The author's observation is relevant to a number of recent Institute publications which similarly highlight the need for the international community to pay close attention to the most far-flung conflicts. These recent volumes include *Council Unbound: The Growth of UN Decision Making on Conflict and Postconflict Issues after the Cold War,* by Michael J. Matheson; *Twenty-First-Century Peace Operations,* edited by William J. Durch; *Taming Intractable Conflicts: Mediation in the Hardest Cases,* by Chester Crocker, Fen Osler Hampson, and Pamela Aall; *Preventing Violent Conflict: A Strategy for Preventive Diplomacy,* by Michael Lund; *Building Peace: Sustainable Reconciliation in Divided Societies,* by John Paul Lederach; and *Engaging Eurasia's Separatist States: Unresolved Conflict and De Facto States,* by Dov Lynch.

In short, *How We Missed the Story* serves not only as a "first draft" of the pre-9/11 Afghanistan story but also as a natural complement to a number of volumes within the Institute's publication catalog. It also informs the applied programs of conflict management of the Institute's Afghanistan Working Group and activities in Iraq. Sure to attract a wide audience and to occupy a prominent place among the Institute's publications relevant to the role of media in conflict, *How We Missed the Story* makes an original, fascinating, and insightful contribution to the policy, academic, and public debate over how and why the Afghanistan story was missed in the leadup to 9/11. It also highlights the need for the West to get Afghanistan's present story right.

Richard H. Solomon
President
United States Institute of Peace

Preface

Almost everyone knows where he or she was on the morning of September 11, 2001. I was in the basement pressroom of a downtown hotel in Lima, Peru, waiting for U.S. secretary of state Colin Powell to emerge from talks. It was beyond any of us reporters who were accompanying him to assimilate the massive crime we watched unfold on the small screen. But no one was in any doubt where the attack had originated. "You had better send someone to Afghanistan," I said on the phone to my foreign editor. Flying into Andrews Air Force Base that evening, we could see the smoke rising miles away from the fire at the Pentagon.

The question gnawed at me: How did Osama bin Laden get the sanctuary to launch such an attack? The answer had to lie in politics, Afghan local politics. A few weeks later, Zalmay Khalilzad, the Afghan-born South Asia specialist on the Bush National Security Council, gave voice to my gut instinct. Speaking before a Washington think tank, he said bin Laden, a terrorist, had in effect "hijacked" a state. But that raised other questions: When did it happen? Was the U.S. government aware? Did they tell anyone? It would have made quite a headline; why had no reporter broken the story? I also felt culpable: Though I had never covered South Asia from the field, I had focused on so-called "small wars" throughout my reporting career. In the 1980s, I kept close tabs from a great distance on the epic struggle by Afghans to oust Soviet occupiers, and I wrote a book about the wars in Nicaragua and El Salvador. In the 1990s, I covered the wars in the Balkans and then coedited *Crimes of War*, a book whose aim was to put a spotlight on obscure faraway conflicts where war crimes usually occur. How had I missed the cues?

With the help of Afghanistan experts, some of whom I had known since the Soviet-Afghan war, I developed a working theory. Bin Laden amassed power over the Taliban regime by supporting them in the civil war, which began the day they came to power in 1996 and lasted until their removal in 2001. From 1998, when bin Laden organized the deadly attacks on two U.S. embassies in East Africa, the U.S. government was fixated on bin Laden the terrorist, but bin Laden was preoccupied with building his power base and planning for more terror attacks. Bin Laden's support was in the strategic deployment of trained ground forces, which enabled the Taliban to capture territory from the renowned anti-Soviet guerrilla leader Ahmed Shah Massoud. To test the theory, I had to investigate the relationship between bin Laden and the Taliban in war. There was value in understanding what had just happened, but an explanation of Afghanistan's transformation into a sanctuary for bin Laden to attack the United States might also offer, as a postmortem, insights into why the sole world super-power has to address small wars in the twenty-first century.

In the days after 9/11, politicians were scrambling to find their equi-librium; the Defense Department was at sea, lacking even a contingency plan for intervention; the CIA had the only real contact with the only anti-Taliban force inside Afghanistan; the United Front was leaderless since Massoud's assassination just two days before 9/11; and the media, knocked off balance by the attack, was chasing events.

I took my proposal to the United States Institute of Peace, one of the capital's premier think tanks, and had the luck to be named a Jennings Randolph fellow starting in October 2002. I began by researching the crimes as well as the strategic turning points of the Afghan civil war. Crimes in war, I knew from the Balkans, was one way a journalist could interest the public in a seemingly obscure conflict. It also stood to reason that the side bin Laden attached himself to saw no obligation to protect civilians in conflict. My first finding was that the research was going to be some task. There had been almost no media reporting of the internal conflict, modest attention to the world's biggest humanitarian crisis, with four million refugees, and only a sporadic focus on bin Laden's fire-breathing threats from his Afghan base. Next I called upon the humanitarian aid organiza-tions for which I had come to respect in reporting the Balkan wars: the International Committee of the Red Cross, the UN High Commissions for Refugees and Human Rights, and Médecins Sans Frontières to obtain their accounts of the internal conflict. No one in Geneva was more encouraging than Prince Sadruddin Aga Khan, a former UN high com-missioner for refugees and top UN representative in Afghanistan after the Soviet troop withdrawal, whose passionate concern and behind-the-scenes activism made a crucial, if unsung, difference during the Bosnia conflict. He urged me on with the project and suggested sources I would not have thought of; his untimely death in May 2003 robbed the world of one of its greatest humanitarian voices. In Pakistan, I pieced together a picture of that country's deep involvement in Afghanistan but found that nearly everyone, apart from a few journalists, claimed ignorance of the role bin Laden played in Afghan internal affairs. I spent about a month in Afghanistan and almost as much time in Pakistan, and I then returned to both countries again before beginning the final phase of research—approaching U.S. policymakers.

At the end of the day I concluded that Zal Khalilzad had stated a ground truth: A nonstate actor had hijacked a state. A number of key fig-ures in the Clinton administration had reached that very judgment by early 1999, but they did not made it public at the time and did not press it effectively upon those at the top of the administration. No doubt the White House did not want to hear the news that bin Laden and the Tal-iban were inseparable, for the aim of U.S. diplomacy was to secure his extradition. Successive administrations also were not interested in the political dimension of the saga. They preferred to view bin Laden as a lone terrorist to be extradited or assassinated, rather than as a political player who had planted deep cultural roots and created a wide political following. Washington's narrow focus precluded developing an overall strategy, as did the aversion prior to 9/11 to name a special envoy responsible only for Afghanistan. In fairness, it must also be noted: neither the experts inside the administration, the overseers on Capitol Hill, the watchdogs of the media, nor indeed the smart minds in think tanks around Washington figured out a way to challenge and change this state of affairs, not even Zal Khalilzad.

Could the media have gotten the story? Certainly not if reporters were not on the scene. There is no substitute for independent journalists going into the field and covering small wars. Without a media-trained spotlight on those places government would prefer to ignore, who will get public attention and focus the energies of government?

This one we missed.

Acknowledgments

This book would not have been possible but for the generous support of the United States Institute of Peace from conception to publication. I happen to have been in the Capitol the day Sen. Spark Matsunaga of Hawaii announced passage of the bill that he and Sen. Jennings Randolph introduced to set up the Institute. During the 1990s and the four Balkan wars, I was frequently in touch with experts at the Institute and its then executive director, Harriet Hentges, who were genuinely interested in developing an independent perspective about the facts on the ground. One of my best State Department sources on the region, fellow Haverford College alumnus Dan Serwer, moved to the Institute in 1998. I knew Richard Solomon, the current Institute president and a former assistant secretary of state, as one of the city's leading experts on Asian issues. Joe Klaits, then director of the Jennings Randolph fellowship program, supported the project from my application to the completion of the book, and John Crist, the senior program officer, found every possible resource to allow me to do it right. Kay Hechler devoted her prodigious energies to promoting the book. The Institute's fellows program is outstanding, and it is a very lucky thing that one place is reserved for a journalist. My editors at the United States Institute of Peace Press, Nigel Quinney and later Kurt Volkan, were highly professional, efficient, and always supportive. I also thank copyeditor Roz Rosenberg for sorting out the footnotes and inconsistent spellings. Patti Taft, a very capable researcher, dug out every known bit of journalism on the period I was researching.

Among those who suggested sources were Mohamad Bazzi, *Newsday's* exceptional Middle East correspondent at the time, Ed Gargan, then *Newsday's* China hand, Mark Hosenball and Owen Matthews of *Newsweek,* and especially Ron Moreau, a cool head in the hottest of places, at the time *Newsweek* Islamabad bureau chief. Kashi Zaman, then with the *Newsweek* Pakistan bureau, pulled out every stop to be of help. Five reporters provided vital assistance in my research: Anthony Davis, the single most careful chronicler of the internal Afghan war, who gave me a strong critique of the chapter on Massoud; Stefan Smith, AFP's man in Kabul during the first part of the Taliban reign, who brought alive the reality of reporting in near Stalinist conditions; Hamid Mir, the independent minded print and television journalist in Islamabad, who is also bin Laden's biographer; Rahimullah Yusoufzai, the veteran reporter for the *News* and the BBC in Peshawar; and Sami Yousafzai (no relation) of *Newsweek,* one of the most intrepid reporters I have known. Asad Hayauddin, then the Pakistan embassy press officer in Washington, and Gen. Jehangir Karamat, the retired chief of staff, steered me toward the best sources in Pakistan.

On the ground in Pakistan, journalist Ahmed Mukhtar opened the doors to all the leading experts, including what may be the first U.S. reporter's interview with "Col. Imam," a key figure in Pakistan's activities in Afghanistan; and in Kabul, fixer-interpreter Sayed Wadood not only did his utmost to get me to the people I needed to meet but was a source of continuing encouragement long after I had left Kabul. Haron Amin, then of the Afghan embassy in Washington, was indispensable in providing introductions in Kabul. I also thank Jeff Bartholet, then Newsweek foreign editor, for his support as I got under way; Richard Sambrook of the BBC, for generously allowing me to look through archives of BBC broadcasts; attorney Joshua Dratel, for providing the material on the U.S. vs. bin Laden case in New York; Haroon Azizpour of Afgha.com, for guiding me to on-line information troves I could not otherwise have located; Rupert Colville of UNHCR, for opening his files and giving every assistance on untangling the events in Mazar-i-Sharif of August 1998; Sarah Horner, for un-earthing her notes on the coverage of that event; Zahid Hussain, a veteran reporter in Islamabad; Hamid Wardak, a Georgetown University student who did his own on-the-ground investigations of the Taliban; Suzanne Bilello of UNESCO, for guiding me to sources on the destruction of the Bamiyan Buddhas; and Tom Blanton, for throwing open the stacks of declassified documents at the National Security Archive.

Among the former U.S. officials who generously gave their time to answering my questions were former national security adviser Sandy Berger, secretary of state Madeleine Albright, assistant secretaries Rick Inderfurth and Robin Raphel, and National Security Council senior director Bruce Riedel.

Those who critiqued the book included Wolfgang Hauptmann, my esteemed German colleague; Henry Bradsher, one of the great American Afghanistan experts; Sarah Chayes, the gutsy former NPR radio journalist who moved to Kandahar and set up a small organization to help local women; my cousin in Austin, Bernard Snyder, an astute student of history; AFP reporter Stefan Smith; Peter Bergen, who defined the bin Laden story with his book, *Holy War, Inc.*; and Marvin Weinbaum, one of the leading analysts of South Asia. I would also like to thank William Maley of the Asia-Pacific College of Diplomacy in Canberra, whose work on the Taliban is second to none, for his support at several stages; and Tom Gouttierre of the University of Nebraska at Omaha, a pioneer of Afghan studies in the United States, for his guidance at critical moments.

For any errors, I assume sole responsibility.

Due to the paucity of media coverage, I relied to an extent way beyond my expectations on UN reports and the insights of UN personnel who served in Afghanistan during the Taliban era. My special thanks to Michael Semple, who helped save the people of Hazarajat during the worst days of the Taliban and who shared his unique insights into the nature of the regime and of bin Laden; and to Mervyn Patterson and Eckhard Schiewek, who are examples of the difference determined individuals can make in monitoring human rights violations and of the UN system at its very best.

Last I thank my wife, Betsy, who showed not only forbearance but encouragement at every stage, despite the vicissitudes of job and house moves and the sacrifice of weekends, evenings, and holidays. To her I shall be forever grateful.

A Note on Styles

In the interest of transparency, I used footnotes throughout; both in my original research and in drawing on the work of others, I tried wherever possible to corroborate every fact of significance.

Transliteration of names and places from the two languages of Afghanistan, Dari and Pashtu, varies from expert to expert, and my rule of thumb was to adopt what seemed to be the most common usage. I refer to the ever-shifting military coalition led by Ahmed Shah Massoud after his ouster from Kabul by the name they preferred, the United Front, shorthand for the National Islamic United Front for the Salvation of Afghanistan, rather than the name widely used by U.S. and Pakistani officials, the Northern Alliance.

How We Missed
the Story

Introduction
The Death of Foreign Policy?

Much has been written about the attacks of September 11, 2001, but a simple question remains largely unanswered six years later: why were two successive U.S. administrations unable to head off the assault?

Two presidents have allowed the blame for the lack of preparedness to fall on intelligence and law enforcement agencies. America's intelligence services, in fact, provided ample and repeated alarms to the country's policymakers, detailing Osama bin Laden's goals and the methods he intended to use against U.S. citizens and property. It is true that the Central Intelligence Agency (CIA) failed to connect the dots and provide tactical warning of the exact attack, but that task—given the openness of American society and the conspiratorial operation of bin Laden's al Qaeda cells in the United States—may have been beyond the capacity of any intelligence agency anywhere. The Federal Bureau of Investigation's (FBI's) dysfunction is a different story—the result of a long-term failure to adapt to the computer age, to improve communications up and down the chain of command, and to extend its list of threats to include foreign terrorism against American targets. Still, law enforcement was in no position to go to the source of the problem. As an FBI agent told the Joint Congressional Inquiry in December 2002, this was "like telling the FBI after Pearl Harbor, '[G]o to Tokyo and arrest the emperor.'" It was beyond the FBI because the U.S. attorney's office in the Southern District of New York "doesn't have any cruise missiles."[1]

The strategic failure was in the field of U.S. foreign policy, which is the responsibility of the president himself. Both Bill Clinton and George W. Bush failed to see bin Laden as a political challenge. The rise of jihadis eager to sacrifice their lives was at its heart a political phenomenon that originated in a little-known corner of South Asia, in an arid, poor, landlocked border state where more than one empire has come to grief. Bin Laden's charismatic political leadership was born during the jihad, or holy war, against Russian occupiers of Afghanistan in the 1980s; emerged after the Soviets withdrew in defeat in 1989; and grew as he developed ties with the Islamist Taliban movement, which took control in 1996 but found itself in a prolonged conflict against domestic opponents for the next five years. Bin Laden's ability to articulate widely shared political grievances about the closed political system in Arab states and his demagogic talent in focusing the blame on U.S. support for Arab regimes enabled him to attract thousands of jihadis to his military training camps in Afghanistan and to disseminate his antimodernity dogma throughout the Islamic world. But both Clinton and Bush treated bin Laden as a military threat that could be eliminated through an intelligence or military operation.

Top Clinton aides acknowledge that they crafted the U.S. response to bin Laden not by examining the U.S. national interest and the facts on the ground in Afghanistan, but by making a political judgment of what course of action they thought American public opinion would bear. The president thus reduced his options to a military-style in-and-out quick fix. But even if a CIA-organized assassination or surgical military strike had come off, it would not have worked. Decapitating the movement would have left the infrastructure in place, along with a dedicated successor leadership and thousands of motivated killers.

George W. Bush had little time to grasp the threat before the 9/11 attacks; he all but ignored the explicit warnings from his predecessor about the danger and the political origins of the assault. The intervention Bush ordered after the 9/11 attacks quickly toppled the Taliban regime, but the president drew two erroneous conclusions from this: (1) that a miniscule ground deployment of U.S. forces (fewer than one hundred special operations units in northern Afghanistan) had carried off an enormous political victory, and (2) that the United States could go it alone anywhere. In fact, the top Taliban leaders, in time-honored Afghan fashion, had abandoned Kabul without a fight in the face of a stronger foe. Meanwhile, hundreds, if not thousands, of al Qaeda fighters—whose destruction or capture should have been the aim of the intervention—escaped, as did the Taliban leadership. Bush subsequently sent thousands of troops to Afghanistan to pursue al Qaeda, but he ignored the local politics that had given rise to the Taliban, and in so doing, he opened the door to a revival of a Taliban military challenge. However, the setback in Afghanistan seems modest compared with the consequences of Bush's 2003 decision to overthrow the Saddam Hussein regime in Iraq without adequate troops, plans, or preparation and with almost no examination of the politics involved.

The failure to head off the 9/11 attacks lay not only at the very top of the foreign policy pyramid but also within the bureaucracy—both at the upper level of political appointees, who have responsibility for policy decisions, and at the level of permanent and highly skilled civil servants, who toil in distant and dangerous locations. There were warning signs that a terrorist had hijacked a state; but if anyone in the foreign policy arena connected the dots and foresaw the dangers to U.S. security in a timely manner, he or she failed to sound the alarm within government, before Congress, or with the public at large.

No regime readily acknowledges error. After, and at the time of 9/11, there was no appetite at the top of government—or in the previous administration—for self-examination. The Bush White House agreed with great reluctance to the demand by families of the victims for a national commission. The resulting report provided an invaluable account of what the U.S.

government knew and how it responded. Books by several leading journalists also provided essential background. But the Bush administration had no interest in a government-wide postmortem focusing on foreign policy lapses. This postmortem is long overdue.[2]

Furthermore, those who have spent their careers carrying out U.S. foreign policy or reporting on it had cause to wonder: had foreign policy died? Successful policy is the outcome of a conscious and deliberative process that requires a solid grasp of the reality on the ground. The president orders an assessment of U.S. interests and chooses a goal that will preserve those interests. An effective approach integrates the resources and tactical capabilities of every relevant branch of government into a strategy. The strategy relies first and foremost on diplomacy, supported by intelligence and ultimately backed by military power. A statesman-president rallies bipartisan support; enlists civil society; and invites U.S. allies, friends, and even rivals to take part.

That is the paradigm. However, because of the influence the United States wields in world affairs, its ability to build coalitions, and its capacity to project and use military power, no administration has a well-thought-through policy for every corner of the world. The default policy in many places is no policy at all or "more of the same."

The most successful foreign policy in modern times was the U.S.-led defense of Western Europe during the Cold War and the smooth transition to a new order in Europe after the collapse of communism. When Saddam Hussein invaded Kuwait, George H. W. Bush built an enormous international coalition and waged a brief war that forced Saddam to withdraw and successfully caged his military ambitions. In the mid-1990s, the government's Balkans policy, led by Secretary of State Madeleine Albright and special envoy Richard Holbrooke, saved Bosnia-Herzegovina from total destruction, rescuing it from Slobodan Milosevic's depredations. Additionally, it helped oust the Serbian leader from power and send him to the Hague tribunal, where he died during his trial on charges of genocide.

No such process occurred in the U.S. government when the Taliban turned Afghanistan into a religious police state and granted sanctuary to the Saudi renegade Osama bin Laden—not even after he directly and lethally assaulted U.S. interests by organizing the bombings of two U.S. embassies in East Africa and the attack on the USS *Cole*, which killed seventeen servicemen.

As demonstrated in the following chapters, American inaction was based on a profound misconception. On the assumption that the public would not tolerate a long-term, broad-spectrum approach, the Clinton administration pursued an "Osama bin Laden" counterterrorism tactic. It hoped to end the threat through a CIA or military quick fix, instead of by crafting a foreign policy worthy of the name—one that would change the environment in Afghanistan in which bin Laden was thriving. In fact, there were many points at which two successive U.S. administrations could have shaped an outcome more favorable to U.S. interests; instead, they opted to do the absolute minimum.

During the anti-Soviet jihad, the United States was the indispensable source of political support, arms, and cash for the Afghan resistance, but Washington showed no interest in the political outcome in the event of a Soviet defeat. After Moscow's troops withdrew, the United States made only a brief effort to organize leadership among the resistance. Then, from 1992 to 1994, Washington all but abandoned the region, refusing to back a weak, pro-Western government in Afghanistan and providing mostly rhetorical support to a futile UN effort to bring about an all-party government there. From 1994 to 1996, the Clinton administration leaned toward supporting Taliban religious extremists, who were attempting to impose a primitive version of Islam on a country in chaos, but Washington then backed off. In May 1997, Washington looked on in silence as Pakistan encouraged the Taliban to conquer the north, where thousands of their ill-trained fighters found themselves in a trap and were massacred. In the mid-1990s, after long delay, the Clinton administration focused its human rights spotlight on war crimes in Bosnia and Rwanda. But when the Taliban, with bin Laden's guidance and financing, conducted its revenge match for the 1997 massacre and committed mayhem against innocent civilians in Mazar-i-Sharif in August 1998, the administration said next to nothing. After the bin Laden–directed destruction of two U.S. embassies in East Africa, which coincided with the Mazar massacre, Clinton ordered a cruise missile strike against largely empty training camps. He made no attempt to collect the facts on either massacre in Mazar-i-Sharif.

After six months of fruitless diplomatic efforts to press the Taliban into expelling bin Laden, senior U.S. officials concluded in early 1999 that bin Laden was inseparable from the Taliban regime. But those who reached this ominous assessment never shared it with the public or with Congress, and Clinton ordered ever-more pointless diplomatic exchanges. In October 2000, the president chose not to identify bin Laden as the originator of the attack on the USS *Cole*, even though his own intelligence apparatus said there was no other conclusion. And in spring and summer 2001, the Bush administration had clear and consistent strategic intelligence about an impending attack but failed to act.

The narrative that follows tracks a systemic failure involving the U.S. executive branch—policy lapses, omissions, and misjudgments—but it also examines the role and failures of the U.S. Congress, the United Nations, and the news media. Indeed, even though the U.S. government failed, journalists should also acknowledge their own negligence. News organizations are free agents, able to decide what to cover and how to cover it; but with few exceptions, journalists paid little or no heed to events inside Afghanistan after its takeover by religious extremists. It was as if reporters were following the lead of the U.S. government, which hoped the story would go away, instead of digging for their own information and using facts to define the issue. Reporters and editors seemed to accept a mindset that saw bin Laden as an exotic, faraway actor and therefore did not devote resources to uncovering his role in the creation of a global movement and a military infrastructure.

Ultimately, however, the media's failure to sound the alarm is a sad but short story—that of the watchdog that did not bark. In fact, this omission may be alert may have knocked the media off balance after 9/11 and led to the overly credulous coverage of the Bush administration's case for going to war in Iraq. As a result, the media may now be paying the price in the form of a loss of public confidence. As major American news organizations pare back or eliminate their capacity to produce strong international coverage in the face of falling circulation, advertising revenue, and share prices, and as the new media (which recycles but does not gather the news) takes the lead, editors and reporters in the so-called mainstream media should ask themselves some important questions: Whatever happened to their role and standing? Where were they when it really counted? Why were reporters not engaged in the independent investigative work that is the unique franchise of the news profession?

Just as the media has some hard questions to face, so too does the U.S. government. Perhaps its central failure was to categorize bin Laden's murderous assaults as "terrorism" and to develop only a counterterrorism policy rather than a proper foreign policy that would engage Congress, the American public, the peoples of the region, and American allies. When government believes military strikes or law enforcement can destroy a movement led by a charismatic political figure and built upon shared political grievances, it underestimates the task and gives new sustenance to the movement. Underestimating the task is the primary characteristic of this story.

1

Comrades: The End!
(1989)

Unlike America's pullout from Vietnam, with its unscripted image of local staff clinging in panic to the runners of the last helicopter, the Soviet retreat from Afghanistan had the appearance of decorum. Banners proclaiming "Glory to the Soldiers of the Fatherland" and "Glory to the Sons of the Motherland" were strung across the bridge between Afghanistan and the Uzbek Soviet Socialist Republic. Music blared forth from loudspeakers at a small reception area on the Uzbek side. At precisely five minutes to noon on February 15, 1989, Gen. Boris Gromov drove the last armored personnel carrier out of Afghanistan onto the bridge crossing the Oxus River and climbed out. Maksim Gromov, a military cadet, approached with a bouquet of carnations, and father and son walked arm-in-arm the last hundred yards back into the Soviet Union.

The event was staged for the media; in fact, Gromov had spent the previous night at a hotel in Termez on the Soviet side of the river.* But no performance or props could conceal the humiliation of this moment. It was over the same "Friendship Bridge" that Soviet tanks had poured nine years and fifty days earlier to begin the most pointless of invasions, leading to the deaths of at least a million Afghans and fifteen thousand Soviet troops. Even the aura of peace at the scene was a deception—in the course of withdrawing, Gromov's 40th Army, with the personal approval of Soviet leader Mikhail Gorbachev, had launched air and artillery attacks that devastated dozens of villages and killed hundreds of civilians. Witnesses reported Soviet tanks rolling over the dead bodies of victims. Meanwhile, Moscow's handpicked and well-armed regime remained in Kabul.[1]

Everyone knew the war had ended in debacle, yet few could have imagined the magnitude of the unraveling that was about to begin. Gromov's brief formal remarks at the time seemed perfunctory but would prove to be prophetic. The Red Army, he intoned, had "fulfilled its international-ist duty to the end." It was the end—but of much more than the "Soviet Vietnam."

---

* "Actually, I slept here last night," Gromov told a Reuters reporter as he returned to check in at his Termez hotel. "I went back over to the other side this morning for the final pullout." But the hotel staff thought he had checked out, and Gromov had to get another room. *Los Angeles Times*, February 17, 1989.

The scene in Washington on February 15, 1989, was almost as unreal. As Gromov crossed into Termez, the teletype at CIA headquarters in Langley, Virginia, clattered a two-word message from Milton Bearden, CIA station chief in Islamabad, Pakistan: "We won." That was an overstatement. Cofinanced by Saudi Arabia, organized by Pakistan, and with Muslim volunteers from the Arab world fighting alongside Afghans, this had been a proxy war. It had cost $6 billion in arms and support for what U.S. officials at the time proudly called a jihad or holy war against the Soviet Union. The fact that not a drop of American blood had been shed and that others paid much of the bill made the victory all the headier. CIA director William Webster threw a raucous party for staff and invited as guest of honor Texas congressman Charlie Wilson, the Democrat whose near-fanatical commitment to the cause generated the budgets to fuel the Afghan resistance.

With that as a start, 1989 proved to be a year of extraordinary surprises. No one could have predicted the cascade of events. The bloodletting in Afghanistan had demoralized the Red Army and weakened its standing at home. When unrest began in east Central Europe a few months later, Gorbachev refused to call out the troops, and that spelled the end for their forty-five-year occupation. In May, Hungary opened its borders to the west, and East Germans streamed out by the tens of thousands to start new lives in the West. In June, Poland acquired a new noncommunist government led by Tadeusz Mazowiecki of the Roman Catholic opposition. The Berlin Wall opened in November; a month later, Czechoslovakia ousted its hard-line Communist Party rulers. Thus, the withdrawal from Afghanistan signaled the beginning of the end of the Soviet empire and, with it, the end of the Soviet Union and of one-party Communist rule. "Comrades: The End!" was the iconic poster in Hungary during the first free elections in May 1990. The Cold War was over. Gone was the bipolar world of the previous forty years, to be replaced by a new world order with a sole superpower that would prove "indispensable," as Bill Clinton would later say, to resolving world problems.[2]

Champagne corks popped giddily throughout the West as the year's events unfolded. But not every celebration was equally auspicious. Three hundred miles southeast of the Friendship Bridge—and far from the cameras—a rather different group of foreigners met that autumn to celebrate what they considered *their* victory over Soviet Russia. They had come from around the Arab world as volunteers, and now, at the al-Farouk camp (a training facility run by Egyptians), they were being recruited to continue the jihad. "We don't want to stop the jihad even if the Russians have left Afghanistan," Abu Ayoub, an Iraqi, told the dozen or more jihadis in attendance. "We will use this group outside Afghanistan." Ayoub asked them to swear a *bayat* (loyalty oath) to him. He reported, in turn, to the "general emir," Osama bin Laden. Son of a billionaire Saudi contractor, bin Laden had recruited Arabs for the Afghan jihad, built and run training camps, and seen combat. He had established an infrastructure and a database of names, and he had developed a following throughout the Islamic world. Bin Laden and his mentor, Abdullah Azzam, a Palestinian, had formally launched the organization in Peshawar, Pakistan, a year earlier in late summer 1988. Bin Laden was not at al-Farouk camp on the day the recruiting began, according to Jamal al Fadl, a Sudanese who went on to become bin Laden's paymaster and later testified about this meeting in a New York courtroom. Ayoub and two Egyptians circulated a set of papers for everyone to sign. Those who swore *bayat* agreed to continue the jihad against other countries and to do "whatever work they ask you to." The targets had not yet been selected—that was the job of a committee of "scholars."

The group would be known as al Qaeda—translated from the Arabic variously as "the base," "the basis," and "the database"—or, alternatively, the Islamic Army. Al Qaeda was the name that stuck. Committees were set up, including a ruling *shura* (council) with members from Egypt, Iraq, Yemen, Saudi Arabia, Algeria, Oman, and Libya; a military committee to carry out training, led by two Egyptians, Abu Ubaidah al Banshiri and Abu Hafs al Masry; and a financial committee, dominated by Saudis. There was also a committee of Islamic scholars (including Saudis, Egyptians, and an Iraqi) and a media committee headed by Abu Musab, a journalist nicknamed "Reuter."

The new members, all graduates of training camps, received a first quick lesson in tradecraft for the undisclosed holy war they were soon to begin. When they traveled, they were to look like anything but the bearded Islamists they were. They were to wear Western clothes, shave their beards, carry cigarettes, use cologne, and leave all their Islamist and jihadi tracts behind. An "immigration" committee was set up to issue false passports, noms de guerre, and airline tickets.

Abu Ubaidah, whose nickname, al Banshiri, indicated that he had fought in the Panjshir Valley with legendary guerrilla leader Ahmed Shah Massoud, told the group that this was al Qaeda's first meeting. (U.S. intelligence officials believe the actual founding of al Qaeda took place a year earlier at bin Laden's Peshawar residence.) Missing from the introductory session was a statement of the targets of al Qaeda's future wrath. "In Afghanistan, everything is over," al Fadl quoted bin Laden as saying. Bin Laden's vague new aim was to remove the major Arab governments and install "Muslim governments" in their place. He aspired to create a caliphate and become the "one Muslim leader for all Muslims."[3]

The Soviet withdrawal from Afghanistan was celebrated in Pakistan as well. The man most responsible for the withdrawal, President Zia ul-Haq, was no longer on the scene, the victim of an unexplained plane crash in 1988; but others would claim the right to determine the succession to Soviet rule. In actual fact, the Soviet withdrawal was not Pakistan's victory either. True, Zia had taken enormous political risks, but he did so with enthusiastic bipartisan political backing in the United States, the financial support of Saudi Arabia, and the general approbation of the Islamic world. Pakistanis had not suffered heavy losses from on-ground fighting.

Conspicuous by their absence from the celebrations in Washington or at al-Farouk were Afghans. Under the deal negotiated through a UN mediator in the absence of Afghan representatives, Moscow's appointed communist government was to remain in Kabul under Najibullah Ahmadzai, the former intelligence chief. The mujahideen, who had fought for almost a decade, were nowhere close to taking power. This face-saving outcome for Moscow was acceptable to Washington, until it became clear that the Soviets had no intention of giving up their residual control in Kabul. As its power crumbled at home, in Europe, and in Central Asian republics such as Uzbekistan, Moscow's rivalry with Washington continued in Afghanistan. On the day Gromov crossed the Oxus, *Izvestia* reported that the Red Army had left behind military installations worth $1 billion, and TASS reported that dozens of IL-76 cargo planes were ferrying in "supplies." Moscow set up an air bridge unequaled since the 1948 Berlin blockade to prop up Najibullah. The United States, announcing a policy called "negative symmetry," stepped up its arms shipments into Pakistan until the end of 1991. It would be three years before power would change in Kabul.

The unsettled state of affairs in Afghanistan was one of the unpleasant surprises of 1989, with repercussions that would last throughout the 1990s, culminating in the attacks of September 11, 2001. U.S. officials closest to the developments (the U.S. intelligence community) had confidently predicted the quick fall of Najibullah's regime after the withdrawal of Soviet troops. In March 1988, the CIA's authoritative special national intelligence estimate stated, "We believe that the Najibullah regime will not long survive the completion of Soviet withdrawal, even with continued Soviet assistance. The regime may fall before withdrawal is complete." The estimate went on, "[D]espite infighting, we believe the resistance will retain sufficient supplies and military strength to ensure the demise of the communist government."

"It was one of the worst miscalculations that Bearden and Anderson made," said a CIA officer, referring to his colleagues Milton Bearden and Frank Anderson, head of the CIA's Afghan task force. They had predicted, "[A]s soon as the Soviets leave the country, Najibullah will collapse." They were not alone. Shortly before the last Soviet troops departed, Jon Glassman, chargé d'affaires of the U.S. embassy in Kabul, called the Kabul government "a house without girders" and predicted that it would fall to the rebels in a matter of weeks, months at the most.[4]

Yet the CIA's own analysis of the military success of the Afghan resistance against the Soviets illuminated the causes for its later political failure. "Paradoxically, some of what we might perceive to be strategic weaknesses became strengths at the operational and tactical levels," the CIA summed

up in a "lessons learned" analysis in 1989. The disunity of the Afghan resistance political leadership made it difficult to infiltrate. The disorganization
of their planning made it impossible to intercept plans, "because they simply did not exist, except for local, short-range ones." The decentralized
leadership, the dispersal into small elements, the flamboyant individual
actions, and the spontaneous operations—all made it hard for the Soviets
and the Kabul regime they installed to find large-scale targets to attack.[5]

With Washington relying on an overly optimistic intelligence assessment and Moscow determined to hang on, Soviet troop withdrawal brought
no respite in the proxy struggle between Afghan insurgents and the communist regime. In fact, it opened a second phase, in which Moscow and Washington pumped in supplies to counter each other rather than to achieve a
clear strategic goal. The conflict had uniquely Afghan characteristics, but
the questions raised had much in common with struggles the Red Army's
retreat unleashed all along the periphery of the Soviet empire: What sort
of government would replace the communist regime? Would it be nationalist or outward-looking, theocratic or secular, autocratic or democratic?

In east Central Europe, communists gave way to pro-Western democrats, many of whom had gained their political legitimacy by spending time in
jail for their beliefs. The attractions of NATO as an alliance of collective security and the European Union as a partnership for economic growth made the
decision an easy one. In south Central Europe, the regime of Slobodan Milosevic shifted from internationalist communism to Serbian nationalism, which
led straight into a decade of wars against the other Yugoslav nationalities.
Afghanistan's war, by comparison, seemed like an anachronism from the
Cold War—neither Russia nor the United States had a real stake, but each
stayed engaged chiefly to balance the other. In the absence of a strong American guiding hand, the vacuum was filled to a limited extent by the two
regional actors that had done most to facilitate the jihad: Pakistan and Saudi
Arabia. But Pakistan's unsteady civilian government and powerful military,
with close ties to radical factions in the Afghan conflict, were ill-suited to
manage anyone else's interests in Afghanistan or even to achieve its own con-
flicting aims, which centered on the delineation of borders, the repatriation of
Afghan refugees, a desire to reach out to the newly independent Central
Asian republics, and an ill-defined quest for "strategic depth" in its competition with India. Saudi diplomacy and financing had achieved a great deal in
the service of U.S. foreign policy aims in Afghanistan, but after 1989 U.S.
involvement was vastly diminished and increasingly adrift. The outcome was
a seemingly unending civil war.

Devout Rivals

Out of the cauldron of war emerged three figures who would dominate
the landscape over the next decade with rival leadership claims: Ahmed

Shah Massoud, Mullah Omar Akhund, and Osama bin Laden. All were devout Muslims, and all practiced Sunni Islam. All three had benefited from U.S. engagement during the war against the Russians, but none of them had good relations with the United States. America's indifference during the postcommunist period helped undermine Massoud but worked to the benefit of Mullah Omar and later of bin Laden.

Massoud, born in one of Afghanistan's most inaccessible valleys, was Russia's toughest foe during the jihad. He was the most open to the world, but he was never able to develop a close relationship with the U.S. government. Omar was the least educated of the three. Raised in obscurity, he lived in seclusion but stayed in power the longest—for five years. The U.S. government tried repeatedly to develop a friendly relationship with him. For bin Laden, as his star rose in Afghanistan, America's sank—he rose to prominence by deciding that his enemy was the sole remaining superpower.

Born into immense wealth on March 10, 1957, bin Laden was the most educated of the three and gave up the most when he turned against his home government and its American ally. Bin Laden's association with Afghanistan, according to his own account, began in 1980, just months after the Soviet invasion, when he traveled to Peshawar, Pakistan, to see what role he could play in the jihad. Unlike most of his twenty-four half-brothers (his father had four wives and some fifty children) who had studied abroad, Osama received his higher education in Saudi Arabia, studying economics, public administration, and engineering at King Abdul-Aziz University in Jeddah. There, two professors of Islamic studies introduced him to the Muslim Brotherhood, the anti-Western movement that attracted so many middle-class students in the Arab world. One of the professors was Muhammad Qutb, brother of a jailed Egyptian philosopher of jihad, and the other was Abdullah Azzam, who felt so strongly about the war in Afghanistan that he moved to Peshawar to set up a "service center" for Arab volunteers in the war.[6]

On that first trip to Pakistan, at age twenty-two, bin Laden met two Islamist resistance leaders, Burhanuddin Rabbani and Abdul Rasul Sayyaf; he returned home to raise money and rally support. He traveled regularly to Peshawar; in 1984, he moved there to set up Beit ul-Ansar (House of the Supporters) at about the time Azzam organized the Maktab al-Khidamat (Office of Services). Azzam published an Arabic language magazine, *al-Jihad*, and traveled through the Arab world recruiting volunteers.[7] "To spend one hour in the battle line in the cause of Allah is better than sixty years of night prayer," he preached. As many as twenty-five thousand Arabs descended on Pakistan as volunteers.[8]

As the scion of an extremely well-connected family championing a cause the Saudi royal family had also made its own, bin Laden had access to extraordinary resources, which he at first put at the service of the Afghan fighters. He could import construction equipment from his family's firm and raise enough funds to promise any fighter a $300 monthly stipend for his family. He had the means to support Azzam's guesthouses and subsidize major commanders. But he was also looking out for himself—he built one training camp exclusively for his own use. It was called al Ma-asada (the Lion's Den) and was built in Jaji, a remote border village in Paktia province; it opened in 1986.[9] It was in Jaji that bin Laden had a major combat experience in April 1987, when Soviet helicopters and bombers attacked the site of his new compound, a clinic, and an arms cache built into caves. Bin Laden recounted in one interview that he was stuck in a trench for several days amid shelling and bombing: "We could hear the enemies' footsteps. Despite the situation, I fell asleep. When I awoke the enemy had disappeared."[10]

It was at Jaji that bin Laden launched a media campaign, giving interviews and speeches and commissioning a fifty-minute video. Shown to Islamic groups around the world, the video proved to be a powerful tool for recruiting and fundraising.[11]

A portrait by an Afghan commander with the pro-Saudi mujahideen leader Sayyaf gives a flavor of bin Laden the fighter. According to this former commander, bin Laden "always enjoyed taking risks" and kept his cool. On a reconnaissance mission in Nangahar province near Jalalabad at the end of the Russian occupation, he was in a group of four Arabs and three Afghans. "We were just 400 yards away from Russian tanks," the commander said, "but he never hesitated, was never nervous. We had lost all our weapons and retreated." Bin Laden won the commander's admiration because he "never said he was a big shot, but was living and dining with us all, sitting on the floor." At the front lines, he would wear Afghan clothes and a headscarf; he would bring his own supply of water and dates (the best quality, in sealed packages). When bin Laden was not at the front, he kept a supply of pure honey and olive oil. He also brought along portable squeeze packs for warmth and shared them with others. For reading, bin Laden had books on military strategy, fighting in the mountains, and Islam. He never missed the predawn prayer.

His political interests were still unformed, but he had begun his political journey. "At first his motivation was just to give financial support," said this former commander. "He didn't have a political awareness. Slowly he changed. He wanted to become famous and popular, and in the end he sought to be both political and religious. His religious and political motivation goes in parallel." As for his international politics, "He was more anti-American than our leaders. We never heard him say anything positive about America." He was also deeply concerned about other Islamic causes, including the Arab-Israeli conflict. "He was always telling us, 'Behind every rock and mountain, there is the shadow of Palestine.' And when we beat the Russians, he said, 'We should go to Palestine.'" He talked "a lot" about jihad in Kashmir.[12]

Whatever impact bin Laden may have had on the events, the war and its outcome were a life-changing experience for him. "I have benefited so greatly from the jihad in Afghanistan that it would have been impossible for me to gain such a benefit from any other chance," he later told CNN reporters. "What we benefited from most was that the glory and myth of the superpower was destroyed, not only in my mind but also in the minds of all Muslims."[13]

All three men were charismatic, politically astute, and obstinate to a fault. All three had a loyal following. All failed to achieve their goals. Massoud had the greatest impact on his country, especially after his death, when his followers took over key positions in government after the U.S. intervention in October 2001. Mullah Omar, who could not relate to the outside world or the obligations of government, will be the most quickly forgotten. By inspiring suicide bombers to commit mass acts of terror against civilians in the name of Islam, bin Laden can be said to have changed the world the most. As they clashed or made common cause, these three men shaped Afghanistan and, with it, the world in the 1990s and well beyond.

The most cunning of the three, bin Laden, decided that he needed a bigger stage for his political aspirations. He returned to his home in Saudi Arabia in 1989, intending to make it the base for his goal of changing Arab world governments. By the end of 1990, he was moving his operations, training facilities, and personnel from Afghanistan to Sudan, which had just gained a new radical Islamist government and was eager for the presence and investment potential that bin Laden represented. That same year, bin Laden commissioned the production of an eleven-volume *Encyclopedia of the Afghan Jihad,* a self-styled guide to "sabotage and terror" that was to be used in the camps to teach future jihadis how to blow up a plane, engage an armored vehicle, or spy on a military base. Although bin Laden's own ambition was to move on in the Arab world, a host of videos and published material continued to attract young Muslims to Afghanistan long after he had gone, and bin Laden left behind institutions, infrastructure, and a loyal following to train and integrate them in his absence. He kept four guesthouses, the main function of which was to process volunteers for the training camps. Bin Laden himself had built and was in charge of one training camp near Khost, but his colleagues sent both students and teachers to a host of others, nominally under the control of Afghan jihad leaders whom he had supported during the war, among them Jalaluddin Haqqani, Abdul Rasul Sayyaf, and Gulbuddin Hekmatyar. Typical of some of the recruits was a Palestinian with a Jordanian passport who volunteered for Afghanistan in October 1990 while studying engineering in the Philippines. Mohamed Sadeek Odeh began at al-Farouk camp, proceeded through three levels of training, and swore his *bayat* to bin Laden in March 1992. He would remain in Afghanistan until March 1993, when he moved to Kenya. Later, he took part in the 1998 bombing of the U.S. embassy there. (He is currently serving a life term in a Colorado prison.)[14]

The Soviet defeat in Afghanistan marked the start of one of the great turning points of modern history, but in the euphoria of the moment, its ominous underside went largely unnoticed. Across the globe, Americans, who had helped bring this situation to pass, enjoyed a lifting of the threat of nuclear annihilation. Politicians claimed it was time to reap the benefits of the peace dividend now that the Cold War was over and stopped paying attention to far-off places like Afghanistan. In turn, the men who had humbled the Soviet Union and forced it to leave Afghanistan were treated as actors whose play had closed. Americans had no plan to help them take power. Almost no one in Washington focused on shaping what would come next.

2

A Half Solution
(1989–1992)

George H. W. Bush was sworn in as the forty-first president in January 1989, just as the last Soviet troops were leaving Afghanistan, and one of his first priorities was to review U.S. goals in light of this dramatic shift. Even before taking office, incoming secretary of state James Baker reaffirmed Ronald Reagan's policy aim—that Afghans decide their future in a "free act of self-determination." In plain English, this meant the removal of the Soviet-installed Najibullah regime. At his first news conference, Bush said that the United States would play a "catalytic role" in "bringing about stability" in Afghanistan.

In Afghanistan as in Nicaragua (where Reagan had also pursued regime change through covert aid to rebel forces), Bush's inclination was to wind down the insurgency and seek a political solution. But he had to contend at home with the conservative wing of the Republican Party, which was riding high and would recoil at any compromise as the Soviets pulled out. Baker's first decision after taking over U.S. diplomacy was to close the U.S. embassy in Kabul, in hopes of speeding up the inevitable fall of Najibullah. Bush rebuffed an early offer by Soviet leader Mikhail Gorbachev to resolve the conflict peacefully and instead continued sending arms to the mujahideen.

The challenge before Bush was to bring stability to this unsettled land. The policy he inherited was an epic anomaly. Washington had funneled $3 billion in aid to the mujahideen throughout the 1980s, but it had had no formal or regular contact with commanders or political leaders there and no plan for putting them into power. There was still an enormous well of goodwill toward Washington. But the history of U.S. engagement in Afghanistan made it hard to imagine a continuing activist role.[1]

From the start, U.S. support for the resistance had always been conducted covertly by the CIA, in close cooperation with Pakistan's powerful Inter-Services Intelligence (ISI), which is responsible for intelligence gathering and operations abroad but also plays a domestic political role; American diplomacy was also conducted through Pakistan, with Washington focusing its energies on a military solution.

The Carter administration had begun covert support to anticommunist rebels in July 1979, two months after a procommunist coup and six months before the Soviet invasion. From $500,000 in initial seed money, the annual aid ballooned to $30 million after Reagan took office in 1981. Pushed by congressional champions such as Charlie Wilson of Texas and with broad support from both parties, it grew to $630 million in 1986. Pakistani president Zia ul-Haq imposed tough terms on CIA operations, requiring all links to the Afghan fighters and all distribution of arms to run through the ISI. Washington would not interfere in Pakistan's "internal affairs" and would suspend its complaints about Zia's dictatorship and its criticism and sanctions of his efforts to build a nuclear bomb.[2]

A military man who seized power in a coup and hanged his predecessor, Zulfikar Ali Bhutto, Zia was sorely in need of political legitimacy. At home, he adopted a pro-Islamist policy, allying with religious political parties and adopting policies that led to the creation of a network of Islamist madrassas. The number of madrassas rose exponentially, from about nine hundred in 1971 to eight thousand official schools and twenty-five thousand unregistered ones in 1988. Many of these schools were along the Pakistan-Afghan border and were funded by Saudi and Gulf region patrons.[3] In Afghanistan, Zia primarily supported Afghan Islamists—as opposed to Afghan nationalists—for reasons related to Pakistan's own security goals. Pakistan wanted Afghans to give up a lingering territorial claim in Pakistan by recognizing the Durand line; this line splits Pashtuns in Afghanistan from their fellow tribesmen, the Pathans in Pakistan, who inhabit Pakistan's tribal belt along the Afghan border. The U.S. commitment to confront the Soviets in Afghanistan on his terms enabled Zia to build political capital at home and abroad.

To spread the costs, the administration turned to Saudi Arabia. William Casey, then CIA director, flew to Jeddah to cement the Afghan link. "What can you do to help us?" Casey asked King Fahd. "That's not a fair question," Fahd responded. "What I tell you I'll do, I'll do. But you have your Congress to deal with. So you do what you can, and I'll match it." Casey said, "You've got a deal." The Saudis had their own agenda in Afghanistan, reaffirming their role as the defender of the Muslim faith and the proponent of the Wahhabi school of Islam. They would bring their own baggage in the form of fired-up volunteers who would take part in the holy war and draw other Muslims from around the world to join them.[4]

Thus, all the patrons were lined up for what would become the biggest covert operation in CIA history. The missing voice at the table was the Afghan resistance, the men who would risk their lives and had by far the biggest stake in the final outcome. In 1984, Zia summoned seven Afghan resistance parties to Peshawar and insisted that they establish an alliance as the price for further aid. They were chosen, not so much as representatives of Afghanistan as a whole but for their presumed agreement with Pakistani objectives in Afghanistan. Islamists led four of the parties; moderate royalists, who favored some future role for exiled king Zahir Shah, led the other three. Zia's favorite was Hekmatyar, whose Hezbi Islami (Islamic Party) and Lashkar-i-Isar (Army of Sacrifice) consisted of Pakistan-based refugees. Burhanuddin Rabbani's Jamiat-I-Islami (Islamic Association) included two prominent commanders, Ahmed Shah Massoud in the Panjshir Valley and Ismail Khan in Herat; it was the only one of the seven parties that was not Pashtun-led.* (Rabbani and Massoud were both ethnic Tajiks.)[5]

Parallel to the U.S. decision to ramp up the covert war, the United Nations launched a diplomatic drive in the early 1980s to remove Russian forces through negotiations. Viewed in Washington as a quixotic but useful activity for keeping the spotlight on the Russian occupation, it was taken less seriously than even the internal politics of the resistance. Ecuadorian diplomat Diego Cordovez organized the first round of talks in Geneva in June 1982. Because Pakistan was unwilling to recognize Moscow's puppet government or deal with it directly, Cordovez fell back on the format of "proximity talks," which entailed separate meetings at different hours at the Palais des Nations, the United Nations' cavernous headquarters in Geneva. Moscow sent its ambassador to Kabul as its representative, but the United States notified Cordovez that it would "not be involved" in diplomatic efforts to end the conflict and instead coordinated with Pakistan. The talks began to show promise in the course of the next year but ground to a halt for more than a year in mid-1984 amid a series of political upheavals in Moscow.[6]

Soviet leadership was in a generational transition. Within four years, three men had ascended to the top position of Communist Party general secretary, and each had shifted policy. Leonid Brezhnev, who launched the Afghanistan invasion on Christmas Eve 1979, died not quite three years later in November 1982. His successor, former KGB head Yuri Andropov, had been a voice of caution when the Politburo debated an intervention in Afghanistan in 1979; according to a Soviet defector, Andropov had repeatedly warned Brezhnev against the invasion. When he reached the top of the ladder, Andropov openly discussed the reasons to withdraw. At a meeting with Cordovez and UN secretary-general Javier Perez de Cuellar in February 1983, for example, the Soviet leader cited the expense of keeping troops in Afghanistan, the domestic repercussions from conscripts returned home in body bags, and the confrontations with the United States, the third world, and the Islamic world over Afghanistan. Andropov told Cordovez that he sincerely wanted to "put an end to this situation."[7]

---

* The other Islamists were Abdul Rasul Sayyaf, head of the Ittihad-i-Islami (Islamic Unity) who had very close ties with Saudi Arabia and with the Arab volunteers who flocked to Peshawar, and Yunis Khalis, a respected but elderly former ally of Hekmatyar whose commanders included Abdul Haq, a moderate of great daring who assembled a following in the Western media. The moderates were Maulvi Nabi Mohammadi, who led the Harikat-i-Inqilab-i-Islami (Islamic Revolutionary Movement); Pir Sayed Gailani, leader of the National Islamic Front of Afghanistan (NIFA); and Sibghatullah Mujaddidi of the Afghan National Liberation Front. All three moderates favored establishing a constitutional government.

Eighteen months later, in February 1984, Andropov was dead of kidney failure at age sixty-nine; his successor, Konstantin Chernenko, switched signals. The first sign was at Andropov's funeral, where Chernenko snubbed Zia's request for talks. The pace of negotiations slowed, and Soviet friends told Cordovez that the army had been given "a free hand to hit the mujahideen much harder."[8]

The sickly Chernenko died in March 1985 at age seventy-three and was succeeded by Mikhail Gorbachev, then fifty-four. This most dynamic of Soviet leaders began a reappraisal of policy in Afghanistan (and in practically every other area), but first he allowed a long-planned and ambitious spring offensive using MI 24 and MI 25 assault helicopters to proceed.[9]

As Soviet policy zigzagged, U.S. policy toughened. The U.S. aim had been to harass and bleed the Russian occupiers, but National Security Decision Directive 166, which Reagan signed the same month as Gorbachev came to power, authorized using "all available means" to drive Soviet forces out of Afghanistan. An annex directed the intelligence agencies to provide satellite photographs of the battlefield and other intelligence and assistance to help the Afghan fighters target Afghan and Red Army installations and secure "burst communications" technology and demolition training. Nevertheless, the mujahideen were getting beaten, or so concluded Morton Abramowitz, head of the State Department's Bureau of Intelligence and Research (INR), in September 1985 after visiting the region. Back in Washington, Abramowitz personally lobbied to equip the rebel force with anti-aircraft missiles.[10]

Moscow and Washington were soon totally out of sync. On February 25, 1986, Gorbachev told the Politburo that Afghanistan had turned into a "bleeding wound" and that troops would depart in a phased withdrawal—half by the end of 1987 and the rest in 1988. One day later, the Reagan administration decided to ship in Stinger ground-to-air missiles; it would take another seven months for rebels to be trained, equipped, and effective in shooting down Soviet helicopters. Russian officials later claimed that the new weapon actually slowed the troop withdrawal. They also acknowledged that it had forced them to fly their helicopters and aircraft at far higher altitudes and thus lose their effectiveness on the ground.[11]

Considering that the negotiations began in 1982, it seems incredible that Cordovez did not have his first substantive encounter with leaders of the mujahideen until February 1988, and then only with the Peshawar-based external party leadership. In the judgment of Australian Afghanistan scholar William Maley, "a mark of a truly great mediator's dexterity is an ability to find ways of linking all necessary parties to a settlement, while excluding all unnecessary parties."[12]

Cordovez put the onus on everyone else. He said his original mandate, based on a UN General Assembly resolution, would have required a special resolution to broaden the participants to include Afghans. Moscow, however, was "dead-set against it"; Pakistan insisted on being in "full control of the situation"; and the United States agreed that Pakistan "would be the channel." Thus, Afghan long-term interests became a secondary matter. Moscow and Kabul insisted that the negotiations would never begin if self-determination was on the agenda, and Pakistan readily agreed. Yaqub Khan, the Pakistani foreign minister, was quick to note that there should be consultations with the "refugees" (a euphemism for leaders of the resistance).[13]

The U.S. attitude on a political role for the mujahideen was "one of total disregard and indifference" and reflected, in Cordovez's view, an underlying pessimism. The Americans "didn't believe they could ever win or get a withdrawal, that the UN would be able to mediate it, or that there was a thereafter that mattered," he said. Michael Armacost, the U.S. undersecretary of state, told him that if the Russians withdrew, so much else would fall in place that there was no need for the United States to do anything else.

"We regarded our strategic interest as getting the Russians out," Armacost later recalled. "The general supposition was that the Russians and British had broken their spears trying to govern these people. They resisted outside authority. They were notoriously difficult to govern even when left alone. The question of who governs was not a prime subject for us." Yet another reason for the lack of interest was a geostrategic judgment going back decades—that Afghanistan was outside the U.S. sphere of influence because it is "next door" to Russia. However, after ten years of being bloodied by local commandos, Russia also was ready to walk away from Afghanistan. "Because of this indifference, the ISI took over," said Cordovez.[14]

Ahmed Shah Massoud, the famed mujahideen commander, was incredulous when he learned in 1988 that Islamabad was negotiating on behalf of the Afghan fighters. The occasion was Massoud's first visit to Pakistan in a decade, and Pakistani authorities had flown him to the capital by helicopter. In a meeting room at the Pakistan Foreign Ministry, foreign minister Yaqub Khan asked Massoud whether he had any message to send to the Russians. "Why should I send a message?" the commander asked. Khan responded that Pakistan was talking "to the Russians . . . on behalf of our Afghan brethren." Massoud countered, "Why are you talking on our behalf? Don't we have leaders here to talk on our behalf?" The silence in the room was "like someone was bringing the weight of a tank on a bicycle," recalled Masoud Khalili, Massoud's spokesman and interpreter. But Khan did not miss a beat: "This is how it has been and how it will be. Do you have a message?" Massoud replied, "Nobody who talks on our behalf will have any kind of result." He pressed his back into the chair and muttered to himself, "We do the fighting and others do the talking. What does it mean?"[15]

What it meant was that UN negotiations sought a Soviet troop withdrawal, not a stable successor regime in Kabul. Self-determination for Afghans was not on the table.

By mid-1987, nearly a year before the final accord was reached, the Soviet leadership decided it would seek in Afghanistan what the Americans had failed to achieve on departing Vietnam: a dignified retreat. "We increasingly recognized that we had to make Najibullah strong enough to survive, at least for a decent interval," said Deputy Foreign Minister Yuli Vorontsov. In defining its withdrawal aims, Moscow took into account the lack of clear U.S. goals. At one point in the negotiations, Gorbachev complained that Moscow wanted to leave Afghanistan, but Washington kept "putting sticks in the spokes."[16]

The final impasse centered on Moscow's demand that Washington cease all military aid, even though Russia was continuing to supply its puppet government in Kabul. Cordovez was convinced that Gorbachev feared a massacre; Washington saw a delaying tactic. The final accords, signed at the United Nations' European headquarters in Geneva on April 14, 1988, papered over the differences.

The ceremony was held in the green and gold council chamber of the former League of Nations, an ironically apt setting in light of the false pretenses underlying the act. The signers of the principal document—Pakistan's representative, Zain Noorani, and his Soviet-installed Afghan counterpart, Abdul Wakil—had not met since the talks began in 1982. They sat on either side of Secretary-General Perez de Cuellar at an angle where they could see him and avoid looking at each other. The two guarantor powers, represented by U.S. secretary of state George Shultz and Soviet foreign minister Eduard Shevardnadze, sat at the far ends of the table but had no chance to speak—a good thing, for they would have quickly dispelled any illusions about their pledges to "refrain from any form of interference or intervention" in the internal affairs of Afghanistan or Pakistan.

For its part, Pakistan pledged not to support the overthrow of the Kabul regime; to encourage rebellion or secession; or to train, equip, finance, or recruit mercenaries or send them into Afghan territory. But Noorani later pointed out that the mujahideen "are freedom fighters. They are from among the refugees. Where is there any restriction?" Wakil made clear to reporters that the Afghan Communist Party intended to play a dominant role in any future coalition government, a stance the opposition flatly rejected.

Shultz issued a written statement affirming the United States' right to continue supplying arms so long as Moscow supported the Kabul regime. He repeated this at a news conference: "There is nothing in the agreement that restricts the U.S. in any way. We have made clear to the Soviet leaders before signing that it is our right to provide military aid to the resistance. We are ready to exercise that right. But we are prepared to meet restraint with restraint." Shevardnadze held his own news conference. "Only irresponsible political figures can ignore, reject, or violate the norms and principles of the settlement," he declared.

The flawed outcome illustrated the limits of UN-led mediation between the superpowers in the late Cold War era. Both Pakistan and the United States viewed the Afghan government as illegitimate and unworthy of diplomatic recognition. Yet Pakistan and Afghanistan had, in effect, signed a nonaggression pact. On the other hand, they had not agreed to a cease-fire. And the mujahideen, who were principally responsible for Moscow's turnaround, had neither a voice nor a seat at the table. So there would be no cease-fire. Hekmatyar, speaking on behalf of the seven-party alliance, said the mujahideen would "continue the war until the Russians and their puppets" were gone.

Still, the Soviet Union had made a remarkable commitment: to begin the withdrawal of its one hundred fifteen thousand troops on May 15 and to withdraw half by August 15 and the rest within nine months. Despite the sparring in Geneva, for the United States and the Soviet Union, it was the high point of a burgeoning friendship.[17]

Colin Powell, then deputy director of Reagan's National Security Council, said he was not sure what would have happened had Gorbachev agreed to an arms cutoff, because nothing would have stopped Reagan, who believed intensely in the cause of the resistance. But Reagan's belief, combined with Soviet leaders' worries about their military's bruised ego, raised the price Afghans would have to pay. The Soviet military, in the biggest air supply effort since the allied airlift into Berlin, sent twenty-five to forty IL-76 planes to Kabul every day. By one estimate, they spent up to $4.5 billion in 1989 alone, far in excess of U.S. support for the mujahideen.[18]

America's inattention to the political outcome was not a partisan position; it reflected the judgment of specialists in both major political parties and beyond. Almost everyone shared the myopia. The focus in Washington was on the impact the Afghan withdrawal would have on the rest of the Soviet empire rather than on Afghanistan. In March 1987, Henry Kissinger had told Cordovez that the Soviets were "right" not to want a massacre and that the United States should not set any conditions regarding the government in Kabul. "Washington should only insist on a swift withdrawal," Kissinger said. Zbigniew Brzezinski, national security adviser under Jimmy Carter and the champion of providing covert assistance to the mujahideen, said the United States should not permit the "knotty issue" of forming an interim government in Afghanistan to delay the promised withdrawal of Soviet troops. He said Washington had no interest in becoming "mired in complex negotiations" over an interim government. Even the *Washington Post* editorialized that it would have been "good to nail down a new government and seal off all arms. But the first and rightful objective of the U.N., as of American diplomacy, has always been to get the Soviets out."[19]

Pakistan Takes Charge

In the face of U.S. indifference at practically every level, Zia developed his own brash scheme. Even before the Soviets completed their pullout, the Pakistani leader was celebrating the triumph by Afghan fighters as his own and announcing his intention to capitalize on it. "We have earned the right to have a power which is friendly toward us. We have taken risks as a frontline state, and we will not permit a return to the prewar situation, marked by a large Indian and Soviet influence and Afghan claims on our own territory," Zia said in an interview. "The new power will be really Islamic, a part of the Islamic renaissance, which, you will see, will someday extend itself to the Soviet Muslims."[20] What he had in mind was a government headed by Hekmatyar, the most ruthless and controversial of the commanders, who was expected to be subservient to Pakistan.

Zia died before he could realize his vision, but Pakistan's new government was determined to carry his plan through. Power was divided after his death among the civilian political leadership, namely Bhutto's daughter, Benazir; a president with close military ties, Ghulam Ishak Khan; and the all-powerful military. The heady victory in Afghanistan led Pakistan into major misadventures, not only in Afghanistan but also in Kashmir, where its government sent in "freedom fighters" who had been trained in Afghanistan. Compared with Zia—a strategist with a vision, a godfather-like figure who U.S. ambassador Robert Oakley believed might have been able to dominate the Afghans—this was a gang that could not shoot straight.[21]

Oakley, a respected senior U.S. diplomat with a record of serving well on the toughest assignments, arrived in Islamabad on short notice in August 1988 to replace Ambassador Arnold Raphel, who was killed in the plane crash with Zia. In Oakley's view, Afghanistan was no longer a U.S. vital interest. "The enthusiasm wasn't there," he said, "the feeling it was vital to national interests." He told the administration as much and, in one cable, advised the United States to accept a Pakistani sphere of influence in Afghanistan. Years later he defended that judgment: "Whose sphere of influence was it supposed to be under—the United States?"[22]

About a month after Oakley arrived, with the Soviet troop withdrawal well underway, Edmund McWilliams turned up in Islamabad as the first U.S. special envoy to the Afghan resistance. Conservatives in Congress had created the post in the last year of the Reagan administration out of concern that overdependence on the ISI had given the U.S. government a skewed picture of the resistance. It was McWilliams' misfortune to be based at the mission housing the CIA station that was still administering weapons deliveries to the Afghan rebels, and he quickly found himself in a bitter clash with both Bearden, the steward of the Afghan arms program, and Oakley. McWilliams rejected Oakley's concept of a Pakistani sphere of influence. Pakistan officials claimed the need for "strategic depth" that extended into Afghanistan proper. But in McWilliams' view, as long as any one out-side power dominated, Afghanistan would be under constant threat of subversion from other regional powers seeking to displace that power.

Fluent in Dari and closely familiar with the insurgency and Russian counterinsurgency tactics from his time in Kabul, McWilliams spent every available weekend and weekday calling on rebel commanders, intellectuals, and political leaders in Peshawar and Quetta. In mid-October 1988, he cabled Washington that Afghans across the political spectrum felt "frus-tration, bordering on hostility" toward Pakistan and the United States for backing Hekmatyar. He continued making the rounds of Afghan politi-cians and mujahideen leaders and after Bush's election urged the incoming administration to abandon Pakistan's plan for a military assault and instal-lation of an externally based interim government.[23]

But there was no way to halt the juggernaut. U.S. intelligence analysts concluded in February that the Najibullah regime could collapse "within weeks." That month, largely at the behest of the U.S. embassy in Islam-abad, the ISI organized an Afghan government-in-exile.

The Interim Islamic Afghan Government was utterly unrepresenta-tive, but it revealed the mindset of its Pakistani creators. The *shura* that set it up was held in Rawalpindi, the Pakistan army headquarters. Saudi intel-ligence put up some $26 million, according to U.S. diplomats, and the seven Peshawar parties selected the 519 participants. Sibghatullah Mujad-didi, a moderate Sunni leader who had won respect among broad segments of the Afghan population but was militarily weak, was to be the head of state. McWilliams believed that his presence offered some hope that the interim government could succeed, but it soon came to naught. Mujaddidi traveled to Iran and promised Shia leaders one hundred seats; but Sunni Islamists cut the number to sixty, and the Shia boycotted. Ahmed Shah Massoud, the legendary Tajik commander from northeast Afghanistan, said he was not invited until two days before the event and did not send repre-sentatives. No seats were allocated for "good Afghans" in Najibullah's gov-ernment; and important mujahideen field commanders, Tajiks, Uzbeks, and supporters of exiled king Zahir Shah were underrepresented. Most of those taking part were party bureaucrats from Peshawar.

As a result of this manipulation, perhaps only a third of the Afghan population was represented, Mujaddidi noted. At Saudi insistence, muja-hideen leader Abdul Rasul Sayyaf, a Wahhabi, was named prime minister. Hekmatyar—the most controversial of all the mujahideen leaders because of his brutal battle tactics and his infighting with other commanders—was named defense minister, also with Saudi backing. Although Durrani Pash-tuns from southern Afghanistan had produced Afghanistan's kings for 225 years, none was named to the new government. As a result, Ghilzai Pashtuns from eastern Afghanistan (Hekmatyar among them) were over-represented. In fact, the government never got off the ground, for neither

Pakistan nor the United States ever recognized it. No one knew the phone number except the U.S. consulate in Peshawar, and usually no one answered the phone, reported John Burns of the *New York Times*. This was ISI's political plan.[24]

The military plan involved an attempt to seize Jalalabad—the main city in eastern Afghanistan, close to the Pakistan border—in order to set up a rebel government that would challenge the Najibullah regime. The assault began on March 6, just three weeks after the departure of Soviet troops, and overconfidence was the order of the day. Oakley recalled, "Sayyaf kept saying to me, 'We're going to win.'" And Mujaddidi boldly announced that the first cabinet meeting would be held in Jalalabad just three days later. At a meeting held the same day the fighting began, ISI director-general Hamid Gul promised Prime Minister Benazir Bhutto that the city would fall within a week "like a ripe apple." With Oakley present but no Afghans in attendance, Bhutto approved the operation already under way. By the time it was over four months later, twelve thousand to fifteen thousand people had died, as many as a third of them mujahideen, and one hundred thousand more refugees had fled to Pakistan.[25]

The military rout in Jalalabad was the result of insufficient preparation and a cascade of wrong assumptions. The mujahideen had neither a general staff nor a unified chain of command, and yet, with little political or military planning, they were being asked to shift suddenly from hit-and-run guerrilla strikes to taking territory, the task of an organized armed force. Afghan-style military conquests are often built on forcing or purchasing political shifts among local commanders, but no such preparations were made. In this instance, local commanders in Jalalabad had made accommodations with the Kabul government precisely because more political work was needed to convince the army garrison to defect. The attackers assumed that encircling the city would lead to massive defections from the government, but that was unlikely just a few months after forces under Yunis Khalis, an Islamist leader, had executed more than seventy government defectors from the Torkham garrison near Jalalabad.[26]

Moreover, the mujahideen were ill-equipped, and the government forces well-armed and prepared. The rebels lacked mine-clearing equipment, artillery to attack concrete bunkers, controller-guided antitank missiles, and missile protection from air assaults. In April 1988, an immense quantity of U.S.-provided military equipment had been destroyed in a weapons depot explosion of mysterious origin, and a fire had occurred at the Chinese factory that produced most of the rockets used by the mujahideen.

Additionally, some of the renowned commanders from the anti-Soviet jihad had been sidelined. Massoud and Abdul Haq—both moderate Islamist leaders and uniquely gifted in grasping the essence of guerrilla war—knew that before attempting to capture cities, it was vital to set up governing structures, to develop guerrilla assault tactics, and to encircle them. But neither was consulted before the siege of Jalalabad, and neither participated. Abdul Haq was scathing in his criticism: "How is that we Afghans, who never lost a war, must take military instructions from the Pakistanis, who never won one?" he asked McWilliams, who reported the comment to Washington. Massoud said he learned about the attack from a BBC broadcast, noting that it took place at a time the country was covered with snow.

They were not the only nonparticipants. Many guerrilla groups refused to cooperate with the ISI because of "a perception that Jalalabad was an ISI effort to defeat Najibullah so it could install its favorite, the Ghilzai Pashtun Hekmatyar, in Kabul," wrote Afghan expert Henry Bradsher. "Few Ghilzais outside his party—and still fewer Durrani Pashtuns, Tajiks, or other Afghans—wanted to die for that."[27]

The mujahideen defeat boosted morale for Najibullah and may have extended his hold on power. In the meantime, he had begun burnishing the image of his communist infrastructure by changing the name of the ruling party, limiting its membership to practicing Muslims, reaching out to every sector in society that would hear him, and broadcasting his version of events on radio and television. It was also a delusional quest. Soviet economic and military support alone kept him in power, and most of the country lay outside his control.[28]

For the rebels and their boosters, Jalalabad proved that there was no military solution and that Najibullah could only be removed through direct talks with Moscow. Jalalabad also destroyed any claim of competence by the ISI and their backers in the CIA. Furthermore, it deepened the contempt of independent Afghan commanders for the CIA. "They're stupid," Haq told the U.S. political officer in Peshawar two years later. "They don't know what's going on—like when they told us to attack Jalalabad."[29]

The shambles was completed that summer when Hekmatyar's forces organized a vicious assault on archrival Massoud. In early July, Massoud summoned one hundred of his leading officers for a five-day planning session to organize attacks on Kunduz and other government-held cities and garrisons in northeastern Afghanistan. One of Hekmatyar's local commanders, Sayed Jamal, set an ambush and killed more than thirty of them. Massoud aides said Jamal was in touch with Hekmatyar's Peshawar headquarters at the time of the attack. Mujaddidi later denounced Hekmatyar as a criminal and terrorist who was responsible for the assassination of hundreds of people, and Hekmatyar quit the interim government.[30] Massoud's forces captured four of the alleged perpetrators, presented them before a religious court, and, following the verdict, executed them.

McWilliams had sent ample warnings that the United States was on the wrong track, leading to repeated clashes with Oakley and the CIA station, who saw to it that he was removed. In June 1989 he fired his parting shot through the State Department's "dissent channel" (a method for diplomats in disagreement with their ambassador to communicate with Washington). The interim government was a "failed, transparently foreign-manipulated gambit" that had no capacity to broaden its base, create a bureaucratic infrastructure, or rally Afghans, he said. Instead, he called for creation of a neutral government of technocrats charged with organizing a UN-monitored election or a traditional Afghan grand assembly to form a representative government. Noting that the ISI (with CIA and embassy support) planned "one more fighting season" to defeat the Najibullah regime, McWilliams wrote that "political and military trends as well as humanitarian concerns" argued strongly against waiting until the end of such a fighting season before attempting to find a political solution.[31]

It was clear that the special envoy needed more clout, and, under pressure from Senator Gordon Humphrey of New Hampshire and other conservative Republicans, the administration raised the post to ambassadorial level. Bush tapped career diplomat Peter Tomsen as McWilliams's replacement. Unassuming and bland on the surface but feisty and determined on the job, Tomsen was at the time the second-ranking U.S. official in Beijing. He was senior enough to know how to approach Oakley and to prepare the battleground for the bureaucratic conflict that would follow in Washington. He had served in India and Russia, lived in Nepal as a Peace Corps volunteer, and followed Afghan politics from a distance, although he had never been in the country.

There was ample reason to view Tomsen's as a "mission impossible." The ISI had far more operatives than the Americans and had maintained much closer ties to Afghan insurgents; it was still receiving U.S. arms shipments; and it had a strategy tailored to its capabilities. Afghan factions that were not responsive to Pakistan's direction would be hard for a U.S. envoy to coordinate. The debacle in Jalalabad was the prologue to Tomsen's first visit to the region, and he arrived in Peshawar in July 1989 to an incipient civil war.

Yet the fact that McWilliams had surveyed the territory the previous year and pressed in vain for a major shift laid a foundation within the State Department, and Tomsen brought his own skills to bear in constructing a new policy. "Peter is capable, interested, and passionate, and he listens," was how Robin Raphel, who later ran the Bureau of South Asian Affairs at the State Department, saw him.[32]

After several weeks of surveying Afghan military commanders and politicians in Peshawar and Quetta, covering much of the same ground as McWilliams, Tomsen was convinced of the enormous and growing distrust of Hekmatyar and his Pakistani patrons. Oakley had taken offense at McWilliams, who was attached to his embassy but did not clear his cables with him, but Oakley supported Tomsen. And Tomsen, using his ambassadorial rank and privileges as special envoy, made it a practice to send cables from anywhere but Islamabad.

Back in Washington, he marshaled the evidence, secured backing from conservatives (and some liberals) on Capitol Hill, and guided an inter-agency review that produced a new set of goals. Reviews are the place where policy changes. Tomsen feared that Hekmatyar might capture Kabul with ISI and Saudi support, thereby putting Pakistan in direct control of Afghanistan and changing the strategic balance in Central Asia. The new aim was "to break the monopoly of the ISI, and CIA support, of the extremists and to strengthen the moderates." The CIA would continue arming the rebel forces, but U.S. officials would try to sideline Hekmatyar, strengthen Massoud's role on the political stage, and seek a political settlement with Moscow. Tomsen would also encourage military commanders, the crucial figures in the anti-Soviet war who had been largely excluded from the ISI-organized Rawalpindi *shura* in February, to organize a *shura* of their own.[33]

The ISI, with strong support from the CIA, was well along with a different plan for 1990—namely, to install Hekmatyar in power. In late 1989, even as Tomsen was trying to write Hekmatyar out of U.S. policy, Pakistan sent a delegation to Washington to outline an "action plan" for an early 1990 offensive built around Hekmatyar's Army of Sacrifice.[34]

In fact, what Pakistan's military intelligence seems to have had in mind was a military coup. After false starts in July and December 1989, Najibullah's defense minister Shahnawaz Tanai launched a full-blown coup attempt on March 6, 1990. Parts of the Afghan air force joined in and bombed the presidential palace, narrowly missing Najibullah. To the surprise of many, Hekmatyar announced that he and Tanai had formed a revolutionary council that would rule until elections were held. The alliance—of a hard-line Islamist and a hard-line communist—was tactical, but Tanai lacked the support of troops on the ground. The coup attempt was over within a matter of hours, and Tanai and his rebel officers were soon in flight—to Pakistan in three Afghan air force planes.

Tanai blamed Hekmatyar for the debacle. "He didn't keep his promise. He never came to Afghanistan but stayed in Islamabad," he later told a fellow officer. "He said he was supposed to send people in after 5:00 a.m. I looked at my watch at 5:05. At 6:00 a.m. I told my people: Everyone's name is on this [failure]."[35]

Ahmed Shah Massoud told a different version. What defeated the coup, he told British journalist Sandy Gall three years later, was "our people in the army" who "had penetrated the regime very deeply." The guerrilla force "had a lot of influence in the air force . . . as well as in the 16th Armored Division and the National Guard, which has a very important and effective force," he said.

Tomsen believed the CIA station in Islamabad was "fully aware and involved" in the coup attempt and had given tacit support through winks and nods and by "not banging on the table" to demand that the ISI desist. The CIA reported at the time that some of the money needed to buy off commanders was contributed by bin Laden. But other well-informed observers concluded that funding also came from ISI and Saudi intelligence.[36]

It was another debacle for Hekmatyar, and even though ISI director Hamid Gul lost his job, the ISI continued to back a military solution, reputedly with CIA support. In October 1990, mujahideen field commanders sent word that some seven hundred truckloads of ammunition, including forty thousand rockets, were being moved into the outskirts of Kabul to enable Hekmatyar to destroy and capture the capital. Afghanistan experts Ahmed Rashid and Barnett Rubin reported that the CIA was involved in the offensive, and Tomsen also believed that the CIA station had endorsed it. With one calamity behind them and another looming, Tomsen was able to win Oakley's support for a joint effort to block the next round in the ISI's military solution. Bush sent a secret letter, and the ISI turned the trucks around.[37]

Tomsen, meanwhile, proceeded with the new U.S. plan, which was to hold an alternative *shura* of mujahideen field commanders, the National Commanders' Shura (NCS). With Abdul Haq's assistance, Tomsen helped bring about the first such *shura* in Paktia province not long after the abortive Tanai coup; about three hundred commanders, mostly Pashtun, attended. Further meetings in May and June 1990 drew mostly Pashtun participants, and a national *shura* was called in October, attended by Abdul Haq and Massoud. Hekmatyar boycotted it, but the new ISI director, Asad Durrani, attended uninvited. Finally, a strategy emerged. After condemning the ISI's plan for a direct attack on Kabul, the *shura* endorsed a plan to capture provincial capitals and set up regional administrations. Massoud went to Islamabad and asked for aid to enable major commanders to develop and implement their own plans without ISI direction. Although the NCS was one of the most promising of the military structures set up during the war —in theory, it could have formed the nucleus of a new Afghan military and state—it was killed by internal politics and outside interference. As Tomsen maintains, the ISI saw themselves losing control and began to undermine the NCS by directly funding participants. Rabbani also opposed the NCS, feeling that Massoud and other commanders were treading on his political turf.[38]

Massoud had had an up-and-down relationship with the CIA. He reportedly received lump-sum payments of $900,000 in May 1989 and $500,000 in January 1990, in addition to $200,000 a month. After he refused to join the early ISI-CIA offensives, the CIA cut his payments to $50,000 a month in spring 1990, but it later boosted his payment to $100,000 a month. The CIA also began delivering radio sets, allowing Afghan commanders to communicate with one another. With experienced commanders doing the planning, funding secured, and the infrastructure being developed, the fighting could begin.

The first successful attack on a provincial capital was the capture of Khost in March 1991, with fighting led by local Ahmedzai tribes and forces of Jalaludin Haqqani, a member of Yunis Khalis's hard-line Islamist Hezbi Islami, and with support from the ISI and the CIA. As many as one thousand guerrillas died in the battle, but mujahideen forces captured approximately two thousand government soldiers. However, guerrilla forces were unable to set up a government; instead, they systematically pillaged the town. When the fighting was over, Hekmatyar's well-organized political cadres went in, put up their flags, and claimed victory. The ISI's promotion of Khost as a Hekmatyar victory undercut any propaganda advantage for the NCS.[39]

The fatal blow to the Najibullah regime was struck not in Afghanistan but in Moscow and was the outcome of a titanic power struggle. One day after General Gromov's retreat in February 1989, Gorbachev had proposed a political solution to Afghanistan: the United States and the Soviet Union would both suspend arms shipments and encourage the government and rebels to join in a coalition, with elections to follow under UN supervision. At the time, Bush rejected the initiative, responding politely that Najibullah first had to be removed from power.[40] One year later, the Bush administration had fully absorbed the lessons of Jalalabad, and following diplomatic ground-laying by Tomsen, Foreign Minister Eduard Shevardnadze again proposed a framework accord. This time, the Americans were ready to accept, but the Russians had to back down. Hard-liners were in the ascendant in Moscow; Shevardnadze was unable to sign the accord and had to resign his post. With Gorbachev under heavy pressure, the Bush administration weighed making further concessions. "I got the impression increasingly that Afghanistan was expendable," Tomsen recalled. "They moved perilously close to accepting the Russian position that Najibullah could remain in power through elections."[41] But the hard-liners' coup attempt against Gorbachev in August 1991 was Najibullah's undoing. The Communist Party plotters—who included the backers of the Kabul airlift —were thrown in jail. Boris Yeltsin, president of the Russian Federation, who led the public resistance to the coup, decided to use his newly gained clout to halt all arms deliveries to Najibullah. It happened during a meeting with James Baker on September 11, 1991. "I will tell Gorbachev to do it," Yeltsin told Baker. After making the phone call, Yeltsin informed Baker that arms deliveries would be halted on January 1, 1992.[42] By then, the Soviet Union itself had dissolved, and Gorbachev was no longer in power.

In mid-November, a delegation of top mujahideen leaders (Hekmatyar excluded) arrived in Moscow for high-level talks; a joint communiqué said all power should pass to an Islamic interim government.[43]

Building on understandings reached in the commanders' *shura*, Massoud—with careful planning and political preparation—had begun applying the pincer on the Najibullah regime during the spring and summer of 1991, capturing about a dozen small towns and villages in northern Afghanistan. Tomsen had made his own contribution to strengthening Massoud. He talked the United States Agency for International Development (USAID) into building a fifty-mile dirt road through the mountains of Pakistan that would allow Massoud to ship in supplies from his warehouse near Chitral.

The end was nigh for Najibullah. Out of funds to pay the forces of Abdul Rashid Dostum (the Uzbek commander whose 20,000-strong militia had served as hatchet men for the communist regime), Najibullah in late January attempted to replace the commander of the Hairatan garrison on the Afghan side of the Friendship Bridge, but Dostum balked and organized a revolt. On March 18, in a speech written by UN mediator Benon Sevan of Cyprus, Najibullah announced that he would step down. One day later, Dostum captured Mazar-i-Sharif, the major city of northern Afghanistan. Najibullah's government unraveled, as key generals contacted Massoud, Dostum, or Hekmatyar to offer their allegiance. A month later, the regime collapsed. Najibullah tried to escape on a UN plane, but rebel forces blocked his way at Kabul Airport, and he returned to Kabul. According to Massoud, key figures in Najibullah's National Guard, whom Massoud had won over before the crisis, took charge of the airport and detained Najibullah.[44]

Massoud's forces moved south from the Panjshir Valley toward Kabul. The Kabul garrison invited Massoud to enter the capital as head of state, but he feared a trap and held back. Meanwhile, Hekmatyar's forces had moved to positions south and east of the capital and threatened to seize the city by force unless the government surrendered unconditionally. Massoud held back as he waited for the interim government to establish itself. Then, after receiving intelligence that Hekmatyar would move into Kabul on April 30, Massoud preempted him, arriving in the capital on April 29 in a three-mile armored column, along with ten thousand troops but without fanfare or celebration. The interim government had named Hekmatyar prime minister and Massoud defense minister, but Hekmatyar was unwilling to share power. Acting president Mujaddidi, grateful that Hekmatyar had been kept from power, thanked Massoud for "not allowing the handful of aggressors [to become] too strong."

What had occurred in Kabul was a split within Najibullah's armed forces. Throughout the anti-Soviet war, the army had been divided between the mostly Pashtun-speaking Khalq and the Dari (Persian)-speaking Parcham; now the top officer corps split, with about two-thirds (mostly Parcham) siding with Massoud and the others backing Hekmatyar. Massoud played the division masterfully to his immediate advantage, but it was a perilous way to come to power. The real fratricidal fighting among former resistance factions was about to begin. [45]

Bin Laden Tests the Waters

During the turbulent years between the Soviet troop withdrawal and the fall of the Najibullah regime, bin Laden was no stranger to Afghanistan. For a decade, he had built close ties among influential Afghan commanders and Arab volunteers and set up enough institutions that he did not need to be there all the time. But events between 1989 and 1992 seemed to be beyond anyone's control, and he drew an important lesson: staying abroad could enhance his reputation in Afghanistan. Bin Laden had taken part in the combat at Jalalabad and fought valiantly, but he lost scores of fighters in the bloodbath. He told Arab journalists that the mujahideen failure and Pakistan's leading role "depressed him greatly."

Bin Laden's sojourn in Saudi Arabia from late 1989 to early 1992 was a watershed in his political life. Outwardly, he lived a modest existence, maintaining an office and living quarters in a sparsely furnished house and putting up family and overnight visitors on the floor. But his exploits in Afghanistan, the demise of the Soviet empire, and his own drive for self-promotion in the form of videos, sermons, and other speeches made him larger than life. Still, he was searching for a cause. He had begun organizing Saudis and Yemenis for a jihad in Marxist South Yemen, but when several of them were arrested, he was quickly fingered.

In the year leading up to Iraq's invasion of Kuwait, he had repeatedly warned in public speeches of Saddam Hussein's intentions toward Kuwait and the Kingdom of Saudi Arabia itself, a foresight which gained him credibility. "No one believed me. I distributed many tapes in Saudi Arabia. It was after it happened that they started to believe in me and believed my analysis of the situation," he would later tell CNN. [46]

In August 1990, when Saddam's troops crossed into Kuwait, he volunteered to lead a new jihad. "I am the commander of an Islamic army. I am not afraid of being put in jail or being in prison. I am only afraid of God," bin Laden told a clergyman sent to represent the Saudi government. The government saw signs of megalomania in him and opted instead for U.S. assistance. "I saw radical changes in his personality as he changed from a calm, peaceful, and gentle man interested in helping Muslims into a person who believed that he would be able to amass and command an army to liberate Kuwait," said Prince Turki al Faisal, the Saudi intelligence chief, who had known the family well and met bin Laden several times in Pakistan. "It revealed his arrogance and his haughtiness."[47]

Bin Laden based his case that the United States could not be allowed to defend Saudi Arabia on a theological reading of a hadith, according to which the Prophet Muhammad had ordered that "there be no two religions in Arabia." The Saudi leadership countered that Muhammad meant that Islam should dominate, not that other religions could not help defend the kingdom.

Bin Laden slowly gained adherents, and the war's indecisive outcome strengthened his argument. President Bush's decision not to unseat Saddam Hussein led to a U.S. request for semipermanent bases in Saudi Arabia to contain any future threat from Iraq. Permanent U.S. bases in Saudi Arabia had been on the U.S. agenda ever since Shia revolutionaries toppled the Shah of Iran in 1979, but the idea was fraught with peril. As part of the theocracy created by the Saud family in an agreement with Wahhabi clerics, the legitimacy of the ruling family is based in large part on its commitment to defend the two holy places—Mecca and Medina—where the Prophet Muhammad lived and died; thus, the house of Saudis committed to upholding and defending the faith as the state itself. Arab-world experts at the State Department and elsewhere strongly advised against setting up bases in a country whose political elite was beholden to a religious ideal, but the Bush administration saw no alternative. Bin Laden and other Islamists had their foil.

There are varied accounts of bin Laden's departure from Saudi Arabia. By his own account, he was under house arrest in 1991, when Burhanuddin Rabbani (the political leader of the Jamiat party allied with Massoud), with help from Sayyaf and "other friends," got in touch with Saudi interior minister Prince Nayif bin Abd al-Aziz and requested that he be freed. Once released, bin Laden went to Pakistan, where he called upon Rabbani and thanked him. Rabbani's version is that he did not directly approach the Saudi government, but that a delegation from a number of parties, including those of Sayyaf and Hekmatyar, traveled to Saudi Arabia in late 1991 and saw Prince Sultan bin Abd al-Aziz, the defense minister. "If bin Laden or other Arabs faced any problems, they discussed it. . . . Most probably they asked Prince Sultan to facilitate the travel of these Arabs [to Afghanistan]." This more or less squares with the account of Saudi intelligence chief Prince Turki, who said bin Laden was never banned from travel but had to have permission to leave the kingdom. According to his version of events, bin Laden obtained permission to visit Pakistan in March 1992. A second version, told to CIA officials by a Saudi intelligence source, is that bin Laden was expelled.[48]

The truth may lie somewhere between. Toryali Hemat, the Sayyaf commander who had been holed up with bin Laden in Nangahar shortly before the Russian withdrawal, saw bin Laden in Mecca in 1992, when bin Laden paid their hotel bills. "The Saudis don't want me in Saudi Arabia. The government has decided to expel me," bin Laden told him. "I may come to Sudan or Afghanistan." Commander Hemat said he urged bin Laden to choose Sudan: "I'll go with you to Pakistan," he volunteered. "Don't go to Afghanistan. You'll hurt your reputation."

In March or April 1992, bin Laden flew to Pakistan and Afghanistan and tested the waters. At the time, Massoud and Hekmatyar were in a military standoff. Bin Laden tried to mediate by radio, but it came to naught. "Go back with your brothers," he told Hekmatyar, urging him to accept a grand compromise with Massoud. But Hekmatyar, brimming with confidence and weapons, declined. Bin Laden then headed to Sudan, where he would remain for four years. [49]

Those were turbulent days in Kabul, but the worst-case scenario had been averted. Tomsen's aim in Afghanistan had been to bring about self-determination, in the form of a traditional *loya jirga* (grand assembly), a *shura,* or free elections; falling short of that, his mission was to keep Hekmatyar out of power. In June 1992, he traveled to Kabul to meet Massoud —his first visit to the capital and his first encounter with the legendary commander—to press his point. "An act of self-determination must take place. The Afghan people have not yet chosen their leader. It is imperative that you hold a *loya jirga* or a *shura,*" he told him. Massoud acknowledged that he had failed to persuade Rabbani to hold one.

Still, Massoud was in Kabul and a regime of moderate Islamists was in power. Bush had fulfilled part of his promise to help oust Najibullah. The outcome was imperfect but could be shaped into something more favorable if the United States continued to be the catalyst for a stable outcome. Unbeknownst to Tomsen and Massoud, this was the high-water mark of U.S. engagement; it was about to end, and Massoud would be on his own.

The inattention that followed must be seen in the context of the other events of 1989—the tectonic shifts set in motion by the collapse of communism—which Bush and Baker managed on the whole with great competence. At the same time, Afghanistan illustrated a pattern for Bush, who addressed challenges one at a time, never developed an overall strategy for the new era, and did not articulate a vision. Historic events had occurred in Afghanistan, and regardless of whether the United States was paying attention, more were to come. By contrast, Osama bin Laden had an intuitive grasp of the potential in this location to change history.

3

With Massoud
(1992–1994)

He was the most capable of the resistance commanders, an in-the-trenches leader with genuine charisma and undoubtedly the toughest single opponent the Red Army faced in Afghanistan. Although often compared with Josip Broz Tito, Mao Tse-tung, and Che Guevara, Ahmed Shah Massoud's skill and determination over two decades of struggle put him in a league of his own. The force he organized in northeastern Afghanistan repelled nine Soviet offensives. He led the bloodless mujahideen takeover in Kabul after the fall of Najibullah in April 1992, and for four-and-a-half years defended a government under siege, often from three directions. After the Taliban marched into Kabul in September 1996, he kept control of a small slice of territory for five years, remaining their most potent rival until his assassination in 2001. He was a military genius in vision and tactics. "I doubt there was anyone else at that level in the world," said a top UN official.[1]

But the "Lion of Panjshir" was also one of the most enigmatic figures of twentieth-century military history, a man of action rather than words, whose story is almost unknown because of the dearth of published writings or an authoritative biography. Unlike Tito, who welcomed Winston Churchill's envoy, Fitzroy MacLean, into his entourage during World War II, Massoud had no desire to receive a foreign liaison and repeatedly urged his backers in Peshawar not to send reporters. Five years into the guerrilla war, at a time when his needs were greatest, he wrote to Rabbani that he wanted all contacts with foreigners to be handled in Peshawar. "I am personally not in contact with any foreigner."[2] The following year, he urged his liaison in Peshawar, "Do not send me journalists, because there are no places for them to sleep or food to eat."[3] And in 1985, he sent word to Rabbani, "It is not necessary for the Englishmen to come to Panjshir. . . . Journalists should not come either."[4] A number of reporters did make the 300-mile trek across the Hindu Kush and produced dramatic written accounts and television footage of their encounters with him. But this limited exposure was not enough for Massoud to develop a political following abroad, except perhaps in France, where he became almost a cult figure in political circles.

Massoud had some grasp of the organization of government and created a semiautonomous authority in northeastern Afghanistan, complete with local administration, tax collection, courts, schools, and a military academy. His shortcoming was in political acumen: he failed to develop a relationship with an outside patron and, after arriving in Kabul, was overly dependent on his political ally, former university professor Burhanuddin Rabbani. When Tito wrested control from the Germans in 1945, he could count on the political backing of the Soviet Union, the moral support of Britain, and the financial largesse of the United States. When Massoud marched into Kabul, he was on his own. Unlike Tito, who observed Stalin's brutal leadership up close in Moscow in the 1930s and adjusted his style accordingly, Massoud spent his formative years fighting in the field; despite the structures he developed in the small and rather homogeneous environment of the Panjshir Valley, he never mastered the art of governance on a larger scale while in power in Kabul.

There is no question that Massoud had his flaws, but the issue is whether the regime he installed in Kabul in 1992 was preordained to fail. Could American support have shored up a national leader with such extraordinary credentials against the armed siege of his rivals? Could a stronger central government have prevented the descent to extreme Islamist rule and the rise of Osama bin Laden? Was backing Massoud the major missed opportunity for U.S. foreign policy in the early 1990s? Or have his admirers overstated his role? Years after his death, the answers remain elusive, but some sense of the missed opportunity can be gleaned by examining his leadership during the long anti-Soviet jihad.

Massoud's emergence as a commander owed much to the coincidence of a great military mind and a home base in Panjshir. The river valley is sixty miles long and in places narrows to a canyon. Close to Kabul and located astride the main north-south highway over the Salang Pass and the Salang Tunnel, it is "strategically too threatening to ignore but topographically too rugged for the Russian invaders to control," as journalist Anthony Davis noted. In this redoubt, Massoud was able to develop and hone his theories. A keen student of Mao Tse-tung and his manual *On Guerrilla Warfare* (written in 1937 when Japan occupied China), Massoud saw guerrilla war as a protracted struggle in which forces from the countryside would surround and eventually vanquish the cities.[5]

His choice of base and methods arose from bitter experience. The son of a retired Tajik military officer, schooled in Kabul's French lycée, Massoud arrived at Kabul University at a time when Afghan leaders were breathing new life into a variant of the nineteenth-century contest over Afghanistan known as the "Great Game." The issue was the tribal agencies in Pakistan —the border areas populated by Pashtun tribes, which Britain had made part of the Raj when it drew the Durand line in 1893. When Britain decolonized India in 1947, Afghanistan disputed Pakistani control and cast the sole vote against seating Pakistan in the United Nations. Now the contest was between the heirs to Tsarist Russia and the heirs to the British Raj.

What reignited the rivalry was an internal Afghan power struggle—a series of coups that drew Pakistan into the fray, led to the first American involvement, and culminated in the 1979 Soviet military invasion. For more than two decades after Pakistan came into existence in 1947, Mohammad Daoud, cousin of Afghan king Zahir Shah, built his political career around an irredentist nationalist demand to split off the tribal areas in Pakistan and unite Pashtuns in Pakistan (known there as Pathans) with Pashtuns in Afghanistan. Finally, in 1973, Daoud seized power with the backing of the Afghan Army, the Afghan Communist Party, and, indirectly, the Soviet Union. His coup gave rise to religious-based resistance at Kabul University and the creation of Jamiat-i-Islami (Islamic Alliance); but after an abortive countercoup, the major figures fled to Pakistan. Within a year, Rabbani, Hekmatyar, and Massoud were receiving training and arms from Pakistan's ISI to oppose the Daoud regime.

In spring 1975, the ISI dispatched the militants to attack provincial offices in eastern Afghanistan. Daoud responded by distancing himself from the Afghan communists, drawing nearer to Pakistan, and making overtures even to the United States—all of which raised concerns in Russia. Among the Afghan militants, many of whom were executed or tortured, these developments opened a profound and long-lasting schism. Hekmatyar, an advocate of immediate holy war, moved closer to Pakistan; Massoud and Rabbani went in the opposite direction. With Pakistani backing, Hekmatyar moved against Massoud, who was arrested and narrowly escaped death.

Daoud was ousted in a Marxist coup that had Russian military support in April 1978 and replaced by Nur Muhammad Taraki, a communist reformer, but his reforms only provoked wider Islamic resistance. Pakistan, with a national agenda of its own (to protect its tribal areas from Afghan claims), continued to train Islamists, and the CIA began to provide support. Coup followed upon coup. In September 1979, Taraki was murdered by his deputy, Hafizullah Amin. As Soviet troops rolled into the country in December 1979, Amin was executed, and another communist leader, Babrak Karmal, was installed.

Even before the Russian invasion, Massoud had returned to the Panjshir Valley to organize against communist rule, while Hekmatyar remained in Pakistan.[6] In building his base in the northeastern corner of his occupied homeland, Massoud was making a statement about the kind of war he wanted to wage. He was willing to accept aid from abroad, but not direction. He saw the war as an Afghan national struggle, not a proxy war. This put him at odds with Pakistan, whose ISI was eager to influence the fighting and hoped to use the U.S. aid it distributed to further its own national agenda in Afghanistan. Additionally, Massoud found himself at indirect odds with the United States, which had decided (primarily for Cold War reasons) in the early 1950s to treat Pakistan as its key ally in the region and viewed Afghanistan as coming under the Soviet sphere of influence.

Pakistan needed a compliant Afghan commander who supported its position, and it found him in the person of Hekmatyar, who remained in Pakistan. As Massoud went his own way, Hekmatyar, with Pakistan's backing, did everything possible to thwart him.[7]

The deadly rivalry with Hekmatyar is a constant theme in letters Massoud wrote to Rabbani and Mohamed Eshaq, a close associate from his school days. Massoud's letters attest to his isolation in those early years. Lacking even radio communication, he had no alternative but to write in longhand. Couriers carried his missives from Panjshir to Peshawar, a journey of up to two weeks on foot or horseback. A collection of letters published in Kabul in 2003 tells a story of extreme deprivation, continuous adaptation, and, ultimately, triumph over the odds.[8] The absence of bravado, the tone of near-desperation, the criticism of political figures, and the discussion of intelligence and plans all suggest that the letters were not intended for publication. In the course of developing a military force, he continually emphasized the importance of discipline, training, intelligence gathering, and tactical innovation. And while his struggle began in his native Panjshir Valley, by late 1984 his mujahideen controlled 80 percent of both sides of the Hindu Kush mountain range.

His biggest worry in the first letter, dated August 1981, was supplies, and he believed that Hekmatyar's Hezbi Islami (the favorite of the ISI and the CIA) was blocking them. "[Hezb] unfortunately is trying to escalate the war against us," he reported. "[Hezb] has blocked all our supply routes," he similarly wrote in September 1982.[9] In the dire straits of December 1982, he reported that Hezb was taxing passing convoys and closing roads. If the road to Khawak is not opened, he wrote, "We might declare war on Hezb."[10] But from the start, he reveals his political ambition to bring "unity and harmony" to the mujahideen of the region, by inviting representatives of twelve provinces to create an alliance in Peshawar to replace Jamiat i-Islami. (However, headed by Rabbani, it remained the instrument for obtaining U.S. and Saudi aid.) The earliest military innovation mentioned in the letters was the development of a network of mobile strike forces that would move against a target then disappear—the *zarbati* that he organized and trained for every *qarargah* (forward command post).

The letters illustrate the development of his military genius. Ever the tactical innovator, Massoud took a direct interest in planning and structuring a force in layers of semitrained local units, mobile strike forces, and trained main units. He was also a compassionate commander—constantly on the move, showing hands-on concern for the well-being of his troops and the civilian population. To avoid "the trap of a one-valley war," Massoud knew he had to develop a regional approach. He built alliances with other regional commanders, trained them in military theory and practice, and, in the process, re-created the tactics and force structure he had established in the Panjshir Valley. But Massoud was also a strategic thinker, perhaps the only Afghan leader with an integrated vision. His aim was to build the corps of commanders in the field into a *shura nazar* (supervisory council) —the heart of an officer corps that would lead a unified Islamic army to rebuild the war-shattered state.[11] Amazing as it may sound, Massoud did not travel abroad until he visited Pakistan in 1988.

No doubt his most controversial decision was the sixteen-month cease-fire with Soviet forces in the Panjshir Valley from January 1983 to April 1984. Hekmatyar and far more moderate Pashtuns, such as Abdul Haq, criticized him bitterly at the time, and ISI and CIA operatives hold it against him to this day. His letters set the context: after fending off two major Soviet offensives—one in May 1982 and the second in August– September 1982—in which the mujahideen captured bases, prisoners, and weapons, they were running out of supplies.

He had good reasons for suspending military operations in Panjshir, even while continuing them on the Shamali plains north of Kabul.[12] In November 1982, after receiving intelligence of a "massive" Soviet offensive planned for midwinter, he urged Rabbani to form a war council that could organize attacks from behind enemy lines. He pleaded for weapons, cash, food, and, finally, for "the people to go to the mosques and pray for the success of the mujahideen."[13] But the supplies did not arrive. Hekmatyar's forces had blocked the way, and now the first snows blocked all supply routes. "You would be surprised if you saw how the mujahideen sit in ambush on snow with no proper clothes or bring fifteen kilograms of rice on their backs from Salang," he wrote Rabbani in late December 1982. The lack of food, warm clothes, and boots; the closure of supply lines from Andarab and Khoistan; and sustained aerial bombardments in lower parts of the valley "have made life almost unbearable," he said in a letter to Eshaq the same day. "The living conditions of the displaced people in the mountains and those who have gone to the north of the country are extremely critical. The economic situation of most of the Mujahidin is worrisome." He summed up, "We pray to God to solve our problems because solving them is beyond the ability of man." What worried him most was a Soviet attack. "If we are attacked in the spring, I do not know what will happen to our people and to the Mujahidin."[14] He did not consult with Rabbani about the cease-fire but brought in Eshaq to witness the making of the deal, which at his insistence took the form of direct negotiations with a team of Soviet generals.[15]

Throughout 1983, he made repeated pleas to Rabbani and Eshaq for aid that would enable him to break the cease-fire by October. What he got back was reports of convoys under way but far fewer supplies than he needed. "I do not have the needed resources to implement the plan, and I do not know how to continue the work." Three thousand sets of boots and uniforms he had requested a full year earlier had still not arrived. "Do you realize under what difficult circumstances we are working?" he asked Rabbani in June. If the aid cannot be supplied, "I should be told openly about it." He quoted the Afghan proverb: "I should not be walking in the dark and extending my feet beyond my rug."[16] In September, he reported that he had to feed one hundred thousand civilians and thousands of mujahideen. "Either I should be provided with what I need, or I should be told openly that nothing is coming. This way I will be able to plan my future work accordingly." Nevertheless, he disclosed plans for attacks in four different districts, all outside Panjshir.[17] That same month, he reported that the Soviets had decided to break the cease-fire in response to attacks in Salang and Kohdaman that "have angered them." But he was hopeful: "I have made secret preparations for war. Let us see what is the will of God." By late October, with supplies still held up, he had to put off his planned offensive.

The seventh Soviet offensive began on April 21, 1984; it was a combined assault designed around new counterinsurgency tactics. It began with three days of heavy aerial bombardments, the mining of mountain passes, and the heliborne landing of Russian commandos in the Panjshir Valley and the strategic heights, with armor sent into the main valley. Massoud had received intelligence "in full detail" three weeks in advance and had ordered a tactical withdrawal. He divided his forces into three. One group launched preemptive attacks on the Salang Highway and against Russian bases; a second was stationed in neighboring valleys to act as a reserve; and the third remained in Panjshir to plant mines, perform reconnaissance, and launch surprise attacks. Even before the Russians arrived, mujahideen blew up one bridge and destroyed five others. They closed the Salang Highway for twelve days, and other mujahideen closed the other main roads to Panjshir from Kunduz, Mazar, and Takhar. Afterward, Massoud could report amazing results: some 2,500 Soviet casualties, 200 armored vehicles destroyed or disabled, and 11 jets and 15 helicopters destroyed.[18] In fact, according to Eshaq, Massoud's men were inflating the numbers; later, when he took over Kabul and found the correct figures, he corrected them.[19]

Massoud's biggest problem was the 150,000 internally displaced civilians who had "nothing to eat."

His biggest asset was intelligence. By this time, Massoud had become the "master of intelligence gathering," according to one aide. He knew where Russians were stationed, the locations of their bases, the communications systems they were using and their wavelengths, and even how much they were paid. "I know what the Russians are up to," he would tell aides. "All Russians are not fighting for the Russians." Significantly, a number of apparent Afghan turncoats, who had received military training in Russia and were employed in positions of trust in Kabul, were in fact reporting regularly to Massoud. Intelligence was his "first priority," his aide, Masoud Khalili, later recalled. "He never thought a war could be won except with intelligence." Once Khalili asked Massoud whether he had a spy in the Russian military planning office. He said yes, that his name was Taj. "That is my cousin!" Khalili said. "We had all abandoned him." Massoud replied, "That man is a hero." On another occasion, Russian commanders designated an Afghan military aide named Kamran to assassinate Massoud, and the man's wife sent word to the commander. Massoud responded, "Have him get the training. But keep me informed who trains him. Talk to them. Find out their weak points." The training lasted three to four months, and every second or third day, Massoud would receive a report. Finally came the day of the assassination, and Kamran, equipped with poison and a pistol, crossed the front line. Massoud welcomed him warmly. "Thank God, you're alive," he said. "What kind of pistol is that?" Massoud used the intelligence he gathered to support allies elsewhere in Afghanistan, among them Ismail Khan, who was fighting the Russians hundreds of miles away in Herat. The network depended on a corps of couriers who carried messages by sewing them into the lining of their clothes and slept en route in mosques where the imams were friendly to Massoud's resistance struggle.[20]

By 1984, Massoud had demonstrated many of the qualities that make a leader. He had shown the ability to organize from the grassroots up, had developed a sophisticated intelligence network, had adapted military tactics in highly unfavorable circumstances, and had been able to make a difficult command decision (on the cease-fire) and stand by it. He showed other qualities of proficiency under fire and never underestimated the stamina of his opponents. Step by step, he began to build a regional—and later a national—force.

From his letters, however, it appears that he was never able to surmount his supply problems. He wrote in June 1984 that he was eager to begin the next phase of mobile warfare against the Russians but could not until he received food, clothes, and medicine. Hekmatyar's commanders had blocked supply lines since the seventh offensive began in April. Adding to his woes, a group of Hekmatyar commanders newly arrived in Parwan province from Peshawar launched what Massoud called "unprovoked attacks" against Jamiat i-Islami, creating "problems for us when we want to attack the enemy." Massoud predicted that an eighth Russian offensive would begin soon.[21] Instead, the Soviet troops departed the valley and sent word they would like another cease-fire.[22] By late 1984, Massoud was holding meetings in Kapisa and Parwan provinces, where he won agreement from commanders and administrators to train and organize assault forces at every forward position.[23] By late November, he could report that Jamiat i-Islami controlled some 80 percent of the mountainous regions of northeastern Afghanistan north and south of the Hindu Kush. He went on to meet the commanders of Baghlan, Kunduz, and Takhar to organize the flatlands.[24]

The victories buoyed the mujahideen of different parties, and Massoud wanted to expand his reach to the entire east of Afghanistan.[25] It was a natural follow-on to organize, together with other regional commanders, a *shura nazar* of the north, which established committees to administer military affairs as well as educational, health, and political structures. Massoud was beginning to cast his eye on a broader canvas, calling on his fellow mujahideen to shift from a regional defensive posture and to start planning an offensive using a centrally organized force. "I am determined to create such a force in 1985," he wrote in March 1985. The biggest obstacle was Hekmatyar. "Now that we have survived, Hezb will have no choice but to make peace," he wrote to Rabbani. "If you can reach an understanding with the leadership of Hezb, it will improve the situation," but he warned Rabbani not to go too far.[26]

The effort was doomed from the start. From Hekmatyar's perspective, Massoud's ability to command and coordinate ever-larger units, coupled with the establishment of the *shura nazar,* transformed the long-standing rivalry into outright confrontation, with Pakistan backing Hekmatyar. Because he lived in Peshawar, "Hekmatyar would have access to us twice a day," said Amir Sultan Tarar (aka Colonel Imam), Pakistan's lead trainer of the mujahideen. "[Massoud] was inside, and it was difficult to have access to him." Tarar felt that Massoud had made "a correct decision" to develop the *shura nazar* beyond a military alliance into a political party—to obtain greater manpower and resources, Massoud had to develop political relations with other commanders. But Tarar said Hekmatyar "feared that his people would be ejected from the area. So they were using arms against each other." Tarar acknowledged that Hekmatyar, in attacking Massoud's forces, "earned his bad name."[27]

To broaden the front, Massoud relocated from Panjshir. By 1986, he was organizing allies throughout the northeast and had begun an officer training program for the new central army. When the Soviets began their next offensive in June, Massoud's units were more or less ready. An enormous, coordinated attack began with ten days of intense bombing raids from 3:00 a.m. to 10:00 p.m. and as many as 100–150 sorties each day against bases and areas controlled by the mujahideen. Units from five Red Army divisions massed in Kunduz on June 11; at 6:00 a.m. on June 16, they began their attack on the Khelab Valley. A wave of helicopters swept into the valley, carrying the first of three thousand Soviet commandos, but the mujahideen were waiting. Three helicopters came under fire but were able to disgorge their troops; a fourth was set on fire by a rocket-propelled grenade (RPG). RPGs and ground artillery destroyed two other helicopters, and the offensive was suspended. Massoud said his forces downed seven helicopters and three jets that day, and killed two hundred Russian commandos. Among the casualties was the Russian commander, who landed in the first wave. From his body, the mujahideen recovered a map laying out the entire operation. The Russians captured only one mujahideen base, in Khelab.

The defeat of so large a force, Massoud effused, "could not be described by the rules of war. Our victory was a God-given one." Once again, Massoud's intelligence appeared to be invincible. He said thousands of Red Army troops and hundreds of tanks were stationed on the road from Kunduz to Faizabad and predicted, on the basis of his intelligence, that they would remain in the north for three months, until they were resupplied, and then would launch new offensives. He could report a "relatively good" overall situation in the mountains of northern Badakshan, but on the plains his situation was "very bad." The Russians, together with Hekmatyar's Hezbi Islami, were able to capture vast areas from Jamiat-i-Islami, he wrote on April 22, 1986.[28]

But Massoud was on the move. By September, mujahideen mobile strike forces had captured enemy garrisons in Taloqan, Kunduz, Khanabad, Andarab, and Farkhar. Morale was up, and "the people are now more confident in the fighting abilities of our forces." Additionally, commanders were coming to Massoud, especially from Badakshan, asking him to organize more mobile strike forces. "They are very popular and more people are ready to join them," he wrote.[29] Meanwhile, he reported that five clandestine sabotage groups were deployed in Kabul, each operating independently, and they would soon be ready to carry out missions.

By June 1988, he held the fifth and most critical meeting of the *shura nazar*, an eight-day session in Farkhar that drew representatives from ten provinces. He called for a shift from defensive to offensive strategy, necessitating the creation of a regular army and a new organizational structure. The commanders formally launched the plan in March 1989, agreeing to establish an army of three thousand.

Massoud was well on the way to an achievement of greater significance than just a larger military formation. His strategic vision might have led to the creation of a secure state built around a military structure whose major figures had earned their legitimacy in the struggle against the Soviets. Unfortunately, he was the victim of his own success. By the time the commanders agreed to establish the core of a future national army, the last Soviet officer had crossed the Friendship Bridge, and Moscow's Afghan proxy Najibullah was consolidating his power base. Massoud called for continued attacks and for seizing areas evacuated by the Russians "at any cost." He also proposed an organizational structure to rule the liberated areas using experienced military officers, a radio station, and a printing press, and based on links with other fronts.[30]

But Massoud and the council of his internal commanders were out of sync with developments. Even as he was meeting with his commanders, Pakistan, operating on its own unrealistic timetable, had decided to bring down the Najibullah regime by launching Hekmatyar and other

Peshawar-based mujahideen leaders in an offensive against Jalalabad. The amateurish planning that sent ill-equipped irregulars in a massed offensive against a trained conventional force, and the impulsive manner of execution, made Jalalabad something of a South Asian "Bay of Pigs." Moreover, as they gambled away the lives and morale of the Afghan forces they had been supporting, Pakistan officials failed to coordinate with Massoud or other commanders who had fought the Soviets from within. That was probably a lucky break for Massoud, who emerged from the debacle with his reputation intact. His record was strong, his confidence was high, but the outlook was cloudy. Without the enemy that had united his disparate forces, Massoud required time and outside support to organize a national army, and neither was in ample supply. "The Soviet withdrawal and the fact that it came so soon took us by surprise," Massoud would later admit. "We didn't have the maturity, and we hadn't gone through the national process which we expected to go through."[31]

In the circumstances, the most serious missing element was a stable relationship with an outside patron, although it would not have been easy for so independent an operator to build a relationship with the United States at this stage. The United States was quickly disengaging from Afghanistan, motivated by the disinterest of the new George H. W. Bush administration in the confusing and complex situation on the ground, and disagreement in Washington over how to address the growing mess following the Russian withdrawal.

America's abdication began on October 1, 1990. With Russian troops gone and no compelling strategic reason for close cooperation with Pakistan, the Bush administration imposed sanctions on Pakistan for its continuing effort to develop a nuclear weapon and the means of delivery.

"When the sanctions came in, our influence started to fade," said Robert Oakley, a senior U.S. diplomat. Nonproliferation came to dominate U.S. policy aims in the region. "We had no imagination with the nuclear issue. We had a sterile back-and-forth with Pakistan. It was the height of heresy to say anything different," recalled Robin Raphel, who served as assistant secretary of state for South Asian affairs in the first Clinton administration. She argued that the "horse is out of the barn door" and there was a "lot of logic" on the part of Pakistan for wanting a nuclear weapon to counter India's acquisition of nuclear weapons. "What in the world are we trying to do here?" she asked. As a result, U.S. aid to Pakistan was suspended, all military assistance was trimmed back, and fighter jets destined for the Pakistan Air Force were put on permanent hold.[32]

There were immediate repercussions, largely for Afghanistan. Pakistan Army chief Aslam Beg and ISI director-general Hamid Gul devised a policy of "strategic consensus, strategic defiance, and strategic depth," in the phrase of a Pakistani journalist. Strategic depth meant a direct attempt by Pakistan to ensure that a friendly government took control in Kabul, a policy goal that translated into continuing support for Hekmatyar. Meanwhile, Beg traveled to Iran and, aware that the United States was adamantly opposed to nuclear proliferation, strongly hinted that Pakistan was willing to transfer nuclear technology. The public outcry that followed his trip led the government to retire him from his post several months ahead of schedule.

Washington's resumption of sanctions not only proved counterproductive in terms of U.S. goals but also put the United States at loggerheads with the country through which aid of any kind would have to flow to get to landlocked Afghanistan. If a single action undercut U.S. foreign policy and Massoud's prospects, this was probably it.[33]

The effects were not immediately evident. Peter Tomsen skillfully brought enough support to bear that Massoud was able to outwit Hekmatyar in the race to Kabul. But there was no follow-up. Fighting broke out within hours of Massoud's arrival in Kabul at the end of April 1992; by the next morning, Hekmatyar and the army units of the Khalq communist faction had begun seizing ministries and barracks. But after tank battles in the city center, the combined forces of the *shura nazar,* Dostum's militia, and the Parcham communist faction drove Hekmatyar and the Khalqis out of the city.

It was the start of a four-and-a-half-year civil war, throughout which the capital was constantly under siege, with two major exceptions: from May to October 1993 and from March to October 1995. Kabul, mostly unscathed during the jihad period, was largely destroyed. And while much of the rest of the country was relatively calm during those years, chaos and anarchy reigned in some cities, such as Kandahar.

The United States disengaged with dispatch. Tomsen's unannounced trip to Kabul on June 14, 1992, was his first—and last—official face-to-face meeting with Massoud. "I am proud to come to Kabul to congratulate the Afghan people on their victory against oppression," he said. "We will definitely open our embassy here," he continued, before adding the escape clause: "But it will depend on the security in Kabul."[34] Tomsen returned to the United States to train in the Dari language, but in the autumn, with Kabul under daily rocket fire from Hekmatyar, he was told he could not return because of security concerns. In January 1993, the Clinton administration took over in Washington, and no one mentioned sending an ambassador. Tomsen accepted a post as principal deputy to the assistant secretary of state for Asia, Winston Lord, Tomsen's former boss in Beijing.

Disengagement

In the meantime, Richard Smyth had arrived in Peshawar to take up the post of political officer at the U.S. consulate. A Dari speaker with a fascination for the politics and leaders of Afghanistan and a gregarious nature befitting his oversized build, Smyth traveled to Kabul that autumn to call on Massoud. It was the first of a dozen trips into the country over four years. Smyth's responsibility was to monitor and report on internal Afghan politics; but he was in no position to negotiate or even prod the players. Tomsen's mantra, which he had repeated to every Afghan politician he met, was that to legitimize their government they had to carry out an act of self-determination: a *loya jirga*, a *shura*, or free elections. Smyth's instruction was to remain equidistant from all players. "We were not going to support anyone," he said. "I was supposed to be 'close to all,' no matter how obnoxious they might particularly be," he recalled. (In practice, he kept a polite distance from Hekmatyar, whom he viewed as "a psychotic.")

Smyth knew he would have to address a fundamental question from Massoud: "What can you do to help me bring peace and security to the country?" Translation: what to do about Hekmatyar, who at the time was rocketing Kabul? Smyth had prepared a not-so-artful dodge: "You know and I know that foreigners don't understand Afghanistan. Every time foreigners have tried to shape things here, they have been unsuccessful. Afghans have to come up with an Afghan solution. Nothing can be imposed from outside." It was the rhetoric of disengagement, words that were "absolutely" irrelevant to Massoud's existential challenge, as Smyth recalled a decade later. The second cop-out was to urge Massoud to cooperate with the UN special envoy, who was trying to arrange an all-party settlement. But the United Nations, after Cordovez's mediation, had sent in mediators who failed to grasp Massoud's key role as the engineer behind the scenes and rarely called on him. The U.S. attitude was insincere, for Washington did not inform the United Nations how it would support UN efforts to achieve U.S. goals. Clinton's feisty UN representative, Madeleine Albright, was an advocate of assertive multilateralism. But in the case of Afghanistan, U.S. policy, said Smyth, "was passive multilateralism."[35]

Massoud impressed Smyth. "He was one of the few who had a real sense of Afghan nationalism. He was much less ideological than any of the others I talked to. He was very pragmatic. I did not see him as one motivated by a desire for personal power. He seemed to be actually a tempered idealist."[36]

Smyth's boss, Robin Raphel, who took charge of South Asian affairs at the State Department in spring 1993, did not share this view, although she admitted, "He was very engaging. . . . If you had to line up the guys, you'd pick him over Hekmatyar." Raphel, a career diplomat, had been married to Arnold Raphel. She considered Massoud a warlord: "It wasn't for us to choose between warlords who were tainted. Let them choose amongst themselves." She felt that Massoud charmed his visitors by his openness to Westerners and, in effect, was saying, "Choose us because we are smart, because we read books, and can talk to you—not because we have the ability to be tolerant for the other 80 percent of the population."

In her mind, Massoud was "in it for himself, and for power for the Tajiks."* When an AP reporter thanked Raphel for interceding to free him from "the bastard's clutches" (a reference to Hekmatyar), she replied, "They're all bastards."[37]

Massoud thought his problem was that Washington had never anticipated that he could take control and had been guided by its hope that UN mediation would place someone else in power. He also knew that Washington was divided. "There was a two-track policy," he said. "The CIA, through ISI, was supporting Hekmatyar, and the State Department was working towards a UN peace program. Everybody thought that if there was a military solution, it would be through Hekmatyar and the Pakistanis, and if there was a political settlement, it would be through the Benon Sevan peace plan." The problem was that Washington did not know "much about the situation" on the ground, and was "on the whole . . . not focusing on the activities" of Massoud's *shura nazar.* As for UN special envoy Benon Sevan, Massoud sent him a message urging him to pay attention to the role of the internal commanders and to not spend all his time dealing with the external leaders in Peshawar. "I asked him for a meeting. He said 'yes,' but later he didn't come."

Even under siege, Massoud was still supremely confident of his ability to achieve his goals. Western powers, he said, "knew from past experience that we did whatever we promised to do, even if it was later rather than sooner." What were his goals? "Naturally, we need an interim government." It would represent all the parties, but two-thirds of the seats should be given to technocrats, and the rest to party people. A *shura* of commanders would choose the defense and interior ministers. "Since an election is one of the things we insist on, we want to make the [run-up] period as short as possible." A general election "is our strategic aim, and we want to see it sooner or later." He offered to remove his own troops and heavy weapons from Kabul if all other parties did the same. His aim was to ensure Afghanistan's future "through elections and parliamentary government, and we will cooperate with all our heart with anybody who is ready to accept" such a policy.

America's departure from the scene left a vacuum and was an open invitation to Afghanistan's neighbors to back one side or other in the civil war. The lines of support shifted, sometimes reflecting an internal realignment, sometimes prompting one. The constant factor was that the United States was a nonplayer. A major beneficiary was Hekmatyar.

Hekmatyar had always been an all-or-nothing political leader with whom there could be no middle ground, and he took up his role as spoiler with a vengeance. Although for most of the civil war period he was officially

---

* In the view of veteran correspondent Anthony Davis, Raphel's remarks prove "how totally she misunderstood the man, totally . . . ludicrously." Davis, e-mail message to author, May 29, 2004.

prime minister of the Afghan government, he gathered his forces in Charasyab—fifteen miles south of Kabul and separated from the capital by a craggy mountain range—and periodically launched rocket attacks against the city. The behavior pattern that had emerged during the jihad, of eliminating those who blocked his path to power, continued in the first months of the postcommunist era, when his forces attempted to assassinate the first two presidents, Mujaddidi and Rabbani. As it was landing at Kabul airport, Mujaddidi's plane came under rocket and artillery attack. Shrapnel destroyed the cockpit, just missing the copilot. Hekmatyar had publicly threatened Mujadiddi's life before the attack, and his spokesman's half-denial—that if he seriously intended to kill Mujadiddi, he would have used twenty missiles—stopped just short of taking responsibility. (When Tomsen flew into Kabul in mid-June for his only visit, it was unannounced.) Rabbani took over as president in late June; on July 4, Hekmatyar launched his biggest rocket barrage against the city, killing at least one hundred people and wounding another three hundred. One rocket fell in a courtyard of the presidential palace less than one hundred yards from where Rabbani was holding a meeting.[38]

In the early months of the civil war, Hekmatyar asserted that his motive was to oust the remnants of the former regime and that his attacks were directed at Abdul Rashid Dostum, the former communist general whose Uzbek militia were now defending parts of Kabul. But this was the man who had made common cause with Najibullah's defense minister Shahnawaz Tanai and had incorporated Khalqi army officers and communist interior ministry troops in his forces. His targets were Massoud and Rabbani.

Bombarding the very city where he was to take up residence as prime minister would appear to be the work of a psychopath. A more sympathetic explanation was that he lost his bearings. One long-time observer said, "He's a strategist. He's a smart cookie. He was the only one [in Peshawar] with a sense of organization. He wasn't a woolly headed intellectual." But when Hekmatyar saw Massoud take over in Kabul, he went "around the bend."[39]

Massoud was on his own, aware of the need to legitimize his government but with no visible outside means of support. "There hasn't been a dollar of foreign aid for us," he told British journalist Sandy Gall in the spring of 1993. The government's only resource was the funds its predecessor had in the bank—some $200 million in gold reserves by one estimate—and printing money. Hekmatyar had the support of Pakistani intelligence officers, Pakistani Islamists, and elements of the Pakistani military, Massoud told Gall. Dostum had the backing of Uzbekistan, the Shia of the Hezbi Wahdat (Islamic Unity Party), and the support of Iran. A wire reporter who was in Kabul at the time said that Pakistan's military provided "vast quantities" of rocket, tank, artillery, and other ammunition to

Hekmatyar commanders during and after 1992, according to receipts Massoud obtained from "a Pakistani source."[40]

Few options were available, and Rabbani picked perhaps the worst one. Unable to win agreement among the parties to hold a *loya jirga*, Rabbani decided to stage what he called a "Council of Resolution and Settlement" in mid-December, with delegates flown in from Peshawar and around the country. Nine hundred sixteen of the 1,341 delegates voted to extend his term another eighteen months. It was a fateful error. Massoud felt the *shura*'s vote had been "85 percent genuine," although he was well aware that it had not been elected and therefore was not representative; five other factions boycotted the *shura* and dismissed the result as rigged.

The diplomatic picture was equally ominous. The regime had no friends abroad, and anyone in Washington who even thought of helping Massoud and Rabbani would find the proposition untenable. "From my perspective, the Rabbani government, from the way it was established, was unsustainable," Smyth said. After the December *shura*, there was "no way we could have named an ambassador to Afghanistan without alienating all the other groups."[41]

The *shura* settled nothing but led to a political realignment with immediate military repercussions, as the five opponents agreed in writing to try to defeat the regime militarily, according to Massoud. Dostum shifted positions in Kabul in support of the Hezbi Wahdat and by mid-January had formally begun cooperating with Hekmatyar. The next round of bombardment lasted five months, broken only by a cease-fire to hold negotiations in Pakistan.

During the fighting that winter, which devastated large parts of Kabul, a great many civilians were killed, and there was a massacre of Hazaras for which many blame Rabbani and Massoud. When Wahdat fired artillery into civilian neighborhoods, Rabbani and Massoud launched two offensives into Shia neighborhoods where Wahdat was operating. The February 11, 1993, assault on the Afshar neighborhood was the most costly in civilian lives. "Massoud was the first one to do ethnic cleansing," maintains Kathy Gannon, a veteran AP reporter based outside Afghanistan. Although John Jennnings, another AP reporter who was in Kabul at the time, calls the Afshar massacre allegation a "myth," an independent commission determined that seventy to eighty people were killed in the streets, and seven hundred to seven hundred fifty arrested men and boys either died in captivity or were killed. Human Rights Watch laid responsibility on Massoud's radical Islamist ally, Abdul Rasul Sayyaf.* More than ten years later,

---

* As for Massoud's commanders, Human Rights Watch noted that "Jamiat commanders may in some cases be liable for the abuses committed during the Afshar campaign by allied Ittihad troops, if it is shown in any cases that they had de facto command over such troops." *Blood-Stained Hands* (New York: Human Rights Watch, 2005).

Masoud Khalili, Massoud's spokesman at the time, did not deny the atrocities: "There was brutality from both sides."[42]

The rocketing came to a halt only when Dostum shifted sides again. Massoud believed the near-defeat of Wahdat isolated Dostum in Kabul, and when Pakistan, the mediator of the cease-fire, proved unable to deliver the top cabinet post it had promised him in an interim government, he became disenchanted. Whatever the reason, from May to November 1993, Kabul was relatively calm. The different factions met repeatedly to try to divide up the top government positions, but with little confidence of finding a peaceful way out. It was during this five-month lull that Massoud sat down for a long and revealing television interview—mostly a monologue —with Sandy Gall. He said his big mistake in the first stage of fighting was not to defeat Hekmatyar completely. "Each time Hekmatyar was on the verge of defeat . . . we stopped our offensive and started negotiations." He had feared the defeat of his archrival would provoke a north-south tribal conflict, between Farsi and Pashtu speakers, Tajik and Uzbek. "Experience showed this was not a wise policy," because Hekmatyar "is a selfish dictator like Saddam Hussein. He wants everything for himself." The clear implication was that during the next round, Massoud would finish the job. But there was another reason why what Massoud called his "limited fighting strategy" had failed: foreign aid to the competing factions. Pakistan invited Dostum to Islamabad in an effort to draw him closer to Hekmatyar, and Iran's deputy foreign minister made several trips to Afghanistan, attempting to draw Hekmatyar and Wahdat closer together. "The foreign aid prolonged the war," Massoud said. As for a long-term solution, Massoud acknowledged that "the leaders have failed in both cases—militarily and politically," a reference to the Peshawar political leaders, including Rabbani. He said he intended to call a new *shura*, with commanders elected from their districts, and then proceed to national elections.

The concept of the *shura* was rooted in Afghan political culture, and staging one conceivably could have led to the act of self-determination Tomsen had insisted on. However, it is hard to see how Massoud could bring about such a forum at the same time he was preparing to annihilate Hekmatyar, in the absence of foreign backing, and with neighboring countries working to undermine him. Massoud was embittered about the stance of Western powers, led by the United States. "By taking a neutral position, they allowed interference from Pakistan, Iran, and Russia. By simply monitoring and observing, they prolonged the war." Many U.S. officials agree.

His disenchantment would soon grow. Rather than respond to the opportunity created by the lull in the crisis, Washington was walking away at top speed. The United States had had a long and successful aid program in Afghanistan, dispensing some $500 million from 1950 to 1979. U.S. funding underwrote construction of the ring road around the country as well as dams, power plants, and other infrastructure, and the United States had sent Peace Corps volunteers from the founding of the agency up to the Soviet invasion. During the Afghan jihad, the United States launched an ambitious aid program to stop the outflow of refugees. The Cross-Border Aid program supported schools and medical clinics, provided food and other supplies, and underwrote private agencies that sent in American medical volunteers. As funding rose from the initial seed money of $6 million in 1985 to $90 million in 1990, the program turned into the "indispensable second front" in the CIA's covert war, according to author George Crile. (In addition, the United States was providing almost as much in relief assistance to refugees.) The donkey convoys and the highways and bridges built inside the country with USAID funding carried more than humanitarian aid: U.S. assistance was doled out to mujahideen political leaders in Peshawar or Quetta for civil-society development, winning goodwill, and helping the United States develop personal relations at a time when the CIA, under Pakistani restrictions, had few mujahideen contacts. Tomsen had prevailed upon the USAID program to build the road from Shogut in Pakistan's Chitral to Topkana on the Afghan border; this was the road that ensured Massoud a critical flow of supplies as he moved toward Kabul in early 1992.[43]

Bush and Baker made the initial decision to cut the aid, but Clinton and Secretary of State Warren Christopher completed the process. U.S. development and grant assistance dropped by two-thirds, from $60 million in 1992 to $20 million in 1993; it was cut by another 90 percent in Clinton's first year, to just under $2 million. Even food donations were zeroed out. Rather than fight for the aid, the administration heeded the warning from conservative senator Jesse Helms that foreign aid was "so unpopular among the American people" that there was growing support for closing USAID altogether. At his confirmation hearing, Christopher said the agency needed to "take on fewer missions, narrow the scope of its operations, and make itself less bureaucratic." The translation: USAID director Brian Atwood had to close twenty-seven offices around the world. After dispensing the final $2 million in grant aid to Afghanistan for the year beginning September 1, 1993, the Clinton administration closed the program; it sent $38.5 million to UN agencies or private agencies for refugee relief. As Atwood later explained, "The Cold War is over. We don't have to be in some countries [where] in the previous era we thought foreign aid was a way of fighting communism." The following year, direct aid to Afghanistan and Pakistan ceased altogether. Margaret Carpenter, Atwood's assistant administrator, told Congress that the civil war in Afghanistan made it "impossible to deliver assistance efficiently and effectively from Pakistan, or inside Afghanistan." That was a subject of controversy at the time.

While there was fighting in and around Kabul, and a descent into chaos and anarchy in Kandahar, there was relative calm elsewhere, according to Richard Smyth. At the most important point of confrontation between Massoud and Hekmatyar—near Sarobi on the trunk road from Peshawar to Kabul—neither side appeared to have more than one hundred men on the front line. "There was no real ideological incentive to fight. And they were unwilling to," said Smyth. Yunis Khalis, a Massoud ally, explained why: "The jihad is over. There's no point to killing other Afghans." But not many were listening to this assessment in Washington.[44]

There were other reasons to cut off aid. According to Carpenter, there had been an "incredible bump-up in aid to the former Soviet Union" and to some countries in Latin America. Asia took a "nosedive," largely because there was "no lobbying group for anyone in Asia." That was not entirely the case. Thomas Gouttiere, head of the University of Nebraska's Center for Afghanistan studies and one of the foremost U.S. experts on Afghanistan, lobbied everyone in Congress who had supported aid during the anti-Soviet war. But so many had become disillusioned in the absence of a settlement that he found no traction. The impact of the Cross-Border program on health care, education, and civil society had been astonishing. Gouttiere's own university had produced 15 million textbooks and delivered them to 1,300 sites inside Afghanistan. An elaborate monitoring system verified that the books arrived and were in use. Smyth felt he was well positioned to monitor the impact of aid. "There were 6,000 teachers and 4,000 health workers who were essentially on the AID payroll via nongovernmental organization cut-outs," he said. Dropping the program meant that "health care disappears and education disappears." The émigrés, the educated moderate elite among refugees in Pakistan—all eager to revive civil society in the postwar era—were abandoned as well. "These are the people we really dumped in 1994," said Gouttierre. "They lost any of their influence. They had no resources behind them any more." The only people who had the resources and money were the religious zealots in Pakistan, who supported their counterparts inside Afghanistan.

The excuse Smyth received was that aid was being cut to Pakistan, and it was untenable to have an Afghan USAID mission in Pakistan if there was no Pakistan mission. "I would argue that they could have run it out of Afghanistan," Smyth said. He suggested a provincial capital, if not Kabul. Carpenter said Smyth was "hopelessly naïve" about politics, because USAID officials "do not go into countries where we do not have an embassy." As a matter of fact, Smyth had checked this out and learned that USAID can obtain special authorization to operate in a country where it has no physical presence. Ultimately, the decision was made in Washington to ignore the advice from Smyth and others at the embassy in Islamabad. As Carpenter put it, "What people in Washington heard from the field didn't carry a lot of weight in the context of larger considerations. . . . What is said in the field is only a small part of what goes into the decision." A USAID official carried out the coup de grace through bureaucratic sleight of hand: combining the Afghanistan and Pakistan offices in the guise of avoiding duplication, and then folding the program altogether.

While the start-up of the Cross-Border program in 1985 had changed the environment in Afghanistan by raising the American flag and identifying the Afghan cause with America's cause, cutting off aid had exactly the opposite impact. The decision was "extremely stupid," said Smyth. "People would say it was the closing of the AID mission that led to the Taliban." Gouttierre concurred that the absence of a USAID presence "had a lot to do with the rise of the Taliban. We wielded no influence anymore in Afghanistan of any credible, solid nature. So the capacity of the U.S. to leverage anything in this period was nonexistent. The real leverage belonged with the Pakistanis, with ISI, with fundamentalist funding sources, and eventually, into 1997–1998, with al Qaeda." A decade later, Atwood did not doubt the impact cutting aid had on the Afghan tragedy: "I have no problem with people second-guessing decisions we made in those days. They were made because of resources."

Robin Raphel also felt strongly about the need to continue aid and reengage U.S. diplomacy in Afghanistan by returning somehow to Kabul. "I would say if you walk away because you got what you were after when the Russians left, and not considering the mess you left this country in, you are going to pay. It is not the right thing to do." For Raphel, this was a period of enormous frustration. "I did everything except dance naked on the secretary's staff table" to draw attention, she said. Gouttierre said Raphel was an ally inside the administration who was unable to convince those above her.[45]

Abandonment

No one felt the loss of aid more than Massoud: "Our request to other countries, especially the West, is that they should not forget Afghanistan because there is no Soviet Empire any more. . . . They have a moral responsibility because of the sacrifice which our nation has made." And the way to assist was to support reconstruction. "The excuse that there is fighting in Kabul is not good enough. They can start reconstruction work through the central government in the other provinces, like Herat, Jalalabad, Mazar-i-Sharif, Parwan-Kapisa. If there is fighting, it is only in Kabul." Noting that Hekmatyar's soldiers were being paid less than $20 a month, he said reconstruction aid would give people work; small sums could restart factories that employed thousands. "We are ready to do anything in our power to facilitate their work," he said. But the die had been cast.[46]

The cutting of U.S. aid at a time of civil war had an impact on Afghans. Afghanistan was already close to the bottom of the nations of the world in development when the Soviets invaded; after a decade and a half of war, the CIA ranked it as one of the top seven humanitarian disasters.

That was no exaggeration. In January 1994, Pakistan closed its borders to Afghan refugees, and those fleeing the fighting in Kabul were forced into subhuman conditions. The sprawling camp for displaced persons outside Jalalabad was an example. Set up on a barren plateau, surrounded by mine-fields, beset by snakes and scorpions, the camp housed 118,000 people living in tents and growing by thirty families a day, almost all fleeing Kabul. A *New York Times* reporter noted that there were neither trees nor a natural water supply and a daily temperature of 105 degrees.*

In a psychological sense as well, Massoud was now on the losing end. This was partly because of the role war plays in Afghan political culture. Afghan forces compete mainly in skirmishes and rarely fight to the finish; rather, they tend to shift allegiances according to whom they think will be the winner. Alliances are the currency of trade. "You can be someone's mortal enemy one day and closest ally the next," said a senior U.S. analyst. And the perception of outside support, "if not identical to reality, is 90 percent of the game here." In this context, Massoud could hardly have appeared anything but a loser.[47]

Although Massoud was exposed, Hekmatyar was in no position to take advantage. Under the Islamabad agreement, which he and Rabbani concluded under Saudi sponsorship in March 1993, Hekmatyar had become prime minister and Massoud stepped down as defense minister, to be replaced by a multiparty commission. But after chairing one cabinet meeting, Hekmatyar never returned to the capital, fearing, perhaps, a lynching by Kabulis infuriated over his role in destroying their city. Even his close aides were embarrassed. Hekmatyar spokesman Qutbuddin Helal was still setting up shop in the prime minister's palace when the city came under Hezbi rocket fire late that month. "We are here in Kabul and he is rocketing us. Now we have to leave. We can't do anything," he told Massoud aides.[48]

This was the backdrop to Dostum's decision to switch sides again. Dostum had played kingmaker once before, when his defection to the mujahideen helped precipitate the downfall of the Najibullah regime; now he saw the opportunity to play this role again. Paying his first visit to Kabul in July and smarting over Hekmatyar's failure to offer his party the promised cabinet posts, he said he would no longer recognize Hekmatyar as prime minister, only as party leader. Rabbani gave him the red carpet treatment, and Dostum, who stayed at the presidential palace, described himself as a "caretaker president." For a brief period, Dostum appeared to be drawing closer to Massoud. In fact, he was pursuing another strategy—to build up his own force with the intent of installing himself as king.

---

* U.S. food aid bounced up and down in the early 1990s: $20 million in 1991; $4.3 million in 1992; $18 million in 1993; zero in 1994; and $12.4 million in 1995. Considering the circumstances, these were modest sums at best. Margaret Carpenter, interview by author.

Born in 1954 to Uzbek peasants in Jowzjan province, Dostum dropped out of school in the seventh grade. He received his military education in the Soviet Union and rose through the ranks of the communist Afghan Army to become commander of three northern provinces. He became known as "Dostum" because of the forceful salutation he delivered to everyone in Sheberghan. A *dost* is a friend, and a *dostum* is "everybody's friend." Under Soviet rule, he developed a loyal and much-feared militia that brutally carried out his instructions. After the Russian withdrawal, Dostum's ill-paid troops gained a reputation for pillage, rape, and murder against non-Uzbeks. But like Ismail Khan in Herat, Dostum also had an eye for business and commerce. With natural gas deposits as a resource, electricity from Uzbekistan, a militia of twenty thousand, and forces in the region of one hundred twenty thousand, he built up the north to become the most prosperous of the Afghan regions. His ministate had its own flag, its own currency, and even its own airline. Unlike Massoud, he played the diplomatic game, winning recognition in the form of diplomatic missions from the neighboring Central Asian countries, Iran, and Turkey, all of whom saw him as a secular buffer against the Islamists who were attempting to take over Afghanistan. Still, he is best known, in the words of one Afghanistan specialist, as "the champion side-switcher" of the late twentieth century, "in bed at one time or another with almost everybody and against almost everybody." But he was also a secular regional leader.[49]

The prelude to some of the worst fighting in the civil war was a visit in mid-November 1993 by Robin Raphel. It was her first visit to Kabul as the State Department's top South Asia official. She met with Massoud and Hekmatyar and was quoted in one account as holding out the prospect of $60 million in aid to rebuild Afghanistan. No one in Afghanistan was listening.

Meanwhile, other regional players—Pakistan, Uzbekistan, and Iran—were ready to use such coin of the realm as they possessed. The ISI and other Pakistani officials pressed Dostum to link up with Hekmatyar, and Uzbekistan provided encouragement in the form of heavy weaponry. In mid-December, "everybody's friend" reached a secret agreement with Hekmatyar to oust Rabbani and Massoud by force. Both men sent close relatives to Tashkent, Uzbekistan, to conclude the deal, and the Hezbi Wahdat joined them in a new Supreme Coordination Council. Bolstered by arms from Uzbekistan—at least thirty T-54 and T-62 tanks—and presumably by funding as well, Dostum attempted a predawn coup on New Year's Day, 1994. But he overestimated his capabilities. Hoping for advantage over Hekmatyar, he attacked alone. Massoud may not have been a skilled diplomat, but his intelligence gathering was as good as ever. Thanks to advance warning, he quickly tied down Dostum's force of some five thousand over a front of many miles. Dostum's attacks destroyed large parts of central Kabul, leaving ten thousand civilian casualties. As many as one-quarter of Dostum's own force were killed, captured, or wounded. Undaunted, Dostum began a second offensive in the north, this time in cooperation with Hekmatyar. They captured Kunduz, but Massoud sent commandos in a late-winter expedition over the mountain and seized the Salang Tunnel, thereby ensuring his own resupply to Kabul and blocking Dostum's. By mid-March, Dostum's forces had lost the initiative on three northern fronts and found themselves on the defensive. Uzbekistan stepped up its aid, including fuel and spare parts, refueling and maintenance facilities for aircraft, and more than fifty additional main battle tanks and armored personnel carriers. Massoud's forces—lacking aviation fuel, spare parts, financial resources, and foreign aid—were unable to defeat Dostum.[50]

Still, Dostum's aura of invincibility had been shattered, and once again Massoud had survived. If Afghanistan were a laboratory experiment, the situation in mid-1994 might be seen as proof of what happens under the U.S. formula of aiding no one and remaining equidistant to all. In fact, it was the beginning of the end of the experiment of mujahideen rule.

4

"A Very Exciting Development"
(1994–1996)

Military stalemate fed the power vacuum and accelerated the breakdown of central authority in Afghanistan. Rabbani's regime could not ensure security for Kabul. It was unable to raise tax revenues, and it had no control over the countryside. So the major players had to fend for themselves. The fragmentation of power was nothing new to this land, for local leaders had never expected much from Kabul and had long before improvised local arrangements to keep their regions in business, but it was taking on a new dimension. In Herat, Ismail Khan set up a strong provincial authority under his personal domination; in eastern Afghanistan, local politician Haji Qadir assembled an all-party *shura*, which provided a semblance of comity. Dostum controlled much of the north and northwest. The roads between them became the source of tax revenue.

Richard Smyth, the U.S. consul general in Peshawar, traveled the country by road and described the picture: "The governor of a province, theoretically a member of Rabbani's government and party, would say, 'Send me some money.' But Rabbani could only reply, 'I don't have any money. Do what's necessary.' That is why they started doing 'security on the roads.'" Checkpoints and tolls sprang up everywhere, but the system broke down in Kandahar. The gateway to the south, Kandahar (named for Alexander the Great), was "chaos and anarchy, absolutely," with four local warlords controlling different parts of the city, all under the nose of the governor, Gul Agha Shirzai. "Elsewhere in the country, things were more or less working. The one exception was Kandahar," said Smyth. Who could unblock the roads? Certainly not the central government.

It was in Kandahar that Afghans tried a homegrown solution to the chaos. Smyth first heard about it from the scion of one of the region's most prominent families, the Karzais. In the spring of 1994, Hamid Karzai visited Smyth at his home in Peshawar. "Richard," he said, "there has been a very exciting development down in Uruzgan. A new group has formed, and you've got to get behind them right away. They are going to bring peace and security to the country." He reminded Smyth of the chaos, where just driving across the city meant being stopped by armed men, who would demand tolls, steal goods, and rape female passengers. The new group was the Taliban, and Karzai pleaded, "The United States has to support them right away."

Smyth responded, "Well, Hamid, who are they?" Karzai said they were "out there, busy, cleaning up all the roadblocks." Smyth said they were "basically nobodies at this stage," but he wanted to meet them. Muhammad Omar Akhund, the village mullah who started the movement, and the Talibs (from the Arabic for "seekers") he gathered around him found a resonance in Kandahar, but at the time Karzai was speaking, they did not control the city, and certainly not the surroundings.

But by autumn 1994, the Taliban had been transformed into a military and political movement with the stated goal of seizing power in Afghanistan; just two years later, they marched into Kabul. How did they do it? The Taliban would explain their meteoric rise with a Robin Hood analogy: by rescuing molested children from the clutches of depraved warlords, by clearing the roads of illegal checkpoints, and by disarming the villages they conquered, they swept through the Pashtun south on a wave of popular adulation. There is also a conspiracy theory that says Pakistan created, directly aided, and steered the movement. Certainly, the government of Pakistan assisted the Taliban in a number of ways, but some of the allegations of direct support came from Rabbani or Massoud and have never been backed by documentary evidence. While much about their internal organization and strategy remains murky, non-Taliban sources have shed light on who backed them and how. Pakistani and U.S. officials say that the ISI did not offer unsolicited aid to the Taliban but that the ISI readily agreed to a Taliban request for limited logistical facilities after being approached by the Taliban leadership. Aides to Benazir Bhutto took further steps to help the Taliban in support of Pakistan's own agenda, which was to open trade routes across Afghanistan to Central Asia. The movement also received significant outside military, political, and financial assistance at its formation. But the aid was largely unsolicited and came from—of all places—Rabbani and Massoud.

In mid-1994, the Kabul leadership did not have a lot of cards to play. Dostum's assault was a military failure, but it delivered a strong political message beyond the capital. The Rabbani-Massoud regime, its energies and limited resources tied up in protecting Kabul, was in no position to ensure security in the provinces except where it suited appointed governors and putative allies. In the security vacuum, local commanders, all former mujahideen, took matters into their own hands. Military checkpoints sprang up on every major road where armed men—under the guise of weapons checks —exacted a "toll" of cash and goods, and sometimes abducted women or boys and raped them. Ordinary citizens had no protection, farmers could not get their produce to market, and intercity and international commerce, conducted largely by the ubiquitous transport mafia, was severely impaired. Kandahar was the quintessence of the breakdown, with its division into four major zones and countless smaller ones.

Different versions are given of the specific origin of the Taliban movement, but nearly every account begins with a mujahideen commander raping adolescents and Mullah Omar and young Talibs mounting a vigilante response. Then, after experiencing a divine revelation, Omar convinces Kandahar merchants to provide the seed money that finances his campaign to clear the roads. The crucial link was the trenches of the anti-Soviet war, where Omar, a minor commander, was injured three times, the last time from shrapnel that destroyed his left eye. Omar's major benefactor was Haji Bashar, his commander in the Hezbi Islami force headed by Yunis Khalis and a prominent Kandahar merchant (also, according to U.S. drug enforcement sources, an alleged opium trader). Although brave in battle and with a reputation for honesty and sincerity, Omar was not a standout commander; however, when he related his vision, in which the Prophet Muhammad appointed him to bring peace to Afghanistan, Bashar believed him. Bashar raised 8 million Pakistani rupees ($250,000) through family connections, the local Jamiat-i-Islami commander Mullah Naqibullah, and local business contacts and obtained six pickup trucks, as well as arms left over from the jihad.[1]

Omar's village of Singesar in the Maiwand district lies close to the road linking Kandahar with the Pakistan border; his first aim, according to Smyth's sources, was to clear that road. Before proceeding, Omar sent a delegation headed by Mullah Mohammad Rabbani to call on President Burhanuddin Rabbani (no relation) to seek his approval. President Rabbani granted his wish and even promised funds. Of course, President Rabbani had his own agenda. The Kandahar-Chaman road was under the control of Hekmatyar commanders, and it suited the Kabul leadership, who were at the time under rocket attack from Hekmatyar, to help anyone who would dislodge Hekmatyar. Mullah Fatah Mohammad, a freelance commander who extorted tolls and merchandise from traders en route to Kandahar, presented the first challenge to the Taliban. When he refused an order to open the road, the Taliban, most of them teenage and older religious students, opened fire, captured him, and—after a summary sharia trial—hanged him for brigandage. They then shifted to the Kandahar-Herat artery.[2]

It is here that Rabbani and Massoud made their fateful investment in the fledgling movement. The funds, approximately $1 million in cash, were reportedly delivered to the Taliban in a suitcase. Ismail Khan in Herat publicly confirmed that money had been provided; according to one account, it came from federal customs revenues already in Khan's coffers. Massoud believed the Taliban's aims were his aims. A former senior aide said, "Commander [Massoud] was not against this uprising. Their main goal was to open the highways and clean up gangs from along the way, collecting arms, disarming bad people, and providing security. He would say, that is why we are fighting—for security, to open the highways, and to have good government. He was not at all worried about them coming; he was even optimistic about the Taliban and thought they could help for security." The commander also had another aim in mind: to use the Taliban to free the blocked arteries that were strangling Kabul. But his cunning may have been mixed with naïve faith in the piety and apolitical claims of the Kandahar "seekers." The cash infusion was no doubt a big boost to Omar, who at this stage had only a few hundred seekers in the movement; it gave him an imprimatur from the central authority, such as it was.

President Rabbani ordered all commanders to back Omar, and Mullah Naqibullah provided public support, funds, and weapons.[3]

The Return of Colonel Imam

In mid-1994 Pakistan sent its most knowledgeable Afghan hand into the restive south—Amir Sultan Tarar, or Colonel Imam, who had been its chief trainer of Mujahideen during the anti-Soviet Jihad. Colonel Imam was well placed to observe developments—and to nudge them along them as well. The six-foot-plus retired officer, besides having trained thousands of Afghan mujahideen in guerrilla warfare, knew practically every commander and politician in the land, including Massoud and Hekmatyar. Additionally, Hamid Karzai had been his assistant and interpreter for one-and-a-half years in Quetta. "He was brilliant," Tarar recalled. "I needed interpreting at first, and he helped me out." Tarar had a strong link with the United States as well. He had trained at Fort Bragg, North Carolina, and, during the anti-Soviet jihad, had given personal tours to Congressman Charlie Wilson and Senator Gordon Humphrey. A grateful Reagan administration presented Tarar with a plaque on which a chunk of the Berlin Wall was mounted. It was dedicated to "Colonel Imam. With deepest respect to one who helped deliver the first blow."

Although Colonel Imam no doubt assisted the Taliban in their rise to power, the single biggest factor in the group's rapid success has to have been the power vacuum in southern Afghanistan. Indeed, the Taliban steamroller recalls the peasant revolt in medieval England. According to Colonel Imam, Omar started with forty people, only half of them armed, and the declared intention to clear the roadblocks. "They covered ninety kilometers a day. People from the madrassas joined them en route, and by the time they reached Kandahar, they had got 4,500 people," he recounted. No one would challenge them.

By autumn 1994, the Taliban could boast a major accomplishment: Taliban checkpoints had been set up along the seventy-five miles between Kandahar and the Pakistan border town of Chaman, and on a similar stretch from Kandahar to Gereshk in neighboring Helmand province, although not in the city of Kandahar itself. Some 1,500 Taliban were manning the checkpoints, and they told BBC reporter William Reeve that they were funded by local merchants and fed by local villagers. Individuals told him they were "totally independent" and "not members of any party."[4]

Their next target was the Afghan border town of Spin Boldak, still under the control of Hekmatyar troops. When he reached that border, Hekmatyar, no doubt counting on Pakistan's support, sent word that he would not hand over the international checkpoint. According to Colonel Imam, Omar replied, "Nowhere is it written that international checkpoints will be spared." He gave Hekmatyar supporters seven days to confer with their leader, but there was no response. He then gave them five more days. On October 13, the Taliban raided the garrison, killing four, with one loss of their own. They also captured the Pasha weapons dump, which, according to the ISI director at that time, contained seventeen tunnels full of arms and ammunition—enough to equip three divisions. Well armed, they developed in short order both a diplomatic and a military strategy for the march to Kabul. Their plans meshed so smoothly with those of Pakistan that it raised suspicions that Pakistan was pulling the strings. There is no question that Pakistan played a catalytic role in the Taliban takeover of Afghanistan's major city in the south.

Pakistan certainly was taking a new look at Afghanistan following the election of Benazir Bhutto as president in 1993. Its strategy of backing Hekmatyar was in tatters, his role in the destruction of Kabul was a public embarrassment, and every diplomatic initiative seemed to run aground. Bhutto turned to a retired general, Naseerullah Babar, who had directed Afghan policy for her father in the mid-1970s and whom she named interior minister. Within the Interior Ministry, Babar set up the Afghan Trade Development cell; his vision was to establish a trade route between Pakistan and the fossil-fuel-rich, newly independent states of Turkmenistan and Uzbekistan. An improved relationship with Afghanistan, built on trade, might curb any Afghan longings to alter borders to unite Pashtuns; in addition, it would assist Pakistan's faltering economy and contain Indian influence. In June 1994, Babar announced that the government would seek an overland route from Baluchistan to Turkmenistan via Kandahar and Herat. Three months later, he visited Chaman on the Pakistan-Afghanistan border and announced that he would send the first convoy to Central Asia in October. On October 20, a week after the Taliban captured Spin Boldak, Babar led a delegation of Western ambassadors to Kandahar and Herat to show them the route; on October 29, the first convoy departed Quetta, carrying medicines, consumer goods, and food for Turkmenistan.[5]

According to Colonel Imam, the ISI asked him to "find out who these people are." He approached Mullah Omar for permission to move the convoy across southern Afghanistan. "He advised me not to take the convoy in, because the area was not safe," Colonel Imam recalled. But the Pakistan government insisted that he use his influence to get them through. At the border, Taliban forces stopped the thirty trucks, and demanded to know

the authority under which they were traveling. The confrontation illustrated the extent of the working relationship the Taliban had by this time
developed with Rabbani. But it also made clear that Pakistan's best experts
on Afghanistan—Babar, Colonel Imam, and Lt. Gen. Ashraf Qazi, the
ISI director-general at the time—were behind the political curve. Smyth
reconstructed the conversation.

> Taliban: "Do you have permission to come through Afghanistan?"
>
> Pakistani official: "Well, you give us permission."
>
> Taliban: "No, no, Afghanistan is a sovereign, independent country. Do you
> have permission from Rabbani?"
>
> Pakistani: "We thought you hated Rabbani."
>
> Taliban: "Yes, he is a bad Muslim. But he is the president of Afghanistan."

Rabbani offered no objection, so the Taliban waved the convoy through;
for good measure, they sent two top commanders, Mullah Borjan and
Mullah Nooruddin Turabi, and some of their armed men to ride shotgun.[6]
The truck convoy was now en route, with two senior Pakistani officers
on board, along with Colonel Imam and Colonel Gul (a former ISI officer). When they reached Takht-e Pul, twenty miles outside Kandahar,
fighters from a former communist militia under Mansur Achakzai halted
it. Achakzai and other commanders demanded as a condition for free movement that Pakistan stop the continued entry of madrassa students into
Afghanistan, who were by this time flocking by the hundreds across the
border from Pakistan to volunteer for the Taliban ranks. Colonel Imam, as
former chief trainer of mujahideen (he estimated that 96,000 mujahideen
"were trained by my teams"), anticipated a respectful welcome but in fact
was roughed up with "two or three punches." He was held for three days,
and there was no negotiating. "We will not allow the convoy through," the
commander told him. "If you want, you can go back to Pakistan." But
Colonel Imam said he showed "strong-headed" defiance. "I will not go back
to Pakistan. I will remain," he recalled saying. "This convoy is arranged by
the government of Pakistan, which is hosting your mother, your wife, and
your children. I am not only a Pakistan official, but a friend of the mujahideen, and the mujahideen are going to respond." It was to no avail. Eventually the Taliban's Mullah Borjan offered to release the convoy, and Colonel
Imam was allowed to go into Kandahar, where he spoke with local leaders,
including Mullah Naqibullah. At the same time, he contacted his own
government—both Babar and the ISI—and urged them not to interfere.
He told them that "if they did, it would be beyond my control." On
November 2, Taliban forces attacked the Achakzai force; two days later,
they freed the convoy. They then continued into Kandahar. In two days,

the Taliban had taken control of the former royal capital. Vital to the takeover was the fact that Jamiat-i-Islami's commander in Kandahar, Naqibullah, with 2,500 men, escorted the Taliban into town.

The mystery is how the Taliban pulled this off so smoothly. Some people credit Pakistan, but circumstantial evidence points in the other direction. According to General Qazi, the movement was indigenous. "The movement was not engineered from outside or trained from outside. If someone had had to plan and launch the Taliban, I would have had to do it. I certainly did not do it."* Smyth and CIA officials concur. And while it is true that Colonel Imam had had countless contacts from the days of the anti-Soviet jihad, he did not take up residence in the south until August 1, 1994. Also, in attempting to clear the way for the convoy to pass through the city, he had negotiated not with the Taliban but with several of the commanders in Kandahar. Finally, when Babar led the delegation of Western ambassadors to Kandahar on October 20, he said there were "no Taliban as such. But when the convoy went in . . . a movement started that later became the Taliban."

A second explanation is that in the context of the political vacuum in southern Afghanistan, the movement coalesced at record speed, its growth coincided with Babar's rush to open a Central Asian trade route, and events developed in a kind of spontaneous combustion. A third explanation is that the Taliban had a partner as they took over Kandahar—namely, the Kabul government, which was desperately seeking an ally because its

---

* Qazi states that the Taliban initiated the first top-level contact between the ISI and the Taliban at about the time that the convoy was moving through Afghanistan. A delegation headed by Omar's deputy, Mullah Rabbani (later head of government), and including Mullah Ghaus (later foreign minister) asked for a meeting and traveled to see him in Islamabad. Except for Rabbani, every one of them had a war wound. Qazi remembered them as "simple village folk" who were "totally unaware" of the rest of the world and thought that by imposing their brand of Islam, everything would fall in place in Afghanistan. He also recalled their primitive ways: "They didn't know how to sit on a sofa. They would sit with their legs up. I said, 'You are dirtying the sofas.'"

Mullah Rabbani's request to Pakistan was, first, to remain neutral and to not help any mujahideen faction. "They thought Hekmatyar was our favorite mujahideen," Qazi said. They did not request funds, weapons, or training, only the agreement that they could purchase fuel for tanks and vehicles and food and that Pakistan would not prohibit this. They would pay cash. It was at this meeting, Qazi said, that Babar asked the Taliban to help free the convoy: "He contacted me when the delegation came, requesting a meeting. He wanted to get a convoy freed." Qazi added that this was Babar's "first contact with the Taliban." (Babar denies being at the meeting.) According to Qazi, the Taliban, in response to Babar's request, released the convoy. Colonel Imam does not dispute that the Islamabad meeting took place, but he does maintain that it did not occur when he was leading the convoy through southern Afghanistan.

Having taken charge of the ISI in 1993, Qazi believed the agency was overexposed in Afghanistan, to no purpose. "We are not funded by anyone. Why are we still there? All we want is that they are friendly to us," he recalls saying. He left one ISI representative in Kabul, one in Mazar-i-Sharif, and Colonel Imam in Herat to keep an eye on both Herat and Kandahar. Qazi did not need convincing of the Taliban's modest requests: "I had no objections. I said so long as I don't have to provide funds." Qazi, interview.

very survival was in question.* Much evidence points to a mix of the second and third explanations.[7]

Colonel Imam's account of events seems to check out. Some months after the incident, a Massoud aide explained to Smyth that when Taliban officials arrived in Kandahar, they approached Mullah Naqibullah with a request for support. After Rabbani and Massoud instructed him to cooperate, Naqibullah "welcomed" the Taliban to Kandahar.[8]

Energized by their breakthrough, the Taliban leadership raised their sights. The Taliban now had advanced weaponry, including at least two hundred tanks, of which one hundred were operational; eleven MiGs piloted by former militia members; and nine transport helicopters. Diesel fuel, previously obtained from Iran, was now flowing from Pakistan. Young Afghans and Pakistanis from madrassas on both sides of the border were rallying to the Taliban ranks. By early 1995, the Taliban had set up camps at Spin Boldak and Kandahar for two-month military training courses, reportedly using former communist militia officers to conduct the training. To man their mortars and artillery, the Taliban reportedly imported former Khalqi Pashtuns who had fled with Tanai to Pakistan. U.S. officials were requesting visits to Kandahar to find out what was going on, and Pakistan announced a $16.7 million grant to repair the roads through Kandahar to Torghundi on the Turkmenistan border. Meanwhile, support of a different type was about to come from the government in Kabul.[9]

Before the end of 1995, the Taliban had captured Uruzgan and Zabol provinces north and east of Kandahar. After two months of fighting, they captured Helmand province in January 1995, then moved into Ghazni, which lies astride the main road to Kabul. Although its governor, Qari Baba, was a government appointee, this was Hekmatyar territory, and he had issued a warning to the Taliban in December that his forces would not yield their weapons "under any circumstances," nor would they allow the Taliban into government. But ousting Hekmatyar from Ghazni was too great a temptation for Massoud to resist: as the Taliban attacked, Massoud ordered his aircraft to bomb the positions. A few weeks later, he provided air support as Taliban militia approached Hekmatyar's base at Charasyab, south of Kabul. In both instances, a former Massoud aide said, "We sent jets to bomb the Hezbi Islami targets to support the Taliban." The air support was not coordinated with the Taliban in either instance, according to another former Massoud aide. Charasyab fell on February 14. Massoud's forces took control of the town and captured all of Hekmatyar's heavy

---

*Yet another anecdote illustrating the tenuous nature of Taliban contacts with Pakistan at this early stage is contained in a December 12, 1994, cable from the U.S. embassy in Islamabad. Pakistan's consul in Kandahar, Major Gul, was approached by Taliban representatives and asked "point-blank" whether he was a Pashtun or a Punjabi. Gul replied that he was a Pashtun, at which point the Taliban told him he should "stop working for the Punjabis and join with them." "Talibs in Kandahar," cable, U.S. embassy, Islamabad, December 12, 1994, released by NSA.

weapons; when the Taliban arrived, Massoud vacated the city, taking the weaponry with him.[10]

At this point, the Taliban controlled six provinces and had extended their reach to Maidanshahr, just west of Kabul. Massoud and Rabbani maintained a cool exterior about these developments but were clearly rattled. Massoud treated the Taliban as a welcome ally and, in a conciliatory gesture, sent doctors, medical supplies, and technicians to maintain their helicopters; he even sent cash. Meanwhile, Rabbani dispatched his central bank director, Ashraf Shah, to warn the United States that in view of the Taliban's gains and Hekmatyar's losses, the latest UN plan (which called for Rabbani to give up his presidency to an interim council) was in jeopardy. The issue was whether the Taliban would agree to share power. Unless they did, the envoy told the U.S. ambassador to Tajikistan, the council set up by UN representative Mahmoud Mestiri would be a "dead letter." Implicit in the message was the assumption that the Taliban had no plan to share power with anyone, but the U.S. ambassador had no instructions on how to respond. A week later, a second emissary delivered a stronger message to the U.S. consulate in Peshawar: the Taliban had demanded that the government turn over its heavy weapons. Massoud prepared for war.[11]

Apparently, a secret meeting had been held in the interim involving Massoud, Mullah Rabbani, and other senior Taliban officials. It took place in Maidanshahr, a dusty, nondescript crossroads of shops and low mud-brick buildings that had served as the launch point for Hekmatyar to rocket Kabul. Hekmatyar's forces were gone and Maidanshahr was now Taliban territory; for Massoud, this was a voyage into the unknown. The Taliban placed two-man watch posts every hundred yards on the two-and-a-half miles between the front line and the meeting place, but that was not the only thing that disturbed Gen. Ahmed Muslem Hayat, Massoud's chief of security, who had gone there on a reconnaissance mission. "Please, commander," he said, "do not forget the history." He was referring to Habibullah Ghazi—also known as Bacha-i-Saqao (son of the water carrier)—a Tajik peasant who led an uprising and held Kabul for nine months in 1929. He was ousted by Nadir Khan, a Durrani Pashtun. Nadir had invited Bacha to a conference, then hanged him and seventeen followers.

Muslem knew what Pashtuns thought of Tajiks running Kabul. "My assessment was to inform the commander he should not enter Taliban territory. I told him, 'It could be your last mistake.'" If he insisted, Muslem said he should "come in an armored personnel carrier with 200 of your best troops." But Massoud would not be dissuaded. "I want to go," he said. "I don't care about security. If you do not want to come, I will go anyway." He asked Muslem for a pistol and an extra magazine and put it in his vest. With Abdullah Abdullah (later Massoud's emissary abroad and foreign minister in the post-Taliban government), they drove the several hundred yards in three cars with a handful of bodyguards.[12]

The meeting took place in midafternoon in a one-room government security post. The participants sat on the roof on Afghan blankets: Massoud, Mullah Rabbani, Mullah Borjan, Mullah Abdul Razzaq, and five other Taliban leaders. The Taliban demand was the same one they had imposed on Hekmatyar and everyone else they had overrun: "Disarm all parties." Massoud agreed, but with a major caveat. "We are not a party. We are the government. We have tanks and warplanes." He said this had to be a government decision, and there should be a complete disarmament program. "Clean up Hekmatyar, and Dostum, and [Abdul Ali] Mazari [the Hazara leader of Wahdat] in Kabul," he said. "We are ready to work together—to open highways, bring security to the country, and, after that, have elections." He said the Taliban insistence that women be banned from public schooling and jobs was "no problem. We can make a decision." The most important thing, Massoud said, was to "clean out the bad people." At one point, Muslem overheard a voice squawk over the Taliban radio: "Arrest this man." But Mullah Rabbani responded that it was not necessary, because Massoud was willing to work with the Taliban. Muslem later learned that Pakistani advisers had urged Massoud's capture and that Mazari also had urged the Taliban to attack the government.

A second round of talks was held in Kabul, at which President Rabbani proposed summoning *maulavi* (learned Islamic scholars) from every province to determine the country's future. The Taliban demurred. Confrontation was looming. Massoud informed Washington that his plan was to avoid launching a first strike against the Taliban but to fight back if the Taliban attacked Kabul. Smyth noted in his cable that Kabul had misjudged the Taliban, its "expectations for a power-sharing agreement reaching further than reality." But Smyth was in no position to offer any advice or assistance.

The showdown began on March 6, 1995, after reconciliation efforts broke down and Massoud moved against the Wahdat forces in Kabul. Two days later, Mazari made a deal with the Taliban to hand over Wahdat's weapons in exchange for the Taliban taking up frontline positions. A Taliban column moved into the Deh Murad Khan quarter. Massoud gave the order, and government artillery and aircraft began to bombard the militia. Mazari's militia refused to hand over their weapons to the Taliban and divided, with a large number going into a pro-Massoud Shia militia. Massoud struck again at the Taliban and forced them out of the city. Dostum's remaining troops, disarmed by the Taliban, were evacuated to Mazar-i-Sharif. Believing that Mazari had intentionally betrayed them, the Taliban arrested him, bound and gagged him, and killed him in what was viewed as a summary execution en route to Kandahar. On March 19, Massoud's forces expelled the Taliban from Charasyab and Rishkor, south of Kabul.

The siege of Kabul was over, and for once Massoud and Rabbani were in control. For seven months, the capital enjoyed relative calm, but it was no time for euphoria. Effective government control was limited to the capital, Herat, the five mainly Tajik northeastern provinces, and, in a limited sense, to the region controlled by the Eastern Shura in Jalalabad. Massoud was "desolate and desperate, deeply fatigued politically and psychologically," according to a close associate at the time. "He was suffering morally. He couldn't support the mujahideen government sincerely because he saw its errors and its problems, but we couldn't flee from the field." Still, the experience of Maidanshahr was an eye-opener. "All the Mujahidin leaders were dissatisfied with the situation. But in comparison with the Taliban, they believed they were right. They said to themselves: 'You are the lawful government. You have taken some losses, some setbacks.'"[13]

If anyone in the West had cared, this might have been a final opportunity to save the mujahideen regime and to stave off the Taliban. If Massoud had any remaining illusions about the Taliban, he shed them at Maidanshahr. The Clinton administration also knew full well what to expect, because the Taliban themselves informed the U.S. government of their plans. Maulavi Abul Abbas, the mayor of Kandahar, told visiting U.S. diplomats in February 1995 that the Taliban intended to take Kabul, disarm all the commanders, and install one government across Afghanistan that would institute sharia. "Anyone who gets in our way will be crushed," he warned. He refused to identify the Taliban leaders or even say how many members were in the ruling *shura*. He left an "overall impression" of "disingenuity and a degree of deception." As Anthony Davis put it, the choice facing the United States was between a forward-looking, avowedly revolutionary Islamist who sought modernization within religious constraints, or a traditionalist, "often obscurantist, fundamentalism that blends the instinctive conservatism of the *ulema* (clergy) with the narrow view of the Pashtun villages." Washington waffled, urging Massoud and Rabbani to yield power to a broad-based transitional government that the United Nations had planned to set up but realistically no longer could.

Afghanistan's northern and western neighbors took a different approach and began sending aid to Massoud for the first time. In a secret cable, the U.S. embassy in Islamabad catalogued the backers of each side. After Mazari's murder, Iran—worried that the Sunni Taliban would turn on the Shia Hazara—started supporting the new Wahdat leader, Karim Khalili, with an initial $2 million and encouraged other Shia groups that cooperated with the government. Uzbekistan cut back its aid to Dostum and urged him to cooperate with the "moderate" Massoud rather than the "fundamentalist" Taliban. India and Russia also provided modest assistance, with Russia allowing the supply of arms through Tajikistan. Turkey was providing humanitarian aid to both Dostum and the government. On the other side, Pakistan was providing assistance to the Taliban and Dostum, but the cable said the aid to the Taliban was "not likely to be enough to give Islamabad much leverage over the inchoate [Taliban movement]." Turkmenistan was donating aid to Massoud's ally in Herat, Ismail Khan.[14]

Meanwhile, Pakistan's intelligence and diplomatic machinery had swung into gear and, taking advantage of their links with local commanders dating back to the jihad, officials prepared the ground politically for the crucial months ahead. Colonel Imam, after actively supporting the Taliban takeover of Kandahar, established himself in Herat. Using his ties with the Taliban, he received a full briefing on their plans to capture Herat. But Imam, by all accounts, also enjoyed an excellent rapport with Ismail Khan, the autocratic but widely admired strongman of Herat. With conflict looming, Colonel Imam in late 1994 or early 1995 briefed Khan in detail on the Taliban's plans to capture the city. He brought maps and planned troop movements, laying out how the Taliban would then advance as far as the Shamali plains north of Kabul. His idea was to convince Khan not to fight the Taliban but to join them. As an inducement, the Taliban were willing to let him govern two other provinces. But Khan, who was highly regarded by Babar, Qazi, and Amir, insisted on remaining governor of Herat. "I believed Ismail Khan could play a greater role . . . at the national level," Colonel Imam later recalled. "I told him, 'Avoid fighting the Taliban. You will be defeated.' But he thought he would be able to stop them. And he failed." The Taliban would make two attempts, in March and September 1995, but in the end Colonel Imam was proven right.[15]

To improve the Taliban's chances, Pakistan moved forward on a second diplomatic front by drawing closer to Dostum, whose fiefdom in northwest Afghanistan abutted that of Ismail Khan. In mid-November, Babar's convoy had transited Dostum territory and dropped off several truckloads of aid in Mazar-i-Sharif. A month later, Taliban and Pakistani envoys called on Dostum in Mazar and told him they would oust Hekmatyar from Ghazni and open the road to Kabul. They asked him to block any countermove by Hekmatyar. Pakistan government officials gave Dostum the same message and asked him not to consider an alliance with Massoud but to keep his lines open to Hekmatyar. In return, Pakistan agreed to continue limited financial support, gave Dostum's small airline landing rights in Peshawar, and offered medical treatment to his VIPs. Dostum was ready and willing to play along. Noting Ismail Khan's vulnerability on his southern flank, he seized Murghab, a key junction town in Badghis province, north of Herat.[16]

The Taliban turned westward and, in late March, made a first attempt to seize Herat. But Massoud outfoxed them by airlifting two thousand troops to aid Ismail Khan, helping save the city in a series of battles that lasted through late April. In late summer, Khan broke out and captured Gereshk in Helmand province, the last major town on the route to Kandahar, but he failed to establish defense lines or command and control.

The Taliban, by bribing a pro-Khan commander, were able to encircle the city and trap Khan's troops. They killed hundreds and captured hundreds more, with the rest fleeing in disarray. By this time, Dostum's air force was bombing Herat Airport and his ground forces were advancing in Badghis province in what had been Ismail Khan territory. He closed the air space over northern Afghanistan to prevent the resupply of government forces. The Taliban next turned to Shindand Air Base. Khan had no time to organize a defense, and when it fell on September 4, he reportedly emptied the local bank and fled with one thousand of his troops to Iran. Massoud aides said the government was to blame for flawed logistics (food and water ran out), but according to an American who witnessed the town's fall, Heratis put the blame on Khan's political and military stumbles. Most Heratis, according to this witness, thought that the United States, the United Nations, and the international community were behind the Taliban.[17]

The fall of Herat was an enormous blow to morale in Kabul, and when angry Rabbani supporters rioted and set fire to the Pakistani embassy, the government unwisely failed to intercede. Whatever divisions had existed within Pakistan's diplomatic and military establishment over linking their fate with radical Islamists in Afghanistan quickly dissipated as the elite rallied behind the Taliban.

By October, Kabul was again under siege. The Taliban picked up where Hekmatyar had left off and fired on Kabul from newly recaptured Charasyab as well as from Maidanshahr. With Dostum blocking access on the main route north, the Taliban blocking the main route south, and Hekmatyar's forces blocking the main route from the east, Kabul was effectively surrounded. That winter was said to be the most cheerless in Kabul's memory. Kabulis, short of food and fuel like their brethren in Sarajevo, had to chop down orchards and ornamental trees to stay alive in the subzero temperatures. Because of Hekmatyar's blockade, Kabul had been without electricity for three years, and only emergency convoys of the World Food Program and a Red Cross emergency airlift kept the city of 1.2 million supplied with food.[18]

That winter, Massoud showed uncharacteristic caution. Blaming the uncertain political outlook, he held back from launching an offensive, something he later regretted. Meanwhile, the Taliban continued assaulting Kabul, firing 287 rockets into the city in January alone, killing dozens of civilians and wounding hundreds. In a final desperate turn of the revolving door of alliances, Burhanuddin Rabbani, with Iranian backing, reached out to Hekmatyar. And in early March, Massoud's lifelong rival, Hekmatyar—no doubt disappointed that Pakistan had switched sides—announced an alliance with him. It proved to be one of Massoud's greatest regrets, but he had few options at the time.[19]

Kabul's Fall

In mid-April 1996, U.S. envoy Robin Raphel visited both claimants to power for what must have been a surreal discussion all around. With the capital under Taliban bombardment, she met Rabbani and Massoud in Istalif, a picturesque village near Bagram Air Base. Stressing that the United States was a "neutral player," she called for an arms embargo against all parties, which would have disadvantaged the government far more than the Taliban. The two Tajik leaders, Massoud and Rabbani, represented themselves as the legitimate government of Afghanistan, which Raphel found a "highly questionable" claim. In what Raphel dismissed as "self-righteousness," they asserted that the government had a legitimate right to import weapons. Rabbani laid out his plan for setting up a transitional government, which would draft a constitution and hold elections, and Massoud set out his vision for a bottom-up democracy. Raphel was unimpressed. Missing from the discussion, she said in her cable, was "a sense of how to get from the current stalemate to the rosy, democratic future both Rabbani and Massoud envisioned." In Kandahar, by comparison, the Taliban had few ideas to put forward about the future government except to say its shape would be "determined by the people" once the nation was disarmed (and under their control). She found their message "naive, simplistic, and rigid." However, the Taliban gave a warm welcome to the proposed arms embargo. But the idea died the following month when Albert Chernyshev, a Russian deputy foreign minister, told Raphel he could not imagine an effective monitoring mechanism. The emptiness of American rhetoric was captured in the headline to her cable: "Chernyshev fails to take the bait." "Why should they have listened? We were not in position to demand anything," she later said.

Raphel's other major talking point was equally unreal: that "economic opportunities here will be missed" if political stability is not restored. In fact, during the conversation in Istalif, according to a Massoud aide, Raphel spent a surprising amount of time discussing a project to build a gas pipeline on Afghan soil linking Turkmenistan with Pakistan. The promoters, a U.S.-Saudi consortium led by UNOCAL of California, had been seeking diplomatic support for their ill-timed project. The White House showed no interest, according to top National Security Council officials, and the State Department had taken up the issue in the vain hope that it would provide leverage in dealing with the parties. In the midst of war, it was unlikely to take off.[20]

Kabul's worst day was June 26, 1996, when Hekmatyar returned to take up the prime minister's post. Having abandoned the moral high ground, the Taliban fired three hundred BM-21 rockets, killing sixty-four and wounding one hundred thirty-eight; fifty of the rockets were aimed at the area around the Intercontinental Hotel, where Hekmatyar was being sworn in. The return of Massoud's lifelong foe did not sit well with his military, and there was little he could do to save the regime. In August, the Taliban launched their final offensive against Kabul, first ousting Hekmatyar's forces from Paktia and Paktika provinces, then sweeping into Nangahar. Haji Qadir's Eastern Shura divided into pro- and anti-Taliban groups, and he fled Jalalabad for Pakistan.

Now Pakistan called in its chips. Hamid Gul, the ISI director-general who had forged a close relationship with Hekmatyar during the jihad period and had masterminded the abortive 1989 assault on Jalalabad with the aim of installing Hekmatyar in power, pulled every string available on behalf of Benazir Bhutto's government. The objective was simple: to undermine Hekmatyar's defenses. The method was equally so: to circumvent him. "I went and told Hekmatyar, 'Please don't fight the Taliban,'" Gul later said. "I told him, 'Your commanders are telling me this.'" Gul said he was in a position to tell Hekmatyar about the views of his commanders "because they used to confide in me directly."

The government's last stand took place west of Sarobi, a town on the Kabul River that sits astride the trunk road at the entrance of the "Silk Gorge," linking Kabul with Jalalabad and Peshawar. Sarobi fell to the Taliban on September 24, after what Gul termed a "purchase, not a battle." That evening Massoud had sent his aide, General Muslem, and three hundred men to Sarobi, along with ten tanks and fifteen trucks. During the night, the Taliban moved close to their front line. When the battle commenced the next morning, government troops ran out of ammunition within an hour, and a Hezbi commander "changed sides in the middle of the battle," Muslem later recounted. "He turned over two truckloads of ammunition, including all the antitank mines in his possession, and then showed the Taliban where we had planted our mines." The Taliban fired mortars. "All we had to defend ourselves were Kalashnikovs." At one point, his troops resorted to dumping rocks from the mountaintops. Muslem lost sixty men and ordered those remaining back to Kabul.[21]

Nighttime Retreat

At three o'clock in the afternoon on September 26, two days after the fall of Sarobi, Massoud ordered a general withdrawal. The people of Kabul should be spared "street fighting," Massoud told his aides. But the canny commander also intended to spare his own forces to fight another day. Massoud's final act before withdrawal was to send his chief of security to the UN compound, where Najibullah had been living since his overthrow in 1992. He urged him to join them. Najibullah replied that the Taliban had not only Pakistan's backing but also that of the United States, and he would be safe under the protection of the United Nations. UN personnel had a different perception of the Taliban and caught the last plane out that afternoon. Massoud's forces organized to withdraw. An orderly nighttime retreat through an urban area with an enemy at its heels is as risky a maneuver as any army can attempt, but Anthony Davis, who was in Kabul at the time, judged the anabasis remarkably successful: Massoud managed to evacuate thousands of government troops as well as most of his heavy armor and artillery. The last troops departed by midnight.[22]

The Taliban forces moved uncontested into Kabul. Full of religious fervor, imbued by a sense of divine mission, and euphoric over their rapid victory, their first act of state was one of primitive vengeance. At one o'clock in the morning, five bearded men in turbans entered the blue steel gates of the UN compound and broke into Najibullah's quarters. A former boxer, Najibullah had grown fat while he was president, but he subsequently began working out three times a day and had gotten back in shape. He decided to fight for his life. He struck one of the Taliban and grabbed his Kalashnikov. One of the other Taliban fired at his head and shot off part of his skull. His two Afghan bodyguards escaped through a window, across a roof, and into the dark street. Either at the UN compound or at the presidential palace where they dragged him, the Taliban mutilated his body and, according to some reports, castrated him. They also killed his brother, who was visiting Kabul from his home in India. The next morning, Najibullah and his brother were found hanged from a traffic post at the Ariana traffic circle in central Kabul; Najibullah's body was bound by ropes to keep it from falling apart. Banknotes were stuffed into his mouth and pockets and cigarettes were shoved into the nostrils of his brother, symbolizing corruption and betrayal. Taliban militiamen danced before the corpses and posed for foreigners' cameras.[23]

Long after the bodies were removed and returned to the family, the site was a highlight of city tours organized for visiting foreign diplomats by the newly installed government. Why the desecration? Why the spectacle? According to unconfirmed reports, one of the men who came for Najibullah was Gen. Shahnawaz Tanai, his former defense minister and implacable foe. For nearly two years since the Taliban capture of Kandahar, Tanai's officers had been providing the skilled expertise needed to maintain and operate all the advanced weaponry and planes the Taliban had captured. According to many accounts, Tanai arrived with the Taliban in Kabul. In addition, Mullah Rabbani harbored a "very personal vendetta" against Najibullah—Najibullah's Khad intelligence had reportedly killed Rabbani's father and two brothers by pushing them out of a helicopter.[24]

Suddenly the social order of a medieval Pashtun village was imposed on the most cosmopolitan, open, and free city in Afghanistan. Kabul Radio, renamed Voice of Sharia, carried the orders. All "sisters" were fired from their government jobs. All women henceforth were to cover themselves from head to foot in burqas in any public place, where they must be accompanied by a male relative. Girls' education was halted, and boys' schools closed for want of teachers. Men were ordered to grow chest-length beards and replace their Western garb with the *salwar kameez* (a long shirt and loose trousers). They were to worship five times a day at the mosque and to forgo toothpaste and use the natural root that the Prophet Muhammad used to clean his teeth. Bans were also placed on televisions, kite-flying, the possession of homing pigeons or birds of any kind, music, dancing, singing, chess, marbles, cigarettes, and photography. Anyone who broke the rules was subject to a public beating. But there was also a positive side of the ledger: security was enhanced, roads were reopened, food and fuel prices fell, and commerce resumed.[25]

From the official U.S. perspective, the Taliban takeover was seen, all in all, as a hopeful development. Najibullah and the Heratis were not alone in believing that the United States favored the Taliban takeover. "From the day the Taliban captured Kabul, it was clear that the U.S. was largely sympathetic to the movement," recalled Agence France-Presse (AFP) correspondent Stefan Smith. "At our end, we had the very general impression, including from U.S. diplomats in Islamabad, that the Taliban were not such a bad bunch at all."

This was not just one reporter's impression. On the day the Taliban took Kabul, the State Department offered them more than an olive branch. "On the face of it, there's nothing objectionable at this stage" to the imposition of Islamic law in areas under Taliban control, State Department spokesman Glyn Davies said. He played down the execution of Najibullah as a "regrettable development."[26]

Twenty-four hours later, the Clinton administration launched a diplomatic initiative to demonstrate its willingness to deal with the Taliban as "the new authorities" in Kabul. Warren Christopher cabled the embassy in Islamabad, authorizing it to send an envoy to Kabul as soon as feasible and safe. He also set out seventeen talking points. To facilitate a dialogue between the United States and the Afghan government (a bold assumption, as there was nothing of the kind), the Taliban were to be urged to appoint an envoy to represent them in Washington. The United States would reopen its Kabul embassy when security permitted; in the interim, it would send an envoy on frequent trips there. Rabbani's representatives would be denied visa extensions. The talking points omitted any mention of the sudden loss of women's rights. Well down the list, at point nine, was a tepid expression of American "dismay" over the summary execution of Najibullah. Raphel approved the cable.

The envoy was to be Lee Coldren, director of the State Department's Office of Afghanistan, Pakistan, and Bangladesh. Raphel tracked him down in Pakistan's far north, where he was visiting Hunza, a region widely thought to be the inspiration for Shangri La of James Hilton's *Lost Horizon*, to attend the opening of the newly restored Baltit Fort. "You've got to get back to Islamabad," she said. "We may want you to go back to Kabul."

With no flights or ground transportation, he hired a local driver and four-wheel jeep for the hair-raising trip through mountain gorges and secondary roads. It took a day and a half to reach Islamabad, but when he got there he found he had new orders: "Under no circumstances are you to go to Kabul, and don't even talk to the Taliban in Peshawar." Coldren recalled, "Within twenty-four hours, her chain was pulled. This cable had a life of thirty-six hours."[27]

Suddenly, Afghanistan turned into a domestic U.S. issue. Theresa Loar, a Foreign Service officer, had just been appointed the first State Department coordinator for women's affairs; she immediately went to State Department spokesman Nicholas Burns to protest the friendly welcome to the Taliban. "We have got to get the secretary of state to say this is not business as usual," she said. Burns asked her to provide new language. His statement that day amounted to a revision of Raphel's cable. "It's not at all clear that the Taliban have control over all of Afghanistan. In fact, it's fairly clear that they do not," he told reporters. "It's not at all clear to us that they have established a functioning government in Kabul or in the areas that they control." He also expanded Raphel's list of topics to include human rights, such as due process "and the treatment of women, which is a major issue in the United States. And we'll continue to raise those issues." As for Najibullah's summary execution, the United States joined in the worldwide condemnation. But this was not the only reason the diplomatic initiative died: the Taliban had sent word that they were not ready to receive a U.S. emissary.[28]

Raphel later acknowledged that the public statement was "not quite right in the heat of the moment." She said the reason for sending Coldren in was "to get in right away and lay down some markers. . . . We reconsidered it because of the way it looked. Then we started down a whole different track."

The upshot was a good deal of confusion and two competing policies within the State Department and throughout the U.S. government. One approach favored embracing the Taliban, even if it meant overlooking the implications of their domestic system, in hopes of effecting positive changes in behavior. The other favored public condemnation of their medieval concept of society, even if it stripped Washington of the means to affect their behavior. In the absence of top-level interest in deciding on a single course or a willingness to bring financial or military resources to bear, both approaches existed in a kind of foreign policy schizophrenia. This was the case during the five-year-long Taliban era, beyond the Clinton administration, and even after 9/11.

Looking back at the civil war from the distance of a decade, Raphel now believes that the policy she implemented was a mistake. "We didn't want to choose for the Afghans. That was the view at the time, which, in retrospect, may have been incorrect. . . . We'd have been better off if we had chosen a side." The problem was that "we weren't engaged enough to stay with a side."[29]

By the time the Taliban captured Kabul, there was a compelling new reason for American attention to Afghanistan. In May 1996, as the Taliban captured one Pashtun province after another, Osama bin Laden had returned to Afghanistan. Soon he was issuing fire-breathing fatwas against the United States and looking for the opportunity to influence the Taliban regime. Washington was in no position to counter him.

5

"An Endless Tragedy of Epic Proportions"
(1997)

Indifference to Afghanistan was no accident during the two Clinton administrations; it was the result of a judgment call. Hotter issues were on the table—such as stabilizing democracy in Russia, restarting the Middle East talks, pacifying the Balkans, and developing relations with China—and Clinton's top aides believed that the Afghan civil war was unlikely to have a lasting impact on U.S. interests or the peace of the region. "I don't recall a debate about Afghan policy in the first term," said a former top White House aide. "Afghanistan was not . . . on the radar screen. . . . I don't think Cameroon was either. . . . And I don't know what our policy was toward the Maldives."

A historian might take a different perspective. Afghanistan has been the burial ground of empires, thwarting British expansion in the nineteenth century and helping to ensure the demise of Soviet power in the twentieth. But a buffer between major land powers can be a very unstable place when the outsiders leave. And when an empire collapses, it is not unusual for a power vacuum to develop along its periphery, leading to civil war and wider chaos. Sometimes, only intervention can bring it under control.* For example, the collapse of the Soviet Union and communist rule produced a power and security vacuum in independent Yugoslavia. The local strongman, Slobodan Milosevic, sought to exploit the vacuum for his own political gain by going to war in Slovenia and Croatia in 1991 and Bosnia-Herzegovina in 1992, with the explicit goal of creating a greater Serbia. The intervention in Bosnia led directly to genocide against the Bosnian Muslims. Eventually, the United States intervened at a minimal level, chiefly to save its own alliance-based security structure. It brought fighting to a halt and recognized the Bosnian Serb entity created through "ethnic cleansing." Nevertheless, the suspension of active hostilities and the long-term stationing of U.S. troops in Bosnia and later Kosovo brought stability and set a

---

* The slow-motion collapse of the Austro-Hungarian and Ottoman empires created a vacuum in the buffer states between them, provoking a series of Balkan wars that set the stage for World War I. After World War II, the defeat and collapse of the German Reich created a vacuum in east Central Europe; Stalin's rush to fill it led to the Cold War.

precedent in Europe. Eastward expansion by both NATO and the European Union gave the continent its best hope for lasting peace in centuries.

Nothing like that occurred in South Asia. A similar power vacuum emerged there, but the United States disengaged beginning in 1992. Washington watched in silence as the pro-Western Rabbani-Massoud regime succumbed to the battering of other factions, and tacitly welcomed the takeover by radical Islamists. Afghanistan had become a political black hole, where, as the UN secretary-general summed up, "Responsible local political authorities, let alone a central government, have ceased to exist." Pakistan, a regional power with profound problems of self-governance and a continuing conflict with India, attempted to fill the leadership gap left by the United States. But Islamabad's diplomacy centered more on a narrowly conceived national agenda—hounding India from disputed Kashmir—than on Afghanistan. A discontinuity in domestic government owing to coups in 1990, 1993, 1996, and 1999; steady support by the military for the Taliban regime next door; and a lack of focus on Afghan internal politics facilitated developments that would take most Pakistanis by surprise.

"The Americans do not have a real policy in this region," observed Massoud not long after his retreat from Kabul. "They rely entirely on the Pakistanis, who told them the Taliban would bring stability [and] an end to drug trafficking; . . . thanks to them, Afghanistan would no longer be a sanctuary for international terrorists. However, we still do not have peace, opium production is continuing apace in the zones controlled by the Taliban, and they have given shelter to Osama bin Laden." He summed up the big problem: the Taliban "are now autonomous and are uncontrollable."

"In hindsight," said the former senior U.S. official, "it is obvious we would have been better off to pay some attention to Afghanistan."[1]

Closer monitoring might have detected the process by which one of the world's poorest and least developed countries turned into a platform for global terror. In hindsight, what made it possible was a political constellation whose true nature was cloaked by an ongoing civil war. Three essential elements of this constellation were in place by late 1996: infrastructure, a willing host government, and a cunning predator. The indispensable fourth element was the conspicuous absence of close international scrutiny, including by members of the news media. The United States, largely through its detachment, played an unwitting supportive role at every stage.

The infrastructure took the form of training camps at which volunteers from around the Islamic world could be prepared for combat and martyrdom. Set up during the anti-Soviet war and paid for with American dollars and Saudi funds, the camps took on new functions and new sponsorship during the chaotic struggle against Najibullah and the civil war that followed. In January 1994, Peter Arnett and Peter Bergen reported on CNN that nine camps were in operation, with six of them run by Hekmatyar's

Hezb Islami. This was the same mujahideen leader Pakistan's ISI had armed, directed, and promoted to take power in Kabul. Other Afghan leaders who maintained close ties with the ISI—such as Jalaluddin Haqqani, Abdul Rasul Sayyaf, and Yunis Khalis—also ran camps.[2]

They had all benefited from Pakistani-distributed U.S. largesse; now, with the United States abandoning its role, Pakistan assigned them a mission in line with its own national interests. In 1989—after the upheavals in east Europe, Moscow's defeat in Afghanistan, and the Tiananmen Square uprising—Kashmiri Muslims began a new insurrection against India. Pakistan had backed and trained Kashmiri separatists throughout the 1980s but was under a great deal of pressure from the United States and other countries to close the camps that had sprung up on its soil. Thus, as the Russians left eastern Afghanistan and U.S. funds dried up, the training of Kashmiris began there. Existing facilities were used and new camps were built. Hekmatyar set up at least one training camp near Torkham on the Pakistan border and sent "advisers" into Kashmir; Haqqani hosted Kashmiri youth fleeing the harsh Indian crackdown. "We have had many Kashmiris here with us and they have gained useful practical experience," Haqqani told a reporter in early 1991. At the same time, Muslims from around the world were still flocking to Afghanistan for military training and religious indoctrination in response to the films and literature of bin Laden and Abdullah Azzam. So both groups were being trained in the same camps, although usually separately. The Afghan mujahideen leaders acted as landlords and collected rent for the use of the facilities. "You could make money. People would pay you—the Pakistan government, bin Laden or guys like him. So it was like a business," said Gary Schroen, former CIA station chief in Islamabad. The instructors were Arabs who stayed behind after the anti-Soviet jihad and ISI officials, mostly retired military officers.

The unintended consequences of American disengagement took on a life of their own. The joint training facilities enabled new ties to spring up that linked the volatile Kashmir struggle, the slowly simmering Arab militancy, and, in time, the radicalizing Taliban cause into an unholy alliance. "Look what we did," Schroen said. "*We* created this." He had a point. Regimes could come and go, but the camps stayed in business. When the Taliban took power, they seized control over six camps that made up the al Badr complex between Khost and the Pakistan border. They closed two and turned four others over to the Harakat-ul-Mujahideen (HUM), a Pakistan party of Deobandi Sunnis whose puritanical observance of Islam paralleled Taliban practice. The HUM in turn had close ties to the Jamaat-e-Ulema-e-Islami (JUI), which was part of Benazir Bhutto's government. Other camps opened during the five years of Taliban rule, and nearly all would fall under the authority of Haqqani, who became minister of tribes and frontiers. Bin Laden and al Qaeda never owned the camps but, in effect, rented them.[3]

Thus, through its retreat from the scene, the United States facilitated the continued operation of the training camps after the Soviet withdrawal.

The second element in the constellation was the seizure of power by a regime of messianic amateurs, whose naiveté and ineptitude in government opened them to an outsider's manipulation. American passivity smoothed the way. The initial U.S. sympathy for the Taliban was "more as a hope than a hard judgment," Clinton's close aide noted. "I think there was some attraction [to the Taliban]. There was some hope that the Taliban, because of their discipline, might be able to bring order out of chaos . . . that maybe the Taliban was the tough medicine that would stabilize Afghanistan."

But the Taliban would prove incompetent at governance, other than in the enforcement of sharia. They had no interest in the country's economy or the well-being of the population and were dismissive of the fate of the millions displaced by the constant war.

The third element in the constellation was bin Laden, whose religious bearing and pious utterances concealed an ego and political astuteness that were second to none. His direct knowledge of the territory, the personalities, and the culture, and his smooth operating style enabled him to exploit the regime's vulnerability in exchange for permanent sanctuary. One of the greatest ironies of the bin Laden story is that it was U.S. concerns about terrorism, coupled with its lack of interest in the region, that led to his return to Afghanistan.

Looking back, bin Laden's four years in Sudan were a dress rehearsal for Afghanistan. The Sudanese government, newly installed in 1989 and eager to prove its Islamist credentials, extended the original invitation in 1990, promising hospitality and support if bin Laden, Ayman al Zawahiri, and their supporters would move their operations to Sudan. But after meeting with three intelligence officials who brought a personal letter from President Omar Hassan Ahmed al Bashir, the al Qaeda rank-and-file were unsure of the regime's ideological purity. Suspicions centered on Hassan al Turabi, the leading behind-the-scenes figure in Khartoum, who had spent time at the Sorbonne. "How do we trust him? He studied in Europe," one al Qaeda member asked bin Laden. A delegation went to meet Turabi. Higher education in Europe "doesn't make the person bad," the visitors were assured. But it was only when they learned that Turabi had been a Muslim scholar for forty years and had memorized the Koran that they gave the go-ahead.

Zawahiri and hundreds of his and bin Laden's followers moved to Sudan in late 1990. By the time bin Laden arrived in mid-1992, after two years in his native Saudi Arabia, more than one thousand al Qaeda foot soldiers were in Sudan, and his associates had set up a network of guesthouses, businesses, and military training camps using his funds.

Bin Laden's leadership style evolved as he issued anti-American fatwas through al Qaeda's religious committee and dispatched trainers and weapons to conflicts throughout the Islamic world. Generally, bin Laden took whichever side the United States opposed. A big exception was Bosnia, where the United States and bin Laden were on the same side, although that seems to have been a minor interest for the latter. His first fatwa attracted little notice. In late 1990, some months after Iraq invaded Kuwait, bin Laden called on the world's Muslims to fight the U.S. Army and expel it from the Gulf region on the mercantilist grounds that the United States wanted to seize Arab oil and other resources. A second fatwa at the end of 1992 focused on religious grounds, calling for the expulsion of Western troops from "our lands" based on the Prophet Muhammad's statement that there could not be two religions in Arabia. A third fatwa followed the Bush administration's decision to send U.S. peacekeeping troops to Somalia in late 1992. This one focused on geopolitics: it charged that having already taken over the Persian Gulf area and now moving into Somalia, the U.S. military, if successful, would next march into southern Sudan and then into other Islamic countries. A fourth fatwa made the emotionally charged claim that the United States had occupied the two sacred cities of Islam, Mecca and Medina. No such occupation had occurred, and the fatwa, to judge from international news reports, attracted no attention.

At the same time, bin Laden and Zawahiri began planning military operations. Senior bin Laden aides, arguing by analogy from the fatwas of Ibn Tamiyeh, a medieval Islamic scholar, told al Qaeda members that killing "Tartars" would ensure them a place in paradise and advised them not to worry if civilians were killed during an attack on military targets. (The Tartars in this case were Americans.)[4]

Bin Laden backed his words with action. With the help of the Sudanese government, he shipped four crates of explosives from a hangar-like storage facility at his Soba farm to southern Yemen in early 1993, using a ship owned by al Qaeda. He sent trainers into Somali to instruct different tribes on how to defeat the United States; and in 1993 and 1994 he sent al Qaeda members to Nairobi and Mombasa, Kenya, to set up businesses and scout out the U.S. embassy in the Kenyan capital for a possible future attack. Bin Laden later told a TV interviewer that Nairobi was targeted because the "brutal U.S. invasion" of Somalia originated there. At the same time, he set up an office in Baku, Azerbaijan, to process fighters into the Chechnya war; sent $100,000 grants to antigovernment groups in Jordan and Eritrea; provided training to Tajiks trying to overthrow the government of Tajikistan and funding for an Islamist element of the Moro Front in the Philippines; and smuggled Kalashnikovs into Egypt via camel train. He even attempted, unsuccessfully, to obtain nuclear and chemical weapons. Bin Laden was building a method of operations.[5]

What endeared him to the Sudan government was the money he threw into roads, agriculture, trade, and light industry. It was more development aid than business investment. "Our agenda is bigger than business," he told a group of his managers. "We need to help the government and the government to help our group, and this is our purpose." Thus, in exchange for a new road from the capital to Hayar, on the Egyptian border, the government turned over the state tannery. Bin Laden also acquired a bakery, a furniture factory, a fruit and vegetable export firm, a cattle sperm bank, and an experimental tree farm, as well as vast agricultural holdings where he raised sesame, peanuts, cotton, and sunflower seeds.[6]

But the same attributes that made him attractive to the regime ultimately led to his expulsion. In 1993, with nearly every Islamist radical group in the world operating from Sudan, the State Department placed the country on its list of state sponsors of terrorism, thereby blocking all private U.S. investments there. In mid-1995, the Egyptian terror group al-Gamaa al-Islamiyya mounted a daring assassination attempt against President Hosni Mubarak of Egypt during a state visit to Addis Ababa. A bin Laden employee was the mastermind. Meanwhile, Zawahiri's Islamic Jihad had secretly tried and executed two young boys, the sons of Egyptian Afghan veterans, for alleged espionage. It was a bizarre case. In his memoirs, Zawahiri claimed that Egyptian intelligence had blackmailed the boys into spying on him and other leaders. Their method was to send in Egyptian intelligence agents who seduced and sodomized the boys and filmed the crime. Zawahiri put the boys on trial before his appointed legal committee, which sentenced them to death. This was too much even for the Sudanese government. Accusing Zawahiri of setting up a "state within a state," Sudan deported the entire Islamic Jihad leadership. They scattered to Yemen, Jordan, and Afghanistan.[7]

Bin Laden was also on notice. He was already in deep trouble with Saudi Arabia and Egypt. In 1994, the Saudi leadership froze his assets at home and stripped him of citizenship, citing his continuing public attacks on Riyadh and his close affiliation with Islamic Jihad and Takfir Wal Hijra, an ultra-radical jihadi group operating in Egypt, Libya, and Algeria. That year, in what was widely assumed to be a Saudi assassination attempt, a hit squad armed with submachine guns sprayed bin Laden's house in Khartoum with bullets. According to Prince Turki al Faisal, then head of Saudi intelligence, the attack was "not real"; rather, it was an attempt by "some Sudanese agencies" to convince bin Laden he should look to them for protection.* The Saudis also tried the velvet glove, dispatching members of his family to

---

* According to Nasir Abdallah al-Bahri (Abu Jandal), a Yemeni volunteer who later became bin Laden's bodyguard, bin Laden told his entourage that an Islamic group that had declared him an infidel was behind the attempt to kill him. What had saved him was a family quarrel—with his son, Abdallah, over the family's austere lifestyle—which delayed his arrival at his office. As the attackers began firing at his office, bin Laden and his son, both armed, arrived and attacked the assailants from the rear. Although bin Laden said both Egyptian and Saudi intelligence agencies supported the Islamic group, he did not accuse either intelligence service of organizing the assault. Nasir Abdallah al-Bahri (Abu Jandal), interview by Khaled Al-Hammadi (part 3), *Al Quds al Araby*, March 18, 2005, translated by FBIS.

beg him to apologize to King Fahd and return to Saudi Arabia. "They sent my mother, my uncle, and my brothers on almost nine visits to Khartoum," he later told an interviewer. As late as March 1996, the Saudi government offered to restore his citizenship and his personal property, and allow him to return "in dignity" if he would renounce his denunciation of King Fahd. They also offered $500 million dollars that would go to his family, but bin Laden rejected the offers.

The United States was also on his case. Bin Laden may have helped finance the late 1992 bomb attack on a Yemen hotel where hundreds of American troops were billeted. The U.S. troops were alerted in time and evacuated the building, but a tourist and a hotel worker were killed. In November 1995, a car bomb exploded outside the Riyadh offices of the Saudi Arabian National Guard, killing seven, including five Americans. Shortly before the explosion, bin Laden received a phone call at his farm south of Khartoum with apparent notification. Bin Laden also claimed to have played a key role in forcing the United States to pull its forces out of Somalia, ending the mission there, although little credence was given to this claim at the time.

His move to Afghanistan in May 1996 was the unintended consequence of actions the CIA itself set in motion. After years of monitoring the terrorist groups that had gathered in Sudan, the CIA's Khartoum station found itself under surveillance, reported two incidents of threats to its staff, and demanded that the entire embassy be closed to reduce the risk.[8]

U.S. ambassador Timothy Carney fought to keep the embassy open, but CIA station chief Paul Quaglia, working with the State Department's diplomatic security section, prevailed. On February 6, 1996, his final night in Khartoum, Carney had dinner with Ali Othman Taha, the Sudanese foreign minister. Carney demanded that Sudan expel bin Laden. A month later, Maj. Gen. Elfatih Erwa, the Sudanese minister of state for defense, appeared in Washington for talks at which senior CIA officials repeated the demand. "Where should we send him?" Erwa asked. "Just ask him to leave the country, but don't let him go to Somalia," the U.S. officials responded. Informed that bin Laden would probably go to Afghanistan, they said, "Let him."[9]

This was one of the most fateful decisions of the Clinton presidency, and the casual way in which it was transmitted seems incredible in retrospect. Why so little attention to the risks? One reason was the neglect of Afghanistan by U.S. diplomatic, intelligence, and national security apparatuses. No senior official was concerned about the unfolding events and there was no ambassador to beat the drum, so no effort was made to determine the impact. And yet everyone knew the chemistry that might develop when a determined terror mastermind took up residence under the protection of a radical Islamist regime, for that is what had occurred in Sudan. "It was insane to force him out," commented a senior State Department expert on Afghanistan, who was not consulted. "Anyone who knew anything knew where he would go."

A second reason was a mindset in Washington that saw terrorism and terrorists not as an existential threat to U.S. national security but as a pesky problem that could be addressed through intelligence gathering and traditional law enforcement. Quite possibly, top officials simply did not understand what a sophisticated organization al Qaeda had become. It was not until well into 1996, when a top operative defected to the United States after eight years of membership in al Qaeda, that U.S. intelligence began to grasp the dimensions of bin Laden's ambitious project. Jamal al Fadl, a Sudanese who had functioned as bin Laden's treasurer, turned up at the U.S. embassy in Asmara, Eritrea, with the story of the founding of al Qaeda; the operation of the training camps; the operations in Somalia, Yemen, and Saudi Arabia; the financing; the numbers of participants; and bin Laden's methods of operation.

A third reason for the lethargy was the reluctance of law enforcement to address international terrorism as a potential domestic threat. White House counterterrorism aides Daniel Benjamin and Steven Simon reported a "lull in work on international terrorism" at the FBI from 1995 until early 1997 and little interest in looking beyond the immediate actors in the first major international terrorist incident in the United States, the 1992 bombing of the World Trade Center. That, plus the "historically poisonous" relationship between the FBI and the CIA, the reluctance of either agency to share with the other,* and the disdain of FBI chief Louis Freeh for almost any request from the Clinton White House left top officials without many options.[10]

The Clinton White House laid the onus on the FBI: "The FBI did not believe we had enough evidence to indict bin Laden at that time and, therefore, opposed bringing him to the United States," said Sandy Berger, then deputy national security adviser. Simply removing him from Sudan was seen as a better option than allowing him to stay. His expulsion "was seen as a major way of limiting his capability to maintain his network of terrorism, which had been based in Sudan," recalled Nancy Soderberg, at the time also a deputy national security adviser. "While there was concern he would rebuild it once in Afghanistan, there was a sense that moving him from Sudan would seriously disrupt his capabilities. It would take him time and be more difficult to re-create in the hills of Afghanistan."[11]

Saudi Arabia was also not an option. According to Turki al Faisal, Sudanese president Omar al Bashir made a "conditional offer" to turn bin Laden

---

* The FBI also would not share intelligence with the State Department, even to avert an attack on a U.S. installation. Richard Smyth said that the FBI, while investigating the murder of U.S. citizens in Karachi, uncovered a plan to hit an American target in Peshawar. "We didn't get that information for weeks. My family, the people working for me, were the target. The FBI told me, 'We're doing a criminal investigation. We're not an intelligence-gathering organization.'" Smyth, interview.

over to the Saudis, the condition being that no legal action would be taken against him. "Bashir was told that no one is above the law and that we could not give such guarantees," Turki said.[12]

Hegira

Bin Laden, his wives and children, and a large retinue of followers departed Sudan on May 18, 1996, and traveled in two aircraft to Jalalabad. Bin Laden flew in on a small private plane. The plane refueled in Doha, but Qatari officials were not aware that bin Laden was on board, according to Turki. Sudanese officials chartered a second aircraft from Ariana, the Afghan state airline, for $50,000. President Rabbani denied having anything to do with the invitation or with facilitating bin Laden's move, but the money, paid in cash, went straight into the depleted state coffers, Ariana officials said. More than ninety men, women, and children, all well-groomed and looking "healthy and handsome," prepared to board the 727-200 in Khartoum. There were more passengers than expected, so the Sudanese state airline donated an extra thirty seats, according to the copilot. The checked baggage included eight large sacks of sugar, generators, oil lamps, oil camping stoves, school supplies, general household items, and a large quantity of luggage. When they landed at Jalalabad, mujahideen in pickup trucks, complete with rocket launchers, surrounded the aircraft. They loaded up and disappeared into the night. When the pilot and copilot flew back to Kabul, they were grounded for a full month. Abdul Rahim Ghafoorzai, Massoud's foreign minister, shouted at the airline's executive vice president, "You have placed the country in a very big problem!"[13]

Eastern Afghanistan was familiar territory to bin Laden from the jihad period, and it had many attractions for him. Being in Jalalabad put him close to the Tora Bora complex of caves, which he had helped build and operate during the jihad, and close to the Lower Kamas Valley, where Wahhabi proselytizers had arrived a century earlier and Wahhabi converts still lived. One of the compounds at which he reportedly stayed—a guesthouse at the intersection of the Kabul and Kunar rivers—offered easy escape into the Mohmand agency in Pakistan's tribal area. His base near the Hadda Farms (an old collective agricultural complex that had been under Hekmatyar's control) put him close to Jalalabad Airport, useful for an airborne getaway if needed. He maintained one or more bases in the Tora Bora area and on some occasions received visiting reporters in a cave. He also held court at the governor's quarters in Jalalabad, maintained at least three safe houses in Kabul, and later built a compound in Kandahar.[14]

The invitation had been delivered by three former mujahideen commanders: Maulvi Saznoor, a commander with Abdul Rasul Sayyaf's Ittihad-i-Islami (Islamic Union), who had spent time pinned down with bin Laden under Russian fire but was otherwise apolitical; Engineer Mahmoud, a commander under Hekmatyar who had built the Tora Bora training facilities and was politically well connected; and Fazl al Haqq, who was with the Yunis Khalis breakaway branch of Hekmatyar's Hezb-e-Islami. The three men offered bin Laden asylum. It was during a visit to Sudan national day celebrations that the three men offered him asylum. Formally, Haji Qadir, a businessman-politician and ostensible ally of Massoud, who governed the Eastern Shura by the juggling act of trying to accommodate the disparate factions from royalists to Islamists, was bin Laden's formal host, but exactly whose guest he was is a matter of dispute. Din Muhammed, governor of Nangahar province, said there were two major factions in the *shura,* and it was not the faction of his late brother, who had been assassinated in 2002, but the second one, of Saznoor and Mahmoud, which invited bin Laden. Then-president Rabbani, denying any role by the central government, said the Eastern Shura was not cooperating with Kabul but was claiming independence under the guise of "federalism." In any case, reporters who visited Jalalabad at the time said bin Laden was put up at Qadir's guesthouse. Qadir's driver said the governor had received bin Laden at the Jalalabad Airport, but Qadir said he did not know of bin Laden's presence until a few days after he arrived. "I had no idea that Osama bin Laden was coming. The whole thing was organized without me knowing about it," he told AFP reporter Stefan Smith in 2001. According to the CIA, there is no doubt that Sayyaf and Yunis Khalis, two other prominent mujahideen leaders, did welcome him.[15]

Sudan notified the United States just after bin Laden's departure, but no one bothered to inform Richard Smyth in Peshawar, who was a frequent visitor to Jalalabad and a close friend of Qadir. "A lot of things we weren't told," said Smyth. But even if he had he known, Smyth could not have talked Qadir out of hosting the Saudi firebrand.* "Bin Laden would have been an honored guest of any self-respecting mujaheed. Ronald Reagan would have been." Smyth said that he had "no doubt that Haji Qadir would have seen it as his responsibility to host bin Laden. And if I were to go to him, and say, 'You cannot see this guy,' he would reply, 'Richard, how can I not? I would be going against everything that I am.'"[16]

It was not long before the thunderbolts began to fly. Interviewed by Robert Fisk of the London *Independent* in mid-July, bin Laden said the United States had ignored his advice to withdraw its troops from Saudi Arabia. Now, he was "declaring war . . . against the American regime, which is against every Muslim." He denounced the Saudi regime as having "lost its legitimacy," and warned Britain and France to remove all military

---

* Haji Qadir told Stefan Smith that he had offered to cooperate with the United States on a "snatch" operation in 1996. "I said to the consul in Peshawar that Osama is here. 'If you want him, come and get him,' I said. The Americans just laughed at us." But according to Richard Smyth, who was consul through late 1996, "Neither Qadir nor Abdul Haq (his brother) suggested a snatch mission to me or any member of my staff." Smith, e-mail message; and Smyth, interview.

personnel from Saudi Arabia or face attacks on them. The interview took place at a remote grass encampment several hours' drive from Jalalabad. At this point, bin Laden, his wives, and two sons were living in tents.

The CIA took note, and in mid-August the State Department published a fact sheet on bin Laden, calling him "one of the most significant financial sponsors of Islamic extremist activities in the world today." The handout charged that Ramzi Yousef, the alleged mastermind of the 1992 World Trade Center attack, had resided in a bin Laden guesthouse in Peshawar for three years before his arrest in February 1995 and said bin Laden had sponsored terror training camps in Sudan and Afghanistan. Containing important elements of the sealed indictment that the FBI was still not ready to present, the fact sheet raised a major question of why the CIA had concurred in allowing bin Laden to return to Afghanistan. However, the content appeared to be largely based on al Fadl's data, and it is possible the CIA did not have that information at the time of his return.[17]

Ten days later, bin Laden issued an attack on the Saudi leadership and a call for all good Muslims to go to war against the United States. The eight thousand-word "Declaration of Jihad on the Americans Occupying the Country of the Two Sacred Places" attacked the Saudi leadership for mismanagement of the economy and for its failure to implement sharia law. "Cleanse the land from these occupiers," bin Laden said of the Saud family. "Expel the occupying enemy out of the country of the two holy places," he said of the United States. The presence "of American crusader forces in the Muslim Gulf states . . . is the greatest danger and the largest harm which threatens the world's biggest oil reserve. . . . Pushing out this American occupying enemy is the most important duty after the duty of belief in God." He called for martyrs and promised that those who died fighting the aggressor would go "to the highest levels of Paradise."[18]

The interview and the declaration zeroed in on the U.S. presence in Saudi Arabia, a presence that of itself was uncontroversial in Afghanistan but which had a resonance throughout the Arab and Islamic worlds. For decades before the first Gulf War, regional experts argued that in a kingdom whose political legitimacy is historically grounded on a compact with Wahhabi clerics, the United States should not even consider permanent bases, lest they play into the hands of political opponents. But with the Gulf War outcome inconclusive and Saddam still in power, American strategists ignored the conventional wisdom. The United States raised its profile and established bases that in time became a direct target not only for bin Laden but also for Iran (the Khobar Towers in Dharan, in June 1996). Now an opponent of the Saudi regime could play the religious card and the political card together. Bin Laden had arrived, and the United States began to show signs of worry.

Also concerned were the Taliban, who swept into Jalalabad on September 12. According to Din Muhammad, the same faction that invited bin Laden (Saznoor, Mahmoud, and al Haqq) invited them. One day before they arrived, Haji Qadir fled to Pakistan; they set up headquarters in his house. Bin Laden's fate was high on their agenda for discussion, with Mullah Borjan, the Taliban military commander, among those voicing suspicion of bin Laden. They understood that bin Laden had been making contributions to the mujahideen, and it was possible that he opposed the Taliban; indeed, according to one report, he had fled with retreating government troops. Taliban leader Mullah Rabbani appointed Mullah Sadiq to investigate—his job was to meet bin Laden and find out what he was up to. "Until now he was living under the protection of the mujahideen," Sadiq told Pakistani journalist Rahimullah Yusufzai. "We are out to fight the mujahideen, and he was in a different camp. That is why we have some questions for him." It took several meetings before the Taliban decided to give him the benefit of the doubt. "Until we are sure that he committed crimes, how can we proceed against him? All we know is that bin Laden is a good Muslim and has taken part in the Afghan jihad against the Soviets," Sadiq would later say.[19]

According to one widely quoted account, bin Laden paid $3 million into Taliban coffers and financed the militia as it marched to Kabul. But it is not clear how the man viewed with suspicion by the Taliban could have turned overnight into the militia's main benefactor. He certainly had ample funds at his disposal. Some accounts called bin Laden a "billionaire," while others estimated his net worth at $250 million, but his fortune may have been of a smaller order. Prince Turki, while he was the Saudi intelligence chief, estimated it "at most" at $40–$50 million. Still, in one of the world's poorest places, such sums would go a very long way.[20]

No one was more surprised at the pace of events on the ground than the U.S. intelligence community, which was out of touch both literally and figuratively. Less than a month before Massoud's overthrow, the CIA thought he had enough support, ammunition, and will to hold off the Taliban for years. Robin Raphel's aide, Lee Coldren, was incensed by the CIA's "stupid" assessment and issued a "counterblast" that predicted that the government would fall within weeks. Undeterred, the CIA's Gary Schroen flew into Kabul in the last week of September. Schroen had begun his second tour in Pakistan at the start of 1996, but his bosses took no interest in Afghanistan, and he had neither funds nor operating guidance. His mission, at the behest of the CIA counterterrorism center, was to seek Massoud's help to capture bin Laden. But the only resource he could cobble together was an offer to buy back Stingers from Massoud at the price of $80,000 or more per missile. It was a dubious inducement for a counterterrorism mission, rendered surreal by its timing. Schroen flew in on an Ariana plane, met Massoud in the early hours of the morning, and made a short sightseeing visit to the Salang Pass north of Kabul before returning to Islamabad the next day. He had arrived much too late. Kabul fell two days later.[21]

Capturing Kabul unopposed was a heady experience for the Taliban. No sooner had they arrived in Kabul than the militia headed north in pursuit of Massoud's retreating army. Over the newly renamed Voice of Sharia radio, the interim authorities broadcast a decree granting amnesty to anyone who assassinated Massoud, Burhanuddin Rabbani, Hekmatyar, or Sayyaf. But because the Taliban were unable to set up an effective administration —beyond a religious police apparatus to punish violations of sharia—the power vacuum persisted, and outside parties took up their familiar roles. The U.S. government vacillated between gestures of goodwill and expressions of shock over Taliban excesses, but Washington was consistent in its disinterest in the outcome of the war. By comparison, bin Laden used his jihad experience as the mentor to his actions. He viewed the war as an opportunity to cement his relationship with the Taliban. Moreover, he now had his own political agenda to pursue, and the continuing internal conflict provided the perfect cover. The failure of the media—and everyone else— to monitor this obscure war gave him a free ticket to pursue his own agenda and transform Afghanistan into a platform for global terror.

The Taliban Overreach

Rushing north in hot pursuit of Massoud, the Taliban underestimated the military challenge. No longer a march through friendly Pashtun areas, propelled by a wave of popular indignation against hated warlords, their unplanned, faith-driven venture into predominantly Tajik, Uzbek, and Hazara territories was fraught with risk. As in Kabul, the language of northern Afghanistan is Dari, an Afghan dialect of Farsi, and not the Pashto of the south. In these parts, especially in cities like Mazar, where women were much freer to work, seek an education, and move about as they wished, the harsh and primitive Islam of the Pashtun village was unfamiliar and unwanted. Nothing short of calibrated use of force and diplomacy could win over leaders and the public.

One approach to the north, along the Salang Highway, abutted the territorial base of Ahmed Shah Massoud. The famed guerrilla leader's network of alliances had undoubtedly frayed, and he and his top aides were exhausted and demoralized, but even in defeat he could claim the loyalty of motivated and well-trained forces. Now he was in his redoubt, where his track record of holding off a superpower indefinitely had earned him the reputation as one of the twentieth century's leading guerrilla fighters. The other approaches were controlled by Abdul Rashid Dostum, a warlord who shifted alliances with the seasons and whose sizeable militia, whether in communist or postcommunist times, served first and foremost to protect his own power base. However warily Massoud and Dostum viewed each other, both were skilled operators in the multidimensional Afghan chess game, in which every enemy is a future ally and every friend is a future adversary. Dostum saw no shame in taking support from any and all foreign sources, and these sources suddenly became very worried about the Taliban victory. Massoud's nationalist ethos led him, on the whole, to forgo foreign entanglements, but he was the master setter of traps, and the Taliban immediately stumbled into one: it was called the Panjshir Valley.

Barely a week after capturing Kabul, Taliban forces moved into the Panjshir and advanced several kilometers. Confident that Massoud was now trapped, they issued an order to "surrender or die." Massoud's forces drew back, and the Taliban militia advanced farther into the valley. Then, in a well-honed tactic, Massoud sent units behind the Taliban. Isolated and under attack from front and rear, Taliban were killed or captured by the hundreds. Meanwhile, Russian and Central Asian leaders held an emergency summit in Almaty, Kazakhstan, to discuss the threat posed to their own Islamic populations by the Taliban advance. Separately, Iran denounced the Taliban takeover as a "disaster."

The key to destroying Massoud was Dostum, and the Taliban tried to win him over by offering a government post and recognition of his special status as warlord of the north. Pressed by his foreign patrons, Dostum publicly professed his neutrality. Then the Taliban threw caution to the wind. Ignoring Dostum's warnings, they advanced north along the Salang Highway to try to encircle Massoud. It was one provocation too many—on October 10, 1996, Dostum met Massoud to announce an alliance.

This was only their second meeting since April 1992, when they had agreed on the plan to seize Kabul. As a third partner, they took on the Hazara Hezbi Wahdat led by Karim Khalili. On October 14, Dostum recognized the legitimacy of the Rabbani government; and by the end of October, the Taliban declared jihad against Dostum. But they had overreached —their harsh social order won them no friends. There was an uprising in Jebal Seraj, and the combined forces of Massoud and Dostum captured Bagram Air Base and began advancing toward Kabul. Although they failed to capture the city, Massoud had dealt the Taliban what one diplomat called "a huge bloody nose."[22]

In Pakistan, the Taliban's patrons saw a golden opportunity to press for what they said would be an all-party political solution to the Afghanistan problem. Naseerullah Babar, Benazir Bhutto's interior minister, shuttled among Islamabad, Kabul, Mazar-i-Sharif, and Kandahar.

Pakistan's role in backing the Taliban has been one of the most contentious issues in the journalism and historiography of the internal Afghan conflict. Anthony Davis, whose careful coverage of the region is an essential resource for any reconstruction of events, concluded that as the Taliban advanced on Kabul, Islamabad's backing was "not confined to the map room." The Taliban's "meticulous planning, unrelenting speed, impressive command and control, effective coordination between several key fronts in a fluid tactical situation, and apparently unfailing logistical support" were unlike any operation carried out over the previous seventeen years. "That semiliterate Afghan mullahs could have been capable of such planning and execution defies belief," Davis wrote. Pakistan, he reported, provided armored vehicles and retired army personnel for support, "if not direction, in planning, command and control, and logistics."[23]

Yet, according to Babar, the Taliban "didn't require any support from us." There was "no dearth" of weapons and ammunition; funding "they got from the traders." By Babar's account, Pakistan's main role was to provide political support. A top U.S. official in Islamabad at the time said Pakistan's role has been exaggerated. Pakistan had advisers with the Taliban armies, "such as they were," and had access to the leadership on a selective basis, but its main contributions were oil (subsidized by Saudi Arabia), subsidized wheat, young volunteers, and military spare parts. "Soft contributions don't give a lot of leverage," this official said. And while Massoud made Pakistan's role a constant theme in his interviews and the pronouncements of his aides, CIA station chief Gary Schroen argued that Pakistan "didn't have the wherewithal to supply" the Taliban.

One reason outsiders have a hard time coming to grips with Pakistan's role in Afghanistan during this period is that Babar and Bhutto, possibly for reasons of domestic politics, often boasted of a part in the creation of the movement and of continued influence that exceeded their actual role. Babar's airy account of his diplomatic initiative follows this pattern. "We put an end to their movement forward to the north. We stopped them in Kabul and started the negotiations," he said of the Taliban, overlooking the drubbing Massoud had dealt the Taliban expeditionary force. Pakistan had, in fact, made the gesture of rebuffing Taliban entreaties to exchange ambassadors. "We said, no, you must first have this agreement with all the other ethnic groups and peoples for a share in power," Babar recounted. Building on his supreme self-confidence and contacts going back decades, Babar personally called on Afghan leaders—including Mullah Omar, Dostum, and Ghafoorzai—as he drafted his plan. Both the regime and the budding United Front—often called the Northern Alliance—submitted lists of names for talks on a prepared draft agreement to hammer out terms for a cease-fire and the demilitarization of Kabul. By November 3, 1996, the arrangements were in place for a peace conference. Babar even briefed the diplomatic corps on the talks.

Unfortunately, the next night, the Pakistan Army removed Benazir Bhutto's government and installed businessman Nawaz Sharif in her place. The initiative was dead in the water. "It was a serious effort, seriously intended," according to Tom Simons, the U.S. ambassador to Pakistan, who called it one of the rare "moments of hope in the whole sorry process." Colonel Imam, Pakistan's representative to the Taliban, agreed. "He tried his best," Colonel Imam said of Babar. "He had the capacity to be successful in making an agreement between both sides. But the government changed, and he left his post." But there is reason to ask whether the Taliban, believing their victory was divinely ordained, would have settled for anything less than a military conquest. Babar may have been indulging in wishful thinking.* "Babar shouldn't say that Pakistan did not let them go north," commented the foreign minister who took charge of the Afghan portfolio in 1998. "They were not ready to go north at that time."[24]

Bin Laden, too, was given to boasting, but more often than not his rhetoric preceded action. His media encounters in this period revealed a growing self-assurance. Why were there no new operations after his July declaration of jihad against the United States, Adelbari Atwan, editor of the London-based newspaper *Al Quds al Araby*, asked him in late November 1996. Major operations take time to plan, he replied. "If we wanted small actions, the matter would have been easily carried out immediately after the statement. The nature of the battle calls for operations of a specific type that will make an impact on the enemy, and this of course calls for excellent preparations." The interview took place in a cave, which bin Laden had equipped with an up-to-date computer and a library of finely bound books. "You make these threats from an altitude of 2,500 meters in the mountains of Afghanistan, 2,000 miles or more away from the Arab region. Don't you think there is something odd going on here?" Atwan asked. "You could be right," bin Laden said, briefly taken aback. He recouped in grand style: "This [Muslim] nation is connected like an electric current, and I am addressing the nation as a whole, not just the sons of the peninsula." This interview marked the first time he claimed Arab veterans of the Afghan jihad had inflicted "big losses" on U.S. peacekeeping troops in Somalia.† Yet it was another boast that raised eyebrows in Washington: "Our relations with the Taliban are excellent . . . and we feel completely satisfied with the cooperation with them."[25]

He was already in the catbird seat, as the U.S. government would soon discover. Clearly concerned by the implications of this interview, Secre-

---

* The Babar initiative was a lot more ragged than it was portrayed. Babar launched it without informing Norbert Holl, the UN special envoy, and then asked the United Nations to cosponsor the plan. But Babar's main points of contact were Dostum and the Taliban leadership, and his proposal ducked tough questions asked by Massoud, such as who would guarantee an accord between the warring parties. The top U.S. diplomat dealing with Afghanistan, John Holzman, informed Holl that the U.S. government adamantly opposed sending in UN peacekeepers or any greater U.S. security role, and no one else would act as a substitute. Holl judged Babar's proposal as "slanted to one side—to the interests of the Taliban, who wanted a cease-fire in order to consolidate their territorial gains." Norbert Heinrich Holl, *Mission Afghanistan* (Munich: Herbig, 2002), 123–44.

† Bin Laden's role in Somalia would grow with each telling. He told Pakistani journalist Hamid Mir in March 1997 that his mujahideen were responsible for the "Black Hawk Down" incident. "My associates killed the Americans in collaboration with Farah Aidid. . . . You will be astonished that Farah Aidid had only 300 soldiers while I had sent 250 mujahideen. We got moral support from local Muslims. In one explosion, 100 Americans were killed, then 18 more were killed in fighting. One day our men shot down an American helicopter. The pilot got out. We caught him, tied his legs, and dragged him through the streets. After that, 28,000 U.S. soldiers fled Somalia." Bin Laden, interview by Mir, *Pakistan*.

tary of State Warren Christopher a few days later sent the first formal démarche to the Taliban, demanding bin Laden's expulsion. "Harboring bin Laden and allowing him and his supporters to transit Afghan territory at will and to conduct uncontrolled activities greatly hurt[s] prospects for Afghanistan rejoining the world community," the letter said. The response took several months.

On February 22, 1997, bin Laden issued what amounted to a declaration of war on Americans, Jews, and Christians. "To kill and fight Americans and their allies, whether civilian or military, is an obligation for every Muslim who is able to do so in any country," he said in a fatwa announcing the formation of the World Islamic Front for Jihad against the Jews and the Crusaders. He called upon "every Muslim who believes in Allah and asks for forgiveness, to abide by Allah's order by killing Americans and stealing their money anywhere, anytime, and wherever possible. We also call upon Muslim scholars, their faithful leaders, young believers, and soldiers to launch a raid on the American soldiers of Satan and their allies of the Devil." The fatwa focused on the U.S. troop presence in Saudi Arabia and U.S. use of Saudi territory as a base to attack Iraq. The fatwa was a fundamental call to arms, but it received next to no attention in the news media. The State Department strongly condemned it as "an open invitation for terrorists to attack American civilians."[26]

Rebuff

In March 1997, the Taliban delivered the definitive response to Christopher's letter. There was the direct answer that Maulvi Ehsanullah, a member of the Taliban inner *shura* and later deputy interior minister in charge of intelligence, gave to three U.S. diplomats in Kandahar. The expulsion of bin Laden, he said, is "not a solution." The United States would repeat its demand three dozen times over the next five years and would receive a variant of Ehsanullah's answer every time. The indirect response took the form of a tacit decision to allow bin Laden to continue threatening violence against the United States and Saudi Arabia. Early that same month, a Taliban spokesman told reporters that bin Laden was a "visitor" living under Taliban protection. He said the militia would "never allow anyone to use Afghan soil to make attacks against any other country." Yet that is precisely what bin Laden proceeded to do in interviews later that month with Pakistani reporter Hamid Mir, Robert Fisk of the London *Independent*, and Peter Arnett of CNN. Again bin Laden denounced the Saudi royal family and renewed his call for holy war against the United States.

Then there was the circumstantial evidence. After heavy lobbying of the Taliban's observer by Saudi and Pakistan officials at a meeting of the Organization of the Islamic Conference, Mullah Omar, according to his official spokesman, "summoned" bin Laden to Kandahar "for his own safety." Yet, this first meeting between the two was anything but a dressing down.* During Friday prayers, Omar singled out bin Laden from the large crowd and introduced him as "a friend, a brother, and a great holy warrior." Together, the two men led prayers for thousands. Mullah Omar's official spokesman reported that the Taliban leader had reaffirmed the gag order on further anti-Saudi propaganda by bin Laden. However, Omar's first foreign policy pronouncement was a demand for the withdrawal of all U.S. troops from Saudi Arabia. There was "no need for them" to remain in Saudi Arabia, because threats from Iraq "no longer existed," Omar said. Thus, the untraveled, unlettered "seeker" suddenly acquired a foreign policy adviser. And not just any adviser but a mujaheed from the land of the Two Holy Places, a holy warrior who had abandoned princely life in the name of religious principle, and the son of the devout Muslim who had helped rebuild the three most sacred shrines of Islam: the al Aqsa mosque in Jerusalem and the key sites in Mecca and Medina. At Omar's request, bin Laden moved to Kandahar from Jalalabad. Soon the Taliban leader was living in a compound built by bin Laden, while the latter moved to Kandahar Airport. The camel was inside the tent.[27]

Bin Laden for his part began sending Arab fighters to join the Taliban in the struggle against Massoud, treating every military setback for the Taliban as a chance to show largesse and curry favor. "The blood of the Arabs and Afghans was spilled at the Afghan fronts and this was an important factor in strengthening the relationship and bolstering links between the Al-Qaeda Organization and the Taliban Movement and their leaderships," said Abu Jandal, who later became bin Laden's bodyguard. With every Massoud advance toward Kabul, "the relationship was strengthened and consolidated." After one such rout on the Shamali plains, bin Laden was spotted visiting Kabul in the company of Arab fighters who arrived in new Toyota pickup trucks, sixty of which he had donated to the Taliban cause. "In each defeat, they became more dependent on bin Laden," said a Taliban sympathizer who was monitoring events in the capital. Gary Schroen made a similar observation.[28]

For the handful of U.S. officials who focused on Afghanistan, late 1996 and early 1997 was a period of deep frustration. The Clinton White House was preoccupied with presidential elections and the start of a new term, and showed no interest in foreign affairs other than to keep a lid on the war in Bosnia. The State Department's South Asian bureau had hoped to seize the moment as soon as the Taliban took Kabul in September and move

---

* According to Abu Jandal, Mullah Omar sent the "summons" by helicopter after receiving word from Taliban intelligence that foreign assassins had arrived to kill bin Laden. But that could not have been the whole story, for according to the newly arrived Pakistani envoy in Kabul, Aziz Ahmed Khan, Pakistan had sent word to Omar that bin Laden's press conferences "will bring you a bad name and will not gain you international approval." Omar responded in seeming outrage: "Is he the Emir Momineen (commander of the faithful) or am I?" For a brief time, bin Laden stopped giving interviews. Abu Jandal, interview by Al-Hammadi (part 9), *Al Quds al Araby;* and Aziz Ahmed Khan, interview by author, Islamabad, April 2003.

toward full relations, but it was forced to beat a retreat. The first formal encounter was in early November between Tom Simons, U.S. ambassador to Pakistan, and Mullah Muhammad Ghaus, the Taliban's acting foreign minister. Simons urged the Taliban to show greater "modesty" and renounce its "winner take all" approach to the conflict. Ghaus responded brashly that Dostum and Massoud would "have to submit to the will of God and the will of the people, which are manifested in the Taliban movement." Shifting from Taliban theology to Taliban political theory, he asserted that the Taliban were "the majority, and in democracies minorities must always submit to the will of the majority." They agreed on one thing—that widely circulated reports that the United States and Pakistan had lavishly supported the Taliban on the march to Kabul were untrue.

Ghaus returned to the U.S. embassy in Islamabad a month later with a letter formally requesting American recognition and support for taking over Afghan's UN seat. To encourage Washington, the Taliban named Hamid Karzai as its UN representative. But the initiative, which Karzai undertook in the hope of moderating the Taliban from within, proved futile. "The U.S. government is not in the position to recognize any group as the government of Afghanistan, including the Taliban," the deputy chief of mission in Islamabad, John Holzman, told Ghaus. Two days later, Robin Raphel delivered the same message to Karzai in Washington. Karzai portrayed the Taliban as "intrinsically Afghan and as a force that cannot be assumed will go away" and said most of the movement were "very simple, unsophisticated people," totally unaware of the broader implications of Taliban policies. "They don't have the worldliness or inclination to counter these policies," he said. He appealed for Washington to become more "actively and directly" engaged in Afghanistan to moderate Taliban policies, but there were no takers. Washington had "neither the funds nor the inclination to back any group," Lee Coldren told Karzai. Raphel added that the U.S. government wanted "to avoid giving signals of a deeper engagement than could be sustained." The one thing they seemed to agree on was the extent of Pakistani aid to the Taliban. Contradicting Mullah Muhammad Ghaus, Karzai said Pakistani support ranged from cash to supplies to logistical support on the ground, as well as military and intelligence advisers; furthermore, Pakistan's Foreign Ministry was drafting letters for the Afghan ministry and may have been suggesting individuals for top posts. Raphel's cable on the encounter backed up Karzai's view on Pakistani military support, thereby reaching a rather different conclusion than that of Tom Simons.* She

---

* The cable's title, "Afghanistan: Taliban Rep Won't Seek UN Seat for Now," tells the story, but Karzai's statement to that effect was redacted from the cable. In fact, he did not abandon the post for another month. In mid-January, while he was visiting Islamabad, a Pakistani deputy foreign minister urged him to represent the Taliban at the United Nations and handed him plane tickets, according to a family source close to Karzai. At that point, Karzai turned down the position, which he had not formally accepted, the source said. "Afghanistan: Taliban Rep Won't Seek UN Seat for Now," State Department cable, December 13, 1996, released by NSA.

said that the State Department had recently received "more credible information" about the extent and origin of Pakistani assistance and that Karzai's account was consistent with this new information. Whether bin Laden's name came up is not clear in the redacted cable, but it certainly did in Warren Christopher's letter to Ghaus, the original of which Raphel handed to Karzai. Karzai's mission had failed.[29]

Any remaining doubt as to the direction Mullah Omar had chosen should have disappeared by March 1997. When three U.S. diplomats traveled to Kandahar early in the month—among them Brad Hanson, Smyth's successor in Peshawar—they were unable to call on Omar because he refused to receive non-Muslims. Beginning in late March, bin Laden frequently called on Mullah Omar. As Omar's spokesman put it, Kandahar was the decision-making center of the Taliban movement, and if bin Laden wanted to discuss anything with the Taliban, "He can go and see the leader directly." And so he did. "He had almost unlimited access to Mullah Omar," Gary Schroen said. "He could see him any time. They met regularly."[30]

Only one outside power believed it had significant influence in the early days of Taliban rule, and that was Pakistan. Even before the Taliban took Kabul, Babar, who knew the key players and the country's needs, helped repair the ruined infrastructure. Kandahar was incorporated into Pakistan's domestic phone system and could be called at domestic rates through the Quetta exchange. Pakistani government agencies repaired the roads, improved the electricity supplies into Kandahar, and provided technical assistance to restore operations to Kandahar Airport. Babar ran a special Afghan cell in his Interior Ministry, and the Foreign Ministry had an Afghan wing directed by its own secretary.[31]

Colonel Imam's Blind Spot

Islamabad's problem after the ouster of the Bhutto regime in early November was a shortage of the right people in the right places. To head its mission in Kabul, Nawaz Sharif dispatched the ambassador to Malaysia, Aziz Ahmed Khan, in early December 1996. A Southeast Asia specialist with no previous experience in Afghanistan, Khan had barely ten days to prepare himself for the job. But his main handicap was that his embassy was in Kabul, far from the real seat of power in Kandahar. Pakistan also had a consulate in Mazar-i-Sharif, the country's second largest city and the capital of the north. The burden for relating to the Taliban leadership fell on Colonel Imam.

But a Special Forces trainer does not necessarily a diplomat make, certainly not an intelligence gatherer. The criticism of Colonel Imam among many Pakistan officers and diplomats was that he had "gone native." By growing a chest-length Taliban beard, donning a tight white turban and traditional *salwar kameez,* and observing the five daily prayers, he had indeed set himself apart from most Pakistani diplomats. But what made his mission to the Taliban unusual was that even after they took power in Kabul, he continued to base himself in Herat, where he had served since mid-1994 as Pakistan's consul-general and which is 265 bumpy miles northwest of Kandahar. "Herat is a beautiful place," he explained in a rare interview with a Western reporter. Additionally, Colonel Imam saw his mission to the Afghan leadership "not as a diplomat but as an ex-colleague." He would travel regularly to the seat of power but clearly was not enamored of the hot and dusty town. With a salary of $3,000 a month and an expense account that allowed him to invite his visitors in for tea, he was hardly poised to exercise great influence over the Taliban.

If his words are to be believed, he had a massive blind spot where Osama bin Laden was concerned. He remembered the Saudi militant from the anti-Soviet war as "a typical civilian prince," who built roads and shelters for the mujahideen in the mountains of eastern Afghanistan but had "no eye for fighting." As for bin Laden's own account of dozing off during an artillery barrage, Colonel Imam's recollection was that bin Laden was in fact "nervous about fighting" and had not participated in any military operation until 1989, the year the Russians left Afghanistan. In the five years between bin Laden's return and the fall of the Taliban, Colonel Imam never laid his eyes on him. "After 1993, we never met," he said.

His view of bin Laden and al Qaeda places him almost on a different planet from most other observers. "Al Qaeda was not there in Afghanistan when I was there. That was all fiction," Colonel Imam said. And the idea of "bin Laden as a politician who wanted a country of his own is disinformation." He admitted that the Taliban at times had some 1,500 non-Afghan fighters at the front, a figure well below Massoud's estimates, but he never visited a training camp and never saw Mullah Omar with bin Laden. Further, he asserted that Omar "never saw or met" the Saudi dissident. That is because, according to him, bin Laden stayed in Jalalabad. "He probably never saw the complex [that he built] in Kandahar." It would appear that Colonel Imam either went out of his way to avoid bin Laden or spent far too much time in Herat; Pakistan officials affirmed that bin Laden was barely mentioned in the cables from Herat.

But at a time when Pakistan's policy in Afghanistan was adrift, Colonel Imam, by most accounts, wielded disproportionate influence there. In his view, the Taliban should move north and capture Mazar-i-Sharif, and Pakistan should recognize the regime. "When the mujahideen were in government, they were recognized by a number of countries. It was my view that if you could recognize the mujahideen, and the Taliban now controlled most of the area, why not recognize them?" Colonel Imam noted that although he "wanted" the Taliban to be recognized, he did not advise or persuade the Pakistan government to do so. Hamid Mir, a close observer of Pakistan policy, had a different assessment: "Imam delivered the Pakistan government." In any case, Pakistan did shift its stance and encouraged the Taliban to go north. And while it may be argued that Pakistan's influence was overrated by both Pakistanis and outside observers, in this instance Pakistan offered so much open political support that leading officials believe it shared responsibility for the outcome. "The Taliban were on a roll," ambassador-designate Khan said. "We knew they would capture all of Afghanistan. Considering it as something inevitable, we did not do anything to prevent them from doing that."

But Pakistan was not just bowing to the inevitable: it was offering the Taliban a powerful incentive for capturing northern Afghanistan by force. Besides removing all other contenders for power from the scene, this would open the way to broad diplomatic recognition, with Islamabad leading the way. "Some of our people gave bad advice," commented a former ISI analyst. "They said, 'Forget about the [return of] King [Zahir Shah]. Go for the rest of the country.'"

Slaughter in Mazar-i-Sharif

The Taliban drive to impose a military solution on a political dispute was built around a strategy of assaulting Mazar-i-Sharif from three directions. It involved the usual elements of Afghan internal war fighting—bribes, betrayals, and brute force—and, when these failed, the somewhat less familiar tactics of terror, war crimes, and ethnic cleansing. Most widely reported at the time was the offensive from Herat and the west, in which the Taliban bought into a mutiny by Dostum's second in command, then supplemented his forces by sending some 2,500 troops of their own. Less noted was a second offensive from the south, in which the Taliban bought the allegiance of a Massoud subcommander and sent 2,000 troops through the Salang Pass. From the southwest, the Taliban sent the biggest force of all, some 10,000 troops through the Ghorband Valley to the two-mile-high Shibar Pass, the other major route across the Hindu Kush. If they could subdue Hazarajat (Afghanistan's central highlands and the home territory of the country's Shia minority), they could deny a potential sanctuary for their political opponents in the north and ensure the lines of communication in the warm weather months.

But Taliban military strategy was more ambitious than their intelligence, political skills, or tactical abilities could sustain, and Mazar produced the biggest military setback during their first year of power. As they encountered resistance along every front, the Koranic students adopted the shortcuts of the ill-prepared: rallying local Pashtun minorities to serve as a fifth column for attacks on other ethnic groups (thereby turning a political dispute into an ethnic conflict) and using tactics that provoked the mass flight of civilians.[32]

It seemed to begin as a counteroffensive to Massoud and Dostum, who had failed to capture Kabul in mid-November 1996. In late December, the

Taliban seized the picturesque village of Istalif, north of Kabul, where Massoud had received U.S. officials a few months earlier, and the town of Qarabagh on the Shamali plains, sending twenty thousand civilians fleeing. The plan required the capture of Charikar—a nearby provincial center that controlled routes to the north through Salang and the west through Shibar—and they succeeded in January, overrunning Bagram Air Base, Charikar, and Jebal Saraj, Massoud's interim headquarters. To ensure their safe passage for the events to follow, the Taliban introduced a new tactic: the systematic evacuation of whole towns on the grounds of disarming them and preventing rebellion. The displacement of some hundred thousand civilians in subzero weather from Charikar and surrounding villages fell short of an ethnic cleansing or other irreversible war crime, but the precedent had been set. Mass expulsion became a routine tactic for the Taliban, and watching in silence became a habit for the international community.[33]

As Taliban intentions to conquer by force became clear, neighbors to the north and west stepped up their covert involvement on either side. Iran armed and trained Afghan troops loyal to Ismail Khan; set up an air bridge between Mashhad, in eastern Iran, and Bagram to supply ammunition and logistics; and, with the help of Iranian transports, flew two thousand Ismail Khan troops and hundreds more Hezbi Wahdat forces to reinforce his flanks. Uzbekistan started conscripting all available manpower, Dostum was reported to have received enormous quantities of Russian arms, and Tajikistan indicated that it was willing to provide Massoud with a rear base if Taloqan came under Taliban threat. At the same time, according to Dostum, Turkmenistan permitted Taliban fighters to transit its supposedly neutral territory to attack his troops and transport munitions.[34]

The leader of the mutiny was Gen. Abdul Malik Pahlawan, the urbane second in command to Dostum who served as the head of the Jumbesh alliance's foreign affairs bureau. Considering the zigzags of Afghan politics, including those of a master player like Dostum, a falling-out among his subcommanders was predictable. Under Dostum, Jumbesh had shifted its alliance more than once in the past. The one-time mainstay of communist power under Russian and later Najibullah's control had pulled the plug on the latter and helped place Massoud and Rabbani in power, only to help bring them down, too. The fact that Jumbesh held together as long as it did seems remarkable. Malik's animosity toward Dostum was personal and came to a boil in June 1996, when Malik's half brother Rasool was assassinated in Mazar, along with fifteen bodyguards. Rasool had been Dostum's commander of Faryab province and a rival for power, and was the leading hard-liner in the Jumbesh alliance. Anthony Davis describes Rasool as a "ruthless, brooding man, given to explosive outbursts of violence." He had close ties to Gen. Shahnawaz Tanai, who had attempted to overthrow Najibullah in March 1990, and to the Khalqi wing of the Communist Party. Malik exacted revenge on the family of the assassin but

viewed Dostum as the author of the action. He had unsuccessfully pressed
Dostum to carry on with Rasool's preferred course of action, which was to
back the Taliban in the overthrow of Massoud. Instead, Dostum had
signed a cease-fire in August and by October had recognized the Rabbani
regime as legitimate. With the Taliban on the march and Pakistani officials whispering encouragement (the ISI had facilitated Taliban contacts
with Malik, according to a Taliban official), Malik saw a chance to get even.
Showtime Afghan-style was an orchestral suite of betrayals.

The Taliban assault began from the west on May 19, 1997. That was
the day Malik switched sides and raised the Taliban white flag in Mai-
mona, the capital of Faryab province. A close Dostum adviser, Gen. Abdul
Majid Rozi, changed allegiance in Badghis province and arrested Dostum's
commanders, including Ismail Khan and seven hundred of his troops. Taliban commander Mullah Abdul Razzaq, the governor of Herat, arrived with
his forces that day and was handed Rozi's prisoners. On the same day, Malik
allies assassinated the governor of Samangan province. Dostum found himself outflanked on the west and south; soon Taliban forces were advancing
from Parwan in the southeast as well. The mutiny spread to units in Jowzjan, Dostum's home base, and his entire front collapsed. Dostum sent his
family out on May 23, and he escaped on May 24.* Malik forces took over
Mazar that evening.[35]

On May 25, the Taliban arrived in the last Afghan city not under their
control. This was a historic opportunity for the movement, which was on
the verge of seizing the entire country. The secret deal worked out by Malik
allowed the Taliban free passage to the northeast, thereby completing the
encirclement of Massoud. President Rabbani fled Taloqan for Tajikistan;
and the defection of Basir Solangi, Massoud's commander on the Salang
Highway, opened the way for two thousand Taliban to move north and
seize the town of Pul-i-Khumri. But the Taliban quickly overplayed their
hand. At 7:00 a.m., Razzaq arrived with about a dozen bodyguards armed
with AK-47s at Malik's two-story lodge at the edge of town. Malik invited
them to the upstairs sitting room for what was to be a discussion about power
sharing, but the visitors promptly began to demolish his furnishings. First
they destroyed a painting on goatskin of Omar Khayyam, the Persian poet,
and a beautiful woman offering him a goblet of wine. One of Razzaq's
men slashed it apart. A bodyguard destroyed Malik's sixty-inch color television, breaking the glass with his bayonet. "I was really upset," Malik recounted. "It was not the television, but I really liked the painting." He did
not offer tea, but he kept his own counsel. "To say something [in anger] to
a guest in your house is not Afghan culture." And, of course, his guests
were armed and ready to shoot.

---

* The once-mighty Dostum, overwhelmed by the speed of events, was alone and stranded at a small
town near the border.

Despite the rocky start, Malik continued reading from the prearranged script. That afternoon he appeared with Mullah Razzaq at the Hazrat Ali mosque—the spiritual center of Mazar and one of the great works of Islamic architecture—and announced that sharia law had been implemented. Razzaq harangued the crowd in Pashto, imposing the burqa, banning women's education, and announcing that thieves would have a hand or leg amputated. Unable to understand Pashto, many of Malik's troops walked out. But the impact in Mazar was immediate: women began covering themselves from head to toe, men began wearing turbans, and five Afghan women working with an international aid agency were beaten in public.

Malik had understood that he was to become the main commander of four northern districts; his forces were not to be disarmed, and the Taliban troops were to return to Kabul. Instead, he found himself relegated to the post of third deputy foreign minister and summoned to the capital. A joint operation "against their enemies" had turned into a military takeover.* More than 150 Talibs landed in transport planes at the Sheberghan Airport, the vanguard of 2,500 who poured into the town, bringing with them tanks, mobile antiaircraft guns, and multiple-rocket launchers. From Malik, the Taliban requisitioned all available four-wheel-drive vehicles.[36]

Pakistan announced full diplomatic recognition of the Taliban regime and abandoned its long-standing, if fitful, drive for a broad-based government. "The new government fulfills all criteria for de jure recognition," Foreign Minister Gohar Ayub Khan informed reporters. "It is now in effective control of most of the territory of Afghanistan and is representative of all ethnic groups in that country." The statement was premature, to say the least.†

---

* The memorandum of understanding (MOU) consisted of four points: (1) a joint operation against their enemies; (2) the establishment by the Taliban and Jumbesh (Dostum's party, now under Malik's control) of a joint northern military council; (3) noninterference by the Taliban in the inner matters of Jumbesh and the establishment or completion of an administration; and (4) the formation of a central government and parliament by means of elections in line with Islamic law and the appointment of a commission to form a broad-based cabinet in line with northern law and with representation of all ethnic minorities. In the view of Norbert Holl, the UN special envoy, "The document confirms that General Malik at no time expected to subordinate himself to the Taliban, rather to ally himself as a free coalition party." Holl, *Mission Afghanistan,* 227.

† It was even more remarkable that no one in the Pakistan government would take responsibility. The decision was made without the knowledge of Prime Minister Nawaz Sharif and carried out by the Foreign Ministry, according to Muhamed Akram Zaki, head of the parliament's Foreign Relations Committee. But Foreign Minister Gohar Ayub said he was carrying out Nawaz's order. "I myself was not that eager," he said. "When the prime minister issues an order, the minister has either to say 'I resign' and go home or you carry on a policy that was there." The government spokesman at the time said Nawaz could not have ordered Ayub to grant recognition, because Nawaz himself sent an aide to demand an explanation for the action. "I don't know who ordered him, but it was certainly not the prime minister." Indeed, Nawaz invited Hamid Mir to coffee and asked him to write a column criticizing the plan to grant recognition to the Taliban. Mir responded that Nawaz should raise the matter with the director-general of the ISI, which is where many Pakistani observers believe the decision was actually made. Muhamed Akram Zaki, interview by author, Islamabad, April 2003; Gohar Ayub, interview by author, Islamabad, April 2003; and Mushahid Hussain, former government spokesman, interview by author, Islamabad, April 2003.

Pakistan's new ambassador to Kabul, Aziz Ahmed Khan, and Mullah Ghaus, the acting foreign minister, flew into Mazar the next day as the two sides began sharpening their knives. Malik called a meeting of the Executive Council of the North, at which some forty leaders from northern Afghanistan told them what had occurred and said they should negotiate with the twenty visiting Taliban. Over lunch, the cultural gap turned into a yawning gulf. Although tables and chairs were provided, the guests insisted on moving to another room, sitting on the floor and eating the traditional pilaw rice with lamb with their hands. Malik told them they had not kept their promises and were not behaving in an Islamic manner. The Taliban leaders responded that they were the real Muslims and the true Afghans—"everything you are not." It went downhill from there. "These were wild people, illiterate, without any culture. They didn't want to use couches and chairs. Their behavior was not traditional Afghan culture," Malik said. He characterized Taliban behavior as "pre-Islamic Arabic culture."

Khan, the Pakistani envoy, witnessed the encounter. He had already observed a shoving match between the Pakistani consul and Mullah Razzaq when the latter insisted that Pakistani reporters who had flown in with Khan put away their cameras. Mullah Ghaus had been conducting the talks with the northern leadership when Razzaq, the hard-line military commander (who by this time had been named governor of Balkh province) took charge. Malik, he bluntly informed all assembled, is "not strong enough to rule the entire north." At that point, Khan said, "I could see the whole thing unraveling. We left." And just in time. According to Malik, street clashes began before the meeting had ended.[37]

It was not a single provocation but a series of spontaneous clashes in poor Shia neighborhoods that led to the melee. Acting like conquerors but untrained for close combat, certainly for urban warfare, Taliban militiamen went to local shops, smashing banned goods and demanding weapons and ammunition. In Saidabad, Gen. Majid Rozi accompanied the Taliban and told the Hazaras to disarm, but they refused, and Rozi left the scene, saying there was nothing he could do. Malik's troops disappeared from the streets. By one account, the Taliban sought to disarm members of a Hezbi Wahdat faction linked to Dostum and, in the ensuing gun battle, lost eight militiamen. The Shia agreed on a cease-fire to clear the battlefield but later the Taliban returned and launched a second attack. Shia and Uzbeks throughout the district began shooting all the Taliban they could find. Civilians in another area were angered by the Taliban having stolen a vehicle. Street fighting raged for eighteen hours.* Malik switched allegiance once again,

---

* The Taliban militia was completely unprepared for the uprising. BBC reporter Philip Goodwin, in a memorable first-person account, captured the ensuing panic in June 1997. "About forty Taleban soldiers were sauntering down the road. Their weapons were not raised at the ready and some were talking to each other. I only had a moment to take in how strangely unaware they seemed to be of the danger before
(continued on next page)

and by midday on May 28, the Taliban had departed. It was a rout—by one estimate, 350 Taliban were killed, including Razzaq, and 2,000–3,000 Taliban surrendered to Malik's forces, among them Mullah Muhammad Ghaus. Total Taliban deaths in the north were estimated at upward of 2,000.[38]

The Taliban's woes were not over. At the Shibar Pass, the Hezbi Wahdat, fighting for their lives and on their home ground, repulsed a string of frontal attacks. An estimated 2,000 Taliban were killed, and many times that number were wounded, according to AFP bureau chief Stefan Smith, one of a handful of Western journalists reporting from Kabul at the time.* Seizing on Taliban disarray, Massoud moved his forces out of the Panjshir on May 29, capturing Gulbahar at the base of the valley and Jebal Saraj, which controls the entrance to the Salang Tunnel and the route north. The Taliban force of some 2,000 was cut off from resupply and the survivors of Shibar from easy retreat. In July, Massoud went on to recapture Bagram and Charikar and advanced toward Kabul. This time, at least formally, Malik was on his side. "The people rose up against them," Malik said of the Taliban. "They went away. The people did not allow them to come back." Malik clung to power until the autumn, during which time those under his command disposed of the captured Taliban by loading them into containers where they suffocated, tossing them into wells, and burying them in mass graves. For months, the International Committee of the Red Cross, at the request of the Taliban leadership, appealed for access to the detainees, sending Malik forty-seven démarches. It was to no avail. The systematic execution of surrendered prisoners constituted a major war crime, but once again the international community watched in silence.[39]

Exactly what was Pakistan's role in the debacle? There is little doubt that Islamabad was the leading outside actor. Its support was mainly in the form of political and diplomatic backing, but there was also indirect military assistance, for Pakistan had "ordered" Kashmiri militants to go to Afghanistan and join the Taliban. Moreover, Pakistan had assured the Taliban that they could capture Mazar-i-Sharif without a fight and, according

---

* (cont.)
they started dying. From windows and doors around them, local people opened fire. And many of the Taleban stood still as their friends were being spun about by bullets. Some panicked and fired into the air, but I didn't see a single one take cover. Seconds later I was unwittingly leading by example when a burst of fire hit the wall above my head. Within moments of me crawling down the street and running into the one open doorway visible, there was the sound of feet behind me. And a group of Taleban soldiers rushed into the room, breathing heavily, turbans awry, limply carrying guns. . . . Their presence began to attract fire, and there was no way to back out, so I made a run for it, leaving them shouting at each other and pointing in different directions." Goodwin's account was broadcast in early June 1997, transcript courtesy of BBC.

* A Hezbi Wahdat commander recounted several months later that Wahdat fighters who had fled south after Malik's takeover had been tipped off that the Taliban forces were massing at the foot of the Shibar Pass and could even see them clearly from high ground. Huge numbers were "just driving up the pass"—a very steep, unpaved, switchback road—in pickup trucks with loudspeakers blaring out Koranic verses in what would have been a very naïve full-frontal attack. Stefan Smith recalled the commander saying, "We just killed them all." Smith, e-mail message.

to Taliban foreign ministry official Vahid Mojdeh, had facilitated Malik's contacts with Mullah Ghaus, the foreign minister, through the ISI. Gohar Ayub Khan announced Pakistan's intention to recognize the Taliban on May 21, then he and every other ambassador or high commissioner in the diplomatic apparatus lobbied the international community to recognize the Taliban. Only Saudi Arabia and the United Arab Emirates took the bait, and both recognized the Taliban just as the deal was unraveling. Gohar even tried his pitch in person on Madeleine Albright, newly sworn in as U.S. secretary of state, but he was rebuffed. Albright said Pakistan was "isolating itself" by backing the Taliban.* Gohar replied that if Pakistan was fully isolated, other countries would not be approaching it asking it to influence the Taliban. "We had some influence," Gohar said. However, "people kept on saying, 'They're under the control of Pakistan.' That control was just imagination." Gohar was not the lead player; it was the military. "ISI brokered a deal, and it was the wrong one," said former ISI director-general Hamid Gul. "ISI said [to the Taliban], 'Do a deal with Abdul Malik, and we will recognize your government.'" It was indeed the wrong deal.† But no deal could have worked for a movement that showed such deep contempt for the culture of non-Pashtun peoples.[40]

With two important exceptions—Ahmed Shah Massoud and Osama bin Laden—everyone was in disarray. Malik's days were numbered, but he was able to hang on by performing the familiar Afghan pirouette, shifting

---

* The United States was closely monitoring events but doing nothing to affect them. U.S. officials were in daily telephone contact with Malik, Dostum, and the Taliban, a U.S. diplomat told UN peace envoy Norbert Holl. Nevertheless, they were as surprised as anyone by the outcome. On the day Pakistan's ambassador flew to Mazar, John Holzman, deputy chief of the U.S. mission in Islamabad, joked to Holl that the UN envoy would soon be jobless, because the "Afghanistan problem" was about to be resolved. A few days later, he conceded that his prediction of a rapid victory had been premature. Holl, *Mission Afghanistan*, 222.

† Among the indicators pointing to ISI was the role of Shahnawaz Tanai, who was living in Pakistan as a guest of the ISI and, since 1995, had played a critical role in the integration of former communist officers into the Taliban militia. In June, Tanai had attended a memorial service for Rasool in Peshawar; in September, he or his Khalqi allies were thought by many, including Hamid Karzai, to be responsible for the killing and mutilation of Najibullah; by October, rumors began to circulate in Pakistan that Malik was contacting the Taliban through Tanai. At the same time, Malik had his own direct links with the ISI, which led more than one observer to view him as Pakistan's Trojan horse. A UN official recalled sitting in the lobby of the Marriott Hotel in Islamabad, when "Malik drives up in an ISI car." Malik was also one of Babar's favorite Uzbeks. During the negotiations for an all-party government, Babar said he used Malik "as a sort of interpreter" for Dostum, who he said did not understand English. And Malik provided Babar with a detailed description of the arms Dostum was receiving from Russia and Tajikistan. To stay in touch with Malik, Babar had telephones integrated into the Peshawar exchange installed at Malik's home and at the foreign affairs office he headed. Even after Babar's departure, Pakistani officials were in daily contact with Malik, both by telephone and through the Pakistani consulate in Mazar. And finally, according to Malik's former deputy, Gen. Mohamed Payenda, Pakistani representatives were present at the signing of the secret agreement. They came in a helicopter from Herat and, according to Pakistani reports, included Colonel Imam. On Tanai's role, Anthony Davis, *Jane's Defense Weekly*, August 1, 1997; on Malik and the ISI, UN official Sultan Aziz, interview by author, January 2004; on Babar's relations with Malik, Babar, interview by author, May 2003; and on the telephone links and Pakistanis present at the secret deal, Payenda, interview.

sides again and helping to reconstitute the United Front. Pakistani diplomacy, based on a lack of local knowledge and an overestimation of Taliban competence, wound up looking amateurish and incompetent. Even years later, key Pakistani officials such as Colonel Imam were in denial about the extent of the debacle. The Taliban who invaded Mazar-i-Sharif were not soldiers and were not armed, Colonel Imam later claimed. "Most were traders, other Afghans who wanted trade with the northern people," he said. Colonel Imam put the onus for the debacle on Iran, whose officials, he said, had instructed the Hazara people to resist. Iran had also "backed the massacre." Less ideologically committed Pakistanis recognized the disaster for what it was. A Pakistani diplomat who had been forced to flee to Uzbekistan said, "Recognizing the Taliban was a big mistake."

But it was much more than just a mistake. In a summary to the UN General Assembly in November 1997, Secretary-General Kofi Annan said, "What we are witnessing is a seemingly endless tragedy of epic proportions, in which the Afghan people's yearning for peace is being systematically and continually betrayed by leaders and warlords driven by selfish ambitions and thirst for power." He said that outside players who continued to support their respective Afghan clients "must be held responsible for exacerbating the bloody conflict in Afghanistan. They must also be held accountable for building a fire, which, they should be aware, is unlikely to remain indefinitely confined to Afghanistan."

Most distressed of all were the Taliban. Stefan Smith recalled, "There was a real sense of crisis, of them losing their grip, after having suffered such massive defeats and humiliations. There was unease in the tribes, affecting Taliban recruiting. And there was a sense that the Taliban were absolutely furious over Malik's betrayal and, indeed, their own naiveté." Mullah Omar got the blame. "A lot of the boys didn't return home," recalled AP reporter Kathy Gannon. "Entire villages were enraged with Omar." To compensate for the losses, the Taliban began using nighttime sweeps to conscript Afghan teenagers in Kabul, Jalalabad, Herat, and Kandahar; these conscripts were sent to the front after only a few hours of training.[41]

"We Know the Russian Mentality"

The crisis for Mullah Omar turned into an opportunity for Osama bin Laden. The Saudi dissident had positioned himself well. He had sent Arab volunteers to support the Taliban during the contest for Mazar, and while they had not entered the city, he could claim that he knew what had gone wrong by virtue of having a force in the right place at the right time. The main contingent consisted of about three hundred Yemenis, according to Hamid Mir, who was embedded with a half-dozen of them. (His "logistics" unit would kill twenty to twenty-five sheep a day and deliver them to the troops.) From this vantage point, it became clear that the Taliban had

stepped into the trap. There were a number of reasons: flawed tactical intelligence, a simplistic understanding of the politics of the north, impulsive
hard-liners as negotiators, and the rapid pace of events. But the perception
from outside the city was slightly different. Mir reported that what drove
the Taliban into the ambush was the perception of a power vacuum owing
to the dramatic removal of Dostum's forces, followed by the disappearance
of Malik's troops. The Arab contingent warned the Taliban leadership that
this could be a trap, but the Taliban responded that common people were
unhappy with Ahmed Shah Massoud. That was a compounded misjudg-
ment, for whatever the common people thought of him, Massoud did not
dominate in this region, and his opportunistic ally, Dostum, had just been
ousted. Thus, when the trap was sprung, the Taliban did not know what
hit them.

As bin Laden discussed the disaster with Mullah Omar, he offered a
purposeful—if self-serving—analysis. "We cannot participate further in
your battles. Your commanders are immature. They cannot read the situation correctly. It is very easy for the Uzbeks to cheat them." Waxing hyper-
bolic, bin Laden averred that Mullah Omar had had very little experience
fighting the Soviets, whereas he had spent eleven years in battle. "I know
the Uzbeks use Soviet tactics. Dostum has Russian equipment." Bin Laden
conveniently disregarded the facts that Dostum played no role in the
uprising, that Taliban boorishness had provoked the fighting, that it began
among noncombatants in poor Shia neighborhoods, and that the Uzbek
and even Shia military commanders were mostly far from the scene when
the uprising began. "We know the Russian mentality," bin Laden continued.
"We would enter an area and they would attack us. You fought only one
year among the Russians."

Bin Laden said Omar solicited his advice: "You give me a commander;
we are ready to fight under your commander." Bin Laden offered the services of Muhammed Atef (Abu Hafs), his military chief and third in command after Ayman al Zawahiri. A former Egyptian police officer who had
fought in Afghanistan in the 1980s and a cofounder of al Qaeda, Atef was
a codirector, along with Abu Ubaidah al Banshiri, of bin Laden's military
committee. The main function of the committee was training. After Banshiri died in a drowning accident in 1996, Atef became military chief. He
had helped bin Laden reconnoiter the U.S. military in Somalia in 1993 and
would help plan every subsequent major operation.* Now his task was to
prepare a major military operation for Mazar-i-Sharif. Astutely, bin Laden
did not accept Omar's offer to put Atef in command of the troops but
teamed him up with Jalaluddin Haqqani, a former mujahideen commander

---

* These would include the 1998 bombings of two U.S. embassies in East Africa, as well as the 9/11
assaults. In 2001, bin Laden's nineteen-year-old son married Atef's daughter. Atef was reported killed
in Kabul in November 2001 by a hellfire missile fired by a U.S. Predator drone.

whom Omar had put in charge of the training camps. Bin Laden had his own agenda, which would become apparent in time.[42]

But for a stroke of terrible luck, Massoud might also have profited from the disarray of the Taliban after their abortive assault against Mazar-i-Sharif. In the summer of 1997, he and other leaders agreed on a new political face for the United Front and selected a technocrat named Abdul Rahim Ghafoorzai as shadow prime minister. Should the fighters manage to recapture Kabul, this former deputy foreign minister and UN representative would take over the government. But just a week after being named to the post, Ghafoorzai was killed in a plane crash in central Bamian province. "This is really a disaster for us," Massoud's spokesman Abdullah Abdullah told a reporter.

Massoud did his best to recoup. Like bin Laden, he saw the Taliban's distress as a leveling of the playing field and as an opportunity to reach out to Mullah Omar, but he was at a disadvantage compared with bin Laden. Sometime in September, Massoud telephoned Mullah Omar to ask if there was a way to resolve their differences peacefully. He got the telephone number from the address book of Mullah Muhammad Ghaus, who was captured in Mazar-i-Sharif. His secretary, Jamshid, dialed it through the Quetta exchange. "Is Mullah Omar available?" Massoud asked, speaking in Pashto. "Yes," Omar's aide replied, "the emir is here." Using his most diplomatic language, Massoud urged Omar to "please come and let us solve the problem" of Afghanistan. Omar asked what Massoud would propose as a solution, and Massoud suggested a cease-fire, an interim administration, a *loya jirga* or other meeting of representatives of the Afghan people, and free elections. Omar was "at first sensitive and emotional," according to Jamshid, but then he asked for time to think about it "and finalize it in another call."

At nine o'clock the next morning, Massoud phoned again. Omar's mood had changed. "We want your support," Omar said. "What type of support?" Massoud asked. "Look, you are a mujaheed. You are different from the others. You are not corrupt. But you have become an obstacle for the Islamic Emirate. Don't do that. You can play a role in Tajikistan. The Tajiks like you. You can expand the Islamic Emirate to Tajikistan." Massoud replied, "We are talking about Afghanistan. There is a war going on in Afghanistan in which the people are suffering. This is not the way to stop it. This is all we want." Omar said that Afghanistan should have a single army, because it was not possible to have different armed groups in different places. Massoud said that until there was a solution all the people could accept, the war would continue. The conversation got more heated. "We have the power. We have most of the population," Omar said. "We can capture the rest in one night and the next day. Put down your guns and surrender." The losses at Mazar were clearly on his mind. "I have not given these 4,000 Taliban martyrs to allow the people on the street to decide about this country." The Taliban, he said, wanted its emirate. "We have made these sacrifices for the emirate, and we will continue to do so." The conversation was drawing to a close. If Massoud did not want to cooperate, he could leave the country, Omar said. "Tajiks should go to Tajikistan, Uzbeks to Uzbekistan, Hazaras to Iran. We are Afghans. This is our land." Omar said goodbye.

Between the two conversations, Omar no doubt conferred with his inner *shura* of advisers; his daft proposal that Massoud take over Tajikistan on behalf of the "emirate" suggests that he may have consulted his Saudi "foreign policy adviser" as well. This was the first indication that Mullah Omar, a village preacher with almost no direct knowledge of the outside world, had become an international jihadi, prepared to foment changes of government in other countries. The conversation also revealed a credibility gap. On the first day, Massoud proposed an exchange of prisoners, saying that the Taliban was holding Ismail Khan and otherwise mostly civilians, while he was detaining combatants. When they spoke the second time, Omar denied holding Ismail Khan. The most remarkable aspect of the conversation was that even at the nadir of his military fortunes, Omar could not imagine a solution other than Massoud's complete surrender.

The context for the conversation was set on the battlefield. Omar was determined to recapture Mazar, no matter what, and to punish the Hazaras for the humiliations in Mazar-i-Sharif and Shibar. He had taken the extraordinary step, for him, of paying his first visit to Kabul in June to rally morale and call for fresh volunteers from Pakistan to fill the depleted ranks. In August, he imposed a blockade of all food into the Hazarajat from the south, east, and west in an attempt to force Shia Hazaras to leave or surrender or both; at the time, no food was coming in from the north because of the chaos in the region. Starving the civilian population is a clear breach of international humanitarian law, as is collective punishment; but in this case it went unnoticed except by the UN human rights rapporteur and humanitarian aid groups. Meanwhile, Taliban forces in northern Afghanistan captured Kunduz and made another abortive attempt to seize Mazar; as they departed, they killed dozens of Shia in Qezelabad. Omar renamed the country the Islamic Emirate of Afghanistan and styled himself "commander of the faithful," the title adopted by the Prophet Muhammad and subsequent caliphs, which carried with it the responsibility to lead the *umma* (world Islamic community). For good measure, he also named himself head of state.[43]

Omar and Massoud were very different leaders, with very different mentalities and understandings of the role of institutions in building a nation. The former claimed the divine right to fashion the country in his image and to disenfranchise half the population, with no concern for such common Western institutions of government as a constitution, rule of law, or independent secular judiciary. The latter expressed a pro-Western outlook, promised that if he regained Kabul he would restore the rights of women, and sought to build institutions that would establish a nascent democracy. As far as American foreign policy was concerned, however, both were just "factions" in a civil war in which the United States would not take a stand.

In October 1997, Albright's assistant secretary for South Asian affairs, Karl (Rick) Inderfurth, told the Senate Foreign Relations Committee, "Let me be very clear about our policy toward Afghanistan: The U.S. is neutral between the factions." He emphasized, "We intend to persevere in our *strict neutrality* among the factions."* This was his first appearance before Congress, and it set the tone for the second Clinton administration. Only one member of Congress challenged him, and that was Dana Rohrabacher, the conservative California Republican who, as a speechwriter in Ronald Reagan's White House, was credited with inventing the Reagan Doctrine.

"Good does not prevail by the United States remaining neutral among factions," Rohrabacher countered. "In Germany in the 1930s, it was not right for us to remain neutral among factions. There were egregious human rights abusers in the form of Nazis and Communists, and we should not have been neutral in that situation. Our neutrality in Afghanistan the last decade has been part of the fault that people are still dying over there, and there is such chaos over there at this time." He added that if the Taliban remained in control of Afghanistan, they "will be the worst terrorists in the world."

It was a voice in the wilderness. Inderfurth did not respond. He had the backing of his boss. "We did not think it useful to get in the middle of a civil war," Albright would later explain.

In mid-November, the secretary of state went out of her way to avoid sounding middle-of-the-road as she publicly denounced the Taliban treatment of women as "despicable." Her strong, unscripted words at a press conference in Islamabad made it clear that Washington was not quietly supporting the Taliban, according to Inderfurth.

In early December, a delegation of three Taliban ministers set off for the United States, seeking support for a gas pipeline that the U.S. firm UNOCAL wanted to build across Afghan territory to link energy-rich Turkmenistan with the growing markets of Pakistan and India. Visas in hand, they toured an oil platform in the Gulf of Mexico and visited UNOCAL's headquarters in Houston. Then they flew to Washington, where Ahmad Jan, the acting minister of mines, was received at the State Department. But instead of blessing the pipeline plan, Inderfurth decried

---

* The term "strict neutrality" has a long and unhappy history in American foreign policy. It was first used by pacifist secretary of state William Jennings Bryan to justify America's noninvolvement during World War I; and pro-Nazi campaigner Charles Lindbergh used it to argue against U.S. intervention in World War II.

the plight of Afghan women, the resurgence of opium growing, and the stalled peace process.

The signals were mixed—to the extent that there was a policy, it was one of disengaged neutrality.[44]

6

"Silence Cannot Be the Strategy"
(1998)

With the United States in strict-neutrality mode and no other major power willing to engage, Afghanistan became just another forgotten conflict, and it was left to the United Nations to lead the search for peace. For years, the United Nations had dispatched low-profile envoys who made the rounds of the warring Afghan parties, arranged cease-fires that never took hold, and issued reports that no one read. In July 1997, Secretary-General Kofi Annan tried to break the pattern by naming Lakhdar Brahimi, his ablest troubleshooter, as special envoy.

Why take on another "mission impossible," reporters asked Brahimi. "I'm foolish enough to accept them," he gamely countered. "No one else will."*

Unlike most career diplomats, the former Algerian foreign minister brought something special to the table, the bona fides of an ardent nationalist and revolutionary who was at home in a land in turmoil. Brahimi would not base himself in Pakistan or keep Massoud and Rabbani at arm's length, as had the three heads of the UN Special Mission to Afghanistan before him. Nor would he suffer snubs, as had Norbert Holl, a German diplomat who was never received by Mullah Omar and could rarely call even on Pakistan's deputy foreign minister. Omar refused to meet infidels; Brahimi—although a secular Muslim—could get in the door.†

Yet, without the backing of a major power or the ability to call in political, economic, and military resources, even the ablest mediator could not do much more than convene meetings. The United States advocated a negotiated outcome but felt it had no interest at stake and adopted a policy of benign neglect. Brahimi had to wait for events to provide his opportunity.[1]

---

* Brahimi had a strong track record: he mediated an end to the 1989–1991 Lebanese civil war, led the UN observer team in monitoring and assisting in Nelson Mandela's 1994 election in South Africa, and helped end the Yemen civil war that same year. Less successful were his attempts to resolve Zaire's internal government feuding in 1993 and his two years as UN mission head in Haiti from 1994 to 1996.

† One of Brahimi's predecessors, former Tunisian foreign minister Mahmoud Mestiri, who served from 1994 to mid-1996, had defined his mission as "to wrest power from Mr. Rabbani." The other two were Holl and UN bureaucrat Benon Sevan of Cyprus, who held the job from 1990 to mid-1992 (and later went on to manage the problem-wracked Iraq Oil for Food Program). Mestiri remark reported by Reuters, March 18, 1995, and quoted in Maley, *Afghanistan Wars,* 211.

At the time of his appointment, the Taliban were still reeling from their setback in May, and the anti-Taliban alliance was in disarray. It would be difficult to exploit the moment, as Massoud's testy exchange with Omar had shown, and Brahimi refrained from taking any initiative until he sounded out the United Nations and the region and met with the Afghan factions. His opportunity would come in the disclosure of a horrific war crime.

With thousands of captured fighters still unaccounted for after their ill-planned assault on Mazar, a worried Taliban leadership asked the International Committee of the Red Cross (ICRC) to confirm that their soldiers were alive or arrange repatriation of their remains. On behalf of the Taliban, the ICRC delivered forty-seven requests to Malik, asking to visit and register the prisoners. He rebuffed every one. Finally, Malik called Massoud and told him what had happened.

"Our troops made this mistake," Malik said. The detainees had been executed. According to his secretary, Massoud was furious: "You really made a big mistake. You should never kill prisoners," he said. Until then, Massoud had considered Malik to be a "brilliant politician." After all, he had defeated Dostum, invited the Taliban in, and then destroyed the Taliban. But on learning about the execution of the prisoners, Massoud decided that Malik "could not be counted on." It would be some months before the full story emerged.[2]

In mid-September 1997, four months after his humiliating removal and flight, Dostum staged a dramatic comeback. By Malik's account, the Pakistani ISI first secured the assent of the Taliban, then sent officials to Ankara to clear the way. According to the Turkish Foreign Ministry, he had departed "of his own will." Dostum would later claim his return had been facilitated by support from Massoud, the Shia Hezbi Wahdat, and the government of Uzbekistan. He no doubt received guidance from the Turks, who kept a diplomatic presence in Afghanistan and a close watch on the politics. So low was Malik's standing in every quarter that all these explanations may be true.

Dostum returned at a moment of confusion and chaos. Mazar was once again under siege, this time from a Taliban offensive involving artillery, ground troops, and air strikes. Wahdat officials were the first to announce his return, boasting that Uzbek fighters soon would join Hazaras to fight the Taliban. Meanwhile, Malik—more politician than frontline commander—had withdrawn to Sheberghan. It took Dostum two months to rebuild his command and restore some of his lost authority. But then he fell out with the Hazara leadership and had to return to his former headquarters in Sheberghan. Malik retreated even farther west, to Samangan province.

Dostum delivered the coup de grace to Malik in an extraordinary manner that at once discredited his one-time deputy and rebuilt his own battered credibility: he dug up the mass graves. On November 17, he announced that he had uncovered twenty mass graves in the Sheberghan region and invited UN investigators and the international media to inspect them. He told the Associated Press in a phone interview that he had seen seven hundred bodies and believed that Malik had executed at least two thousand Taliban fighters.

The brutal killing of so many by an obscure warlord made no waves abroad, as few observers outside Pakistan had any sympathy for the Taliban; but it rang alarm bells at the United Nations. An atrocity like this could be the death knell of any peace initiative. Brahimi seized the moment.

Although Taliban officials condemned the United Nations and the international community for watching mutely as the killing proceeded, the United Nations moved with unusual alacrity. Annan ordered a special mission to Afghanistan within a day after Dostum's announcement. They reached Mazar in twenty-four hours, well ahead of the news media. After a guided tour by Dostum, the team called for a rapid follow-up probe to determine whether the dead had been killed in action or executed after being taken prisoner. Meanwhile, Brahimi approached the newly appointed UN high commissioner for human rights, former president of Ireland Mary Robinson, and asked her to organize an investigation.

When reporters arrived the following week in Sheberghan, they described stomach-turning scenes. At Nine Wells—an uninhabited area in the Dasht-i-Laili desert about thirty miles west of Sheberghan—the air was "thick with the stench of rotting flesh," the BBC reported. "The area is strewn with ribcages, limb bones, and skulls." One corpse, partially decomposed, "had clearly been taken from a hospital bed to be killed—from its arm protruded an intravenous drip." Reuter correspondent Tim Johnston took advantage of the upheaval to visit the Mazar jail and found eighty Taliban fighters in "appalling physical condition." Jail officials told him they were the remnant of 1,570 Taliban once held there. Malik, contacted by reporters, said he had had nothing to do with the massacres. But an aide who was released from jail told the BBC's Alan Johnston that Malik had personally forced him to participate in the executions in the desert; he said Malik had been there in person.[3]

The UN human rights rapporteur on Afghanistan, Choong-Hyun Paik, traveled to the area on December 13 with a Canadian forensic pathologist in tow. Malik, who by this time had fled the country, was rattled. "No Taliban POWs have been killed," he wrote Mary Robinson in a letter dated December 4. "Utmost attention and care has been accorded them in our custody." Paik's first verbal report December 16 bared the lie. "The manner of death was horrendous," a UN spokesman quoted him as saying. Evidence at the site of one mass grave showed that the prisoners "were lined up and mowed down with heavy caliber machine guns." Paik visited Nine Wells and interviewed witnesses. "Prisoners were taken from detention, told they were going to be exchanged, and then trucked to wells of a type used by shepherds. They were thrown into the wells alive; those who resisted were shot and then tossed in," he reported. Their captors threw grenades down the shafts and bulldozed earth over the openings. Paik found spent cartridges and pins from hand grenades in the vicinity. In early January, the pathologist who accompanied Paik reported that nearly all the corpses recovered from the shallow graves had their arms tied behind their backs. He recommended autopsies at the Nine Wells site, where there might be as many as one hundred bodies in each of the nine wells, and at a shallow grave east of the Mazar-Hairatan road, where dozens of corpses were found tied individually and together, with numerous spent cartridges in the vicinity.

In February, the UN General Assembly unanimously called on Annan to "continue to investigate fully" the allegations about mass killings of prisoners of war and civilians and about incidents of rape. Annan agreed. These developments warranted "urgent action" on the United Nations' part, he said in mid-March, calling for "credible efforts" to establish the facts.[4]

But Paik feared that the United Nations was about to duck for cover. In his March 1998 report to the UN human rights commissioner, he said it was "indispensable" for the United Nations, as the universal defender of human rights, to respond to massacres; he called for a thorough and full-scale investigation of all sites by a neutral team as soon as logistically possible. The outcome should be for "those accused to be found, investigated, and punished by the competent authorities if found guilty." The United Nations "must be vigilant and give priority to protecting the human rights of large segments of the Afghan population against atrocities such as massacres." He warned, "Silence cannot be the strategy of the international community."

The admonition went unheeded. Not until six months after Paik's initial visit did Robinson dispatch a reconnaissance team headed by two human rights researchers. Their counsel was the same as Paik's—the United Nations should launch an investigation "as soon as possible," before the sites were tampered with. "The UN should not undertake any more exploratory missions," they urged. "It is clear that all sides are losing patience with the United Nations and now want results. . . . Either an investigative mission begins, or the UN should acknowledge its limitations and drop the attempt."

Silence in the Face of Crime

Although this had been one of the worst slaughters of the war and the UN bureaucracy had done all the right things, months later no investigation had yet been launched. What had gone wrong? One factor may have been that the United States—champion of human rights everywhere else in the world and the principal sponsor of the special UN war crimes tribunals for the former Yugoslavia and Rwanda—was silent.

By coincidence, Madeleine Albright was in Pakistan one day after Dostum's announcement. At a press conference in Islamabad, she condemned the "despicable" attitude of the Taliban toward Afghan women; in Peshawar, after hearing a story about a girl jumping out a window to avoid being raped, she denounced the Taliban as being "especially backward and harsh" for denying health care, employment, and education to women. "I reacted to what I was hearing," she later said, explaining her strong language. Albright had been the champion of human rights and international humanitarian law in the Balkans and a prime mover behind the establishment of the International Criminal Tribunal for the Former Yugoslavia (ITFY). But she said nothing about the mass graves in Sheberghan, nor did she direct her staff to support the investigation.*

Mary Robinson took a dim view of the challenge Brahimi threw her human rights oversight body, which had been established in 1993 and had yet to develop a strong investigative capacity. She was more at home speechmaking than overseeing fieldwork, her staff said. She may also have had a personal antipathy to this project. "I will not be a gravedigger," she was quoted as telling staff.[5]

The final report, which might have led to charges against Malik and a trial, was not completed until late 1999, long after it could have affected the course of events. Great Britain, the Netherlands, Norway, Sweden, and Denmark paid the $427,000 cost of the investigation. The United States was not among the contributors.[†]

---

*Albright's staff selected the Bibi Mariam School at the Nasir Bagh Afghan refugee camp for her photo op—an unfortunate choice. To demonstrate American-style women's empowerment, Albright invited all her top female staff and two women reporters to join her. But her advance team failed to inform her that Pakistan had begun razing the camp and had ordered its inhabitants to return to Taliban-controlled Afghanistan or find another camp. The situation was one of utter despair and had been fully detailed in a UN report issued a month earlier. Refugees were dying for lack of food, Choong-Hyun Paik wrote. "Some refugees stated that there were those among them who could not afford the cloth in which to wrap a corpse. People had to share a single piece of bread and had no energy to work." They had no money for medicines when they fell ill. He quoted refugees as saying that a chicken on a farm in a developed country got more food than they did. They asked him for food, for direct deliveries by the United Nations, and for warnings should the camp be destroyed. They also asked Paik if he knew of any other country that would be willing to accept them. A reporter accompanying Albright said the news that the camp was being dismantled "took us all by surprise." UN report #A/52/493, October 16, 1997; and Carol Giacoma, interview by author, July 2004

† Robinson did not take the lead in the investigation until November 1998; she announced it in May 1999, and it began in July. The mission turned into a fiasco, and the final report was never made public, although a summary was distributed. The team, headed by Andreas Schiess, a former ICRC official, arrived in Mazar-i-Sharif two years and two months after the event. They visited the sites recommended and located a number of witnesses but were unable to carry out forensic work. By this time, the front had changed. Except for three provinces controlled by Massoud, the Taliban were in control of northern Afghanistan. Taliban leaders blocked interviews unless a Taliban minder was present. They had also removed the evidence. When the Schiess team arrived at the Nine Wells site, "no human remains could be seen." Its conclusions were all but useless. "It could not be established how many persons were detained overall in the context of the events, where these people were detained, and what happened during their detention; it could not be established when, by whom, and where and under what circumstances *(continued on next page)*

Brahimi was not the only one to detect Taliban vulnerability in mid-1997 or the need to reach out to them. Even as the Office of the High Commissioner for Human Rights (OHCHR) dallied, bin Laden had already offered his plan to make good the defeat of 1997, and the Taliban, with his support, were reorganizing their forces for a return engagement.

By early 1998, the militia was ready to announce its plan to build a regular national army of two divisions that would replace the tribal and regional task forces. Air assets were to be reorganized in a corps at Khoja Rawash Air Base. U.S. officials were aware of the army reorganization, but bin Laden's deepening links with the Taliban leadership escaped notice. "I don't think we saw or understood his connection with Mullah Omar," Gary Schroen would later say. He added, "I don't think we understood exactly this whole role of the reorganization until later." The main reason for overlooking the development was that "we weren't focusing on . . . what was going on at the battlefield. . . [and] we were focusing on where is bin Laden today."[6]

For journalists on the ground, the first sign of significant change was a clampdown on frontline access. Throughout 1997, the few foreign reporters in Kabul were welcomed—even invited—to tour the front lines. "We would chat with the Taliban, drink tea, and look at the front," recalled AFP's Stefan Smith. Sometimes the information minister, Amir Khan Muttaqi, would knock on their doors in the morning and invite them for a drive. However, the United Nations reported that in August 1997, the acting deputy minister of information cautioned reporters to send stories that "truly reflected the situation" and not to resort to analysis or witness reports that might give "a false impression" of the situation. The atmosphere worsened in early 1998: checkpoints were set up to block journalists from the front unless the visits were organized in advance.

The apparent reason for the tightening of security was that Arabs began to play a more important frontline role. Smith said, "We regularly spoke with travelers coming from villages north of Kabul who told us about foreign fighters who had taken over large sections of the front line." In Kabul, they spotted Arabs from Yemen, Algeria, Saudi Arabia, Kuwait, and other countries, as well as Muslims from Chechnya and Burma, even though the Taliban supposedly had asked them to stay out of sight. Three training camps in the Kabul area—one in Shekar Dara, about twelve miles north on the road to Charikar; a second in Paghman; and a third just south of the Darul Aman Palace southwest of Kabul—became "no-go" sites. "But we knew what was going on there from a whole variety of sources," Smith said,

---

† (cont.)
prisoners were killed; command and responsibility could not clearly be established. Evidence at numerous potential massacre and/or mass grave sites was destroyed," the report said. But the report contained graphic details from witnesses the staff had interviewed and left no doubt of Malik's culpability. Robinson declined to be interviewed for this book and offered no comment on textual references to her role. UN Investigation Team for Afghanistan, "Confidential Report to the High Commissioner for Human rights,: September 30, 1999.

"the military training of foreign fighters." Khost became off-limits, as did areas around Jalalabad and Tora Bora, and reporters were discouraged from visiting Kandahar. The warnings that writing about foreign fighters was not permitted were unmistakable. "We had a 'red line' drawn along our reporting regarding foreign fighters. That was something that we were simply not permitted to mention," Smith recalled. "The slightest mention of a Pakistani would get you in enormous trouble." The AFP reporter said he had "the general impression that I was on the verge of expulsion."

By the summer of 1998, the tension was high. The Taliban gave the impression "that they were starting to resent, if not hate, the few expatriates left in Kabul. Our lives were restricted. Our reporting was restricted. We started to need to have bits of paper to do anything."* The pressures on the international press indicated creeping Arabization. The Taliban developed a plan to move all foreigners—the UN staff, nongovernmental organizations (NGOs) and charities, and foreign reporters—into Kabul Polytechnic, the university quarter largely destroyed during Massoud's battles with the Hazaras. Reporters were told that the pressure for the move came from Kandahar and inspired by the system in Saudi Arabia, where all expatriates live in compounds. Although the scheme never went anywhere, "It reinforced the impression that we were not really welcome," said Smyth. "The Taliban as I had known them from when they arrived in Kabul were no longer the same people. They stopped caring about what the rest of the world thought of them, which was a dangerous direction."7

For Osama bin Laden, 1998 presented a window of opportunity to strengthen his ties with the Taliban and to pursue his own agenda. He slowly raised his profile as he carefully laid the groundwork for a spectacular debut as a world actor.

His first move was to unite the various factions of Islamists that had drifted apart in the years since fighting the Soviet Union—in particular, his own al Qaeda and Ayman al Zawahiri's Egyptian Islamic Jihad—and to lead them in a new jihad, this time directed against the United States. He set out his political aim in a blood-curdling fatwa that twisted facts and Islamic theology into his service. Claiming that the United States was occupying the Arabian peninsula in the service of Israel and had killed a

---

* Smith said Muttaqi summoned him on several occasions for "long explanations on what I meant by 'independent sources' or 'eyewitnesses,'" with Muttaqi picking through my copy line by line." If Smith made the slightest mention of foreign fighters, he was told to be "very, very careful." He managed to cultivate friends in the Taliban's Foreign Ministry, who provided private pointers on "what we could not write and where we could not go." The Foreign Ministry was run by Taliban from Logar province, who were far more open than those from Kandahar. "They bailed me out of serious problems on more than one occasion," Smith said, "mostly when I had gone to a front line or Kabul hilltop where I was not allowed."

In early 1998, the Logaris and former communists at the Foreign Ministry told him to keep a low profile with regard to the other key ministries—justice, defense, vice and virtue, and interior. Smith said, "The Foreign Ministry even asked us not to request interviews with these ministries, so as 'not to advertise your presence here.'" The Taliban were not explicit with threats, but when Smith encountered an Arab, there would be "some hassle—guns in my face, and so on." Some Taliban officials started to refer to him as an infidel, "which is never a good sign." Smith, e-mails.

million Iraqis, the fatwa declared, "The judgment to kill Americans and their allies, both civilian and military, is an individual duty of every Muslim able to do so and in any country where it is possible. . . . We, in the name of God, call on every Muslim who believes in God and desires to be rewarded to follow God's order to kill Americans and plunder their wealth wherever and whenever they find it." The fatwa was dated February 12, 1998, with the subtitle "a legal fatwa," and first published ten days later in the London-based Arabic newspaper *Al Quds al Arabi*. It received almost no other media notice at the time, but the announcement that civilians would be primary targets shocked some of his own associates. Bin Laden's London representative said it was "not Islamic" to kill civilians. The fatwa also marked the debut of the grandiosely named International Islamic Front for Jihad against the Jews and the Crusaders.* Bin Laden and Zawahiri signed it, along with other extremist leaders from Egypt, Pakistan, and Bangladesh. Unbeknownst to anyone outside the inner circle, bin Laden now moved from the planning phase into deployment of personnel for a major operation against American diplomatic missions in East Africa.

The U.S. government protested the fatwa to the Taliban on March 2; the next day, the Taliban sent back word that bin Laden was living "under restriction." But bin Laden was not cowed and in mid-March sent a fax to the Associated Press calling for jihad against U.S. troops in the Persian Gulf or, as he called them, "Christian occupying invaders." To compensate for the fatwa's principal flaw—namely, that it was not legal in view of bin Laden's lack of standing as a religious scholar—he rounded up *ulema* to endorse it. By late April, some forty Afghan clerics and a group of their counterparts in Karachi had declared jihad under Islamic law against the United States; in June, an imam from the Prophet's Mosque in Medina called for the withdrawal of U.S. troops. These endorsements carried little weight with the man-on-the-street but would certainly have impressed the credulous Mullah Omar, a true believer in religious edicts.[8]

A tug-of-war for the favor of Mullah Omar was thus under way, pitting bin Laden against the United Nations' Lakhdar Brahimi. Bin Laden, working to bring about a Taliban military conquest, was better plugged in with Omar and other leaders and better able to summon financial assistance. Brahimi had few inducements to offer beyond the prospect of taking over the UN seat still occupied by the Rabbani government, as well as international recognition. On the deficit side, his pledge to have the United Nations investigate the Mazar killings had stalled, as Paik had feared, and the United States was playing a passive role, sending mixed signals.

---

*The name of the group was an expansion of the former International Islamic Front, and its reemergence signified that two Egyptian groups—Zawahiri's Islamic Jihad of Egypt and al-Gamaa al-Islamiyya, led by Rifai Ahmad Taha—had reconciled. Other signers were Sheikh Mir Hamza, secretary of Jamiyat Ulema Pakistan (the Pakistan clerics association), which was said to be a social aid group, and Sheikh Fazel al Rahman, the leader of the Harrakat al-Jihad group in Bangladesh.

Brahimi had moved deliberately. The previous autumn he had set up an advisory body consisting of Afghanistan's six neighbors—Pakistan, Iran, Turkmenistan, Uzbekistan, Tajikistan, and China—as well as the United States and Russia. He drafted a mission statement that the advisory body endorsed on March 3.* The central premise was that "there can never be a military solution to the Afghan conflict because no one faction (whatever the composition of its current alliance) can win an outright victory or impose an exclusive dominance over the whole country." The underlying assumption was that both sides could accept a political solution. The mechanism for the talks had been proposed by the Taliban: an apolitical commission of Islamic religious scholars or *ulema* from both sides to propose modalities for a cease-fire and an interim government. The notion that a theological ruling could end the war aroused great doubts within the United Front, and the Taliban themselves were ambivalent. Nevertheless, with Brahimi in the background, Pakistan hosted Burhanuddin Rabbani to start the talks in December 1997. The Taliban did not send a delegation but left the door open to further talks; however, in February 1998, when Rabbani submitted a list of forty-five scholars, the Taliban rejected it, claiming that not all had been properly trained.[9]

Bill Richardson Tries His Hand

With Brahimi's encouragement, the Clinton administration attempted to kick-start the process by flying UN ambassador Bill Richardson into Kabul for one day. The self-styled troubleshooter had negotiated with Saddam Hussein, Fidel Castro, and North Korean leaders to free hostages or prisoners, and he was a "friend of Bill." But when he landed in Kabul on April 17, 1998—the first cabinet officer to visit Afghanistan in nearly two decades—he found that he had met his match. Pakistan's ambassador in Kabul, Aziz Ahmed Khan, welcomed Richardson on behalf of the entire active diplomatic corps, namely himself. In preparation for the visit, Khan had met Mullah Rabbani three times to review the U.S. concerns and to coach Rabbani on his response.

After one-and-a-half hours of talks, followed by lunch (at a table), Richardson believed that he had achieved most of what he had come for. The Taliban agreed to a cease-fire and to join face-to-face talks with the United Front in Islamabad within ten days; they offered to allow higher education for women, but no coeducation; they would allow Afghan female

---

* The Clinton administration welcomed the "six-plus-two" forum and continually cited it as evidence of its interest in Afghanistan; in fact, the Americans saw it as a way to emphasize the role of other countries, although those countries either had a conflict of interest or too much historical baggage to take the lead. As Albright put it: "We were working through a process where we thought the others might have more influence than we did . . . the Russians and Iranians and various other members of the six plus two." Albright, interview.

doctors to provide care for women; and they would prohibit all opium poppy cultivation.

But they would not expel bin Laden. "They just said no," said a White House official. Mullah Rabbani said, "Bin Laden is our guest here. He is under our control." Rabbani claimed that no one would listen to bin Laden because he was not an *alim* (religious scholar) and had no credentials to issue fatwas. The Taliban would not allow terrorism to emanate from Afghan soil, Rabbani said.

Richardson headed north to talk with the opposition. A detour to Badakshan to see Massoud fell through, so he settled for a late afternoon encounter in Sheberghan with Dostum, whose military and political situation was once again precarious. They were joined by Burhanuddin Rabbani and Karim Khalili, head of the Shia Hazara movement, the Hezbi Wahdat.* "Everybody's friend" staged a lavish reception and, for good measure, organized an exhibition game of *buzkashi,* the Afghan answer to polo, played with the headless carcass of a slaughtered goat. The United Front readily agreed to attend the talks.

Back in Islamabad that evening, Richardson was in a celebratory mood. "I believe the Afghan people want this war to end. I saw it in their eyes," he exclaimed. "It appears we have a breakthrough." Among other things, the Taliban had agreed in principle to lift the food blockade on Hazarajat, where aid workers said tens of thousands of Hazara were on the brink of starvation.

Pakistani officials rushed to take credit. The foreign minister, Gohar Ayub Khan, boasted that Pakistan had laid the groundwork, even coaching Richardson on his manners: "We told him how to talk, shake hands, or hug so that the Afghans would feel at home with him."

The triumph was short-lived. Shortly after Richardson's visit, a representative of Omar told the BBC that there was no question of starting "any comprehensive dialogue at this stage." Although both sides met on April 26 as Richardson had asked, the first three days were spent wrangling over the definition of *ulema.* The deal breaker turned out to be the United Front's demand for an unconditional lifting of the food blockade on Hazarajat. Taliban representatives argued that this action had to await the advice of the religious scholars. On May 3, all but one in the Taliban delegation left for Kandahar to seek new instructions; they never returned. Two weeks later, Taliban officials, charging the United Nations with "bad

---

* Massoud was "so desperate for a Western audience" that he would have met any diplomat at any level, recalled his spokesman, Masoud Khalili, but he preferred to meet VIPs in nearby Dushanbe, Tajikistan, or in Tashkent, Uzbekistan. Khalili said, "We heard there were more than forty people . . . we had no facility to receive them in, and [if] they had to stay overnight, it would have been a nightmare. Our people informed them about the lack of facilities, and they chose not to go." But a top White House aide came away with the impression that Massoud was "not that crazy to be identified as America's guy. . . . The fact is, he wouldn't meet Richardson." Masoud Khalili, e-mail to author, January 2004; and former senior U.S. official, interview by author, December 2003.

faith," abandoned their own proposal for an *ulema* commission and asked the United Nations to find a new basis for the talks.*

According to U.S. ambassador to Pakistan Tom Simons, this was the best chance for a negotiated solution since Babar had tried it in October 1996. But there is reason to wonder whether it could have succeeded. Richardson had little more to offer the Taliban than Brahimi—essentially, a vague promise of reconstruction and development assistance. Full recognition seemed out of the question, because the administration was by this time deeply conflicted. Clinton himself had promised women activists gathered at the White House on March 11, 1998, that there would be no recognition until treatment of women improved. To win U.S. backing to take over the Afghan seat at the United Nations, which Rabbani's government still controlled, the Taliban would have had to change its policy denying girls and women access to health care. Albright laid down a marker shortly before Richardson landed in Kabul: "If the Taliban or any other Afghan faction want international acceptance, they must treat women not as chattel but as people, and they must respect human rights," she said in a radio interview.

If Rabbani's commitments had been implemented, Richardson could have portrayed the changes as meeting the Clinton and Albright hurdles. But it seems highly unlikely that Rabbani could have delivered, and there is every reason to question how Clinton (whose foreign policy tended in many parts of the world to be built around the interests of political constituencies at home) could have reciprocated.

The Taliban were deeply ambivalent about seeking a negotiated peace, as evidenced by their reluctance to enter the *ulema* process in early 1998 and the fact that they had not invited Richardson to the real seat of power. "We were in Kabul, not Kandahar," noted Rick Inderfurth, who accompanied Richardson. "We were seeing Rabbani, not Omar. And for there to be any major decisions taken with respect to the fighting, with respect to bin Laden, it had to be done with Omar." Why didn't they go to Kandahar? "We were not invited to Kandahar. When they said we could come, they said, 'Come to Kabul.'"[10]

A flying visit to Kandahar might not have done much good. Omar's messianic worldview was built around the fatwas of sympathetic religious scholars and had no place for political compromise. He saw the internal conflict as a holy war against sinners. "These people have sinned and rebelled against Islamic sharia" and should be "fought to the end," he told an Arab interviewer shortly after his negotiators abandoned the Islamabad talks. "We have a fatwa from our *ulema* that we should fight them and force

---

*The Taliban relented at the end of May and temporarily lifted the blockade, allowing limited shipments of wheat to two affected areas of Hazarajat, but the United Nations said the severe food shortages put tens of thousands of Hazara at continued risk.

them to submit to sharia, especially since our Islamic princedom's rule is the sound and correct rule of sharia." In Omar's world, opponents who fell on the battlefield did not merit a Muslim prayer or burial. "Our *ulema* do not permit it," he said.

A political settlement was inconceivable for Omar. "A political solution starts with asking questions about who started the fight . . . who is to blame, and so on," he said. He preferred a solution based on sharia, in which "the esteemed *ulema* have the last word. They understand sharia, and they rule between us and our opponents."

But his decision to call off the conference of *ulema* suggests that he did not really trust the scholars unless they agreed to an outcome that would keep the Emir il Momineen in power. An interim coalition government was "impossible and unacceptable to us under all circumstances," he said. The Taliban "refuse to have any others participate in rule. We want a government based on sharia and the fatwa of *ulema* known to us. We do not accept a government in which the others participate." For Omar, the decision could not be handed over to just any *ulema*; it had to be pro-Taliban *ulema*. There was no middle ground.[11]

In short, Omar's absolutism made it unlikely that a high-profile U.S. role could have achieved a breakthrough. At the same time, diplomacy was never really put to the test. Aside from that one day in Afghanistan, the administration had no focus on Afghanistan. Top aides said the real reason Richardson was in South Asia was to visit India and Pakistan and address the tensions between them, rather than to settle the Afghan conflict. Clinton rarely threw himself into diplomacy, but he was preoccupied with expanding economic ties with India, and Richardson, acting as advance man for Clinton's forthcoming trip to India and Pakistan, was signaling a change in U.S. priorities. There was no way Clinton could undo congressional restrictions centered on demands that India and Pakistan call off their respective drives for nuclear weapons capability, but he could play down the concern. The message Richardson took with him was that "we would not let nuclear proliferation be a veto" over strong ties.

Inderfurth told the Indians that commerce "should be the centerpiece of our relationship," while Richardson told the Pakistanis that "there are other issues than nonproliferation." "The United States recognizes Pakistan's right to set priorities for defense and security needs," Clinton told Prime Minister Nawaz Sharif in a letter, implicitly accepting Pakistan's drive to develop a nuclear arsenal and the means of delivery. The timing of the policy shift proved to be a colossal miscalculation.[12]

Unfortunately for Richardson, and for Clinton, the CIA was not watching the South Asian test sites—on May 11–13, India conducted a series of nuclear tests; on May 28–30, Pakistan did the same. Democrats in Congress were apoplectic, and the Clinton initiative was "blown out of the desert," said a former White House official.

In mid-June, Clinton named Richardson secretary of energy, and congressional delays in confirming his successor, Richard Holbrooke, spelled the end of U.S. Afghanistan diplomacy. "There was not sufficient follow-through on this," was the judgment of Richardson's deputy, Calvin Mitchell. "Bill wasn't there to push this forward."

The damage was not only to U.S. authority as a mediator but to the UN–led peace process at a time when Brahimi's credibility was in question. The special envoy had seized on a major war crime against the Taliban as an opening for the peace process; Robinson's failure to follow through undercut his effort. "I asked for the investigation. They [the Taliban] agreed to it," he would later say. "Our human rights people were far too slow, as usual." And now the United States showed that it had no interest in a negotiated outcome to the Afghan struggle beyond a single flying visit.[13]

But bigger forces were also at work. The Taliban were determined to vanquish Massoud on the battlefield. In the first week of May—even before the collapse of the Islamabad talks—the black turbans scored a significant gain, capturing a district center called Ishkamish in what appeared to be a two-pronged assault to seize Massoud-held Takhar province in northeastern Afghanistan. A local warlord blocked a second planned advance through mountainous Nuristan to capture the Tupkhanah Pass, and that element of the offensive was put on hold. Meanwhile, to the west, the Taliban organized an assault on Dostum's forces in Sheberghan as they planned a major offensive against Mazar-i-Sharif. On May 17, as the political leadership abandoned its peace initiative, Taliban aircraft bombed Massoud-held Taloqan, the provincial capital of Takhar, hitting a market and killing more than thirty civilians. Later that month, the United Front fired fusillades of rockets at Kabul Airport; they sometimes missed their target and hit residential areas of Kabul, killing civilians.

One of the most striking features of the Taliban offensive—according to Anthony Davis—was the crucial support role played by Pakistan. In late December 1997, just as Burhanuddin Rabbani was working out the modalities for an *ulema* commission in Islamabad, some two hundred Taliban crossed from Pakistan into south Badakshan through the pass, an operation "clearly impossible without the concurrence of Pakistani border authorities," Davis wrote in *Jane's Intelligence Review*. They were repulsed some weeks later. The spring offensive to capture Tupkhanah from the Afghan side was to have opened the pass for some one thousand Taliban to cross to capture Faizabad, the capital of Massoud-held Badakshan province. Throughout the spring and summer, truckloads of Pakistani "volunteers" were driven into Afghanistan and dispatched to the different fronts. But the moment for the big push in the north would have to wait for some further Afghan-style diplomacy: the buying of the other side's allied commanders.

Pakistan was not alone in pursuing a two-track policy, but it was the most blatant example in the run-up to the 1998 spring and summer offensive, and the U.S. government was well aware of it. A top Pakistani official confirmed in March 1998 that Pakistan had supplied arms and ammunition, although not since the end of 1997, and that Pakistan was the sole source of fuel to the Taliban. The U.S. consulate in Peshawar reported an apparent "major escalation in Pakistani assistance" in March, when twenty-five large Mercedes Benz trucks covered with tarpaulins transported an estimated two thousand "Pakistani Taliban" to Kabul Airport for air transport to Kunduz. In June, the United Nations quoted "reliable witnesses" reporting that the Taliban had received a "large delivery" of military supplies loaded on two hundred trucks. And in July, Pakistan pledged some $6 million to pay the salaries of Taliban officials and military commanders, according to Taliban and Pakistani sources.[14]

The Clinton administration was also proceeding on two distinct tracks. Starting in late 1997, the CIA's Counterterrorist Center developed a plan to capture and remove bin Laden from Afghanistan. Using local tribesmen, the agency planned a nighttime capture at his primary residence, Tarnak Farms, outside Kandahar Airport. They rehearsed it in autumn 1997 and again in March 1998, and finally did a complete rehearsal in May 1998 with an eye to carrying out the abduction by mid-July. But on May 29, CIA director George Tenet called off the operation, fearing that the risk of civilian casualties was too high.[15]

Bin Laden Takes the Stage

Bin Laden had kept a low profile during Richardson's visit, although he made no secret of his scorn. In a statement, he said the U.S. aim was "liquidating Arab Mujahidin . . . thwarting the project of an Islamic state in Afghanistan, and [forcing the Taliban] to cease applying sharia"—a code phrase perhaps referring to the suppression of women's rights. He said Afghans would not "sell their Islamic state at whatever price," nor end their support for "their Mujahidin brethren, who stood by them at critical moments, irrespective of the lures carried by Richardson." Meanwhile, bin Laden proceeded full speed ahead on *his* second track.

In the first half of 1998, bin Laden had organized his political allies; spelled out his political aims; laid the theological ground for the violence that would follow; and received endorsements from *ulema* in Afghanistan, Pakistan, and Saudi Arabia. By late May 1998, training for the operation was well under way, and he decided to stage a series of news events at the al Badr camp in Khost province. In the first interview (actually more of a monologue) with Pakistani journalist Hamid Mir in mid-May, bin Laden stated that his goals were to expel the U.S. military presence from Saudi Arabia and "liberate" the Haram al Sharif in Jerusalem—a thirty-five-acre complex that includes the al Aqsa mosque (one of Islam's most sacred sites) but which sits above the Wailing Wall (one of Judaism's most sacred sites).

He also planned to liberate Palestine. Sketching out a megalomanic vision, bin Laden declared that jihad to liberate "all the holy places of Islam" was "obligatory upon every Muslim" and warned that anyone "refuting the call to join jihad anywhere in the world is an infidel." Ten days later, he invited a group of mostly Pakistani journalists for a briefing, smuggling them into Afghanistan on a two-day trip that involved a five-hour trek at night across the mountains, hours in jeeps, an overnight in a safe house, and then a circuitous route before reaching the Khost camp.

"Heavy guns boomed as bin Laden stepped out of his sturdy jeep with tinted windows, and rocket-launchers were fired in the air to celebrate his arrival," wrote veteran Afghanistan-watcher Rahimullah Yusufzai. He later discovered that most of the gunners were not bin Laden's men, rather Afghans and Pakistanis staying in the nearby Zhawar camp.

Bin Laden's message to the one Chinese and thirteen Pakistani journalists was that the *ulema* of Saudi Arabia and elsewhere had issued a fatwa to wage jihad "to expel the Jews and the Christians from the Arabian peninsula." The campaign would also topple the ruling Saudi dynasty, and the members of the royal family would be put on trial. The result of this campaign would "be visible in the coming weeks."

Two days later, he hosted John Miller of the ABC network. Citing his own fatwa, he told Miller that civilians would be the targets for his next operation. He foresaw an apocalyptic outcome: "We predict a black day for America and the end of the United States as United States," and he said the leadership of Saudi Arabia "will disintegrate." Miller reported that bin Laden "put a time cap on it, saying that whatever action will be taken against Americans in the Gulf, whatever violence awaits, will occur within the next few weeks." Bin Laden had raised his profile, although he claimed he was operating within the Taliban guidelines. (He had been "asked to avoid" military activities, but there was "no restriction on political activities.")

That wasn't the understanding of Mullah Omar, who first learned of the press conference from BBC radio. He telephoned Yusufzai: "Who was the organizer? How did he travel into Afghanistan without a visa?" The reporter explained the route, and Omar exploded, "How dare he hold a press conference without asking my permission!" He then dictated a statement to Yusufzai. There will be one ruler in Afghanistan, either I or Osama bin Laden. . . . I will see to it." Bin Laden responded with a statement that he accepted Omar's rule and leadership, accepted Taliban decisions, and promised to abide by the pledge. For several months, he did, more or less.[16]

Neither of these media events received much U.S. media attention or public expression of concern by the White House, State Department, or Congress. In June, the U.S. Navy told sailors to exercise caution in the Gulf and canceled shore leave, and the State Department ordered embassies throughout the Middle East and South Asia to tighten their security. The United States did not formally protest the latest bin Laden provocation to the Taliban, but in early July a Taliban envoy informed the U.S. embassy in Pakistan that the authorities had "enacted tough new controls"; henceforth, bin Laden must clear all activities with the Taliban, including interviews. Bin Laden promised he would fully "submit" to Taliban control.[17]

Whatever the restrictions, bin Laden was on a roll. He had big plans in Afghanistan and a burgeoning corps of backers in neighboring Pakistan. He had planted the seeds for suicide ventures among Islamic extremists throughout South Asia and the Middle East, and gained the support of clerics in many countries. Bin Laden had recognized something about distant, small wars that the U.S. government did not: for those who contribute military support when the going is tough, war provides an excellent camouflage for their agendas. Bin Laden had put his trainers, his training camps, his own infrastructure of supporters, and his forces at the disposal of the Taliban, but every asset had a dual purpose—the second beneficiary was his personal jihad against the United States. From his safe haven in a largely inaccessible land, he was building manpower capacity in the form of trained, indoctrinated, and battle-hardened loyalists who had already proven their readiness to die for any cause to which he assigned them.

In their one-dimensional focus, U.S. authorities and the American media failed to recognize that bin Laden the international terrorist was the same as bin Laden the Taliban ally and that the two roles reinforced each other. Bin Laden was not conducting his own military operations —yet. The logic of his investment in the Taliban domestic war machine, combined with Mullah Omar's sensitivity, dictated that the timing for his own major international military operation should coincide with that of the Taliban.

His public threats to the United States and Saudi Arabia were counterproductive in one regard, for they helped coax the sometimes-wary allies into closer coordination. CIA director George Tenet visited Riyadh in late May and early June and won a commitment from Crown Prince Abdullah for an "all-out" secret effort to have the Taliban expel bin Laden. In mid-June, Prince Turki, then intelligence chief, traveled to Kandahar. "I asked Mullah Omar to hand him over and he agreed," Turki later said in an interview. "I was told their interests were with us and not with any individual. Mullah Omar asked me to inform the king and the crown prince that he wanted to set up a joint Saudi-Afghan committee to arrange procedures for the handover." But the joint committee was to be a committee of ulema, Omar's favorite form of procrastination and of avoiding political negotiations. Turki accepted, thinking it provided the Taliban a way to save face. He asked Omar explicitly if the only thing lacking was the modalities. "Assure the king and the crown prince that this is my view," Omar replied. In July, Omar sent Abdul Wakil Muttawakil, his future foreign minister, to Saudi Arabia with an assurance that a joint committee was being set up. It never came about.[18]

The continuing internal conflict concealed a more subtle development that went largely unnoticed by the international media (whose main focus tended to be "beards and burqas") and by government officials such as Albright, who publicly decried the persecution of women. This development was that with each battlefield setback, the Taliban toughened their internal repression. Choong-Hyun Paik, the UN special rapporteur for human rights in Afghanistan, spotted the trend during his regular visits. Setbacks in battle turned relative moderates into hard-liners on human rights issues. In October 1997 he wrote, "Violations of human rights by the Taliban and their crackdown against the populations in areas they controlled were commensurate to the pressure they faced on the battlefield." The decrees severely curtailing women's freedom "were aimed at humiliating people and showing them who was in power and that their actions were governed entirely by military goals."

From mid-1997 to mid-1998, such degradation became the public face of Afghanistan. Richardson's pleas had gone nowhere. In July 1998, the U.S. embassy protested three more edicts: the Taliban had closed home-based schools for girls in Kabul, denied medical treatment to women not accompanied by a close male relative, and required all NGOs in Kabul to relocate their offices to a single isolated compound.

Women could not go anywhere without a male escort, although even a four-year-old boy was deemed a suitable chaperone. At a checkpoint, boys up to age ten could search a woman. On public transport, no male older than ten years could collect a woman's fare. Women's health became a political football. In September 1997, the Ministry of Public Health shut down all services to women at Kabul hospitals and concentrated all services for a city of six hundred thousand in a single forty-five-bed medical facility that lacked equipment and qualified staff. Male and female doctors were already forbidden to talk or associate with each other, and male doctors were forbidden to enter a female patient's room unless called upon.

Men were also routinely humiliated. If their beards were not two fists in length (a Coca-Cola can was an alternative measure), they were subject to lashes by the Department for the Promotion of Virtue and the Suppression of Vice, and time in jail "until their beard gets bushy," one man told Paik. In Maidanshar, some seven hundred men were arrested for having short beards and no turbans, an offense that could be punished by confinement in a shipping container. "The fate of animals in Europe [is] better than that of people in Afghanistan," wrote Paik. In March, the Taliban banned television sets, videocassette recorders, and satellite dishes.[19]

Bombings, Executions, and Slaughter

The offensive that was to bring down opposition control over most of northern Afghanistan began July 10 with a Taliban assault on Dostum's forces in Maimana, the capital of Faryab province. In early June, Dostum had attempted to head off a Taliban attack by launching an operation in Badghis province on the Turkmenistan border, but the Taliban repelled it. Now it was payback time. Aided by two bribed defectors, Taliban forces moved along two axes: one a column of infantry in pickup trucks arriving from Qaisar and Almar, and the second a column of tanks arriving from the Turkmen border. The Taliban captured Maimana on July 12. A second paid defection—of Hezbi Islami troops from Balkh province—allowed the Taliban to press north to Andkhoi. They captured Sheberghan on August 2. Following the defection of another of Dostum's commanders in Balkh province, the way was now open to Mazar-i-Sharif, which they fought their way into on August 8. The initial task force of eight thousand was quickly augmented by reinforcements sent by road and air, and the Taliban seized the city in a pincer movement, with one column advancing from the west and a second from the airport, six miles to the east.

According to Anthony Davis, their rapid march north was facilitated by the "incompetence and feuding" within the United Front. Dostum attempted in vain to reestablish his dominant position in Mazar, which put him into confrontation with the Hazara Hezbi Wahdat, and then in clashes with Massoud's Jamiat in Tashkurgan, east of Mazar. Massoud had counted on Dostum's support to recapture the town of Kunduz, but the aid never came. Dostum was "fixated with Mazar," Massoud told Davis. "On Kunduz, he delayed, delayed, delayed."

In addition to the sale of fuel, the provision of cash, and the proffering (it is widely assumed) of military advice, Pakistan's major contribution to the Taliban offensive was in the form of manpower.* The UN mission in Islamabad said it had reports of "large numbers of non-Afghans"—most of them of Pakistani origin—engaging in "all aspects of the fighting alongside the Taliban." Western aid workers who were in Maimana when it fell reported that a quarter to a half of some Taliban units appeared to be Urdu-speaking Pakistanis, according to Davis. Western diplomatic sources also said that in the two weeks before the fall of Sheberghan, hundreds of Pakistani volunteers were airlifted to Herat and then taken by truck to the Taliban front lines. Davis reported that more than five thousand Pakistani madrassa students had been mobilized for Taliban service. Massoud's own intelligence indicated that 1,700 of the 8,000-man Taliban expeditionary force were Pakistanis. Later that summer, UN officials interviewed captured

---

* Anthony Davis, the closest journalistic observer of the war, noted in *Jane's Intelligence Review* that the Taliban's professionalism in using water tankers to supply fast-advancing columns in the initial phase of the operation and the well-coordinated use of Antonov transports to fly in reinforcements to air bases at Maimana, Sheberghan, and Mazar within hours of forward ground forces seizing the facilities raised the question of Pakistani military involvement. "It bears pointing out that, despite wild accusations by the opposition, there has never been any convincing evidence of the presence of serving Pakistani military personnel—let alone Pakistani aircraft or armor—in the Taliban campaigns, but circumstantial evidence of Pakistani involvement is powerful." *Jane's Intelligence Review*, November 1, 1998.

fighters in Bamiyan—they all admitted to being Pakistani but claimed to be independent and private adventurers fighting for a cause "without affiliation to any official institution of the Pakistani government."

The main financier of the offensive appears to have been Osama bin Laden. "In Mazar, it was well-known that the financing was by bin Laden," said an ICRC official. "I was at times at the front lines, and you could see the presence of these [Arab] troops, and they probably had commanders in the field." Davis reported that the Taliban conducted the offensive with at least four hundred new Japanese pickup trucks imported from Dubai through Pakistan; Massoud's intelligence concluded that it was actually 1,200 vehicles. "He gave them the cash to buy the equipment," said a close Massoud aide at the time. "Compared to us, they were highly mobile, with a few men sitting in a pickup truck with artillery mounted in back." His calculation was that the offensive cost $16–$18 million, and that it came from bin Laden "or his fundraising."* Massoud also credited bin Laden with a vital role in the war. Schroen quoted him as saying, "Every time I fight the Taliban, the glue that holds them together is the Arab units. Those guys stand and fight. If I pressure the Taliban too hard, they break, because they're not really used to this kind of combat. Those guys [the Arabs] fight to the death. They actually aim their weapons. They shoot straight." But in 1998, even as bin Laden played the role of indispensable ally and financier to the Taliban conquest, the CIA was not tracking the internal war. The agency could have noted the crucial role bin Laden played in helping reorganize the Taliban militia, but it did not. "What was going on on the battlefield wasn't that important to the United States," Schroen said. "We were focusing on 'Where is bin Laden today?'"[20]

On August 7, 1998, without specific warning, Islamic extremists drove explosives-laden trucks into two U.S. embassies in East Africa and blew them up almost simultaneously. In Nairobi, Kenya, Mohamed Rashed al Owhali, a twenty-one-year-old British-born Saudi, threw stun grenades at the U.S. embassy guardhouse as his driver, a Saudi named Jihad Mohammad Ali al Makki, detonated several hundred pounds of TNT and aluminum nitrate. It was 10:35 a.m., a time when observant Muslims would be attending Friday prayers. Altogether, 201 Kenyans and twelve Americans died, and five thousand people were injured.

Four minutes later, a refrigerator truck containing hundreds of pounds of TNT, wired to two oxygen-acetylene cylinders, blew up outside the U.S. embassy in Dar es Salaam, Tanzania. Eleven Tanzanians were killed as well as the truck driver, known as "Ahmed the German." The local who had accompanied him partway, Khalfan Khamis Mohamed, had used a

---

* Bin Laden could not have provided the funds from his personal income, estimated by the 9/11 Commission as $1 million a year through 1994; more likely, it came from the tens of millions he raised from wealthy Saudi and Gulf Arabs. Al Qaeda's annual budget in this period was about $30 million, of which $10–$20 million went to the Taliban.

meat grinder to grind up the TNT and helped in other preparations. After cleaning up at the safe house, he escaped by bus to Cape Town, South Africa. Before departing, he sent the meat grinder to his mother.

The Nairobi bombing was quickly traced to bin Laden. At the time of the explosions, an alert Pakistani immigration supervisor at the Karachi Airport noted a visitor arriving shaved while his Yemeni passport showed him with a beard. "Are you a terrorist?" he innocently asked Mohamed Sadeek Odeh. In fact, Odeh was a Jordanian national of Palestinian heritage who had fled Nairobi on the eve of the bombing, after setting up the infrastructure for bin Laden and helping in every element of the setup. He did not answer the question but tried to convince the immigration officer that the bombing was a religiously correct act. "I did it all for the cause of Islam," he later told interrogators. Bin Laden "is my leader, and I obey his orders." He gave the names of all his collaborators to Pakistan interrogators. Extradited to Kenya, he made a full confession to Kenyan and later to U.S. authorities.[21]

Al Owhali had received lacerations on his hand and face and a large wound on his back from the explosion; he went to a medical clinic to have them treated. He was sent to a hospital where, two days after the bombing, Kenyan police questioned him because he did not have proper papers. Arrested, he confessed that he had met bin Laden during training camps in Afghanistan. He had been with bin Laden at the al Badr press conference three months earlier, in May, where he apparently received his mission: to be a martyr on behalf of the Army of Liberation of the Islamic Holy Lands.

The bombings, with their heavy toll of civilians, were a phenomenon without parallel. Who, exactly, were the perpetrators? Every one of the bombers had been in an Afghan training camp, but not all of them were high-powered. Odeh had pledged *bayat* to bin Laden, but al Owhali had declined the invitation, and Khalfan Khamis Mohamed had not even been invited. The last was a low-level recruit who, after training, was sent off as a sleeper cell. The story he told after his arrest in October 1999 helps explain why impoverished Muslim youth were ready to die for bin Laden. A native of Zanzibar (a largely Muslim island off Tanzania's east coast), Mohamed was born poor, dropped out of high school, and became a drifter. Not long after the Bosnian Serb massacre at Srebrenica, Mohamed began spending time at his mosque, where he found a sense of community. The local imam spoke of the plight of Muslims in Bosnia, in Chechnya, and in Palestine, and the obligation of Muslims to sustain the *umma*, or world community of Muslims. "He really became consumed by a mission to become basically a soldier for Islam," said psychiatrist Jerrold Post, who spent hours talking to him in jail. On television, Mohamed could see planes strafing Muslims, tanks rolling, and heavy armor. Post said, "He saw himself in a kind of unformed way as wanting to become a soldier to fight against the . . . Serb soldiers who were killing innocent Muslim victims, the Russian soldiers who were killing innocent Chechen Muslim victims." He volunteered for an Afghan training camp but did not pass muster to join the Arab fighters in the internal Afghan struggle. Instead, he was sent home with a phone number to contact and drifted to Dar es Salaam, where he worked as a clerk in his brother's grocery. That is where he was activated in the spring of 1998.[22]

No one among the Taliban leadership would have focused on the back-to-back bombings in faraway East Africa. One day later, on August 8 (aided by bin Laden's finances, fighters, training, and restructuring advice), the Taliban captured Mazar-i-Sharif. This sprawling, dusty city of a half million—a center of Shia Islam and cosmopolitan home to Tajiks, Hazaras, and Uzbeks—was about to become a Pashtun village. Its tiled master-piece, the fifteenth-century Hazrat Ali shrine (in Afghan tradition, the burial place of the Prophet Muhammad's son-in-law) was about to be turned into a podium for a Taliban rabble-rouser. Now the militia controlled three-quarters of the country, including every major city.

The city's ultimate fall followed a familiar pattern: overreaching by one militia (in this case, Hezbi Wahdat) followed by betrayal by practically everyone else. In a move to discourage local Pashtuns from joining up with the advancing Taliban forces, Wahdat troops deployed several days before the fall of the city to the Dawlatabad district near Balkh city northwest of Mazar. But they started abusing local women, enraging the citizens. Repulsed by the excesses, two local commanders—one a Dostum loyalist and the other a Massoud commander inside Mazar—switched sides. Another account has the Wahdat forces capturing seventy-six Pashtun men in Chaharak to the northeast and taking them to Mazar, apparently to be massacred. Hekmatyar's Pashtun Hezbi Islami, consisting of Pashtuns from Balkh and hardly a reliable ally of the United Front, also defected.

"A Killing Frenzy"

What followed, according to a Mazar resident who escaped the city and arrived in Pakistan nearly a month later, was a "killing frenzy." But the massacre of at least two thousand civilians was by no means uncontrolled or spontaneous. There is overwhelming evidence of advance planning, central direction, and clarity of purpose, namely, revenge. To carry it out, the Taliban sealed off the town by cutting all communication with the outside world, terrorized the population into mass flight, and eliminated any future threat from Hazaras by killing or removing the male population.

The invaders arrived in Japanese pickup trucks decorated with white Taliban flags, carrying whips made of cable (the sort used to spur on donkeys) and armed to the teeth. They fired rockets into the city center as they arrived at around eleven o'clock in the morning.

Antiaircraft guns mounted on military trucks fired down the four broad avenues that radiate off the main square, sending shoppers and merchants fleeing in panic. Mobile units drove through the main roads, firing submachine guns at anything that moved, including men, women, and children of every ethnic background, and even donkeys and sheep. As some seven hundred Wahdat fighters fled the city in panic, people rushed to their homes. Meanwhile Taliban foot patrols—mostly Balkh or northern Pashtuns this first day—went house to house, killing whoever came to the front door.

At about 11:30 a.m., raiding parties broke into the offices of international aid agencies and seized communications equipment, including walkie-talkies and antennas, threatening staff with execution if they did not reveal every hiding place.* All UN agency staff were told they had to report henceforth to the Taliban intelligence service. Taliban forces stationed monitors in the International Red Cross radio room and restricted ICRC personnel's movements in the town.[23]

At noon, about ten militiamen from a militant Pakistani anti-Shia party—the Sipah-e-Sahaba—forced their way into the Iranian consulate, in what a former Taliban official called a "premeditated plan." They frisked the nine staff members and the reporter for the Iran news agency at gunpoint and took all their cash as well as the keys to their cars. After searching the building for weapons, they ordered the Iranians into the basement.

Three Taliban leaders then arrived and "held their weapons up and threatened to kill us," recounted Allahdad Shahsavan-Qarahosyeni, one of two diplomats who survived the execution and lived to tell about it five weeks later. "They lined us up against the wall [and] immediately opened fire on us." Shahsavan-Qarahosyeni dropped to the floor under a table. "I said my prayers and waited for death," he said. Despite bleeding from a bullet wound to his leg, Shahsavan-Qarahosyeni escaped Mazar-i-Sharif two days later with the help of the consulate guard (who had hidden in the kitchen) by dressing like an Afghan. Before leaving the consulate, he tried in vain to dial Teheran; later he discovered that all public telephones were shut down.

---

* One vivid account by a UN security guard describes the scene. Upon entering Mazar-i-Sharif, the Taliban militia "started confiscation of communications sets and antennas throughout the city. They broke into UNICEF, UNOPS (UN operations), Guest House, WFP (World Food Program), and UNHCR premises. At 11:30 a.m. . . . two pickup trucks with heavily armed militia on board arrived at the main gate of our office at UNHCR. Two of the men jumped on the wall with Kalashnikovs in hand, while another one fired at the lock and opened the main gate. We were in the office. The armed men shouted at our guard, who was exiting from the back door of the building and who ignored the warning. The militia opened fire at him, which hit the wall a few inches from his head. I and the other guard jumped out the office window to the neighboring house, where we spent two days in hiding." This man, a half-Pashtun, stayed in Mazar-i-Sharif until the end of August, then escaped to Pakistan over the land route. "Report of UN Security Guard [name withheld]," written account made available by UNHCR.

As the details began to emerge, the murders in cold blood put Mazar-i-Sharif on the international map.[24] They also generated tension with Iran that brought the two neighbors to the brink of war.*

But so much else was happening to the citizens of the city that never came out, except through the accounts of escaped refugees. The man the Taliban appointed governor, Mullah Manon Niazi, gave a hint of the mayhem in a satellite telephone interview with the Associated Press on August 8. "Last year, we were invited in. But this time, we burned the mountains," Niazi said. It was an understatement. Taliban militiamen slaughtered people like sheep, slitting their throats in the *halal* or religiously prescribed manner for animals. They seized hospitals and shot the wounded. They set up roadblocks to prevent city dwellers from fleeing and bombed and strafed those who escaped. People trying to bury corpses were shot. And that was only the first day. The following is a sampling of eyewitness accounts:

- A Tajik medical student, age twenty-two, rented a room that overlooked the main hospital. He told UNHCR, "Lifting up a tip of the curtain, I saw them bringing the wounded to the garden. They put them in a line and then shot with Kalashnikovs. They shot eight people."[†] This continued for days, according to his roommate, who worked in the hospital.[25]

- A Hazara street trader survived with the help of his Pashtun landlord: "Khodabakhsh was a vegetable seller. . . . They beat him on his head with a stick and killed him. . . . I saw a man trying to escape from our street—he was Hazara—killed by the Taliban with a bayonet in his head, face, and eyes. In our street a sweet-maker named Muhib Ali lived. The Taliban entered his house, where they killed him with twelve members of his family, including children, women, and an old man."[26]

---

* Supreme leader Ayatollah Ali Khamenei actually presented a plan involving the capture of Herat and Shinand, Iranian diplomatic sources told AFP reporter Stefan Smith in 2001. Khamenei backed off when others in the leadership demanded a long-term plan and expressed concern about being drawn into a conflict with Saudi Arabia and Pakistan. Smith, e-mail message to author, March 2006.

† Two days later, medical staff were ordered on the radio to report to the main hospital to meet Mullah Musa, the newly appointed director of public health. A witness described his encounter with Musa. "He entered every room and looked at every patient, saying, 'Is this a Hazara? Is this a fighter?'" That same day, Musa had visited the army hospital with other Taliban, where, according to a colleague there, "They shot all the patients (around twenty) and also a number of relatives who were with them in the hospital at the time of the visit." At the main hospital, Musa instructed staff to provide a list of all staff members, including their ethnic identity. When a staff member delivered the list, Musa told him to return to his hospital with six Kalashnikovs and three pistols. The staff member said weapons were forbidden inside hospitals. Musa said, "If the Amir il Momineen says something, you do it. I'm the Amir il Momineen's delegate, and you're my delegate. So go and get me the guns." Tajik witness, Mazar-i-Sharif/Taliban Case 12, interviewed by UNHCR on October 14, 1998.

- After the first few hours, it was extremely difficult to get out of the city. There were checkpoints everywhere, including at the entrance and exit of all villages and towns on the roads, and not just in the vicinity of Mazar-i-Sharif, but all across Taliban-held areas, including the south. Hazaras were pulled out of vehicles and shot or taken away. Taliban at checkpoints were using sticks with wax on the end. They pushed these up the sleeves of suspicious people to see if they had underarm hair. (The Taliban believe that all body hair except beards must be shaved.)[27]
- Hundreds of civilians headed south on the main road out of the city, some in cars or other vehicles, but many on foot. For at least two days after the takeover, the road was hit by rockets fired from Taliban positions west of Mazar-i-Sharif, most likely BM-21 Grad (Hai) multiple-rocket launchers, commonly known as Katyushas. An unknown number of civilians on the road were killed when they were bombed by Taliban airplanes; witnesses stated that the bombs scattered hundreds of grenade-sized munitions over a wide area on the road. Rockets hit an area called Tangi Shadyan on the southern outskirts of the city at about noon, killing at least fifty—"People were in pieces" along the road. A witness who left immediately when the Taliban arrived [said] he and his family carried with them nine bodies of a family that had been killed in a rocket attack on the road, including two women, three men, and four small children, and buried them in farmland on the way to the mountains.[28]

On the second day, Mullah Niazi, the Taliban's newly installed governor of Mazar-i-Sharif, took personal charge. In speeches at the Hazrat Ali shrine and other mosques, and in radio addresses two or three times a day, Niazi, a Dari-speaking Pashtun from Herat, incited the conquering militia to mass murder on religious and ethnic grounds. "Hazaras are not Muslims. You can kill them. It is not a sin," he would say. To Hazaras, the message was that the killing was in revenge for the deaths of Taliban the previous year. Niazi said, "Don't come to me to ask me to stop killing your people. When Wahdat was killing our people, did you ask them not to kill?" Niazi knew well that the execution of thousands of Taliban was carried out by Malik and his Uzbek militia, mostly outside Mazar-i-Sharif, in Sheberghan, not by Wahdat in Mazar.

His message was not consistent. At one point, he indicated that the "frenzy" of the first day had purpose. "We are here to govern you. Whether you want us or not, we will govern you. If you oppose us, think of the dead people in the street that you've seen. The same will happen to you." Another speech indicated that the aim of the "frenzy" was an ethnic cleansing. "You should consider yourselves lucky," Niazi said. "So far we have done nothing in Mazar-i-Sharif. We had planned to kill everybody, because we suffered so much here." In another speech, he bragged about the bloodbath. "Last year, you people of Mazar-i-Sharif killed 10,000 Taliban. Now we have killed more than that."

What was consistent was the message of sectarian war and the attempt at gunpoint to force a mass conversion of Shia to Sunni Islam. Niazi labeled Hazaras *kufr* (infidels) and told them they must convert to Sunni Islam and attend prayer five times a day "unless they wanted to be treated like dogs and shot on the spot. . . . Hazaras can live with us. They have three choices. They can become Sunni, they can go to the Islamic Republic of Iran, or they can be killed."[29]

Niazi turned neighbor against neighbor, threatening that anyone sheltering a Hazara would be shot: "Oh, people, if we find one Hazara in your house, we will kill all of you."

It was on the second morning of the conquest, according to eyewitnesses, that the Taliban began rounding up the Shia men. "Trucks were brought to the Shia mosques, and anyone emerging was taken away to the prison. Men, particularly Hazara men, were also picked off the streets. Passers-by were asked by the Taliban to point out Hazaras, and some did so." Armed units went house to house, concentrating on those areas where the Shia uprising began in May 1997. According to a witness UNHCR considered "extremely reliable," almost all who were found were either shot three times on the spot (one bullet in the head, one in the chest, and one in the testicles), slaughtered in the *halal* way, or removed to the jail. Hazaras, said to be descended from the Mongols, often have distinctive facial features. One way of trapping those without the distinctive features was to ask them how many verses of the Koran they said during the various prayers.* If someone gave the "wrong" or Shia response, he was arrested on the spot.†

In a short time, three thousand people were packed into the prison, which had only two toilets and one water tap. Captives were divided into two groups, according to ethnicity, Hazaras on one side of the line, the others on the other side. On at least one occasion, Governor Niazi "personally oversaw the process of selecting prisoners for transfer," according to a witness quoted by Human Rights Watch. Those who survived the transfer

---

* During the afternoon prayer, Sunnis recite ten verses, while Shia recite four. During the morning prayer, Sunnis recite four verses, and Shias two.

† According to Choong-Hyun Paik, there were indications that Mullah Omar had issued a fatwa stating that the killing of Shia Muslims is not a crime because they are infidels. This may have been the guide used by Taliban killers. A Tajik eyewitness, trying to find out why he was on the Taliban's blacklist, met a Kandahari Talib while visiting a friend. "I don't know if I'll go to heaven now," the Talib told them both. He had been among those searching houses in the Saidabad district and had personally shot people in about thirty houses as soon as they opened the door. But in one house, after he had shot the men, he suddenly realized that the women and children were speaking Pashto. The men he had shot were Pashtuns. "For this reason," the witness said, "he was very worried that he might be excluded from heaven. That he had killed people in twenty-nine Hazara households seemed not to cause him any concern at all." UN report #A/53/539, October 26, 1998.

were taken to Sheberghan for what the Taliban called "interrogations." The detainee was asked to speak Pashto, according to a UN official familiar with Mazar-i-Sharif. "If they couldn't, it was assumed they were not Sunni," he said. They had little chance to be set free.[30]

Pashtuns, Turkmen, Uzbeks, and Tajiks were gradually allowed to leave the prison. Hazaras were packed into forty-foot-long metal shipping containers, which sat all day in the August sun and were taken at dusk to Sheberghan military base. UNHCR's "highly educated and extremely reliable" witness, who had worked for an aid agency, saw a container with open doors "after all the males inside had died from suffocation." Paik, in his report on the massacre, said two or three such trucks transported Hazara prisoners to Sheberghan every day, and many subsequently to Dasht-i-Leili, site of the mass graves of 1997. When women came to the prison to obtain the release of their relatives, if the men were not inside, "They were told by the Taliban to look for them in Sheberghan, and if they were not there, at Dasht-i-Leili." There one witness said he saw countless corpses.

On the third day, according to numerous witnesses, the "real Taliban" arrived in force. Stung by their ignominious defeat the previous year, the Kandaharis largely allowed Balkh Pashtuns to carry out the killing on the first two days, witnesses said. In their search for Hazaras, the Taliban even offered cash. "One of the Taliban pulled out a hundred dollar note and said that it was mine if I brought him to Hazara houses," said the Tajik medical student. "I said I was just a student from out of town and not very familiar with Mazar."

That was the day Niazi announced that he had forbidden the burial of the dead, ordering the population to allow the corpses to decompose in the streets until dogs and birds of prey began to defile them. "Last year, you killed us and left our bodies on the streets. This year we will kill you and leave your bodies." Starting on the third day of the conquest, Hazara women in Mazar-i-Sharif—their husbands, brothers, and fathers dead or in prison —became easy prey, and Niazi gave the explicit go-ahead. "Shias are like Christians and Jews," he said in one mosque speech. "They are infidels. . . . Once you kill them, their wives and their property are yours." He threatened more than once that if Hazaras did not fulfill certain unspecified conditions, the Taliban would "kill the men and keep the women as slaves."[31]

According to Human Rights Watch, there were reliable reports that young women had been abducted in some neighborhoods. At least four women in their early twenties were abducted from the Kamaz refugee camp, and a witness from the Karte Ariana neighborhood reported seeing teenage girls in the area being forced into Pijaro cars and driven away by Taliban militiamen. A witness reported that a nurse acquaintance had been raped, along with dozens of other women. "At first she did not want to tell us anything," the witness said, but then she said that when she went to her family house in the Ali Chopan neighborhood, the Talibs "abducted her and locked her up in a house with twenty to twenty-five other young girls and women. They were raped every night." All the women were Hazaras, and she was the only one released. One Talib told her that "now she was *halal* [sanctified], [and] she should go to his parents in Kandahar and wait for him to come and marry her."

According to Paik's graphic account, which the United Nations published on October 26, 1998, mass killings took place in the first two weeks after the capture of Mazar-i-Sharif. After that, only those who were denounced by members of the local Pashtun community were detained or killed. But a UNHCR witness recalled that Niazi had declared that normal life could resume just five days into the occupation. He told them that shops should reopen and everyone should come to the mosques for prayers, a witness recalled. But this was not a reversion to normalcy at all, for in a relatively short time the names of all the Shia mosques were changed. Those in charge drew up attendance lists and a roll call was read out before each prayer time five times a day to make sure everyone was present; a great many men started praying in the Sunni style instead of as Shias.

Meanwhile, the Taliban set up enormous obstacles to prevent Hazaras from fleeing. Beginning August 11, the Taliban had stopped all buses heading east from Kabul toward the Pakistan border and removed any Hazaras or Uzbeks from Mazar-i-Sharif and ordered them into a refugee camp consisting of mud huts on a stretch of treeless desert near the main highway. By August 18, Taliban guards said there were one thousand people there; by late October, there were at least two thousand, according to Paik. The provincial governor, Maulvi Satar-i-Azam, told the Associated Press, "We stop them so they do not become tramps in other countries. They are poor. They can go all over Afghanistan, but not out of the country."

The borders remained sealed for months. One Hazara family, the men of whom had grown long beards, managed to escape to Pakistan by pretending they were Pashtuns from Ghazni province. When they reached Kandahar and had to stop at the Taliban security department, they were told the instructions were to prevent any onward movement of Hazaras from Mazar-i-Sharif or Bamiyan. When Taliban inspected their luggage and found, wrapped in a cloth, a doll belong to the witness's four-year-old daughter, "they became furious, abusing the group, calling them Buddhists and *kufr*, shouting that Hazaras and Shias were nonbelievers and should go to Iran, China, or Mongolia." They beat the men with steel cables, arrested them all, and held them overnight. Eventually, the family reached the border at Spin Boldak. There the Taliban accused them of coming from Mazar-i-Sharif or Bamiyan and demanded they confess. Eventually they were let go. As of early November, three months after the conquest, only some eighty families had arrived in Quetta, this witness said.[32]

Just how many noncombatants died in Mazar-i-Sharif may never be known. One conservative estimate at the time was that two thousand civilians, possibly many more, were killed in the city. An investigation by NGOs in 2003–2004 determined that at least 2,500–3,000 civilians were killed in Mazar-i-Sharif and Sheberghan. "The total could, frankly, still be much higher," said Mervyn Patterson, former UN chief representative in northern Afghanistan, who coordinated the study.

However, at the time the atrocities occurred in Mazar-i-Sharif and Sheberghan, almost nothing was known except that the Iranian diplomats had gone missing. The Taliban cut the city's communications, imposed a news blackout, and closed the town to foreign journalists—indeed, to all foreigners.[*] And they did everything possible to prevent refugees from escaping to tell the story. Those who left in the first days and had to trek through the mountains did not arrive in Pakistan until late August or early September and could provide at best an incomplete picture. UNHCR interviewed its first solid witnesses on September 8, a full month after the Taliban arrived in Mazar, and the first news reports based on those interviews appeared the next day. But much remains unknown.[33] For example, at this writing, Mullah Manon Niazi's role has had at best minimal exposure, and even though any number of Mazaris recorded his incendiary speeches, he has not been charged with a crime in any major forum, and his whereabouts are unknown.[†]

If anything in Afghanistan grabbed world attention at first, it was the fate of the missing diplomats. Iran sought assurances from the Taliban on the day of the conquest, asked Pakistan to intervene, and then complained to the United Nations about their disappearance, but the Taliban paid little notice. Niazi first denied they had been captured and said they might be hiding in Mazar-i-Sharif or have retreated with the Wahdat forces to Bamiyan province. More brazenly, on August 11, a Taliban official said the eleven diplomats faced arrest because they had not reported their presence to the new regime. Iran shot back that it had evidence that the eleven had been kidnapped; on August 19, Iran announced that Revolutionary Guards would shortly hold exercises on the Afghan border.

The Taliban were militarily preoccupied with their blitzkrieg advance through northeastern Afghanistan. First they captured Taloqan, a town of sixty thousand where Massoud had moved his headquarters after the fall of Kabul. Jamiat forces withdrew again at night, and the Taliban arrived

---

[*] On August 20, Maulvi Syedur Rahman Haqqani, the Taliban ambassador to Pakistan, explained the news blackout this way: "We are not allowing journalists to visit Mazar-i-Sharif at present only to protect their lives. The situation is calm there, but we want to ensure further peace before we allow visitors." The Taliban allowed the ICRC in only to drop off relief supplies. AP dispatch, Kabul.

[†] A search of the Nexis and Factiva databases turns up only a handful number of media accounts mentioning Niazi (sometimes spelled "Niyazi").

without a shot fired on August 11. A day later, the Taliban captured Pul-i-Khumri, the scene of so many previous clashes, as well as Hairatan, just across the Oxus River from Termez, Uzbekistan, thereby closing down the last resistance gateway to the rest of the world.[34]

"War of the Future"

On August 20, Afghanistan came under attack, but from a completely different direction. "Our target was terror," President Clinton said in disclosing a near-simultaneous cruise missile attack against targets near Khost and in Khartoum, Sudan. Bin Laden had launched a "terrorist war" against the United States, Clinton said, and "our mission was clear: to strike at the network of radical groups affiliated with and fronted by Osama bin Laden, perhaps the preeminent organizer and financier of international terrorism in the world today." Albright was even more blunt. Bin Laden had "declared war on the United States and struck first, and we have suffered deeply," she said that day, and the response would be the "war of the future." When he made his decision, Clinton was under enormous political pressure growing out of the Monica Lewinsky scandal and was about to go through the impeachment process, but he was determined to carry on with matters of state, as if the collapse of his personal standing had no bearing on his duties as president. His decision coincided with the release of a comedy film titled *Wag the Dog*, about a president in deep trouble over personal sexual lapses who decides to invade Albania to distract his own country.

Unfortunately, the seventy-five cruise missiles fired at the Zhawar Kili complex of six camps outside Khost missed bin Laden—by a few hundred miles, according to his bodyguard, Nasir Abdallah al-Bahri, also known as Abu Jandal. The thirteen cruise missiles fired against al Shifa pharmaceutical plant in Khartoum, Sudan, (timed late at night to avoid civilian casualties) almost certainly was a mistake.

Mushahid Hussain, Pakistan government spokesman at the time, said he learned from the ISI on August 19 that bin Laden had planned a summit at the Khost complex on August 20. "The information was public knowledge . . . and of course, bin Laden got wind of [the missile attack] three or four hours in advance, and he got away." But according to Abu Jandal, bin Laden escaped the attack through sheer luck.[35] He was in fact en route to Khost on August 19 but decided on impulse to drive to Kabul instead.*

---

* Abu Jandal recounted, "I remember that when we reached a crossroads between Khost and Kabul in the Wardak Province, Sheik Osama bin Ladin said: 'Where do you think, my friends, we should we go, to Khost or Kabul?' We said we would go to Kabul in order to visit our comrades at the front there. He said: 'With God's help, let us go to Kabul.' We arrived in Kabul and the U.S. attack against the Khost camps occurred the next day." Abu Jandal, interview by Al-Hammadi (part 9), *Al Quds al Araby*.

About a half hour before the missiles struck Zhawar, the phone rang in Rahimullah Yusufzai's home office: "Hello, I am Dr. Ayman al Zawahiri. Do you recognize me?" Bin Laden had asked him to deliver a message. The Muslim umma should "continue jihad against the Jews and Americans to liberate their [holy places]. Meanwhile, he denies any involvement in the Nairobi and Dar es Salaam bombings." Yusufzai got in only one question about their whereabouts before the conversation was interrupted by a foreign voice saying, "Who are you? Who are you?" Zawahiri said, "Somewhere in Afghanistan," then bade Yusufzai goodbye.

Twenty-four hours after the cruise missile strike, Zawahiri called Yusufzai again. "The war has just begun. The Americans should wait for the answer!" was the brief message. He went on to say that "Brother Osama" was safe and sound. "We have survived the American attack. Tell the Americans that we aren't afraid of bombardment, threats, and acts of aggression. We suffered and survived Soviet bombings for ten years in Afghanistan, and we are ready for more sacrifices." Zawahiri extolled Mullah Omar for being "brave enough" not to hand over bin Laden to the United States "as part of some deal." Omar, he said, "is a true Muslim." Yusufzai had the impression that bin Laden was sitting alongside Zawahiri during both phone calls.

There is no question that U.S. missiles struck a bin Laden training camp, Abu Jindal, where bin Laden had held his May news conference, but two other targets—al Badr I and al Badr II—were operated by the Harkatul mujahideen, a militant Islamic group led by Pakistani Fazlur Rehman Khalil that sent volunteers to fight in Afghanistan, Indian-occupied Kashmir, and other trouble spots. There is also no question that those in the camps were forewarned. The death toll at the entire Zhawar complex was only twenty-six, including at most five Arabs, among them three Yemenis, as well as twenty-one Pakistanis, Kashmiris, and Afghans.[36]

The destruction of al Shifa plant was not a near miss but a genuine blunder. The decision to target it was based on a single soil sample collected by a CIA operative across the road from the plant (which supposedly revealed traces of EMPTA, a precursor chemical for VX nerve gas) and a memo drafted just before the embassy bombings, in which staff of the White House counterterrorism office said that bin Laden had invested in and "almost certainly" had access to VX produced at a plant in Sudan. Clinton himself wondered whether they had hit the right target. The State Department's Bureau of Intelligence and Research expressed strong doubts about the evidence, but Albright ordered the publication suppressed. The 9/11 Commission concluded that there was no independent evidence to corroborate the CIA's assessment of al Shifa plant.[37]

Around the Muslim world, the U.S. assault provoked anti-American demonstrations and condemnations. In Kabul, Pakistani Taliban shot dead an Italian UN military observer, wounded a French national working for the United Nations, and nearly murdered AFP reporter Stefan Smith.* At the CIA station in Islamabad, there was some bewilderment about the choice of targets. Gary Schroen said, "CIA headquarters was involved, obviously. But they certainly didn't ask us in the field for targets." At home, conservative Republicans—who days earlier had savaged Clinton for his sexual indiscretions—rallied quickly around him. "Thank you, Mr. President," said Republican Senator Orrin Hatch of Utah. "Thanks for being willing to take this type of action. Don't make it the last time. Let's wage a war against terrorism in this world, and this is a good beginning." House Speaker Newt Gingrich of Georgia called it "the right thing to do at the right time." He dismissed *Wag the Dog* speculation as "sick." And Republican Senator Jesse Helms of North Carolina concurred that "there must be no refuge for terrorists who murder innocent American citizens." Public opinion also backed Clinton.

The missile attack may have missed bin Laden and his aides and barely dented his infrastructure, but it got Mullah Omar's attention. Suddenly he was under enormous international pressure. The United States had mounted a sneak missile attack aimed at his invited guest, and Iran was threatening a ground assault over the disappearance of eleven diplomats in Mazar-i-Sharif. Like Zawahiri, Omar reached for the phone. First he called an Afghan news agency in Peshawar to denounce the American intervention as "a demonstration of enmity" for the Afghan people. He declared defiantly, "We can never hand over Osama to America."[38]

Then, after sending advance word of his plan, he called Michael Malinowski, director of the Pakistan, Afghanistan, and Bangladesh desk at the State Department. The bizarre conversation began in the early morning hours of August 22, 1998, Washington time. Speaking through a translator, Omar gave his "advice": if the United States wanted to rebuild its popularity in the Islamic world and deal with its internal problems, Congress "should force Clinton to resign." He then picked up on the theme of bin Laden's February fatwa, which provided pseudotheological approval for his attack on the two U.S. embassies, and urged the United States to remove its forces from the Gulf, where he asserted it was a threat to Islam's holiest sites. This was his "best advice." Finally, Omar dismissed the charges against bin Laden. He knew of no evidence that bin Laden had planned terrorist acts while on Afghan soil; besides, getting rid of one person would not end the problems posed to the United States by the Islamic world.

The cable summing up the conversation indicates no response to Omar's gratuitous advice. Instead, Malinowski explained that Clinton had acted in self-defense "as a father who had to protect his children from

---

* "I was stopped at a Taliban checkpoint in central Kabul, and a Kalashnikov was put in my face and fired. The gun jammed," Smith recalled. He left Kabul that day. Smith, e-mail.

jeopardy." Further, he said the strikes were "in no way" directed against the Afghan people or the Taliban. Omar "should know that the U.S. had been a friend to the Afghans and wanted only the best for Afghanistan," Malinowski told him. As for bin Laden, he said there was considerable and solid evidence, and he urged Omar to arrest or expel him and other terrorists. Malinowski said he was aware of *Pashtun wali*—the code of behavior requiring protection for guests—but said no Pashtun, including Omar, should allow a guest or refuge seeker to abuse Afghan hospitality. He compared bin Laden to "a guest shooting at neighbors out of the host's window." Despite the gap between the sides, Omar said the Taliban was "open to dialogue" and accepted the suggestion of "establishing a vehicle for secure communication" with U.S. officials using the Afghan and U.S. embassies in Islamabad.

Malinowski's tone of "more in sorrow than anger" reads like an attempt to cushion the impact rather than pound home the reason for the use of force. In the immediate aftermath of the East Africa bombings, the Clinton administration went out of its way to avoid an appearance of coercive diplomacy (that is, the application of force to achieve a political end). Subsequent State Department messages to Omar were couched in even gentler terms.

In fact, Clinton had secretly authorized the CIA to use lethal force to get rid of bin Laden and other members of the al Qaeda leadership.* He ordered two nuclear submarines to be posted on indefinite deployment off the coast of Pakistan. To reduce the ramp-up time for cruise missile strikes to the absolute minimum, he authorized the CIA to support efforts by Afghan tribal fighters or by the ISI to capture or kill bin Laden.[39]

But the diplomatic track was all conciliation. Two days after Omar's call, for example, Assistant Secretary of State Rick Inderfurth drafted a cable to Islamabad for delivery to the Afghan embassy and to Omar, stating that the United States "appreciates" the phone conversation and now wants to follow up with a serious and secret dialogue at the U.S. embassy in Islamabad on the need to bring bin Laden to justice. Like Malinowski, Inderfurth chose to overlook Omar's "best advice" about removing President Clinton from office.

Given the dramatic context in which they were drafted, the American talking points had a tone of unreality. The following facts were known to the U.S. government:

- The Taliban had abandoned the UN-Richardson peace initiative to pursue the blitzkrieg military strategy that was under way.

---

*On two or three occasions, the CIA obtained preliminary intelligence on bin Laden's whereabouts and Clinton authorized preparations for an attack; later the agency said it lacked sufficient confidence and recommended that the strikes not go ahead. In one instance, the CIA had images of high-end sport-utility vehicles but concluded it was a wealthy oil sheikh on a falconing expedition. This plan was abandoned in May 1999, according to the 9/11 Commission. Chronology provided to author by former national security adviser Sandy Berger.

- Twin terror strikes directed from Afghan soil against sovereign U.S. territory in two East African countries had killed more than two hundred civilians, including twelve Americans, and injured five thousand.

- The slaughter in Mazar-i-Sharif had been described by the U.S. consul in Peshawar in a confidential cable titled "Massacres Possible in the North" on the day of the missile strikes. Quoting relief agency sources, the cable said that the Taliban had massacred at least three hundred Hazaras, that the town had been sealed to nearly all foreigners, and that there were rumors of 2,000–3,000 dead.

- Finally, after the Taliban failed to account for the eleven missing Iranians, Iran had announced a major ground exercise and warned of possible armed intervention.

Despite all this, the Clinton administration view of the Afghan internal struggle remained unchanged from Inderfurth's previous testimony to Congress in October 1997.

"The U.S. is neutral on Afghanistan. We want to see an Afghanistan at peace under a broad-based, multiethnic government that is engaged in the great task of rebuilding the country and respects international norms of behavior," Inderfurth's talking points of August 23, 1998, began. "In launching the strike of August 20 against Khost, the U.S. in no way wanted to harm the peaceful people of Afghanistan nor damage the Taliban."

After a preamble that ignored the Taliban's capture of Mazar-i-Sharif (which quashed all hopes of a broad-based, multiethnic government), how seriously would the Taliban leader take the rest of the message—largely public statements of the case against bin Laden? The talking points concluded as softly as they opened: "We have asked you before, most notably when Ambassador Richardson visited Kabul, and others have asked you, including Saudi Arabia, to do the right thing. The eyes of the world are now on the Taliban. It should now do the proper and just thing."

The Taliban saw a public relations opening. The Afghan envoy in Islamabad, Syedur Rahman Haqqani, refused even to receive the letter when the second-ranking U.S. embassy official attempted to deliver it on August 25, and he let that be known to the Pakistani press. He relented three days later, then released the content that would embarrass the Americans.* Meanwhile, Mullah Omar called the Afghan press agency

---

* Aimal Khan wrote in the *Frontier Post* on August 26 that the contents of the letter were not officially released, but his Afghan sources "said the U.S. government had clarified its position in the letter, maintaining that the last month's missile strikes on the alleged terrorist bases of Saudi dissident Osama bin Laden in eastern Afghanistan were not targeted at the Afghans [but] rather [at] the terrorists operating from their country. The sources claimed that the Americans had even offered the Taliban government that if it put certain restrictions on the activities of Saudi dissident Osama bin Laden, Washington would recognize their government [and provide] a very attractive developmental package for the war-ravaged country."

to announce the State Department offer to hold talks and then to dismiss it. "There is nothing left to talk about after the missile raid," Omar said.

The Taliban were already doing "the right and proper thing" by their own lights. Even as Inderfurth was explaining the limits of *Pashtun wali* to a Pashtun ("Bin Laden has violated *Pashtun wali* by not behaving as a guest should behave . . . by launching attacks from Afghan soil. No Pashtun should put up with such abuse"), Omar, bin Laden, or quite possibly both had already rallied key mullahs behind a new fatwa that would mandate permanent protection for the Saudi dissident.

On August 25, a former mujahideen leader with close Taliban ties told the U.S. embassy in Islamabad that the Taliban position was hardening. The visitor confirmed that a fatwa had been issued that required Muslims to protect bin Laden. Having such a religious edict gave Omar the shield he felt he needed to protect his guest. Bin Laden was free to stay.*

"There is no denying that this unassuming Saudi businessman has run circles round the world's most powerful nation and, in the process, become the inspiration for a large number of Muslims who increasingly feel Washington has wronged their religion and its followers," Rahimullah Yusufzai wrote the following week. But Omar also deserved full credit as a student of bin Laden for learning how to manage the U.S. administration.[40]

There is every reason to think that the missile strikes, far from harming bin Laden or his infrastructure, far from splitting bin Laden from Mullah Omar, drove them into each other's embrace.

"A Black Hole"

Through the end of 1998, the administration pursued the goal of extradition through dialogue. But "the search for moderate Taliban," as U.S. diplomats dubbed the process, proved an illusory quest and one that no country other than Pakistan actively supported.

Clinton dealt gingerly with the Taliban leadership, but others responded more forcefully. On September 1, Iran's Revolutionary Guards began 70,000-man war games forty miles from the Afghan border. Four days later, after the Taliban acknowledged the possibility that the diplomats had been murdered, Iran publicly invoked the right to use force in self-defense under the UN Charter and announced a second exercise four times larger.

International criticism began to build over the Mazar-i-Sharif massacre as the major human rights organizations and the UNHCR issued

---

* The visitor, whose name was redacted in the cable, confirmed press reports about the fatwa and mentioned two key mullahs, "Zakiri and Shinwari." Zakiri was probably Amir Maulana Abdullah Zakiri, the chairman of the Ittehad Ulemae Afghanistan, and Shinwari was possibly Jalaluddine Shinwari, the deputy minister of justice. "Security Situation," cable, U.S. embassy, Islamabad, August 25, 1998, released by NSA.

statements of alarm. In mid-September, the UN Security Council voiced "deep concern" over the reported mass killings in Mazar-i-Sharif; on September 21, foreign ministers in the six-plus-two forum agreed that the United Nations should investigate. Asma Jehangir of Pakistan, Annan's special representative on extrajudicial executions, sent a pointed inquiry to the Taliban. In a report to the Security Council, Annan rank-ordered the killings as the "most urgent" of the issues in Afghanistan, even ahead of Iran-Afghan tensions, and dispatched Lakhdar Brahimi to the region to discuss it.

The U.S. government was virtually silent, with a State Department spokesman saying only that this "kind of thing . . . ought to be looked into."* Had the champion of Muslim victims in Bosnia become indifferent to Muslim-on-Muslim atrocities? Did it fear that criticizing the Taliban leadership would derail the hoped-for talks?

According to a top human rights aide to Albright, no one in the upper ranks of government would champion the broad human rights concerns because success seemed so unlikely. In Haiti, U.S. officials had maintained a high U.S. profile on human rights issues, but the results were minimal and everyone had felt burned. In Afghanistan, women's rights were the only subject anyone high up would support. "There were very few people who wanted to get into the Afghan human rights issue in a big way. It was a black hole," said this senior aide. As a result, the Mazar massacre pretty much disappeared from view. "I truly do not remember being asked to [do more] or told more," Albright said. "We knew the Taliban were terrible people. There were not a lot of options there. That is part of the issue." She

---

*Amnesty International (AI) issued the first statement on September 3 that the Taliban had killed "thousands of civilians" following the takeover of Mazar-i-Sharif. "The victims were killed deliberately and arbitrarily in their homes, in the streets where their bodies were left for several days, or in locations between Mazar-i-Sharif and Hairatan. Many of those killed were civilians, including women, children, and the elderly, who were shot trying to flee the city," AI said, citing survivors and eyewitnesses. UNHCR conducted its interviews a few days later, and the BBC and Voice of America (VOA) issued their first reports quoting UNHCR spokesman Rupert Colville on September 10. Human Rights Watch (HRW) put out a strong statement on September 14. "Western diplomats, UN officials, and Western aid workers say thousands of Hazaras, mostly males, were killed in front of their families in Mazar-i-Sharif, the capital of the anti-Taliban alliance in northern Afghanistan, when the Taliban captured the city last month," HRW said, calling for an investigation. But the State Department took practically no notice—a spokesman said the following day that the United States had only "fourth- and fifth-hand information," and "no independent confirmation of these kinds of atrocities." That same day, the UN Security Council, with American concurrence, issued a far stronger statement, voicing its "deep concern . . . at reports of mass killings of civilians in northern Afghanistan" and demanding that "the Taliban fully respect international humanitarian law and human rights." Three months after the bloodbath, Peter Burleigh, acting U.S. ambassador to the United Nations, told a General Assembly committee that Washington was "deeply concerned" by reports of the slaughter of Shia minorities in Mazar-i-Sharif; he also said that the murder of the Iranian diplomats was unacceptable. Amnesty International (AI) announcement, September 3, 1998, www.amnesty.org; BBC and Voice of America (VOA) reports on September 10, 1998, courtesy of BBC and VOA; HRW statement, September 14, 1998, hrw.org; and Burleigh statement to the United Nations reported by BBC Radio's Pam O'Toole on November 10, 1998.

added, "I think we did a human rights report on it," a reference to the State Department's annual human rights review.

Underlying this selective human rights approach was Clinton's deep reluctance to rattle his saber. The Taliban had no such compunctions and showed at Mazar-i-Sharif how brutal they could be if they shut the world out. Given the administration's silence on Afghan issues other than women's rights, they could assume that the United States would not be closely watching them.[41]

Now their goal was to complete the rout of the United Front. Khalili, Massoud, and Dostum had met in late August in Mashhad, a city in eastern Iran, to coordinate strategy for saving Bamiyan, capital of the Hazarajat and the last major redoubt of the Hezbi Wahdat after the fall of Mazar-i-Sharif. Iran subsequently opened an air bridge to Bamiyan, but it was too late. Eight local commanders switched sides, opening the way for a small Taliban force to cross the mountains into the town; on September 13, the Taliban conquered Bamiyan. The American spotlight may have been indistinct, but people like UNHCR's Rupert Colville, Lakhdar Brahimi, and Kofi Annan, by speaking out, managed to train the international spotlight on the massacre in Mazar-i-Sharif and the murder of the Iranian envoys. On the eve of the capture of Bamiyan—and on the express demand of the UN Security Council—Mullah Omar ordered fighters to treat civilians humanely and to allow all Hazaras to flee. When the Taliban arrived, the city of forty thousand was empty. The UNHCHR said the Taliban searched the nearby villages, arrested male Hazaras over thirteen years old, took them to the desert, and reportedly executed a number of them "summarily." Dead bodies "were scattered everywhere." Still, it was not a bloodbath. There were deaths, but "they didn't kill big," Colville concluded.

And despite the fears of Buddhists (and art lovers), the Taliban did not demolish the enormous Buddhas carved out of sandstone in the escarpment across the narrow valley from the town. Naseerullah Babar, though no longer in government, said French and Sri Lankan officials contacted him and asked him to intervene with the Taliban. "That whole evening I was on the phone to them in Kandahar," he said. "They said they not only wouldn't damage [the site], but would give it additional security." A local commander damaged one of the statues, but total destruction was averted.

The capture of Bamiyan secured Taliban control over 90 percent of the country. Dostum's Jumbesh alliance—the largest and best-equipped faction, with an estimated thirty thousand troops—was effectively destroyed, as was Hezbi Wahdat, which had ten thousand. Aside from a pocket of territory in the northwest controlled by Massoud and his force of fifteen thousand to twenty thousand, the Taliban had conquered Afghanistan. True, Massoud was able to hold the Salang Tunnel and to threaten Kabul via the Shamali plains, but compared with where they were just a year earlier, the Taliban were riding high. About all Massoud could do was to rocket northern Kabul—a volley of rockets there one week after the fall of Bamiyan killed at least seventy-five people, possibly twice that number. The Taliban had reason to feel that God was on their side. Despite the pressure from Iran and criticism from the international community over the excesses in Mazar-i-Sharif, they were on the brink of their goal of establishing sharia throughout Afghanistan.[42]

It was at this inauspicious juncture that the head of Saudi intelligence, Prince Turki al Faisal, returned to Kandahar for a second talk with Mullah Omar, an encounter that proved to be a major turning point in relations between Taliban Afghanistan and the rest of the world. Accompanied by the Pakistan foreign minister and the director of ISI—and bearing the hopes of the Clinton administration—Turki quickly got off on the wrong foot, for he had come not to congratulate Omar but to fetch bin Laden. Turki thought he had a deal, but Omar did not.

"I have never told a lie in my life. I never told you I would hand over Osama," Omar said. "He is our guest. It is not in our tradition to ask the guest to leave. And where would he go? He would be arrested." Omar then began to lecture Turki on bin Laden's main theme. "You are keeping troops on sacred soil. And you should first get rid of those troops," Omar said. Turki at this point reminded the Afghan leader that Saudi Arabia had been a major benefactor of Afghanistan in past years, and he indicated that he had an open checkbook, or at least that is how Omar recounted the incident to a Pakistani journalist.

Omar was livid. He called an attendant to fetch a bucket of water and proceeded to pour it over his own head. "I am so angry, I am fearful of what I would say to you," he said. After cooling down, he delivered the final insult: "You know, you are an American pimp. Leave this place immediately." Turki stormed out, but not before delivering a warning: "You will regret it, and the Afghan people will pay a high price." On September 22, the Saudis withdrew their top diplomat from Kabul and declared his Afghan counterpart in Riyadh persona non grata.

"I wished I had not gone," Turki later said. In addition to reversing his decision on bin Laden, Omar "was abusive about the Kingdom and its people." Turki said he realized that Omar and bin Laden "thought alike." He told Saudi television that Omar "made decisions arbitrarily and capriciously, and once made, he was not interested in revising them." Turki later confided to U.S. officials that the Taliban had turned into "fanatics." Pakistani officials also claimed to be astonished at the change in Omar.[43]

But Clinton still seemed determined to avoid a diplomatic confrontation with the Taliban. In a speech to the UN General Assembly that focused on the threat of terror, he listed nearly every spot on Earth where terrorist incidents had occurred but failed to distinguish local terrorism from the global conspiracy of al Qaeda. And while he called on UN members not to provide sanctuary to terrorists, he omitted mention of Afghanistan or bin Laden. It did not help that, as the president was speaking, U.S. television was airing his four-hour-long testimony to the grand jury in the Monica Lewinsky case.

"God Has Obligated Us"

Mullah Omar apparently viewed the UN speech as a signal that the heat was off, and two days later he sent a fax to the State Department reaffirming that the Taliban would not hand over bin Laden. Muslims "believe that the Osama bin Laden issue is just an excuse made by the U.S. and this is harming the U.S," he said. Taliban policy "is real Islamic policy. We cannot change it. . . . Almighty God has obligated us to follow this policy." If the United States disagreed with "the real Islam," it would be hated in the Muslim world. "Our advice is [to] change your policy. If you do, it will be a major success for you." Nevertheless, he said if the United States believed that Taliban policy "is not Islamic, then we can try to convince you." The drafter of the reporting cable inserted parenthetically: "Note: this means we can have a dialogue."

The State Department took the bait, and in early October offered a "serious and confidential dialogue" through the U.S. embassy in Islamabad. But this time a formal warning was sandwiched between the cordial opening words and an appeal for talks to better understand the "views and vision" of the Taliban. "Those who continue to harbor and welcome terrorists must accept responsibility for the actions of terrorists who abuse such hospitality, and we expect the Taliban to honor international responsibilities in this regard." The message said the United States would hold the Taliban responsible for any further terrorism conducted by the bin Laden network, "as long as the Taliban provides sanctuary to members of that network." Thus were the Taliban forewarned.

From that point forward, Taliban envoys had talks with U.S. officials every few weeks, but to little effect. Mullah Abdul Jalil Akhund took on a dual assignment as bin Laden's minder (the man who could unmuzzle the Saudi radical) as well as the highest-level regular visitor to the U.S. embassy. William Milam, the ambassador to Pakistan, recalls "enormously bizarre meetings" with Jalil, at which he would put his bare feet up on a coffee table loaded with pastries and food, and proceed to pick his toenails.

In mid-October, shortly before the Taliban UN representative, Abdul Hakeem Mujahid, called at the State Department, Milam cautioned Albright that the drive for dialogue was not getting results. "The fact is that the leader of the Taliban appears to be strongly committed to bin Laden. It is questionable whether U.S. or Saudi efforts can influence Omar's decisions," he wrote. Milam urged the administration to say it reserved the right to take military action if bin Laden engaged in any terrorist activities. The aim was to "solve the problem politically and do it soon, before the

U.S. strikes on Khost—a wasting asset—become old news to the Taliban leadership." Under Secretary of State Thomas Pickering sat in on the meeting to demand bin Laden's expulsion, but Mujahid responded that the Taliban had his commitment for future "good behavior."

The Taliban stance shifted during this period of "dialogue," but not in any useful direction. The regime demanded proof of bin Laden's terror connections for presentation to its Supreme Court. When a U.S. grand jury indicted bin Laden on November 4 in the August bombings and as the leader of a nine-year conspiracy, the embassy sent the Taliban leaders the text, together with tapes of bin Laden's interviews with CNN in 1997 and ABC in 1998. But a Taliban representative told Ambassador Milam that they saw nothing new and did not pass them on to the Supreme Court. Not surprisingly, the court subsequently ruled that there was no evidence against bin Laden. Worried about a revenge strike, Taliban envoys turned up at the U.S embassy in Islamabad several times, voicing fears that there would be another cruise missile attack or an attempt to destroy the regime outright.[44]

Indeed, for months, U.S. warships were stationed off the Pakistan coast, ready to launch a missile attack if the CIA could pinpoint bin Laden's whereabouts. Now the Taliban introduced a new excuse: their hands were tied. Turning him over to the Americans "would cause internal problems for the Taliban within Afghanistan that would result in their demise," spokesman Abdul Wakil Muttawakil told Alan Eastham, chargé d'affaires at the U.S. embassy in Islamabad. Muttawakil said "the people" would not understand why the Taliban had expelled a man regarded as a "great mujaheed" during the war against the Soviets. U.S. officials were baffled by the excuse, apparently unaware of the crucial role of Arab fighters in the military advances since August and the influence this bought for bin Laden. The facts were out there, but no one connected the dots. "Arab mujahideen . . . fought alongside us in the recent battles in Mazar-i-Sharif and Bamiyan," an aide to Omar admitted to a visiting Arab reporter.

At no point was the embassy asked by Washington to raise the issue of human rights in Afghanistan, and Milam never added the Mazar-i-Sharif atrocities to the agenda. "We had five or six issues with the Taliban, and you had to prioritize," Milam recalled.[45]

So the travesties against human rights, which reached an all-time high for Afghanistan in the second half of 1998, disappeared from public or private debate. The exception was at the United Nations, where Lakhdar Brahimi, Kofi Annan himself, Choong-Hyun Paik and his aides, and some affiliated bodies—in particular, the UNHCR—did what they could within the system. No one sounded the alarm more factually than Paik, who delivered his formal report on the events in Mazar-i-Sharif in late October 1998. Unable to visit Afghanistan, he compiled "the most credible information possible" on the events that took place there from reliable sources—mainly UNHCR refugee testimony.

Paik expressed horror over the latest reports from Afghanistan and shock and dismay at the killings in August and September, and he condemned the "heinous" taking of innocent life. "There can be no justification or tolerance of such outrages and no impunity for their perpetrators, who must be brought to justice," he wrote. He repeated what he had said seven months earlier: "Silence cannot be the strategy of the international community." Paik added, "The scale of violations in Afghanistan and the suffering of the civilian population warrants the urgent attention of the world community." But his report, with language as intense as ever seen in a UN document, drew little attention, and Paik resigned from his post a short time later.

The Taliban leadership dismissed Paik's report as fiction. "He has not verified a single point of what he has claimed but most likely has relied on anecdotes and baseless reports of the press or on the false stories of opponents," they said in a response published as an annex. Then they turned the tables and asked why the United Nations had failed to investigate the 1997 killings of Taliban in Mazar-i-Sharif. Had the author ever tried to explore the crimes of opponents of the Islamic Emirate, they asked? "When thousands of unarmed and peace-demanding Taliban were tortured with different means, where were those alert ears?"

The BBC was one of the few news organizations to report on Paik's summary. "This has to be one of the most shocking reports ever produced by the UN," BBC reporter Rob Watson said in his dispatch. He duly noted that the Taliban had rejected the content as baseless and that some UN officials said privately that few of the allegations in the report could be proved. Still, he put the facts before the public; not many other media outlets went that far. Other than the major news agencies, only two American newspapers attempted to verify the content by doing their own investigation, but they did not follow up to determine what really happened; and no international television network did its own reporting on the crime.[46]

Where was everyone when all this was happening? "From May to August it was 'pool party summer,' and the press were at the pool," was the acid judgment of one UN official. Actually, the reporters who covered the volatile South Asia region (most of them based in New Delhi) and even more so those who covered all of Asia from Beijing had several major stories on their plates, and they were competing for airtime or newspaper space with the Lewinsky scandal. The top story from the region was clearly the bombings in East Africa and the connection to bin Laden. Some distance behind that was the standoff between Afghanistan and Iran, two theocracies where access was particularly difficult. With few exceptions, foreign reporters ignored the Afghan internal conflict, in part because visas were hard to obtain, movement was severely restricted within the country, and visiting media were required to hire drivers and translators from the Taliban and accept an official minder. TV reporters faced the added challenge that the Taliban forbade still photographs or television cameras. Moreover, access to Mazar-i-Sharif was cut off for many months.

But every obstacle has a workaround, and when the front door is closed, there is often a side entrance. In this case, the UNHCR had already conducted a half dozen interviews it deemed authentic, and it offered to help reporters find other refugees and put its own credibility on the line in vouching for their authenticity. Convincing editors of the story's value was the next hurdle for reporters. Freelance journalist Sarah Horner persuaded the VOA to accept one of the first reports based on the UNHCR accounts but had to put her job on the line to get it on the air. After a month of research, she offered a full-blown account to *Newsweek*, with what she said was compelling evidence of Taliban complicity; however, in the flurry of breaking stories on the Lewinsky scandal, nothing appeared other than a brief item in the "Periscope" section. "It was heartbreaking," she later said. "It really devastated me as a journalist." The first print reporter to talk with refugees was Dexter Filkins, then with the *Los Angeles Times;* his gripping 1,200-word, page-one story on September 18, 1998, was based on interviews with a dozen refugees in Peshawar, three of whom he quoted by name. At the end of October, Anthony Davis wrote a three-part, 2,400-word story in *Asiaweek* under the pseudonym Michael Winchester. He based this most thorough account on multiple witnesses. And in late November, the *Washington Post*'s Kenneth Cooper did a solid reconstruction of the attack and the execution of civilians. He estimated the death toll between two thousand and five thousand. But the *New York Times,* America's newspaper of record, never published an investigation of the massacre and was content to run brief accounts of reports from the United Nations, such as those by Choong-Hyun Paik. "All the journalists were very shocked," said Colville, who spent hours visiting individual journalists, trying to sell the story. "Their editors kissed it off."

The BBC provided the most thorough coverage as well as the most controversial. Its staff reported on the plight of refugees as they departed Mazar-i-Sharif and flagged every warning from AI, HRW, and the UNHCR. Regional analyst Jenny Norton led off a five-minute overview on August 28 by noting that a "complete news blackout" remained over the city. Recounting what Taliban opponents were saying about mass arrests, ethnic killings, and ethnic cleansing of non-Pashtuns, Norton concluded, "As long as Mazar-i-Sharif remains closed and it's impossible to verify the situation, it's inevitable that the rumors will continue, as well as the suspicion the Taliban may have something to hide." It was a first-rate example of watchdog journalism—holding the authorities to account and demanding access to ascertain the facts.

The human rights community had a different view of another BBC reporter, Kabul correspondent William Reeve, who (in his own words) was "vilified" for his reporting on Mazar-i-Sharif. "People were saying I was pro-Taliban," he said. "I reported what I saw and heard and was totally non-one side or the other." When HRW issued its carefully researched report in late October based on eyewitness accounts, Reeve played down the conclusions. "As with all such military operations within urban areas, civilians undoubtedly suffered in the heat of battle," he said. Mazar-i-Sharif was "by no means the worst" atrocity, and he urged an investigation of the May 1997 Taliban conquest in which some two thousand Taliban prisoners had been executed. The "more recent events in Mazar-i-Sharif were a direct corollary," he asserted. But Reeve should have been aware that the Hazaras, the principal Taliban target in 1998, were not responsible for the 1997 systematized killings. That was the responsibility of Malik's Uzbeks.

Not having visited Mazar-i-Sharif, Reeve took aim at the accounts of refugees who had fled in terror. "There were certainly quite a few incidents of men with weapons being executed on the spot," he said. "But independent and reliable sources say there was not the impression of a generalized systematic massacre, nor the total indiscriminate targeting of civilians, be they men, women, or children, except for those killed during the fighting on the first day."

When he actually got to Mazar-i-Sharif in December, he described the city as "peaceful, calm, but perhaps a bit tense." Most people say "they are happy with the present security," he said, while noting that "not many" ethnic Hazaras could be seen around town, "certainly not Hazara men of fighting age." By mid-December, his reporting toughened. He said that the Taliban had used "brutal" tactics and killed between five hundred and one thousand people while disarming and subduing Hazara parts of the city. He dismissed UN figures of up to eight thousand dead as based on only six eyewitnesses and not on visits to the city. But Reeve certainly knew about the news blackout that blocked every reporter other than himself and the security clampdown that prevented international organizations from operating freely in the city at that time.

Nor was Reeve the only reporter to belittle the UN reporting. Kathy Gannon, the longtime AP bureau chief in Islamabad, agreed with Reeve's figure of approximately eight hundred killed and called the UNHCR estimate "nonsense." By disparaging the UN reporting, Reeve and Gannon—both old-timers in the region—may well have discouraged other reporters from pursuing the story.*

To Colville, the outcome was tragic, and not only for the Afghans. "If ever there has been a major atrocity in the past twenty years that didn't get the attention it deserved, it is this one. I think it may have been, technically, within the definition of genocide." He puts the blame on the indiffer-

---

* Although both Reeve and Gannon wrote critically of the Taliban on many occasions, (envious) colleagues noted that they were the only reporters the Taliban allowed back into Afghanistan to report on the movement's last days in power.

ence of journalists.* "It never occurred to me that as strong a story as that could evaporate. It broke any law of media logic," he said. "To be honest, the main villain in the piece is the media."[47]

The media were far more willing to make their platforms available to bin Laden. Since the U.S. cruise missile attacks in August, he had observed the Taliban gag order, imposed because Omar wanted him "to stay silent all the time . . . in the hope that time will help the United States and some of the states demanding his extradition to forget him," said an aide to Omar, summing up the policy. But as the months wore on, bin Laden argued that this policy was causing him harm, including frequent official U.S. denunciations, a grand jury indictment, and a $5 million bounty on his head (and that of Abu Hafs). In mid-December, when CIA and Pentagon officials told reporters about intelligence that bin Laden was seriously ill, possibly with cancer, his pleas gained traction with his minder, Mullah Jalil.

It no doubt helped that Taliban "investigations" by this time had convinced Omar of the "falsehood" of the charges against bin Laden. So, written assurances notwithstanding (including one from the Islamabad envoy that bin Laden's "personal activities" had been banned), the Taliban relented. Once again, Yusufzai, as well as a number of Arab journalists, trooped in to see him one-on-one.[48]

He spoke with permission this time and from a new venue—a mountain encampment in Helmand province in southwest Afghanistan—but in other respects it was the same bin Laden. "I had no hand at all in the bombings in Kenya and Tanzania," he said, "but I feel no sorrow over the blasts." He did claim credit for inspiring the attacks, however. "Our job is to instigate and, by the grace of God, we did that—and certain people responded to this instigation." He reaffirmed the jihad against American and British civilians. "The British and U.S. peoples have generally supported their leaders' decisions to attack Iraq. That makes every one of their nationals warmongers whom every Muslim must fight and kill, just like the Jews in occupied Palestine." He said hostility toward the United States was "a religious duty" and expressed confidence that Muslims "will be able to end the legend of the so-called superpower that is America." What got the most attention was his stated determination to acquire weapons of mass destruction. "It would be a sin for Muslims not to try to possess the weapons that would prevent the infidels from inflicting harm on Muslims," he declared.

It was time for another démarche. At a meeting with the local envoy, Syedur Rahman Haqqani, Alan Eastham, U.S. chargé d'affaires in Islamabad, expressed "deep concern" about the latest interviews. Haqqani stopped just short of an apology. The understanding was that bin Laden would use

---

* There were honorable exceptions, according to Colville, among them AFP, *Asiaweek*, the *Los Angeles Times*, the *Sydney Morning Herald*, and VOA. Other reporters pitched stories but were turned down by editors. Television never touched the story, Colville said. Colville, interview.

the interview to deny his involvement in the August bombings and any support for terrorist activities. "However, he did not do what he promised," Haqqani said. The interview "was a mistake" and bin Laden "will not be allowed to give any more interviews." Eastham offered Washington a skeptical judgment of this latest assurance: "We doubt the Taliban will take concrete action (aside from a renewed effort to keep bin Laden out of the public eye)."[49]

The net result of his manipulation throughout 1998 was that bin Laden had strengthened his standing within the Taliban. Extradition through dialogue had failed, as had the "search for moderate Taliban."

It was time for a change of U.S. policy.

7

Hijacking a Regime
(1999)

The Taliban reached a watershed in the second half of 1998, but the Clinton administration could not bring itself to act. Protecting the "Great Mujaheed" had become the supreme interest of the Taliban regime, and with each rebuff of U.S. demands, Mullah Omar made clear that hosting the Saudi renegade had higher priority than establishing relations with the world's number one power, more important than even the security of the state.

More was at work than one man's fanaticism. Behind the scenes, bin Laden had made himself indispensable. The moment of bonding between bin Laden and the regime is not certain, but Omar was unquestionably in his debt beginning in August 1998, when he and his fighters helped the Taliban conquer most of northern Afghanistan. Bin Laden aides had helped reorganize the Taliban force, and he reportedly provided much of the wherewithal for the offensive.

Bin Laden's historical role in the jihad, his part in expanding the emirate to the Amu Darya River, and the tradition of *Pashtun wali* added up to a compelling case for the credulous village cleric to grant sanctuary, and on the eve of the American missile strikes, Omar made an irrevocable pledge: "We will never hand Osama over to anyone and will protect him with our blood at all cost." He repeated this commitment the day of the attack and often thereafter. The Taliban capture of Bamiyan in mid-September with the help of Arab fighters and logistics no doubt reinforced the tie between the two men.

But the Clinton administration paid no heed to Omar's public oath and instead persisted with a diplomatic drive to have the Taliban expel bin Laden. Early in February 1999, after a long string of snubs from the Taliban, Rick Inderfurth flew to Pakistan to meet with Taliban spokesman Mullah Abdul Jalil Akhund.* The day before, CIA director George Tenet told

---

* Some examples of the snubs in late 1998:

August 25: the U.S. embassy in Islamabad learns of a fatwa obliging all Muslims to protect bin Laden.

September 13: Omar waits two weeks before agreeing to a dialogue on bin Laden. Taliban envoy Abdul Hakeem Mujahid informs the embassy that Omar is the key supporter among the Taliban of bin Laden's continued presence in Afghanistan and will not discuss the matter with subordinates.

(continued on next page)

an open Senate hearing that there was "not the slightest doubt that Osama bin Laden, his worldwide allies, and his sympathizers are planning further attacks against us . . . wherever in the world he thinks we are vulnerable." As Inderfurth sat down with Mullah Jalil in Islamabad, the State Department spokesman in Washington demanded that bin Laden be expelled and brought to justice. Privately, Inderfurth warned Jalil that the Taliban would be held responsible if bin Laden undertook any action against U.S. interests. Jalil replied that bin Laden would be controlled.[1]

A week passed, and there was another rebuff: a Taliban spokesman said the movement would "never" expel bin Laden, although he was "free" to leave the country. But everyone knew that no other government was willing to take him in. Next, the Taliban claimed that he had disappeared. Bin Laden had "left his place of residence in Kandahar without informing us of his destination," Omar told an Arab newspaper, adding that contact with him had been broken. "We believe that he has disappeared somewhere, possibly inside Afghanistan's territories, but we do not know as yet his whereabouts, whether he has left Afghanistan, or where he could possibly go." Other spokesmen were equally implausible. "He was there in our control area, but since he left the area, we do not know where he is," Mujahid, now UN envoy, told Inderfurth in Washington. (Bin Laden was spotted near Jalalabad some months later.)

The definitive response to the U.S. demand came once again from Mullah Omar. "We cannot go back on Afghan, Islamic, and Pathan tradition," Omar told journalist Rahimullah Yusufzai. "According to those traditions, we owe protection to anybody who has taken refuge with us, and bin Laden is not just anybody. He fought with us." Omar said that protecting him was more important than staying in power. "Half my country was destroyed by war, and I would not mind if the remaining half is destroyed in trying to protect our guest, bin Laden," he said.[2]

That ought to have been the turning point, for there had been a metamorphosis in Kandahar. Omar and bin Laden had by this time "effectively become one," and the alliance was unshakable, Inderfurth said. Milam took it a step further: "Omar became a bin Laden convert, a believer in bin

---

* *(cont.)*

Mid-September: Omar breaks his commitment to hand over bin Laden and lectures Prince Turki about the need to expel U.S. forces from Saudi Arabia.

October 19: U.S. ambassador to Pakistan William Milam reports that Omar is "strongly committed" to bin Laden. He says it is "questionable" whether any U.S. or Saudi effort can influence Omar's decisions and uncertain whether Pakistan can.

November 28: Taliban spokesman Muttawakil says expelling bin Laden will bring down the Taliban regime.

December 19: Muttawakil says Afghanistan anticipates another U.S. military strike but will not expel bin Laden; he accuses the United States of murdering innocent Afghans in the August 20 missile attack.

December 30: UN envoy Abdul Hakeem Mujahid says bin Laden issued his latest public threats to American civilians as a result of "pressure from journalists."

Ladenism." His analysis suggested that bin Laden would become a major influence on internal Afghan affairs and that Omar now viewed himself as an actor on the Islamic world stage. The State Department's Bureau of Intelligence and Research (INR), headed by Phyllis Oakley, a former Afghanistan desk officer, used a more dramatic turn of phrase: Bin Laden had "hijacked the state, hijacked the [Taliban] movement." According to a senior aide, White House officials had reached a parallel conclusion—that Omar and bin Laden were "effectively merged." The CIA did not speak explicitly of a "hijacking," but its experts referred to bin Laden in internal discussions as the "terrorist sponsor of a state."[3]

Whatever the characterization, the Taliban movement, by providing sanctuary to bin Laden at any cost, had fused itself to a terrorist, transforming itself into a terror regime. From that point on, Inderfurth believed that any effort to sanction the Taliban and seek a change in behavior was increasingly unlikely to succeed. In his view, the Taliban "weren't going to be politically talked out of office. They weren't going to be politically ganged up on. They didn't care about sanctions."

Yet that is the course Clinton chose to pursue: imposing unilateral economic sanctions and lobbying the United Nations to follow suit, coupled with military and CIA plans to capture or kill bin Laden. The U.S. sanctions took effect in July 1999, freezing Taliban financial assets and blocking travel to the United States; international sanctions would follow in October. Inderfurth opposed the sanctions;* Albright's chief adviser on counterterrorism, Michael Sheehan, drafted the language.[4]

Looking back, the U.S. approach may seem difficult to comprehend. Bin Laden followers had attacked sovereign American territory with deadly effect; he had obtained sanctuary in Afghanistan and, with Omar's permission, had publicly incited the further murder of innocents. Clinton was on record in August 1998 saying that bin Laden was fighting a "terrorist war" against the United States. Albright said bin Laden "had declared war on the United States and struck first." Tenet drew the same conclusion late in 1998. "We are at war," he declared in a message to other intelligence officials. "I want no resources or people spared in this effort, either inside CIA or the [intelligence] community." Implicit in Clinton's decision to sanction Afghanistan was an acknowledgment that bin Laden could not be separated from the regime.

Yet to impose economic sanctions on one of the world's poorest countries, a dysfunctional state that had almost nothing to lose, would do nothing to reduce the threat Tenet described. On the contrary, many experts believe that U.S. reliance on sanctions (the weakest arrow in the

---

* "Mike and Rick disagreed on things," Albright noted some years later. The American sanctions blocked more than $34 million in Taliban assets held in U.S. banks, and $215 million in gold and $2 million in demand deposits belonging to the Afghan Central Bank. Albright, interview; and *9/11 Commission Report*, 185.

national security quiver) emboldened Omar and Osama and drove them still closer together.[5]

Why did the administration fail to act? One factor was the apparent disconnect between Inderfurth and his boss. Madeleine Albright considered Inderfurth one of her closest aides and said she had "incredible confidence" in him, but later she could not recall him communicating his judgment on bin Laden's effective takeover of the Taliban regime. From a journalist's perspective, a disclosure of this sort of transformation would be a page one headline and a major story to be pursued on the spot. Albright said in an interview that Inderfurth had "probably" told her, "but I can't remember exactly. . . . I don't specifically remember this."

In any case, whatever Inderfurth told her left little impression. "We know now" about the "symbiotic relationship" between bin Laden and the Taliban, she said, "but for whatever reason it was not quite as evident at the time." In an interview, Inderfurth expressed surprise at Albright's memory lapse: "I don't have any doubt at all that in cable reporting and subsequent updates, and [with] Intelligence Research and Phyllis (Oakley) doing their intelligence side, this wasn't a 'this just in' [development]." Inderfurth added, "I have no doubt at all that there would be reporting and information memos going forward. We did not keep it to ourselves."[6]

The failure of the State Department to sound the alarm about the dramatic shift in Kandahar should be seen in the context of other events. At the time of Inderfurth's epiphany, Albright was leading an international political campaign to change the face of southern Europe—to clear the way for a U.S.-led NATO intervention in rump Yugoslavia and halt the Serbian army's assault against the predominantly Albanian Kosovars. Indeed, NATO's seventy-three-day bombing of Serbian targets began just six weeks after Inderfurth's meeting with Mullah Jalil. Albright's leadership role led some to dub Kosovo "Madeleine's war," a sobriquet that stung at the time but later became a badge of honor.

That was one factor, but it was probably not decisive. The Republican campaign to impeach Clinton over the Lewinsky scandal also distracted Congress and the public from focusing on the real threats to the republic.

Clinton's aides would later cite myriad other reasons for not toughening U.S. policy in Afghanistan. One top aide belittled the significance of the embassy attacks: "We don't go to war over dead Africans," he said. He also gave a quasi-diplomatic explanation that helping to arm the Taliban's opposition "would have legitimized more arming of the Taliban by Pakistan and others and would have violated the six-plus-two process, which was an effort to find some negotiated solution." It seemed a disingenuous excuse, because the six-plus-two forum had always been a diplomatic cover that allowed the United States to duck a leadership role. Moreover, by mid-1999, the process was at a dead end, and the arming of the factions was a fact of life. A more polished explanation from P. J. Crowley, the

National Security Council spokesman at the time, was that there was "no appetite for military options, no good ones, and a crowded diplomatic agenda."[7]

The real reason Clinton stuck with a doomed course in South Asia, according to aides, was his decision to follow the lead of a small group of Democrats in Congress in reacting to the nuclear tests of May 1998. Clinton, a consensus builder who critics said too often set his compass by opinion polls, had yielded to domestic political pressure.

Preventing nuclear proliferation was a passionate cause among a small group of congressional Democrats. In 1994, the antiproliferation caucus won passage of the Glenn amendment, named for Senator John Glenn of Ohio, which imposed automatic, broad economic sanctions, without the possibility of a waiver, in the event Pakistan or India held nuclear tests. Clinton signed the bill into law, and although by 1998 it had clearly failed as a tool of deterrence, it had a remarkable political half-life. After Pakistan's nuclear tests in May 1998, the nonproliferation bloc, led by Glenn in the Senate and California Democrat Nancy Pelosi in the House, insisted that the administration sanction Pakistan and India. According to a close aide to Vice President Al Gore, a small group in Congress was "extremely doctrinaire," had generated a "groundswell" for a very strict policy, and made sure the president stayed within the letter of the law.[8]

The problem before the president was that the only possible pressure that could be brought on the Taliban without using American force had to come from the same Pakistani government that Clinton's liberal allies in Congress insisted on sanctioning over nuclear proliferation. Pakistan controlled the main routes and fuel supplies into Afghanistan and was the transit point for spare parts and pickup trucks for the military offensives, as well as the provider of manpower, ammunition, training, and weapons. The Pakistan military, which believed profoundly that developing a nuclear deterrent was a core Pakistani security interest (a position Clinton had all but endorsed in April 1998), had the power to throttle this support. Interestingly, Gen. Jehangir Karamat, chief of armed services at the time of the embassy attacks, thought that the military could have been won over to a tougher policy. A level-headed career military man who had trained at the U.S. Army Command and General Staff College in Leavenworth, Kansas, Karamat felt that top U.S. officials could have sat down with Pakistan's top military strategists at this stage to pursue a "considered engagement" policy. It would begin with a statement of the obvious—that American sovereign assets had been attacked—then give an estimate of bin Laden's worldwide potential. He believed that a concerted American effort would have convinced Pakistanis that the Taliban was ultimately a threat to Pakistan itself. The Pakistan military had to abandon its own preconception that putting the screws to the Taliban would provoke an extremist backlash and be coaxed into "extricating itself to the winning side." To "strangulate" bin

Laden, the two countries would have to develop a joint strategic concept for dealing with the Taliban.

But that discussion never took place. Pakistan was in economic free-fall and saddled with a corrupt civilian government, led by businessman Nawaz Sharif, that was flirting with pro-Taliban Islamist parties. Karamat resigned in early October 1998, after publicly criticizing the Sharif government for failing to throw all its energies into the country's catastrophic economic situation.

Forced to choose between politically popular but counterproductive sanctions against Pakistan and a radical policy shift to protect directly threatened American interests, Clinton chose sanctions against Pakistan and a mix of covert and military operations targeting bin Laden. The outcome may have quieted critics at home, but it had an equal and opposite effect in the region, giving an incentive to nationalist members of the Pakistan military to support, not undermine, the Taliban. And soon a friendly but unstable civilian government in Pakistan would give way to a stable military regime with zero concern for U.S. national security interests in Afghanistan.

Responsibility for the failure to devise a new policy falls on the State Department as well as the White House. Senior State Department officials seem to have grasped the big picture—namely, that bin Laden had effectively become part of the Taliban regime—but major players from throughout the national security area (top White House officials, a ranking member of the Joint Chiefs of Staff, and senior CIA officials) say State never shared this conclusion in administration-wide counterterrorism discussions. At the same time, the CIA never informed the Senate Intelligence Committee of its assessment that Afghanistan had become a "terrorist-sponsored state," according to the ranking minority member of the committee.*

Among the agencies that would have been most interested in the State Department's assessment of the Taliban was the Joint Chiefs of Staff, which adamantly opposed radical change of U.S. policy in Afghanistan. The heads of America's armed services and the commander for that region feared that any major policy shift in Afghanistan would threaten what little remained of U.S. military relations with Pakistan. If the Joint Chiefs had known of the new political reality in the stark terms described by Inderfurth, they would have changed their thinking, a ranking member said.[9]

---

* Among those who were unaware that the State Department had drawn this conclusion was Leon Furth, Vice President Gore's national security adviser. A year after 9/11, Furth said, "If the premise is true, and bin Laden was the master of the government, then a lot of other things would fall in place." These included Mullah Omar's obduracy, his insistence that the United States furnish proof of bin Laden's role, his willingness to accept any amount of pressure, and his rejection of appeals from people who could help the Taliban. "All would be indicators that power had passed from him. It would explain his almost suicidal stubbornness," Furth said. Furth, interview.

Avoiding Massoud

The State Department's failure to take the lead has multiple explanations. Its own senior diplomats were ambivalent about responding to the Taliban and deeply divided over supporting to the Taliban's sole military opponent, Ahmed Shah Massoud. At the top of the department, Albright, in the judgment of one senior aide, lacked a strategic vision for South Asia. "Her focus was Europe," this aide said. Indeed, from late 1998 through the NATO intervention in Kosovo in March 1999, Albright was an indefatigable promoter of the use of force in that very different theatre, an example of how a cabinet officer could drive decisions under Clinton. But in addressing South Asia, both Albright and her deputy, Strobe Talbott, were deeply distrustful of the Pakistanis. For this reason alone, holding a discussion of the sort Karamat proposed "would have been next to impossible," said a ranking State Department official. Several years later, Talbott—who shuttled frequently to New Delhi and Islamabad after the May 1998 nuclear tests—could not name a single trustworthy official. "Either they were deceiving or lying," he said. Talking to them "wasn't worth anything."

The more fundamental problem was that no one was listening to Inderfurth, the State Department's chief regional expert on this issue. Recriminations from Congress and the White House over the failure to anticipate the nuclear tests in India and Pakistan had stilled the voice of the State Department's Bureau of South Asian Affairs in setting policy for this region. After the five bombs in India and six in Pakistan, nonproliferation and nuclear issues "went bang up to the top" of the agenda, Inderfurth recalled. "Our entire policy toward Pakistan turned on the issue of nonproliferation," said Leon Furth, Al Gore's national security adviser. An Albright aide said, "No one would have confidence in the [State Department] policy apparatus" after its failure to predict the Indian nuclear test. In her autobiography, Albright says that late in 1998 she delegated much of the responsibility for policy formulation to Michael Sheehan, a former Army Special Forces officer whom she named State Department coordinator for counterterrorism. Sheehan "soon developed a strategy for increasing pressure on the Taliban," Albright wrote.[10]

The U.S. military, too, was widely perceived to be dragging its feet. Richard Clarke and his counterterrorism team at the White House felt there was "tremendous reluctance to do anything about Afghanistan" among the military. It seems astonishing in retrospect that neither the Joint Chiefs nor the White House requested contingency plans for military intervention in Afghanistan, and General Anthony Zinni, commander of the U.S. Central Command, never drafted any. "Contingency plans are based on threats to us" and are not drafted "unless you have a specific threat to us," Zinni later explained. "The Taliban didn't represent a specific threat to us." He commented, "We had counterterrorism plans. After 1998, we were looking at T-Lams [Tomahawk land-air missiles], surgical methods, how to get at the cancer without getting at the whole body." However, after al Qaeda–commandeered airliners struck the World Trade Center's Twin Towers on September 11, 2001, the U.S. military deployed its forces in the subsequent invasion without any advance plans.[11]

And that was the paradox: the country's political and national security leadership acknowledged a state of war. But instead of mobilizing the country, demanding that every department produce its best thinking, and then promoting the policy with the public at large and driving it through Congress, the president, like Albright, pigeonholed the bin Laden crisis to his White House counterterrorism team, led by Richard Clarke, a career civil servant.

It was a formula for inadequate response. Though a formidable presence within the White House, Clarke was too low in the chain of command to conceptualize and drive a major policy shift. Operating in what an Albright aide called a "hypercompartmentalized" culture to preserve the "sanctity" of the intelligence that came his way, Clarke was in no position to reach out and build alliances within the bureaucracy. In addition, he lacked the institutional base and staff resources to force the issue through the system or the political stature to articulate the position in public. Turning the ship of state around is the job description of the president. And Clinton's decision to define the issue as counterterrorism, to be fought largely in secret through the CIA, made it harder to lead the government and the country on what everyone agreed was the topmost threat to U.S. security, the Albright aide said.

So Clarke and Sheehan threw their energies into encouraging law enforcement efforts to halt terror plots, advocating plans to decapitate al Qaeda through the capture of bin Laden, and promoting UN sanctions against the Taliban. Sheehan chaired a policy review in late 1999 or early 2000 that produced a plan for punitive steps against Pakistan, among them, naming it a terrorist state and imposing a trade ban and an economic blockade. Top State Department officials headed off that move, fearing it would "precipitate a completely disastrous undoing of Pakistan." But worse schemes were on the horizon.[12]

Afghanistan during Clinton's second term was coming to resemble Bosnia-Herzegovina during his first. The pattern was the same: avoid confrontation as long as possible and refuse to arm and support the opponent. Meanwhile, the United States would wink and nod at foreign arms transfers to the beleaguered underdog, hope there would be no embarrassing disasters, and seek diplomatic "fixes" whose main merit was to remove the issue from the limelight. This pattern did not lead to a resolution in Bosnia and could not in Afghanistan. The difference was that this time almost no one, including the Republican-led Congress, was paying attention.

Even the tactical fix (i.e., to decapitate al Qaeda) turned into a mission impossible. The president had taken a hammering in the news media for the attack on al Shifa pharmaceutical plant, which the State Department's INR had concluded was a mistake.* In mid-December 1998, when the United States and Britain launched air assaults against Saddam Hussein's regime after he ordered UN inspectors to leave, Clinton critics trotted out the familiar *Wag the Dog* accusations. And though conservatives had cheered him on after the August 20 bombings, he never followed up with another strike. Under partisan assault over the Lewinsky scandal and fearing another misstep like al Shifa, Clinton raised the bar for taking military action. Although his aides told the 9/11 Commission that American submarines were standing by, ready to fire cruise missiles as soon as there was "actionable" intelligence spotting bin Laden, Clinton had decided after the al Shifa fiasco that the intelligence "had to be perfect," an aide said. This required intelligence of a quality beyond the CIA's ability to deliver.

In February 1999, CIA Afghan assets on the ground reported that bin Laden was near a hunting camp in southern Afghanistan, and in May they reported that he could be targeted in Kandahar. Both times the military prepared itself for a strike; both times Tenet's uncertainty about the target and White House fears about collateral damage to civilians led to a cancellation. From May 1999 until September 11, 2001, policymakers did not consider a missile strike against bin Laden.[13]

Clinton's other major omission in Afghanistan was his administration's failure to engage Ahmed Shah Massoud. If the United States was at war, as so many of its leaders said it was, ramping up support for an enemy of its enemy—the remnants of the beleaguered United Front—would seem logical. Massoud's repeated denunciations of the ISI made it unlikely that Pakistan would permit direct supply, but significant U.S. cash could have flowed through other routes to the only major resistance leader still operating inside the country.

Massoud was territorially weakened and in difficult financial straits in 1999, but overall it was a year of military stalemate. Massoud claimed to control 30 percent of the country, which contained 50 percent of the population, but most experts think that, with his Hazara allies, he actually controlled 15–20 percent of Afghan territory.

Resourcefulness was in ample supply, however. Once again, he was busy building up a professional military, and his three-month training

---

* Through 2004, Clinton himself, former vice president Al Gore, Sandy Berger, George Tenet, and White House counterterrorism chief Richard Clarke all insisted to the 9/11 Commission that their judgment had been correct in bombing al Shifa. But the commission noted that no independent evidence had emerged to corroborate the CIA's assessment. The commission judged that the failure of the initial strikes, the *Wag the Dog* slur, the intense partisanship of the period, and the nature of the al Shifa evidence "likely had a cumulative effect on future decisions about the use of force against bin Laden." *9/11 Commission Report*, 118.

courses graduated hundreds of junior officers. Some specialist courses were conducted by small groups of Iranians flown in secretly via Tajikistan. Iran—which played a similar role in Bosnia with Clinton's acquiescence—was also providing him with significant amounts of munitions and technical support, and helping to build a bridge across the Amu Darya River with Tajikistan near Dasht-i-Qala.* According to journalist Anthony Davis, Massoud also purchased 120 new Russian jeeps from Tajikistan, then fitted some of them with heavy machine guns or mortars.[14]

But in terms of cash, Massoud was vastly overstretched. His main source of income was the sale of emeralds and lapis lazuli, which reportedly earned only $7–10 million annually. True, he got a cut of the Afghan currency printed in India or Russia and had his men trade it for goods in bazaars or across the front lines. The Taliban had never managed to redesign the Afghani, and Rabbani split the proceeds with Massoud 80–20. Another source of funding was CIA repurchase of Stinger ground-to-air missiles. Otherwise, Massoud managed to survive through his brother's short-term overdrafts. "I borrowed from banks—in 1999, my overdraft came to over one million pounds," recalled Walid Massoud, the commander's brother, who was also his envoy in London. "I was paying 17 percent interest. My payments were sometimes three or four months in arrears." Ahmed Shah Massoud, a pious Muslim, never understood. "My brother didn't believe it was Islamic to pay or get interest," Walid said.†

Massoud may have been practically alone, but he was organized, innovative, and active. But the Clinton White House wrote him off as just "a warlord" who would never gather a bigger following. Officials saw him through the ethnic prism of the Pakistan government and many Afghan émigrés, as a Tajik in a land where Pashtuns had the traditional claim to govern, rather than as a patriot who was fighting for his country. The American focus was on bin Laden, and White House aides felt Massoud's forces at most could harass the Taliban but not defeat it without on-ground U.S. military support. The attitude on U.S. support was all or next-to-nothing.[15]

---

* Iran sent a trainload of arms in October 1998, buried under bags of flour and under the false lading of humanitarian aid. The eleven carloads contained 100 mm and 115 mm tank ammunition for T-55 and T-62 tanks, antitank mines, 122 mm towed howitzers and ammunition, 122 mm rockets for the Grad multiple-rocket launch systems, mortars, and small arms. The shipment was halted by Kyrgyzstan customs officials before it reached its consignee—the Iranian ambassador to Kyrgyzstan—and most of the content was returned to Iran. The Taliban Foreign Ministry interpreted the interception as "a Russian signal toward the Taliban," according to Vahid Mojdeh. At the time, Russia was asking to send a delegation to Kandahar to open diplomatic relations—and trying to prevent breakaway Chechnya from doing the same. The Taliban rebuffed the initiative (assuming that is what it was), dismissing it as "Satan's seductive ways" and refusing to receive the delegation. Mojdeh, unpublished manuscript, 45.

† Walid Massoud said his brother did not receive any income from drugs. "How could a man like that run drugs?" he asked. The HRW report on arms supplies to both sides also did not allege that Massoud's income came from drugs. Walid Massoud, interview.

Although Massoud frequently traveled to Dushanbe, Tajikistan, the administration dealt with him exclusively through the CIA station in Islamabad and, on occasion, by sending officers from Langley.* They would meet roughly twice a year, either in Badakshan or in Dushanbe. According to Gary Schroen, the State Department did not send a representative to any of the seven meetings he attended. And when Abdullah Abdullah came to Washington, he said he had at most a half-hour-long meeting with Inderfurth. "We never saw anyone on the NSC," said Haron Amin, who was then with the Afghan mission to the United Nations. He never once called on a cabinet-level officer. "You are not going to see a spokesman for what at this point was a warlord, unless you are going to say, 'Yes, we will support him,'" said a high-ranking White House aide.[16]

Clinton and his aides, so astute in dealing with places where they saw a domestic political advantage, such as Northern Ireland, had next to no grasp of the internal Afghan context or the impact on the political landscape of receiving a Massoud aide, if only to rattle the Taliban. In a land in which alliances are the coin of the realm and today's mortal enemy can be tomorrow's close ally, the perception of outside support, or even interest, alters the internal reality. By asserting that it was "neutral" but seeking out the Taliban at high levels in Islamabad and by publicly inviting its officials to the State Department, even for high-level thrashings, the U.S. government unwittingly fed the perception that it was backing the movement, said one intelligence analyst. Protestations of neutrality in the Afghan context conveyed the message that the United States backed those in power. "Perception, if not identical to reality in Afghanistan, is 90 percent of the game here. In many cases, it is not the reality, it is the perception," was the analysis of this official.

That certainly was Massoud's perspective. He thought the embassy bombings had offered the basis for a genuine strategic relationship with the United States; he could not comprehend the rebuffs. In his eyes, Washington had turned over its policy to Islamabad.

In a message Abdullah read to a Senate hearing in October 1998, Massoud said that southern Central Asia was in turmoil: "Some countries are on the brink of war.... Ethnic and religiously motivated mass murders and forced displacements are taking place, and the most basic human and women's rights are being shamelessly violated. The country has gradually

---

* The State Department assigned a very able career officer, Robert Finn, to Dushanbe, but for security reasons insisted he maintain his permanent residence in Almaty, Kazakhstan. Despite the restrictions, Finn was a frequent visitor to Dushanbe, but the State Department gave him no role in relations with Massoud, and he later estimated that he received at most 10 percent of the cable traffic about Afghanistan. The department's bureaucracy apparently did not grasp the strategic necessity. Tajikistan and other Central Asian states reported to the European bureau, while Afghanistan was managed under the South Asian bureau. Even though the Taliban welcomed Islamist militants from all the countries to its north, the State Department, according to a diplomatic source, "did not see Central Asia as an extension of South Asia."

been occupied by fanatics, extremists, terrorists, nationalists, drug mafias, and professional murderers." Those facts were incontrovertible, as was his assertion that the Taliban were "unyielding and unwilling to talk or reach compromise with any other Afghan sides." Massoud listed his goals: to end the war, establish a just peace, set up a transitional administration, and move toward representative government. He urged the United States to engage in "constructive and substantive discussions with our representatives and all Afghans" who sought peace and freedom.

Massoud's goals sounded like those Inderfurth listed at the same Senate hearing. Massoud accused outside powers (he had Pakistan in mind) of "misplaced greed, hegemonic designs, and ignorance." But he offered a remarkable mea culpa for his own past failures. "We Afghans erred, too. Our shortcomings were as a result of political innocence, inexperience, vulnerability, victimization, bickering, and inflated egos," he said. But this, he added, "by no means" justified the response of former Cold War allies "to destroy and subjugate Afghanistan."

There was no response.

"The terrorists will grow deep and wide, right and left, up and down to terrorize and entangle the West, and especially the United States," he told a close aide in December 1998. So far, the Taliban, Osama, and the Pakistani fanatics who volunteered to support the Taliban did not have a strong organization. "But if that is established under Osama," Massoud said, "then it would be very hard to stop it." Why, he asked, would the United States not come to his aid? "We have a common enemy. Can it not be that the richest and the poorest have a common enemy?" He viewed Afghanistan as a diseased patient. "Infection affects poor and rich the same way. Just the treatment makes a difference. I am looking for a proper treatment." Proper treatment was one thing he could not obtain.

In February 1999, Clinton authorized Tenet to enlist Massoud as a "partner" in the attempt to capture—but not kill—bin Laden. Considering that his front lines on the Shamali plains were hundreds of miles from Kandahar, where bin Laden spent much of his time, the idea was bizarre. CIA officers who went to see Massoud said he visibly winced at the offer. "You guys are crazy," he responded. "You haven't changed a bit."

By late October 1999, Massoud was in desperate straits. CIA officers visited him in the Panjshir Valley and won his assent to try to gather intelligence on bin Laden. "I need help. I need military equipment. I need money," Massoud told his CIA visitors. "If you can't give me the equipment, give me the money, and I can buy it from the Russians. I've got to have help." The Taliban are "getting stronger. I'm not getting stronger. They have the money to buy the defections of commanders. They're wearing me down. I need help." According to Schroen, "astronomical" sums were available to capture bin Laden but at most $100,000 or $200,000 per visit to keep Massoud's struggle against the Taliban alive.

During one such visit, Schroen made a back-of-the-envelope assessment of Massoud's military needs. More than any weapons system, he needed mobility—Kamaz cargo trucks, Toyota Hilux 4 x 4 pickup trucks, transport helicopters, small aircraft such as AN-12s that can carry two people or cargo and land on short runways. He needed a lot of small arms, new AK-47s, and heavy machine guns. Massoud estimated that $50 million in aid would allow him to buy what he needed, and with $20–30 million, "you could make a huge impact."

Massoud desperately needed a radio station. His was one of the few guerrilla movements anywhere to survive without being able to broadcast its message to its supporters and to the other side, not to mention to the rest of the world. He also needed a permanent, effective lobby in Washington and access to the upper reaches of the executive branch in Washington. His plan was not to defeat the Taliban by capturing the cities of Afghanistan but "to prolong the fight and exhaust them," he said. The key to his success was for the world "to recognize that this man is there." The Taliban claimed that Massoud was not a good Muslim. What he needed most of all, according to his brother Walid, was moral support. "If the Americans just said 'You are fighting a just cause,' it would have raised the morale of our people, given a signal to Pakistan and to al Qaeda that the Americans are coming. It could have demoralized the Taliban. That would have been enough as a first thing." American moral backing for Massoud would have discouraged the Taliban, but that moral backing is precisely what the Clinton administration refused to provide.[17]

The most reluctant officials were in Foggy Bottom, where many saw him as "damaged goods" from the 1992–1996 period. "There was a lot of resistance among Afghan watchers in the State Department," said Milam, who was new to South Asia when he arrived in Pakistan in August 1998. His deputy, Al Eastham, and Mike Malinowski, bureau director for Afghanistan at the State Department and later principal deputy to Inderfurth, were "very much" against helping Massoud, and Milam thought Inderfurth was as well. The argument they made was that Massoud could not win, and more aid would make things worse in Afghanistan. Milam said he "bought that line of thought for a while," but he later changed his mind. "I decided the Taliban would win it all unless we were helping Massoud."

Eastham believed that Iran and Russia were providing "adequate support" to keep Massoud in the game. "Since we didn't think they could win absent a substantial campaign of military assistance plus a diminution of aid by the Pakistanis to the Taliban, it didn't seem to be practical," he said. According to Schroen, who overlapped with Eastham in the Islamabad embassy, Eastham "did not like" Massoud or Rabbani and said they could not be trusted. A Taliban victory, Schroen recalled Eastham saying, "would mean no more fighting, no more civil war, and that would in itself be something good for Afghanistan." In fact, Eastham indicated to Massoud's representative Abdullah Abdullah that the best cure for the Taliban was to let them win. "Don't you think that if the Northern Alliance [United Front] is defeated, the Taliban will collapse of their own weight?" Abdullah recalled Eastham saying. So long as the Taliban opposition was non-Pashtun, Pashtuns would rally behind the Taliban. The moment the opposition was destroyed, Pashtuns would rise up against the Taliban. Eastham quickly added, "I hope this will not happen, but don't you think it could?" Abdullah knew the originator of the idea was another former mujahideen commander, Abdul Haq, himself a Pashtun, and it seemed self-serving.

Considering the paucity of anti-Taliban leaders, the State Department seemed remarkably averse to talking with Massoud. Albright's counterterrorism aide, Michael Sheehan, opposed sending any support. "They had plenty of money, plenty of guns, plenty of everything. They couldn't do shit," he said, unless there was "a major U.S. commitment to start a war against Afghanistan. That was the general consensus." A senior White House aide said Richard Clarke was the driving force in favor of aid to Massoud, but he ran into resistance every time. Even with extensive support, the most Massoud could do was harass the Taliban. "He didn't lack ammunition, weapons, or military knowledge; what he lacked was a support base outside the Tajik community," this official said. "We couldn't do much to help him with that."

A top NSC official agreed: "We debated the proposition of arming and equipping the Northern Alliance. The overall judgment was, one, that they . . . were basically saturated with arms from Iran and from Russia, and that more arms would not have changed the situation; and, two, they simply did not have the capability of making any really significant impact on the Taliban."[18]

And while Schroen, who knew Massoud best, believed that he and his fighters could make a difference, many in the CIA still resented the guerrilla leader's failure to operate on their schedule in the 1989–1992 period. And the naysayers had a top-level ally at the CIA in the person of the deputy director of operations, Jim Pavett. According to Clarke's deputy, Roger Cressey, Pavett "was the roadblock," and Tenet would not override him. "The Agency said, 'We need consensus.'" In the Clinton administration, this translated into a veto, for it was the bureaucracy that drove the White House. "If it is not eager to do something, it takes an act of God or a 9/11," said Cressey.

Pressure from Congress, the expatriate Afghan community, or academic experts might have shifted the debate, but there was no such call. Sheehan challenged: "Find one op-ed, one congressman, anywhere. Find one voice that called for something like that—an article, a symposium, a policy guy. No one cared." Charlie Wilson, the former Democratic congressman from Texas who single-handedly helped fashion the CIA backing for the mujahideen during the anti-Soviet war, could have made the difference. But Wilson had left Congress and was now working as a lobbyist for Pakistan.

In fact, through late 1999, the brain trust among academic experts strongly advised against aiding Massoud. Barnett Rubin, a leading scholar, told Congress in late 1998, "I do not favor military assistance to anti-Taliban forces, as Afghanistan's society, I believe, really cannot withstand the impact of more war and violence." His advice: "Break the lifeline to Pakistan." Zalmay Khalilzad, an Afghan-American veteran of previous Republican administrations but then with the RAND Corporation (and years later U.S. ambassador to Kabul), said the United States should offer the Taliban "a deal": international recognition in exchange for expelling bin Laden, opening peace talks with other Afghan groups, and lifting the ban on girls' education. That failing, he urged a policy of undermining the Taliban by supporting moderate elements and urging Pakistan to cut its support.

In mid-1999, Khalilzad coauthored a white paper for a private foundation calling for actions to weaken the Taliban and transform it into a more benign movement. One means he suggested was "military stalemate," which he asserted could be achieved by pursuing a familiar path: pressuring Pakistan to end support for the Taliban. As for Massoud, he urged only the exploration of ways to assist "foes" of the Taliban in their struggle. This would entail both "succoring" current resistance groups "and, more important, identifying and helping new anti-Taliban foes that have more support outside their immediate communities." The implication was to support Abdul Haq and other Pashtun leaders as opposed to the Tajik Massoud. Another voice in the chorus was T. Kumar, a representative of AI, who urged Congress not to "trade one armed group for another armed group," because "that's not going to give peace to the people of Afghanistan."[19]

Small wonder that, in autumn 1999, Inderfurth laid out a seemingly schizophrenic policy before Congress. "The Taliban's sheltering of bin Laden, who continues to threaten U.S. lives and property, presents a clear danger to the security of the U.S. and its citizens," he told a House hearing. Then he seemed to reverse himself as he declared, "We are prepared to work with the Taliban to rid Afghanistan of terrorist networks." It was clear that the administration had not made up its mind and was leaving the initiative to the other side. "The choice between cooperation and isolation lies with the Taliban," he said.

It would be well into 2001 before the academics would see Massoud as the best possible ally in a dire situation, but by the time the proposal came up for serious White House review, it was the eve of 9/11.

Until then, regime change in Afghanistan was "so far beyond the pale, at that time and under those circumstances, it was seen to be an unsellable option," said Pickering. "Nobody wanted to assume the liability for taking on a train wreck like Afghanistan and trying to bring it right. Everyone's feeling was that bin Laden was the problem and the Taliban was the host. Nobody was willing to say the invasion of Afghanistan was necessary." In hindsight, it was a flawed judgment. As P. J. Crowley put it, "If we knew then what we know now, we would have invaded in August 1998."

And where were those watchdogs of the American government, the news media? Obsessed with the Lewinsky scandal or chasing a story the administration wanted the public to focus on (NATO's armed intervention in Kosovo), American journalists paid scant attention to the growing maelstrom in South Asia. Had reporters been aware of the phenomenon of a terrorist with global reach hijacking a regime, and had they investigated, strong journalism could have emerged that would have stirred public debate. Conceivably, a politician closer to the center than Dana Rohrabacher would have called for a radical policy shift.* "If you guys had sort of been keeping the heat on the administration for stuff like this, it might not have turned out the same way," was Milam's judgment.[20]

Dodging the Bullet

In mid-March 1999, a half dozen feminists who had organized a campaign to protest Taliban discrimination against Afghan women met with President Clinton in the Oval Office. The mainstream press had ignored the Feminist Majority and its crusade against what it called "gender apartheid" in Afghanistan. "They were absolutely impenetrable" said Mavis Leno, wife of late-night television comedian Jay Leno, so she turned the drive into the Hollywood cause of the year and whipped up coverage in the celebrity magazines. The Feminist Majority gathered its own facts on the situation from women's groups throughout South Asia. The group had already claimed one major success against the Taliban—shaming the oil firm UNOCAL into dropping its plan to build a pipeline across Afghanistan, linking the rich fields of Turkmenistan with Pakistan. In late March, they held a glittering event for more than one thousand actors, singers, and guests; Clinton videotaped a message of support.

But in the hour they spent with him, they asked not for moral support but for "global and moral leadership." Plunging in where the experts feared to go, the delegation urged the president to "designate the Taliban as an international terrorist organization." Afghanistan had become a terrorist state, and its export of terrorism throughout Central Asia, together with its leading role in the production of raw opium, "creates major and multiple security risks for the United States and contributes to regional instability." They drew Clinton's attention to the transformation of the Taliban regime.

---

* Rohrabacher's impassioned attacks on State Department witnesses and his demands for internal documents to prove his contention that the administration was coddling the Taliban provoked ridicule from a fellow committee member, reducing his effectiveness. In one hearing, ranking Democrat Tom Lantos of California called Rohrabacher's claims "absurd and delusional" and his statement a "moment of levity and amusement," and challenged him to back up his contentions with evidence. HIRC subcommittee session, October 20, 1999.

"We knew the Taliban were a terrorist entity, one and the same as bin Laden and al Qaeda," said Leno. "We told him this." That no one else seemed aware of this mystified Leno. It seemed to her that the entire country was living "in a fool's paradise."

The women asked Clinton to withhold recognition of the Taliban until women's rights were "fully and permanently restored." And they demanded that all military and economic aid to Pakistan be conditioned on a halt to Pakistani support to the Taliban, and for an end to military sales to Saudi Arabia until its support ceased. Their ten-point memorandum referred in several spots to the plight of Afghan women, who after twenty years of war comprised as much as seventy percent of the refugee population. In essence, the memorandum amounted to a call for bringing down the Taliban. "Our role focused on U.S. policy to remove the Taliban. . . . We saw this as a threat to our own democracy," said Eleanor Smeal, president of the Feminist Majority. "We saw this as a threat to Pakistan, and thereby a threat to regional stability. We said there were major, multiple security risks to the United States."

On the crucial issue of national security, Clinton dodged the bullet. Instead (in typical constituency-service mode dispensed daily from Congress), he seized on a letter Smeal had brought along depicting the plight of two Afghan sisters—one who wanted to become a doctor, the other a lawyer—who had fled to Pakistan and were unable to get permission to emigrate to the United States. Smeal gave him statistics showing that for the previous five years, the United States had admitted only 103 Afghan refugees and asked that the number be increased to 25,000, equal to the number of Bosnians resettled in the United States.* Smeal recalled Clinton's reaction: "He grabs that letter and latches onto it. His whole thing was, 'We should start a scholarship program for girls.' He got obsessed with that."[†] In fact, the meeting led Clinton to issue a waiver allowing admission to any Afghan girl who had been denied education but had obtained a scholarship from an American institution.

Five years later, Smeal regretted bringing the letter. "I shouldn't have done that," she said. About the only comfort they got was on the question

---

* The admission rate dropped precipitously in the 1990s, from 1,233 in 1993 to 21 in 1994. Only four Afghan refugees were admitted in 1995; none in 1996 or 1997; and eighty-eight in 1998. After the Feminist Majority appeal, the numbers rose slightly to 365 in 1999, 1,709 in 2000, and 2,930 in 2001. Department of Homeland Security, *Yearbook of Immigration Statistics*, uscis.gov/graphics/shared/statistics/yearbook/2002/RA2002list.htm.

† The letter, which Leno read at a congressional hearing, was from an Afghan woman whose father was killed by the Taliban and who fled with her sister and mother to Pakistan. "I am 22 years old and, like all Afghan women, I am a victim of war and prejudice. Both my sister and I want to finish school. I hope to become a lawyer and my sister wishes to become a doctor. . . . I am afraid of what will happen to us. We do not have a future. I know I have very bad destiny. I cannot go to school. I do not have a job. I cannot take care of my old mother. I cannot take it any more. Why God made me a woman? Why should I suffer all the time? I feel hopeless and I would like to come out of this country." Leno testimony before Senate Appropriations Subcommittee on Foreign Operations, March 9, 1999.

of not recognizing the Taliban regime. "We asked him to tell us that the United States under his administration would never recognize the Taliban," Leno recalled. "He said it in a way that we actually believed him." He promised not to recognize the Taliban as the government of Afghanistan until the Taliban "improve their human rights record on women and girls."

The Feminist Majority never informed the media of their Oval Office meeting. This time they did not want public attention. "We were serious," said Smeal. "This wasn't a special interest thing. We were talking about something big." The aim was a change of policy. "We didn't care if we got an ounce of credit." Smeal said they left the meeting with "mixed emotions. He did treat us seriously. He did not appear condescending." But they did not get their point across that it was time to bring down the Taliban, according to an internal State Department memorandum summarizing the Oval Office session. The administration did not designate Afghanistan a terrorist state, although in October 1999 it added al Qaeda to the list of terrorist organizations.*

Two years after the meeting, the failure was patent. "We realized they weren't going to do it," Smeal said.[21]

By mid-1999, UN-led diplomacy in Afghanistan was drying up as rapidly as American hope for decapitating bin Laden.

Snow was still blocking the key passes when Brahimi, in late January, launched a new diplomatic round by inviting deputy ministers of the warring parties to secret talks. The February meeting in Ashgabat, Turkmenistan, led to a second in March, at which both sides agreed to form a shared executive branch, a shared legislature, and a shared judiciary, in addition to conducting a prisoner exchange.

The breakthrough was short-lived. Omar's close aide, Abdul Wakil Muttawakil, and Massoud's deputy, Mohammad Yunus Qanooni, could not agree even on a cease-fire. The deal breaker was Taliban insistence that the proposed new government report to the Islamic Emirate. Massoud said he could not accept the emirate, because the Taliban had neither a popular nor a legal mandate to govern or to dictate terms. Omar called a *shura* of clerics and, on April 10, ruled out further talks, insisting that there be a "unified command" under his leadership. "That is what the

---

* The ten "Recommendations for U.S. Policy to End Gender Apartheid in Afghanistan" were as follows: oppose recognition of the Taliban by the United States government and the United Nations; convene a global summit of world leaders on gender apartheid in Afghanistan; do not resume military assistance to Pakistan, but condition Pakistan aid on withdrawal of Pakistan support from Taliban; condition weapons sales to Saudi Arabia on withdrawal of support from the Taliban; designate the Taliban as an international terrorist organization; refuse support to U.S. companies that do business with the Taliban; increase admission of Afghan women refugees to the United States and urge other countries to accept Afghan women refugees; oppose forced repatriation of Afghan refugees; increase aid for programs for Afghan women and girls in Afghanistan and Pakistan; and separate Afghan/Pakistan management desks at the State Department, the United States Agency for International Development, and the United States Information Service. Feminist Majority Foundation, Arlington, Virginia.

people want," he said,* not a joint government with people who had "plundered" the country.[22]

Fighting had already begun. In late February, Hezbi Wahdat forces came down from their mountain refuge and recaptured the town of Yakow-lang at the western end of Bamiyan Valley. Surprised at the overrunning of their garrison, the Taliban arrested more than five hundred townspeople, including those on the quisling Taliban council, and transferred them to faraway prisons.† After local civilians staged an uprising in late March in villages west of Bamiyan, the Taliban destroyed and burned houses and forcibly evacuated other villages. Wahdat held the province for three weeks, but the Taliban massed a force of four thousand and recaptured it on May 9. The Taliban apparently invited traditional rivals of the Hazara, armed Kochi nomads, and Pashtuns with land claims in the region to join in the fighting. Tens of thousands from Bamiyan and Yakawlang took to the mountains; during their absence, much of the housing stock of the valley was systematically destroyed.

"The sheer scale of destruction indicates that it was clearly organized by the military command as a form of collective punishment, rather than as any form of discriminating retaliation against known figures," wrote Michael Semple, a UN humanitarian aid observer. Bamiyan houses, usually consisting of rooms around the edge of a large courtyard, were doused with gasoline on all sides and then ignited. Semple wrote that 15 percent of the houses were totally destroyed and another 21 percent partially destroyed. When the Hazaras returned, the Kuchis exacted their payoff by setting up checkpoints, searching and taxing vehicles, and collecting weapons to be sold.

Kamal Hossain, a former Bangladesh foreign minister who had succeeded Choong-Hyun Paik as special rapporteur for human rights, seized on the events in Bamiyan to develop a new relationship with the Taliban. After interviewing refugees from Hazarajat in Quetta, Pakistan, he reported that there had been "vicious" attacks against civilians, including the summary execution of women and children, forced displacement, looting and burning of homes, arbitrary detention, and the use of forced labor. Hossain presented his allegations in person to Muttawakil in late May.

Something clicked: on June 8, Muttawakil informed Hossain in writing that Mullah Omar had issued a special decree banning house burning. It fell short of Hossain's concerns, and now he insisted that the Taliban

---

*In fact, that is what the Taliban military commanders wanted. According to former Taliban foreign ministry official Vahid Mojdeh, military commanders, who stood to lose substantial income as well as control over the income of their troops, blocked every UN peace initiative. Mojdeh, unpublished manuscript, 32.

† The ousted Taliban administration in Yakawlang blamed the defeat on overreporting of troop numbers by Taliban allied commanders, who were being paid by the Ministry of Defense according to the number of soldiers they claimed. Mojdeh, unpublished manuscript.

issue an order to halt summary executions and arbitrary detentions, hold an inquest into the crimes the militia had allegedly committed, and permit him to travel to the Hazarajat to investigate on the spot.[23] Although the Taliban never gave him permission to travel, Omar eventually issued an edict "forbidding the mujahideen from killing women and children" as well as captured combatants and old men.*

With a Taliban summer offensive in the offing, Brahimi made a last-gasp effort at peace talks in mid-July, inviting Taliban and United Front representatives as observers to a meeting with deputy foreign ministers from the six-plus-two group in Tashkent, Uzbekistan. The Taliban threatened a boycott unless they were invited as the government of Afghanistan but finally attended, at Pakistan's urging, as an Afghan "group." The sole accomplishment at Tashkent was that the six neighboring countries, along with the United States and Russia, signed a pledge "not to provide military support to any Afghan sides and to prevent the use of our territories for such purposes." It was a high-order hypocrisy. Everyone knew that Pakistan was providing vital support to the Taliban; and while the Clinton administration was reluctant to assist directly, it never challenged Russian or Iranian assistance to the United Front. "We called it the "six-minus-two," Inderfurth said.

Brahimi had wanted a six-week cease-fire, an exchange of prisoners to build mutual confidence, and political talks between the warring parties. But the two-hour meeting ended without even a statement. Taliban information minister Amir Khan Muttaqi insisted on recognition of the emirate; a "single, central, and national army and security force"; and a central government, conditions Abdullah Abdullah, representing the United Front, could not accept.

Power sharing was out of the question, and so was peace. American mediation also was not in great demand, certainly not by the Taliban following the imposition of U.S. sanctions two weeks earlier. "It is stupid to make peace in the presence of Americans," Muttaqi said afterward. At a separate meeting, Inderfurth warned Muttaqi that the United States would be "forced to take further actions" if bin Laden was not brought to justice. But he had neither carrot nor stick to hand.

---

* Omar's edict read as follows: "We order you gravely and severely to refrain from killing women and children, irrespective of the party with which they are affiliated. And if there falls into your hands combatants or elderly men, we forbid you from killing them without permission, even if the field commanders order you to kill them. [That is] because, according to Shariah, the order given by the General Emir is more deserving of being obeyed then other orders. So you must give precedence to this priority, as we know that taking a Muslim's life is a cause of defeat. So we order you, O brothers, to exert caution in this matter, adhere to humility, and avoid shortcomings, as the Jihad must be purely for Allah's sake. As for victory and defeat and taking revenge for martyrs, those are things over which man has no power, so leave it for Allah, the able. We order you to abide by what we have commanded you with. And he who transgresses in this matter has no right to complain." The exact date for the edict is not known, but former Taliban say it was after one of the offensives in Bamiyan.

The evening after the talks ended, Ahmed Shah Massoud turned up in Tashkent to call on Uzbek president Islam Karimov, who had previously backed only Dostum, Brahimi, and Inderfurth.

"What is the solution?" Inderfurth asked Massoud at the start of their ninety-minute meeting. The guerrilla leader said it was to strengthen the opposition and apply diplomatic and political pressure on Pakistan to stop supporting the Taliban. He did not ask for military aid. Abdullah, who was interpreting that evening, said Massoud's reluctance was because the United States would not recognize the resistance as legitimate. "If there isn't any moral support, how do you expect material support?" he said. "It wasn't that we didn't see it as necessary. We thought it was just impossible at that stage."

But Inderfurth said neither Massoud nor Abdullah ever sought military aid in meetings with him. "I would ask them, 'How are you doing in the field?' And the answer was, 'We are okay.'" Inderfurth assumed that aid requests were going to the CIA, anyway. Had Massoud sought military aid that evening in Tashkent, Inderfurth would have returned to Washington with the message: "Look, they're saying they need help. Does that change our calculation?" In the absence of such a request, Inderfurth concluded that Massoud's forces were getting what they needed from other sources and that they would not be defeated on the battlefield. The assumption needed a reality check. The bold commander was a reticent politician, loath to plead for help. This baffled his brother Walid. "He never, ever asked. It happened many, many times," he said. The Taliban had delayed their summer offensive at Brahimi's express request, and now the embargo was lifted.

"We are ready to attack the enemy, which will be destroyed," Muttaqi said, as the Tashkent talks broke up. "The opposition has to accept the Taliban system of government. There can be no compromise." Tashkent proved to be the last serious UN-led attempt to mediate a peaceful resolution of the conflict.[24]

At dawn on July 28, black-turbaned Taliban fighters in the Afghan 4WD cavalry (Toyota pickup trucks) launched a five-pronged offensive across the heavily populated Shamali plains north of Kabul. This fertile area—about thirty-five miles long and six to eighteen miles across—was well-irrigated and full of vineyards, orchards, and fields growing wheat, other cereal grains, and vegetables to serve Kabul. With as many as 50,000 troops, including 3,000–5,000 Pakistani "volunteers" and 400 Arabs fighting under the banner of bin Laden's 055 Brigade (according to the United Front), the movement announced its plan to destroy what remained of the armed resistance. Supported by tanks, artillery barrages, and aerial bombardment, the Taliban captured Bagram Air Base three days later and, in short order, Charikar (the capital of Parwan province) and Muhumud-i-Raqi (capital of Kapisa province). Massoud's forces, estimated at 15,000 with another 30,000 less-trained reserves, fell back to the Panjshir Valley, where they dynamited the entrance to the gorge as they had several times in the past. Mullah Omar called on the United Front to surrender and offered a general amnesty.

"This organized withdrawal gave the enemies a sense of victory, euphoria, and the impression that our forces had been routed," Massoud later told a Russian reporter. "They very soon saw that they were cruelly mistaken." The wily commander, master of the tactical retreat, was waiting for the right moment; on August 5, he counterattacked. The Taliban had failed to construct defensive lines or conduct mop-up operations; within two days, Massoud's forces had recaptured Bagram and the two provincial capitals and were back in control of practically all the territory they had lost. It was a rout for the militia, and Omar issued an appeal for help from the madrassas in Pakistan's northwest frontier province. Seminary leaders closed the schools, and thousands of students headed into Afghanistan. But however much Shamali represented a military disaster for the Taliban, it was an immense human tragedy for the mainly Tajik inhabitants. The Taliban had set the pattern in Bamiyan. The level of destruction in 1999, according to Semple, was far in excess of anything seen during the 1992–1995 battles for Kabul. About 250,000 civilians were displaced in the course of the year, the largest involuntary population movement in Afghanistan since the battles for Kabul.

"They shot my father, and I saw it," 10-year-old Mohammad Wali told the *New York Times* in October 1999. Mohammad's mother was taken away, and he was in the care of an aunt in Bazarak in the Panjshir Valley, where 65,000 refugees lived in makeshift tents of cloth and plastic in dread of the coming winter. Mohammad was one of "the irretrievably broken . . . the unbearably sorrowful . . . the children of parents who were killed as they watched or the men whose wives were carried off screaming," wrote reporter Barry Bearak. The witnesses who described the "binge of blood lust and mayhem" spoke in consistent detail. The Taliban and their Pakistani volunteers had gone "on a destructive spree . . . killing wantonly, emptying entire towns, machine-gunning livestock, sawing down fruit trees, blasting apart irrigation canals."

The United Nations accused the Taliban of executing at least seventy-two captured male civilians in groups, but dozens more must have been shot gangland-style, like Mohammad's father. Hossain also charged that the Taliban had forced the displacement of at least 125,000 civilians, separated thousands of women and children in camps, and systematically destroyed homes, fruit-bearing trees and other agriculture in the Shamali plains, and irrigation systems. Taliban officials asserted that they were only clearing a protective strip two hundred yards on either side of the main road, but Kamal Hossain said independent reports noted that homes and villages far from any main road had been destroyed. The Taliban acknowledged transporting 1,800 families to a desolate camp in Jalalabad on the grounds that the opposition had used civilians and their homes "as human shields."

The destruction was methodical. "Initially, houses were burnt, then bulldozers were sent in to flatten the rubble, and teams of conscript workers were deployed to level the area, cutting down trees and vines," Semple wrote. Some three thousand unarmed conscripts were mobilized to carry out the destruction. Many of them were prisoners taken during the Bamiyan conflict, who saw their own houses burned and then were used as slave labor in camps and released only after they had cut their quota of trees. The earth-moving equipment came from government departments. Conscripts who returned from taking part in the destruction related that they had instructions "to raze everything" within a half mile of the main road, but Semple said it appeared more like collective punishment than a military tactic.[25]

In September, the Taliban transferred as many as five thousand men, along with pickup trucks, artillery, and armor, to the north to attack Massoud's strongholds in Kunduz and Takhar provinces, but the operation degenerated into a raid. In the face of counterattacks, the Taliban lost all the positions they had conquered. They also attacked Darra Souf, a trading post in the north central province of Samangan and the base of operations for the Hezbi Wahdat. The Taliban captured the bazaar in July but lost it again in October.

A new pattern of crimes emerged in the course of 1999, with women and civilian property the principal targets. In central and northern Afghanistan, Hossain reported that "many" Hazara and Tajik women and girls had been removed from their houses by force and abducted from their villages. Women from Mazar-i-Sharif, Pul-i-Khumri, and Shamali were rounded up and forced onto trucks, and there were reports of women killed or maimed trying to escape from these trucks. Eyewitnesses saw trucks and cars full of Afghan women on the road to Kandahar and Pakistan, and many suspected that the women and girls were forced into prostitution. Women from Kabul, Mazar-i-Sharif, and Shamali gave accounts of "many instances" of forced marriages. "Taliban reportedly enter houses in Kabul and in new territory they conquer and force the families of young girls and women to conclude a *nikah* (marriage contract) and thus marry them to Taliban members or to give them a large sum of money instead."

"There are endless cases . . . thousands," according to Ali Jalali, the postwar minister of the interior. Girls as young as eleven or twelve years of age were taken from their families at gunpoint and forced to marry. "You could take a girl under that law, under that sharia interpretation of Taliban, and bring a mullah, and he will say something about what sharia requires, and that is it."*

---

*The postwar education minister, Sharif Fayez, said he had evidence from "many sources" that Mullah Omar would issue a "wedding contract" to Taliban fighters that permitted them to take women by force and call them their wives. "Fighters, when they raided a town, raided the women," Fayez said. There were "a lot of rumors" that these women were then sold to Arabs. Sharif Fayez, interview by author, Kabul, July 2003.

Afghanistan had a tradition of the "phony war," in which commanders feign conflict to obtain resources of the war economy but avoid destructive clashes. By contrast, every Taliban offensive in 1999 was marked by wanton destruction of civilian property, wiping out livelihoods and living quarters, according to Semple. The areas they attacked—Bamiyan, Shamali, Takhar, and Darra Souf—had been relatively prosperous despite the years of conflict. By late 1999, Taliban attacks had reduced them to penury. Shamali—the bread, fruit, and vegetable basket for Kabul—was largely scorched earth. In Bamiyan, the Taliban destroyed two-thirds of the livestock and commercial vehicles, and systematically looted shops. Prosperous farmers had bought trucks to carry their goods to faraway markets; 180 trucks were burned or commandeered, an irreversible loss, reducing farmers to relying on international charity. In Darra Souf, shops were torched with their stock, and the wheat harvest was burned on the threshing floors.[26]

Clinton's decision not to alter policy radically but to support sanctions against both Pakistan and Afghanistan would set back U.S. interests in both countries.

In Afghanistan, the strategic failure to see the enemy of our enemy as our friend left a vacuum of American influence in the internal struggle that Pakistan was ready to fill, although in the opposite fashion from that sought by the administration. Repeated U.S. demands on the Taliban to cough up bin Laden, with no coercion attached, drove the Saudi renegade closer to Mullah Omar and Pakistan closer to the Taliban.

The administration's stated aim in Pakistan was to prevent thermonuclear war, but after nearly a decade of military sanctions, and now trade restrictions, for testing a nuclear deterrent in response to the actions of archrival India, the Pakistan military and political elite saw little reason to cooperate on any issue, including the implementation of sanctions against Afghanistan. Without Pakistani cooperation, there was no hope of imposing penalties on Afghanistan. Beyond that, Thomas Pickering, America's highest-ranking professional diplomat, recalled that Pakistanis had a "crucifixion complex"—an attitude of "Go ahead and kill me. I'm ready to take it all. See how bad things will get."[27]

The crisis that finally crippled what remained of American influence in pre-9/11 Pakistan started as an armed conflict between Pakistan and India and ended with yet another Pakistani military coup. In winter 1999, Pakistan's armed forces, under the command of General Pervez Musharraf, Karamat's successor as chief of staff, crossed the agreed-upon line of separation into Kargil, a remote part of Indian-controlled Kashmir. With Kashmiri militants in tow, the Pakistanis occupied a number of Indian army posts that had been abandoned, as was the annual routine when snows blanketed the Himalayan highlands. British reporter Jason Burke observed hundreds of Harkat-ul-Mujahideen (HUM) fighters being "used as auxiliaries" to run supplies "under shellfire up to the Pakistani soldiers in the forward positions."*

Not until May did Indian intelligence discover the breach ten miles into its territory. Alarmed that Pakistan had gained command of the key ridges over the only road between Srinagar (the capital of Jammu and Kashmir State) and Ladakh (the easternmost region), India sent in its ground troops. Fierce fighting erupted in late May and early June 1999, along a 100-mile front, but India could not dislodge Pakistani forces from their positions at fifteen thousand feet, even with Bofors guns and air power.

As casualties mounted into the hundreds, Clinton sent Zinni to Islamabad to demand that Pakistan withdraw. Instead, under Musharraf's command, Pakistani forces seemed to be preparing for a showdown, according to an account by a former White House aide, Bruce Riedel. U.S. intelligence picked up signs that Pakistan's military was preparing its nuclear arsenal for possible deployment. Fearing complete loss of control, Prime Minister Nawaz Sharif flew to Washington on July 4, 1999, to seek U.S. mediation. "He wanted desperately to find a solution that would allow Pakistan to withdraw with some cover," recounted Riedel, who was the notetaker at the discussions. The outcome was a joint statement in which Pakistan promised to withdraw its forces.[28]

The crisis ended within days but led to an internal confrontation between the prime minister and his armed forces chief. Still smarting over the pullback from Kargil, and with public opinion (and the political opposition) on his side, Musharraf threw down the gauntlet by publicly committing his support behind the Taliban. In a speech in Karachi in August 1999, Musharraf said the Taliban military record was a "success story" highlighted by "spectacular military successes," regardless of temporary setbacks such as Mazar-i-Sharif in 1997. The "historic commonality" between Afghan and Pakistani Pashtuns had to be "recognized," he said, a statement that Pakistanis and Afghans might interpret in very different ways. Musharraf even claimed that the Taliban religious radicalism and zealotry could be tempered in due course to bring them around to the Pakistani mindset. Nawaz swung further into the American camp by publicly pressing the anti-Taliban cause, all but ensuring a collision with Musharraf.

The clash between the two men encapsulated Pakistan's quandary. As one commentator wrote, "The dilemma we must face, sooner or later, remains implicit in our traditional dependence on America and our declared recognition of the Taliban Afghanistan. How long could we keep on riding the two mismatched and skittish horses at the same time? . . . We are left with the onerous task of proving our credentials to two sworn enemies as a friend of both."

---

* HUM, through its previous incarnation as Harkat-ul-Ansar (HUA), was on the U.S. list of terrorist organizations; many of those killed at Khost in August 1998 were HUM volunteers.

Nawaz had been playing both sides, reassuring the Clinton administration that he took its concerns seriously but not informing his own cabinet and certainly not taking any action. His top aides professed ignorance about the ties between Omar and bin Laden.

"Bin Laden and al Qaeda was hardly a word known here," said Gohar Ayub Khan, the Pakistani foreign secretary from mid-1997 to mid-1998. "I visited a good thirty-five countries during that one year I was foreign minister, and nobody raised the issue with me. I didn't know what the hell is al Qaeda until these missiles landed in Afghanistan." His successor, Sartaj Aziz, said he was "absolutely" unaware that thousands of Arabs were living in Kabul and taking part in the Taliban fighting. "I was not aware of the influence, scale, and presence of bin Laden and his team. We had hardly heard of al Qaeda as an organization."*

Were they in denial? Was this a self-serving explanation for a flawed policy? Did they base their assertions on the reporting of Colonel Imam, Pakistan's eyes and ears outside Kabul, who claimed to outsiders that bin Laden was only an occasional visitor to Kandahar? Or was Nawaz keeping them in the dark? Nawaz's able spokesman, Mushahid Hussain, said he was unaware of the role the Arab forces played inside Afghanistan until after 9/11, when he heard about it from Colonel Imam.[29]

Amid rumblings of an impending coup, Nawaz decided to switch horses. At encounters starting at the end of 1998, Clinton had pressed Nawaz for help in capturing bin Laden. Nawaz proposed setting up a Pakistani commando group to do the job. His ISI director, Lt. Gen. Khwaja Ziauddin, proposed that CIA officers train a commando force of sixty retired Pakistani Special Forces officers to snatch bin Laden. "I can't have American soldiers come and do that. What if you help me create a unit that can do raids with my guys? You give us the intelligence, and we can cross the border and do these things," he told Gary Schroen. Schroen obtained funding, trainers, intelligence, communications equipment, and Toyota Hilux 4 x 4 trucks.

Clinton was skeptical but approved the project. "The Pakistani military was full of Taliban and al Qaeda sympathizers," he wrote in his memoirs. "But I thought we had nothing to lose by exploring every option." Sandy Berger viewed it as a "cockamamie" scheme, Pickering viewed it as a "charade," and the CIA had "no confidence" in it.

Nawaz sent Ziauddin to Kandahar in early October 1999 with urgent demands. Ziauddin had a powerful dislike for Mullah Omar and for the

---

* The two foreign ministers also denied any knowledge of the August 1998 massacre at Mazar-i-Sharif. "The massacres weren't known in these parts as such," said Gohar, who was departing office as they occurred. According to Sartaj Aziz, "We were not at all aware . . . at the time, this was not even highlighted or mentioned. Otherwise we would have expressed our abhorrence." Sartaj suggested that in killing civilians, the Taliban "took their revenge" for what Malik's troops had done to the Taliban a year earlier.

Taliban. Afghanistan had turned into a "breeding ground for terrorists," he told Omar. More than 200 Pakistanis had received military training in Afghan camps, carried out terrorist incidents in Pakistan, and then fled back across the border. The latest was the killing of dozens of Pakistani Shias in a series of sectarian attacks.

It was a late awakening to a reality that was widely known. When U.S. cruise missiles struck the Khost camp during the August 1998 attacks, most of the victims were Pakistanis training for guerrilla warfare in Kashmir. Ziauddin demanded that the Taliban hand over the two most-wanted men —Riaz Basra and Saifullah Aktar—along with at least 150 others, and close the training camps. Omar promised to look into the matter. "We have asked Taliban to wind up these training camps. This practice should be stopped," Nawaz said at a news conference October 7.

Nawaz's last step (in more than one sense) was to fly to Abu Dhabi on October 11 to seek the support of the United Arab Emirates, the only other country maintaining active diplomatic and trade ties with Kandahar. Accompanying him on the flight were his son Hussain Nawaz, his speech-writer, and Ziauddin. The flight allowed them to talk without fear of being bugged about Nawaz's plan, which had been gathering strength, to fire Mu-sharraf. While in Abu Dhabi, Nawaz proposed a get-tough policy requir-ing the Taliban to close all training camps, extradite the Pakistani militants, and expel bin Laden—exactly what Washington had sought. But that was as far as Nawaz ever got.

On October 12, as Musharraf was playing golf in Sri Lanka, Nawaz decided to remove him and install Ziauddin as head of the armed services. When the nine army corps commanders refused to go along, Nawaz ordered flight controllers to block Musharraf's commercial plane from landing in Karachi, and Ziauddin ordered his U.S.-funded commandos onto the streets to support Nawaz. But after taking a look around, they "disap-peared like a sand castle in a tide," Schroen recalled. Nawaz's attempted ouster of Musharraf gave way to a military coup. The Pakistan military arrested Nawaz, lifted the hold on Musharraf's aircraft, and installed him as chief executive.[30]

In Washington, the speed of the drama came as a shock. U.S. influence in the Pakistani officer corps plummeted, and all hopes for cooperation in Afghanistan soured. Suddenly, the relationship went cold.

In place of Ziauddin, Musharraf appointed Mahmoud Ahmed, an artillery officer who had been the frontline commander at Kargil and on October 12 had ordered troops to arrest Nawaz during the failed coup. Ahmed traveled to Washington shortly after taking over and received the CIA grand tour. "We had a very, very nice visit with him," recounted Schroen, who by now was deputy chief of the agency's Near East division. "We hosted him. Took him to Gettysburg and all that stuff. I thought we had made some progress." On his return, Mahmoud shut down all contact with the CIA station other than perfunctory memos back and forth; CIA officials did not see him until the eve of the 9/11 attack. He was, in Sandy Berger's eyes, a "known Taliban supporter."

Making matters worse, Musharraf appointed as chief of the general staff Lt. Gen. Mir Aziz Khan, former head of the ISI's Afghan bureau, where he had the reputation of being a pro-Taliban hawk. When Inderfurth called on Musharraf in mid-January 2000, the Pakistan leader promised to travel to Kandahar in person. "I intend to meet Mullah Omar. I think I can get through to Mullah Omar," Inderfurth recalled him saying. "I'll take a sleeping bag with me. I will sleep on the floor. We will find a way to make those points to him." Inderfurth doubted his sincerity and reported back that Pakistan was unlikely to do anything, "given what it sees as the benefits of Taliban control of Afghanistan." Musharraf never went. "He never took his sleeping bag," Inderfurth recalled. The sole gain in the debacle was in the U.S. bureaucracy: at the State Department, regionalists recouped some of the voice they had lost to the antiproliferation lobby in 1998.[31]

The year 1999 was a chaotic one in Afghanistan. As the world's governments, NGOs, and the news media turned their focus elsewhere, the country spiraled rapidly downhill.

In late August, Mullah Omar was the target of a truck-bomb assassination attempt; forty people were killed, including two of his brothers, a brother-in-law, fourteen bodyguards, and six Arab nationals staying in a guesthouse adjacent to his home. But Omar emerged unscathed. Earlier, family members of prominent Taliban critics had been assassinated—the wife and son and bodyguard of Abdul Haq were shot as they slept in Peshawar in January; and Abdul Karzai, a former deputy speaker of the Afghan senate and father of Hamid Karzai, was gunned down in Quetta days after he had returned from the United States.

The Taliban turned a deaf ear to UN pleas for a negotiated end to the war but proved incompetent to turn the tide militarily. They instead resorted to a systematic pattern of crimes against noncombatants. Other than the United Nations, the world was not monitoring the internal war, but thousands of Pakistani militants, hundreds of Arabs, and an unknown number of Central Asian Islamics were now involved as volunteers. "This is extremely dangerous," Brahimi said in a July interview. "I think Pakistan, Arab countries, and any Central Asian countries with nationals fighting there would ask themselves, what are these young people going to do when they come home? Some of these volunteers have agendas elsewhere." In August, Nawaz Sharif expressed concern to Brahimi that there were a "large number of Pakistani nationals in a conflict in a neighboring country"; by early October, in a bid to gain U.S. backing in his internal political struggle, Nawaz had changed course. But that policy was reversed by the mid-October coup.

That same month, the State Department formally designated al Qaeda as a "foreign terrorist organization," and the UN Security Council approved sanctions against Afghanistan unless it turned over bin Laden within thirty days. In practical terms, the sanctions only meant discontinuation of Ariana airline flights to its one regular destination, the United Arab Emirates. Neither the designation nor the sanctions "had much additional practical effect," according to the 9/11 Commission. "The sanctions were easily circumvented, and there were no multilateral mechanisms to ensure that other countries' financial systems were not used as conduits for terrorist funding."

This was the end of the road for UN–led diplomacy, and Brahimi, in an almost unprecedented move, gave up the post on October 20. Citing "the meagerness of the results achieved after two years of fruitless efforts" and the disappointment arising from the negative attitudes of the Afghan sides, in particular the Taliban positions, he told reporters, "I have tried everything I know, and it has not been of much use. . . . At this stage . . . somebody like me has no role." One diplomat who worked with him summed up the reasons for his failure as Pakistani sabotage and U.S. lack of interest. As for Brahimi, "He did not have any carrots to offer both sides."

About the only thing flourishing on the plains of Afghanistan at this stage was opium poppy, whose fast-expanding production was having a pernicious spillover effect on neighboring countries as well as worldwide addiction. The United Nations estimated that Afghanistan produced up to half the world's opium in 1998, with almost all the cultivation of opium poppy under control of the Taliban. This got worse in 1999, when Afghanistan became by far the world's biggest illicit producer of opium, producing 75 percent of all opium worldwide. Land under opium poppy cultivation increased 43 percent to some 91,000 hectares (225,000 acres or 350 square miles) in 104 districts, up from 73 districts in 1993. The Taliban profited from production, taking 2 percent profit, according to Foreign Minister Muttawakil.

Any hope for outside investment seemed out of the question. The Feminist Majority believed it had killed UNOCAL's plans for a gas pipeline in 1998, but Pakistan and Turkmenistan, both of which had strategic reasons for developing a north-south pipeline, signed a three-way declaration of intent with the Taliban in late April 1999. "We were very keen that this pipeline go through," said Gohar Ayub Khan, the former Pakistani foreign minister. Inside the Kabul government, however, the plan was already seen as dead. The U.S. missile strike in August 1998 "made it impossible for American companies to continue on the pipeline project" so long as the Taliban were in control of Afghanistan, according to former Foreign Ministry official Vahid Mojdeh. The Argentine firm Bridas (UNOCAL's rival) kept an office in Kabul, but aware that working with the Taliban might raise suspicions that it was cooperating with international terrorism, it was completely inactive.

The Taliban Style of War

If there was little reason for confidence in the prospects for peace or economic development, there was equally little reason in late 1999 to think the Taliban could solve their number one security challenge: taking charge of the state's territory and all its borders. Brilliant strategy in the conquest of Kabul and a determined drive to conquer the north had given way to a lazy reliance on cannon fodder and logistics—enormous numbers of fighters and Japanese pickup trucks, deployed in World War I–style forward charges, followed by scorched earth, terror, and crimes.

The Taliban seemed incapable of creating and leading the military force it needed to assert control over the entire territory. After five years of fighting, Taliban conscripts still went into battle in sandals, disdaining boots because they would interfere with the requirement to doff foot coverings for the ritual ablutions prior to the five daily prayers. "They were fighting 100 percent in flip-flops," said Nic Robertson of CNN, one of the more frequent media visitors to Taliban Afghanistan. Pakistani reporter Hamid Mir said, "I saw many people heading for the front lines with rocket launchers, *barefooted.*" The Taliban had never set up a defense ministry or a general staff. Orders to frontline commanders came directly from Mullah Omar and were to be obeyed absolutely.

Every commander was responsible for his troops, and the defense minister, Obaidullah Akhund, was in charge of logistics. "You went to him to get something from him," said one commander. "I went once every two to three months. I sent my representative weekly for logistics and food." Arabs and Pakistanis had their own areas of command at the front line. There were no tactics or strategy. They would just sit down and say, 'Attack.' If we were on the top of a ridge, they would say, 'Tomorrow we attack this village.'" As battles unfolded, commanders had no way of coordinating the front lines. This commander said, "One part of the front advanced, but another had no advance. When the one was defeated, the other one collapsed."

"Without exaggeration, the Taliban military commanders were probably the most careless commanders in the world with respect to the lives of their subordinates," wrote Vahid Mojdeh. "They never learned their lessons from others' experiences and their own on the battlefield. By employing only one strategy repeatedly in vastly different regions, they ensured a heavy casualty load. They never arranged their line of battle in an orderly fashion so as to cut down on casualties. Time and again this question created conflicts between them and the Arab and Pakistani fighters and resulted in their many defeats." Bin Laden was contemptuous of Taliban fighting style, in particular their preference for fighting without boots. In his 1998 interview with Hamid Mir, bin Laden said he had written a letter to the Afghan clerics stating that "it is against Islam to go into the fight against the enemy unprepared." Both bin Laden and Abu Hafs would say, "It is crazy," Mir said.[32]

HRW quoted a retired senior Pakistan military officer who estimated that up to 30 percent of Taliban fighting strength was composed of Pakistanis serving in units organized by Pakistani political parties. HRW estimated that at least eight thousand other troops were foreigners, mainly Arabs from Gulf states and North Africa. It quoted Pakistani volunteers taken prisoner by the United Front as saying they were trained at Rishkor, a base near Kabul, and that as many as twenty-five Pakistani military and intelligence personnel trainers lived in a guarded area in the camp. They described their trainers as being "in their forties, military in appearance and speech, and frequently multilingual," speaking English in addition to Pashto, and in many cases Arabic or Urdu.

Whatever role Pakistanis played in training, former Taliban commanders interviewed for this book could not attest that Pakistani officers were involved in combat. "I didn't see it," said a former senior intelligence commander. "There were many Talibs and many dressed up as Talibs. But they may not have been Talibs." An Urdu-speaking former UN official said that if Pakistan had senior officials there, he did not spot them. "I would award a prize to the ISI for being discreet. I didn't chance upon senior officers," he said. According to Mojdeh, Pakistan's People's Party sent technicians when the Taliban arrived in Kabul, to advise on logistics, finance, engineering issues, and training. Still, the Pakistanis do not seem in any sense to have swung much weight in the fighting or brought much advantage, other than numbers, to the Taliban.

The Arab contingent was a very different story. Eventually they comprised 10 percent of the front line; they were trained militants ready to fight to the death and were the most feared by Massoud's commanders. Unlike Pakistani volunteers, who fought in what they believed was a jihad against a Russian-backed opponent, the Arabs "did not interpret the war between the Taliban and Massoud as a holy war," according to Mojdeh. "The Arabs were following their own interests. They wanted their troops to get trained." On occasion, bin Laden or Abu Hafs would deploy brigades of highly skilled, highly motivated men from the specialized training camps. Arab jihadis were the most feared and they carried scimitars, but the Taliban probably did most of the killing of civilians, according to UN observers. One former UN observer said the Arabs "did not take on the overall strategy, but let the Afghans think they were running their strategy. Insofar as was a strategy, the Afghans ran it." What the Arabs did, however, often was highly strategic. For example, in the September 1998 capture of Bamiyan, one major contribution of Arab fighters was to force their way through the strategic Ghorband Valley east of Bamiyan, thereby opening the way to the main valley for the Taliban forces.

Their role would grow over time. "They were very important, the hard core, the front line," Abdullah recalled. "To capture one was a very difficult job, because they were fighting to the end." During fighting in Charikar in 1998, four Arabs about to be captured locked their arms around each other in a circle and blew themselves up with a single grenade. In an epic battle for Taloqan, the Arabs controlled the front line and mounted seventeen major offensives against the city, he recalled. "Arabs were very brave," said former commander Gul Haidar. "Because of their courage, they fought to the death. On every front where there were Arabs, we would make very slow progress. When we attacked, unless they were dead, we couldn't catch them. Even if they were caught in a very tight corner, even if they didn't have bullets, they would blow themselves up." He recounted a battle to control a mountain where twenty Arabs occupied the caves. "There was a military post at the top of the mountain. We couldn't capture it until we killed every one of them. One of our commanders, Karandol, controlled it for one hour. He faced a huge offensive from Arabs. It was nighttime. We couldn't see how many there were. We were hearing their voices over the radio." Even for the Taliban, it was difficult to coordinate with the Arab fighters. "They were in the front lines of Shamali," said an Afghan humanitarian aid official who spoke Arabic. "Three or four times, I was asked by [Taliban] commanders to inform the Arabs of something. They said, 'They are not 101 percent within our command. We do not speak their language.'"[33]

Along with Arabs and Pakistanis, fighters began to arrive from around Central Asia, and bin Laden was the welcoming committee. Two Uzbek insurgents, Juma Namangani and Taher Yoldashov, are said to have met bin Laden in 1997. The following year, they jointly announced in Kabul the founding of the Islamic Movement of Uzbekistan (IMU) and a jihad to overthrow Uzbek president Islam Karimov and establish an Islamic state. Bin Laden provided the seed money for the IMU, according to Pakistani journalist Ahmed Rashid, citing U.S. officials. The IMU, in turn, supplied as many as 600 armed fighters from Uzbekistan and other Central Asian states to the Taliban, starting in 1997. After the Taliban conquered Mazar-i-Sharif in 1998, the IMU was given a military training camp close to the Uzbek border. Namangani and Yoldashov used Afghanistan as a jumping-off point for attacks in the Ferghana Valley, which links Uzbekistan, Kyrgyzstan, and Tajikistan. Yoldashov had a headquarters in the Tymeni district of Kabul that became a gathering place for Uzbeks, Tajiks, Chechens, Kyrghiz, Cossacks, and even Uighurs from China's Sinkiang region.

The relationship with the Taliban was symbiotic. "In Afghanistan," Rashid wrote, "these groups fight for the Taliban, and in return they receive military training, battle experience, weapons, funding, access to the drug trade, and contacts with the whole world of Islamic radicalism." This was not the only Afghan-Uzbek connection—for years, as long as he was in Afghanistan and even after his exile in 1998, Karimov provided ample aid to Dostum. Mullah Omar, for his part, hoped the formation of an Uzbek force in Afghanistan—bringing together Uzbeks, Turkmen, and other Afghans—would "forever eliminate" support for Dostum among northern Afghanistan Uzbeks. Instead, what happened was that Yoldashov demanded a voice in any future Taliban party policy toward Central Asia.

"Afghanistan," Kofi Annan said in his final report on the subject in November 1999, "is becoming a breeding ground for religious extremism and sectarian violence, as well as various types of international terrorism, the scope of which far exceeds Afghan boundaries." The Security Council's Resolution 1267 in October 1999 strongly condemned "the sheltering and training of terrorists and planning of terrorist acts" on Afghan territory, especially in areas under Taliban control. But the Taliban felt buoyed by developments. "Our prestige is spreading across the region because we have truly implemented Islam, and this makes the Americans and some neighbors very nervous,"* said Information Minister Amir Khan Muttaqi.[34]

Taliban prestige was not the only thing spreading across Asia. Late in November 1999, Jordan's intelligence service intercepted a phone call from Abu Zubaydah, a long-time ally of bin Laden, telling Khadr Abu Hoshar, a Palestinian extremist, that "the time for training is over." Police arrested sixteen plotters, at least four of whom had been trained in Afghan camps, and foiled a plan to blow up the Radisson Hotel in downtown Amman, Jordan, and attack border crossings between Israel and Jordan and two Christian holy sites. Sheehan sent a stern message to the Taliban, and Clinton sent Zinni to Musharraf with a plea for help. The U.S. government went on high alert and notified U.S. installations the world over; at the CIA's request, friendly governments in eight countries disrupted potential terrorist operations. In mid-December, Ahmed Ressam, an Algerian-born political asylum-seeker in Canada who had trained in Abu Zubaydah's Khaldan camp, drove onto a ferry from Victoria, Canada, to Port Angeles, Washington, with plans to blow up a terminal at Los Angeles Airport. When an alert customs agent stopped him and began to frisk him, he bolted. He was caught and arrested. Both the Jordanian and Canadian plots apparently were initiated in the field, and the plotters sought approval

---

* In an internal government debate following the conquest of Mazar-i-Sharif, Taliban foreign ministry supervisor Mullah Mohammad Hassan Akhund commissioned a statement assuring neighbors that Afghan policy was not to interfere in their internal affairs. Vahid Mojdeh, who drafted it, recalled that Justice Minister Mullah Nooruddin Turabi objected strenuously. "We are fully aware of our nation's intentions. Is it really our policy not to interfere in others' affairs?" Turabi said. Hassan responded that if Afghanistan had the power it would "not hesitate" to "help other Muslims," but it could not at present. Turabi said a promise of noninterference would be dishonest. "In my opinion, according to Islamic law, it is not right for us to make promises we cannot keep. Why are we pressed to claim that we will never, ever interfere? It should be enough to state that we are not in any position to pose a threat at the moment." Mojdeh, unpublished manuscript.

from bin Laden aides. Bin Laden himself was reportedly engaged in organizing an attack on the USS *The Sullivans*, a warship in Aden. The operation failed because the small boat carrying the explosives sank.[35]

The millennium celebration passed without incident, with the exception of the hijacking of an Air India plane that began over India and ended in Afghanistan. It got little attention in the United States but sent a shudder around South Asia and in the White House. The plane, with more than 150 passengers and crew on board, was hijacked after departing Nepal on December 24; it touched down in India, Pakistan, and the United Arab Emirates before arriving in Kandahar on Christmas Day. The hijackers demanded freedom for three Kashmiri separatists in Indian jails, among them Maulana Muhammad Masood Azhar, a Pakistani-born cleric accused by India of belonging to HUM, which was on the U.S. list of global terror organizations. Azhar had been held in an Indian jail since 1994. The other two men —Mushtaq Ahmad Zargar and Omar Saeed Sheikh— had been held since 1992 and 1994, respectively.

According to reporter Peter Bergen, who covered the crisis, bin Laden played a key behind-the-scenes role between HUM and the Taliban, urging the hijackers to "cut the best possible deal" for themselves. After a week of negotiations, India released the three men and flew them to Kandahar. Along with the five hijackers, they disappeared into the dust in Afghanistan.[36]

Azhar turned up in Pakistan four days later, making a fiery anti-American speech at a Karachi park. "I have come back and I will not rest in peace until Kashmir is liberated," Azhar told the crowd. "Muslims should not rest in peace until we have destroyed America and India." The crowd chanted, "Death to India, death to the United States." Pakistani authorities did not detain him, saying there were no charges pending against him. Nor did they arrest anyone else, including the hijackers, all of whom were reported to be on Pakistani soil or en route to Pakistani Kashmir. Sheikh went to ground until January 2002, when he is alleged to have organized the abduction and killing of *Wall Street Journal* reporter Daniel Pearl.

The hijacking troubled Bruce Riedel. "This should have been a wakeup call," said Riedel, who oversaw policy in South Asia on the National Security Council. "Here you had international air piracy directly linked to the Taliban. The Taliban were willing to be directly involved in a terrorist incident. You had Taliban, Arabs, Kashmiris, and Pakistanis all over the place. It was an important point in the evolution of the Taliban–al Qaeda relationship and the Taliban's willingness to be seen as a sponsor of terrorism." The U.S. news media paid little heed, as did the Clinton administration.

Also slipping under the radar was the Taliban decision to recognize the breakaway Chechnya. From autumn 1996, when the Taliban took over Kabul, Chechen separatist leaders had been visiting and asking for recognition. With every visit by a Chechen delegation, Russia contacted the Taliban and requested a visit to Kandahar leading to normal relations. The Taliban rejected every Russian visit and normal relations, but Russian diplomats invariably got their messages through by asking Pakistan to intercede. Finally, on January 16, 2000, Wakil Ahmad Muttawakil, the Taliban foreign minister, and Zelimkhan Yandarbiyev, former Chechen president and now special envoy, agreed to open diplomatic relations and set up embassies in each other's capitals. The Taliban accepted the Chechen assurance that they would not be the first to recognize independence, because Russia already had, and they brought along a copy of a signed agreement between Boris Yeltsin and Chechen president Aslan Maskhadov. Almost simultaneously, the Taliban sent troops to Chechnya.

"Our recognition has become absolutely necessary because of the brutal Russian onslaught against Chechens," said Muttawakil. The Taliban urged all Muslims to follow suit. "We are not afraid if Russia imposes sanctions on us or threatens us occasionally," said Qudratullah Jamal, the Taliban information minister. "The Russians have not recognized us. We are independent. Everybody is doing his own business."

Yandarbiyev certainly was. After completing his trip to Afghanistan, he set off on a whirlwind speaking tour of Pakistan. "All the Muslims of the world need to be united," he told the crowds. "I'm here in Pakistan to mobilize opinion for the recognition of the Chechen government." At a rally in Peshawar, he told Pakistani sympathizers that "the issues of Chechnya and Kashmir are similar in nature," adding that "whenever the Muslims become one nation, no power on the earth can confront them." Of course, he had Russia in mind. Under heavy pressure from Moscow, Pakistani authorities detained Yandarbiyev and ushered him out of the country. Even for Pakistan, this was carrying Islamist militancy too far.[37]

8

Coasting toward Catastrophe
(2000–2001)

Bill Clinton began his final year in office at the turn of the millennium under assault from two rather disparate quarters: political opponents who were determined to hound him until the end of his term over his sexual indiscretions with a White House intern, and Osama bin Laden, who had declared war on the United States but was unable to provoke another American military strike. Clinton could not make the Monica Lewinsky scandal go away, but in the case of the top national security threat he got lucky. Bin Laden–trained operatives had planned terrorist assaults against American targets in three corners of the world, but all misfired. The question before the president was how to respond to a nonstate actor in the middle of nowhere whose latest attacks had failed to cause any damage.

Clinton had just celebrated a political triumph in Europe, where U.S.-led NATO forces freed Kosovo from the grip of Slobodan Milosevic. But Afghanistan was not Kosovo. There was next to no media coverage of the situation and no public clamor for action. In the upper reaches of the administration, no cabinet officer would step forward to champion a policy shift or to marshal support from America's allies as Secretary of State Madeleine Albright had done so ably in Kosovo.

Clinton and his aides were convinced that the public and Congress would not back a major intervention in Afghanistan, an assessment that implicitly acknowledged both the challenge of intervening in a landlocked state and the president's disinclination to use force. He did not rule out a military operation but insisted on near-perfect intelligence before acting; then and only then would he order a surgical strike against bin Laden. But the strike he had in mind would have left bin Laden's network and forces intact, along with the sanctuary in which they flourished.

Instead of force, the president opted for a combination of diplomacy, covert operations, and law enforcement—but he structured the drive without the connective tissue that could have brought results. Effective diplomacy against a determined foe requires the credible threat of the use of force. It also requires close coordination with a supportive regional power and tough but enforceable sanctions. But since Pervez Musharraf came to power in a coup engineered by pro-Taliban senior officers, Pakistan had moved ever closer to the Taliban and become less willing to implement sanctions.

For covert operations to work, the CIA needs an intimate knowledge of the political landscape and close cooperation with an inside partner. But the White House largely ignored the internal politics and failed to recognize its common strategic interest with Ahmed Shah Massoud in defeating the Taliban and al Qaeda. The major CIA covert operation inside Afghanistan was to deploy Afghan tribal elements as spotters for a potential cruise missile strike against bin Laden.

And finally, law enforcement in the form of counterterrorist disruption operations is a function the CIA and FBI carry out with the cooperation of foreign governments. The liaison seemed to work reasonably well in most places, except for the two places that mattered most: Afghanistan and Pakistan.

Putting means before ends made it impossible for Clinton and his aides to devise a strategy to defeat and eliminate the Saudi renegade. This was a formula for inaction.

For Osama bin Laden, the calm at the dawn of the new millennium was no doubt a setback. In hindsight, it seems incredible that a full eighteen months after the twin embassy bombings he was still preparing multiple and simultaneous attacks. But in the absence of effective U.S. retaliation, his ambitions had grown. He had a clear and publicly stated goal—the mass killing of American military personnel and civilians—an obsession with long-term planning, and the flexibility to adjust tactics to circumstances.

The three failed terror attacks on American targets near the turn of the century were the result of flawed tradecraft by suicide bombers; the failures called for course corrections and a rethinking of bin Laden's management style. Yet, as a test of U.S. national security preparedness, the three failed attacks gave bin Laden cause for hope. In Jordan, where the target was a hotel in Amman and sites popular with Christian tourists, the plotters (thirteen of whom had trained in bin Laden camps) were taking orders from Abu Zubaydah, bin Laden's number three man. Phone intercepts enabled Jordanian authorities to disrupt the plot, a flaw that could be rectified through better operational security.

The chief figure in the second plot, the Algerian-born Ahmed Ressam, had undergone nine months of instruction in the Khalden and Darunta camps in 1998. Upon completion of his training, which included six weeks of instruction on bombmaking, he was given $12,000 and the mission to bomb a prominent U.S. site. Ressam reported to an Algerian al Qaeda operative in London and another senior al Qaeda leader with access to bin Laden. He was en route to blowing up a terminal at Los Angeles Airport when an alert customs inspector arrested him in Port Angeles, Washington. That was bad luck.

What thwarted the plan to blow up the American destroyer USS *The Sullivans* on January 3, 2000, in Yemen was sheer ineptitude. The small skiff was overloaded with explosives and sank upon launch in shallow water. But here as well, bin Laden could draw encouragement: the Clinton administration did not know of the attempt, which he had personally directed, at the time, not learning of it until a second, successful attack on a U.S. naval vessel the following October.[1]

He apparently drew several lessons from these ill-fated missions: to take a hands-on role in conceiving and directing future assaults, to select more capable personnel, and to trim his ambitions to match his capacity. He was a shrewd and determined foe.

Clinton went down a familiar path after the millennium assaults, issuing a harsh verbal warning to the Taliban and dispatching General Anthony Zinni, commander of the U.S. Central Command, to Pakistan.* Zinni asked General Musharraf to "take whatever action you deem necessary to resolve the bin Laden problem at the earliest possible time." But Zinni left Islamabad empty-handed, as did every special envoy.

The Pakistani leader was "unwilling to take the heat at home," Ambassador William Milam reported. The underlying truth was that Clinton's aversion to using force to back up his threats meant bin Laden could operate in relative safety for the foreseeable future. There would be no retaliation for the millennium plots.[2]

Grasping at Straws

The first half of the year 2000 saw a series of ever-more abject U.S. appeals to Pakistan and a vain search for proxies, as if policymakers were unaware of the course Pakistan's military leadership had already chosen. Evidence of that course abounded. Early in December 1999, just weeks after UN sanctions went into effect, Musharraf traveled to Iran (his first trip abroad since seizing power) and announced that the two countries henceforth would "coordinate" policies to encourage the peace process in Afghanistan. But the only thing they harmonized on was maintaining open borders for trade with Afghanistan and—later—closing their borders against refugees who were trying to escape drought, conflict, and penury.

The U.S. groveling began in January when Inderfurth and Sheehan called on Musharraf and held out the possibility of a Clinton visit in March, on condition that Pakistan put pressure on Omar. The Pakistan "chief

---

* In the middle of the night after Ressam's arrest in December 1999, Michael Sheehan, the State Department counterterrorist chief, phoned Taliban foreign minister Muttawakil with an emotional message from Clinton. "If you have an arsonist in your basement, and every night he goes out and burns down a neighbor's house, and you know this is going on, then you can't claim you aren't responsible," Sheehan began. Muttawakil did not grasp the parable. "You have a terrorist in your basement," Sheehan continued. "He is attacking us. And you are completely responsible." Muttawakil replied that Afghanistan would do nothing to hurt America. He said there was no proof that bin Laden was behind the plots. Sheehan then read a statement from Clinton: "We will hold the Taliban leadership responsible for any attacks against U.S. interests by al Qaeda or any of its affiliated groups. You will be held personally responsible." *Seattle Times*, December 14, 1999.

executive," as he styled himself, promised to travel to Kandahar, "take his knapsack and sleep on the floor" if it would gain access to Omar. But Inderfurth concluded that he was unlikely to do anything.[3]

Amir Khan Muttaqi, the Taliban's former minister of education and culture, flew in from Kandahar for the latest dialogue of the deaf with the American envoys. If bin Laden commits "any further acts," Inderfurth and Sheehan warned, the Taliban would be held responsible. Muttaqi responded with the well-practiced brush-off. The United States should not make such a big issue of bin Laden, he said, adding that in the future bin Laden would not conduct "any activities" against the United States. Sheehan ended on a flowery note that betrayed the weakness of his position. Americans still shared deep feelings of "respect and warmth" for the Afghan people, he said, and understood "your political problem and your need to maintain the support of the people."* He said there could be a short-term backlash if bin Laden were arrested, "but in the long term the world would be a safer place if he were brought to justice." Sheehan said he was offering this advice "in sincerity and friendship."[4]

Musharraf never made it to Kandahar, but Clinton landed in Pakistan on March 25, 2000, albeit for only six hours after a five-day visit to India. He intentionally avoided the topic of bin Laden in meetings at which ISI officials were present and saved his pleas for his one-on-one session with Musharraf. "I offered him the moon when I went to see him, in terms of better relations with the United States, if he'd help us get bin Laden and deal with another issue or two," Clinton later recounted. But he had badly misread Pakistan military politics—the following month, it was ISI director Mahmoud Ahmed, not Musharraf,† who headed to Kandahar.[5]

Clinton apparently was hoping that foreign proxies would carry out U.S. strategic aims in Afghanistan so he could avoid the use of American military power. There was a precedent in his first term, when he hesitated for two-and-a-half years before authorizing the bombing of Serb positions to halt the ethnic cleansing in Bosnia.‡ Where possible, Clinton preferred

---

* Sheehan seemed to separate the Taliban regime from the government that had given sanctuary to bin Laden. In May 2000, he told reporters that he did not believe the Taliban was hostile to the United States. "In fact," he said, "they repeatedly tell me that they want good relations with the United States, and I believe that to be a sincere desire. However, within the territory that they control, there are numerous terrorist organizations that directly threaten the United States, that directly undermine the security of the region and other parts of the world, and that is a problem." State Department briefing, May 1, 2000, FDCH transcripts.

† Omar made it clear that Musharraf would be unwelcome if he raised the bin Laden issue, although he denied to Pakistani journalist Rahimullah Yusufzai sending a specific message to that effect. "I didn't say General Musharraf shouldn't come to Afghanistan if he wanted the Taliban to give up bin Laden. Pakistan knows it is none of its concern. Pakistan will not and should not ask us to hand over bin Laden." He said Pakistan was well aware that the matter concerned the Afghan government and the United States. *News*, Islamabad, July 15, 2000.

‡ Clinton's hesitations unwittingly played into bin Laden's anti-Western campaign, for some of the militants who carried out later suicide missions fought in central Bosnia with a small mujahideen brigade.

that others do the job. When Iran sent arms to save the Bosnian Muslims from extinction, the U.S. government did not object; when Croatia launched Operation Storm in the summer of 1995 to dislodge Serbs from the Krajina region and some of Bosnia, the CIA provided the Croatians with intelligence, political and moral support, and some training.

The candidates to be U.S. proxy in Afghanistan were Iran, Russia, and Pakistan, and each brought a great deal of excess baggage to the role. Iran, still in the throes of Islamic revolution, was least likely to gain U.S. backing for an armed intervention. In the six-plus-two group, which Brahimi ran, and in the Geneva Group launched by his successor, Francesc Vendrell of Spain, U.S. officials regularly met their Iranian counterparts and made clear that they had no objection to Iran sending arms and cash to the United Front. But the administration was on record since the murder of Iranian diplomats in 1998 as opposing any Iranian intervention in Afghanistan. By the year 2000, Iran was hosting well over a million refugees and also offered sanctuary to the anti-Taliban opposition. On the other hand, as UN sanctions went into effect on November 21, 1999, Iran reopened the border with Afghanistan, restoring an important commercial link to Dubai; this was followed by the accord on cooperation when Musharraf visited in early December. There was yet another reason for staying an arm's length from Iran: the ruling Shia clergy and the Revolutionary Guards allowed Iranian territory to serve as a conduit to Afghanistan for al Qaeda militants. Indeed, as many as ten of the fourteen "muscle" hijackers (as opposed to the ones who flew the planes) in the 9/11 attacks traveled into or out of Iran between October 2000 and February 2001. Iran was ill-suited to serve as U.S. proxy.[6]

Russia was an obvious candidate to conduct military operations, because it had forces in the region and allies such as Uzbekistan that would acquiesce to overflights; but in every other regard, it was totally unsuited for the role. Russian leaders had become deeply concerned over Taliban support for the Chechen rebels and the flow of fighters back and forth between Afghanistan and Chechnya. Boris Yeltsin and Vladimir Putin "tried to open our eyes on what was going on in Afghanistan," Deputy Secretary of State Strobe Talbott recalled. "They would say, 'You're going to be the victims of it.'"

Clinton's response was to throw his support behind a possible Russian-led bombing campaign in Afghanistan. The Soviet leadership that had invaded in 1979 was long gone, and the post-Soviet leadership was popularly elected. Still, for the United States to endorse another Russian-led armed intervention barely a decade after the debacle that caused such suffering begged credulity. Still more bizarre was that the administration asked Pakistan to deliver the threat. Indeed, the man who carried the message in April 2000 was none other than Musharraf's pro-Taliban ISI director, Gen. Mahmoud Ahmed.

At a meeting in Kandahar in April 2000 (according to Pakistani diplomatic records left behind at the fall of Kabul in late 2001), Ahmed warned Omar that "nothing short of the extradition of Osama bin Laden to a place where he could be brought to justice would satisfy the U.S." If Omar did not comply with U.S. demands, Ahmed said Washington wanted Pakistan "to end all support for them," according to the documents. In addition, "Russia and its allies could be given the go-ahead to embark in hot pursuit against terrorists. They could bomb strategic targets north of the Hindu Kush, thereby eliminating the military potential of the Taliban to the complete advantage of Ahmed Shah Massoud." Ahmed said, "The United States and Russia could coordinate their actions in pursuance of the above measures." He told Omar that Clinton might declare Afghanistan a terrorist state, leading to U.S. missile attacks "targeting the Taliban's military assets."

It was not a well-vetted threat-by-proxy. No one at the top of the State Department was even aware of the idea, which apparently originated at the White House. The plan was based on the assumption that Pakistan would put aside its well-known support of the Taliban and deliver a credible threat of Russian and American force against the Taliban. Pickering said he first learned of the gambit a full month after it was delivered, when Ahmed briefed him on his talks with Omar. Inderfurth and the U.S. ambassador to Pakistan, William Milam, said they never heard of it. "To me, this doesn't make sense," said Inderfurth. "I never heard of it." Albright concurred: it was "not something I was aware of." This was a case of grasping at straws.

After delivering Clinton's warning that he would unleash Russian bombers, Ahmed proceeded while in Kandahar to state Pakistan's own national security agenda. This was a logical step as Musharraf's representative, but hardly the message the officials behind the U.S. threat would have wanted. Pakistan insisted that Omar close all terrorist training camps immediately and extradite all wanted terrorists to their respective countries, including Pakistan, China, Uzbekistan, and Arab countries. The demand gave Omar just the opening he needed to split Musharraf from Clinton. He agreed to close the camps but stalled on bin Laden, saying this was an American, not a Pakistani, issue. "He wanted to get rid of Osama but did not know how," Ahmed later reported to Pickering.

The Taliban were playing an old-fashioned shell game, but this time the high-stakes gambler was the government of Pakistan. In mid-May, when Mullah Abdul Jalil Akhund traveled to Islamabad to reaffirm Omar's commitment to close camps, Musharraf did not repeat Ahmed's demand for bin Laden's handover but instead proposed reviving the Taliban plan for an Islamic court. "Perhaps the U.S. would now be amenable to it," Musharraf told Jalil and Taliban interior minister Mullah Abdul Razzaq.[7]

Clearly, Pakistan was also unsuited to serve as the U.S. proxy in Afghanistan. Musharraf was riding a tiger, rushing toward Kandahar and away from Washington at a speed that could hardly serve Pakistani interests. On May 25, the day Pickering arrived to follow up on Clinton's visit, Musharraf threw Pakistan's full weight behind the Taliban, saying that he would never "alienate" the Taliban because Pakistan felt obliged to look out for the interests of Pashtuns on either side of the border. "We cannot alienate the Taliban, as we want the Pushtoons on our side. It is strategically very important for us that the Pushtoon, which means now Taliban, are on our side," he said at a televised news conference.[8]

Musharraf had spoken in a similar vein a year earlier as chief of the armed services, but this time his words were policy—dubious policy, inaptly expressed—but policy nonetheless. He not only had taken sides in a complex internal dispute but was citing cross-border ethnicity to justify siding with the Taliban against their multiethnic northern opponents. At the same time, in equating Pashtun interests with those of the mullahs, he was dismissing the legitimacy of Pashtun opponents to the Taliban, such as Abdul Haq, not to mention all the Taliban's Pashtun opponents in the country. Last but not least, his public statement was a slap in the face for the White House, which, as Ahmed told Omar, had asked Pakistan to cut ties with the Taliban if bin Laden was not handed over. By defining Pakistan's relationship with the Taliban as a matter of national security and by omitting any reference to bin Laden, Musharraf had placed himself squarely on the opposite side of the issue from Clinton.*

In the same news conference, Musharraf said he was deeply concerned about reports that Russia was contemplating air strikes on Taliban-controlled areas of Afghanistan. Any such act would have very serious repercussions, he said. These attacks would be seen as support for the United Front, and the outside powers should refrain from such a policy. Musharraf conveniently overlooked the fact that his own representative had conveyed the same threat to Omar.

The only apparent quid pro quo for the cave-in was a Taliban promise to close the training camps. But after pocketing Musharraf's unconditional declaration of support, the Taliban welshed. Early that summer, they closed two camps temporarily and made excuses for not closing the others, Arif Ayub, the Pakistan ambassador in Kabul reported.† "Whatever the

---

* Musharraf may have had second thoughts. An official transcript of his press conference provided to the author in February 2006 omitted the remarks equating Pashtun interests on both sides of the Afghan border with the Taliban. "Pakistan cannot alienate Taliban," it quotes Musharraf as saying.

† One major camp the Taliban closed was at Rishkhor near Kabul. The BBC's Kate Clark found it completely empty when she visited it in June 2000. But she found big signs in Urdu and Arabic, belying the Taliban claim that it had had been used only to train its own fighters.

explanations, the fact remains that the Taliban seem addicted to international jihad as a means of mobilizing support and a distraction from their own shortcomings," Ayub said. In July, when Interior Minister Moinuddin Haider handed over a list of eighteen camps where Pakistan militants were said to be receiving training, the Taliban responded by demanding proof as well as a reciprocal agreement under which Pakistan would hand over Afghan opponents living in Pakistan opposition figures to the Taliban.[9]

The Taliban were feeling their oats. Early in 2001, Omar issued a thinly veiled threat to destabilize Pakistan by stirring Pakistan's religious parties into revolt. If Musharraf enforced Islamic law "step by step," Pakistan's religious parties would be "contented and avoid raising a hue and cry" that would give rise to "instability," Omar said. "This is our advice and message based on Islamic ideology. Otherwise, you had better know how to deal with it."[10]

The U.S. search for proxies was at a dead end. It had been built on the dubious premise that parties backing opposite sides in the internal conflict would unite to threaten the Taliban. Pakistan sought Massoud's defeat, while Russia hoped for his victory, and only the United States was "neutral." The greater setback was to U.S. diplomacy and influence in the region. Musharraf's public pledge of support for the regime in Kandahar on the heels of Ahmed's meeting eliminated the last shred of ambiguity in Pakistan's position and undercut America's ability to deliver a credible threat to the Taliban. From May 2000 onward, there was almost no way Washington and Islamabad could work together to deal with Kandahar.

All the parties now were coasting toward catastrophe, Pakistan among them, as its leading diplomats were quite aware. For reasons of domestic politics, the Pakistani government was pursuing "policies that we know are never going to deliver and the eventual costs of which we also know will be overwhelming," said Ashraf Jehangir Qazi, the Pakistan high commissioner in India, in a paper for a Foreign Ministry conference on Afghan policy at the start of 2001. "Thus, we are condemned to ride a tiger." Pakistan was stuck, as the closest ally to a movement that responded little to persuasion and not at all to pressure. The conventional wisdom, Qazi said, was that "we cannot abandon them either, because that would lead to a power vacuum in Afghanistan which would be filled with anti-Pakistan elements," and the withdrawal of any support from the Taliban would "immediately lead to political unrest in Pakistan." He advocated a dramatic policy shift, demanding that Afghanistan hand over bin Laden and, if it did not, squeezing supplies to undermine the authority of the noncooperative Taliban leaders.

Squeezing was not about to happen. Papers left behind in the embassy when the Taliban were overthrown in 2001 show that Arif Ayub, the Pakistan ambassador in Kabul, spent much of his time soliciting his own government aid to expand Afghanistan's infrastructure. He also invited firms from Pakistan and abroad to exploit Afghan mineral wealth in exchange for funds to rebuild its roads.* He even arranged the supply of aviation fuel to the Taliban (whose flights outside the country were grounded under the UN sanctions), and responded to requests from the Aviation Ministry for fuel, training, and assistance with repairs of their aging aircraft.[11]

Pakistan's most flagrant breach of the UN sanctions was in aiding the Taliban war effort. Vendrell's quarterly report on Afghanistan in late 2000 called it "deeply distressing" that a significant number of non-Afghan personnel, largely from the Pakistani madrassas, were "taking part in the fighting, most if not all on the side of the Taliban, and there also appears to be outside involvement in the planning and logistical support of their military operations." Stopping the resupply was "a hopeless task," according to Vendrell. "Every time we went to the Pakistanis on this issue, they would say there are no supplies." Pakistan suggested having international military observers on the border, but UN experts said it would take twenty thousand observers along the border to control the traffic. HRW reported that Pakistan was providing and facilitating shipments of ammunition and fuel.[†] In April and May of 2001, as many as thirty trucks a day crossed the Pakistan border, carrying artillery shells, tank rounds, and rocket-propelled grenades.[12]

Russia, meanwhile, continued along the path of confrontation with the Taliban that it probably would have taken regardless of the U.S. threats to unleash Russian air power. In mid-April, leaders of four Central Asian "stans" signed an agreement on "joint action to fight terrorism as well as religious and other kinds of extremism and organized crime" emerging from Afghanistan. In June 2000, as the United States and Russia set up a bilateral working group for "concrete proposals" to counter "terrorist threats originating in Afghanistan," Russian made three air incursions into Afghan territory, or so the Taliban complained. China joined Russia and the "stans" in July for a summit to discuss counterterrorism measures against Afghanistan; and after militant Uzbek dissidents infiltrated Uzbekistan and Kyrgyzstan via Tajikistan, these states, along with Kazakhstan, called an emergency summit. There were more top-level talks, and in mid-October the "stans," with the exception of Uzbekistan, agreed with Russia to revive

---

* In one letter to the Pakistan minister of communications, Ayub listed some of the minerals available: "Large coal deposits are available in Herat, Samangan, 50 million tons under the surface in Darra Souf, which could easily supply the 1.5 million tons annual requirement of the steel mill in Karachi . . . large deposits of hematite, magnetite, 120 million tons . . . available at Hagigak . . . marble, inexhaustible reserves of several km of high-quality onyx, available in Helmand, Kandahar, and Nangahar provinces could be easily transported to Karachi by road, rail, through Peshawar; copper, 750 million tons of copper ore are available at Aynak . . . next to the copper mine is a chrome mine, 58 percent grade, which is already being exported to Pakistan." In addition, there was crude oil, nickel in Kandahar and lithium in Kunar province, beryllium in Nuristan and Badakshan, and radioactive and rare elements in Helmand.

† HRW also claimed that Pakistan's army and intelligence officers had helped plan and execute major military operations and contributed to making the Taliban a "highly effective military force"—on occasion, directly providing combat support. But it did not document these assertions.

the Commonwealth of Independent States collective security treaty, with particular reference to Afghanistan. All this had little impact on the Taliban, who threw all their efforts into defeating Massoud.

In March 2001, Russia announced that it would set up a rapid deployment force for Central Asia and dispatched three thousand paratroops to augment the ten thousand men it had in Dushanbe to protect the border.[13]

A State within a State

As Bill Clinton searched in vain for a foreign state to act as a proxy for the United States after the millennium plots, bin Laden was busy taking over Afghanistan, where he was an honored guest, and making it the launch pad for his terror campaign against the United States. The critical enabling factor for bin Laden in 2000 and 2001 was the protected environment in which he operated: a failed state in whose civil war he played a major supporting role. Afghanistan was one of the poorest and least developed countries on earth, but what drove his Taliban hosts on what they regarded as a holy mission to rule at home and promote global jihad was their inability to control their own territory. As the internal conflict dragged on, bin Laden's military and financial support made Mullah Omar increasingly dependent on him. Omar had little choice but to allow bin Laden to establish training camps, offices, and safe houses; to build a sizeable militia (which he regularly made available for the Taliban's military operations against Massoud); and to tolerate the comings and goings of the militants as they organized operations abroad. Indeed, al Qaeda members could travel freely within the country, enter and depart without visas or immigration procedures, and buy and import weapons and vehicles. At the end, they were even using official Ministry of Defense license plates.[14]

The only real restriction Omar imposed was on his guest's relentless quest for self-promotion. The news blackout presented a real problem to the international media, which, in the face of tough working conditions and a lack of interest from the general public, pretty much walked away from the story. The Clinton administration, having long before abandoned any American presence and the influence that accompanies it, also did nothing to put the spotlight on this far-off place that had become a symbol of American impotence. But bin Laden adjusted to the absence of media exposure by publicizing his exploits in the Islamic world through recruitment videos, which passed from hand to hand in Gulf countries. And there were advantages in operating outside the spotlight. Having an infrastructure, an independent revenue stream, and his own militia in a protected environment allowed bin Laden to set up a state within a state—with minimal attention from abroad. The general public in the United States and elsewhere hadn't a clue this was going on.

Despite his family wealth, bin Laden had surprisingly limited means of his own during the years in Afghanistan, but he had an amazing capacity to elicit support from wealthy sympathizers in the Gulf region. U.S. intelligence estimated that he raised some $30 million a year for al Qaeda and invested $10–20 million a year in the Taliban.* He got a lot of bang for the buck. In the five-and-a-half years between his return to Afghanistan and September 11, 2001, his training camps processed up to twenty thousand militants from around the world. Only a fraction received advanced terrorist training; it was from those ranks that he drew suicide bombers for overseas assignment, troops for his own protective unit (sometimes called Brigade 055), and frontline troops in the internal conflict. At the later stage of the conflict, he was able to deploy 1,500–2,000 frontline fighters, and they were, according to Massoud, by far his fiercest opponents.[15]

The broad dimensions of bin Laden's establishment on the ground were known to U.S. intelligence by late 2000, but nothing could be done to address it owing to Clinton's reluctance to use force. The onus was on U.S. law enforcement to prevent an attack, which was an impossible task. At the joint congressional inquiry in December 2002, an FBI agent said it was "like telling the FBI after Pearl Harbor, 'Go to Tokyo and arrest the emperor.'" Nothing other than a military solution could resolve the issue, and the U.S. attorney's office in "the Southern District [of New York] doesn't have any cruise missiles."[16]

Incubator for Conspiracy

Afghanistan had little to offer in the way of high technology (such as a working phone system), but bin Laden was able to turn it into the center of his worldwide jihad, with a network of al Qaeda affiliates (mostly graduates of his camps) in fifty-five countries. Thanks to lax controls by Pakistan and Iran and the willingness of the Afghan missions in Pakistan to provide cover,† jihadis from around the world traveled freely into and out of the country.[17]

---

* By comparison, Massoud's United Front budget was approximately $60 million a year, most of it raised from the sale of lapis lazuli mined in Badakhshan province or from Afghan currency printed in Russia. Massoud's intelligence aides estimated the total Taliban budget at $250 million a year. The official budget announced in July 2001 was $80 million, according to the United Nations; it is possible that income from opium sales (the Taliban skimmed 2 percent off the profits) made up much of the rest. On United Front and Taliban budget, author interview with senior Afghan government official who spoke on condition of anonymity, Kabul, March 2003; and on Taliban skimming of opium sales, Mojdeh, unpublished manuscript, 38–39.

†According to a former Taliban foreign ministry official, as many as 90 percent of the volunteers arrived via Iran by paying about $1,000 to a smuggler. This was a preferable route for Saudis, for Iranian border guards were told not to stamp visas into passports, so visitors could return to their home countries without fear of being stigmatized for visiting Afghanistan. At least eight of the future 9/11 hijackers traveled in and out of Afghanistan this way. A considerable number also arrived via Pakistan, according to Arif Ayub, the Pakistan ambassador in Kabul. There "seems to be a free crossing for the

(continued on next page)

This was a hospitable atmosphere for building conspiracies. From the time bin Laden returned in 1996, freelance jihadis beat a path to his door, bringing projects for attacking the United States. Indeed, most of the plots bin Laden supported were proposed by persons outside his immediate circle, including the planned assaults in Amman and Los Angeles. The concept behind the biggest plot of all—the 9/11 attack on the symbols of American economic, military, and political power—also arrived over the transom.

What drew them? Bin Laden's charisma (a child of privilege who abandoned his inheritance and risked his life in jihad) no doubt helped, as did a well-oiled publicity machine that distributed interviews and video-tapes throughout the Islamic world. But the two indispensable factors were the message (his ability to articulate the grievances of the downtrodden, the politically dispossessed, and those outraged by travesties such as the ethnic cleansing in Bosnia) and the vision (a highly demagogic and self-serving vision that offered a purpose in life to Muslim men from many countries). Some were nearly illiterate drifters, some highly educated men from well-off families; all were ready to do battle against what bin Laden defined as evil and to risk their lives in the name of their religious beliefs.

One of the first visitors shortly after bin Laden touched down in Jalal-abad in 1996 was Khalid Sheikh Muhammad. Born in Kuwait of Paki-stani parents, Muhammad had fought in the anti-Soviet war along with his nephew, Ramzi Yousef, and had volunteered in Bosnia in 1992. He had studied in the United States but was intensely opposed to U.S. policy in the Middle East. Yousef had trained in Afghan camps funded by bin Laden. It is not clear that he had ever joined al Qaeda, but he was part of the same loose network of Sunni extremists who focused their growing fury on the United States. When Yousef devised a plan to blow up the World Trade Center late in 1992, Muhammad advised him on bomb construction and even wired funds to assist him. With U.S. authorities on his trail in Qatar, Muhammad relocated to Afghanistan at the beginning of 1996, six months before bin Laden got there.

Muhammad first met bin Laden at the latter's Tora Bora redoubt later that year. His nephew's renown opened the door. He briefed bin Laden on the failed attack and on a series of other stillborn plots he and Yousef had cooked up in the aftermath, such as blowing up U.S. passenger aircraft, and later cargo aircraft, in Asia.[18] Now he brought bin Laden an ambitious plan that combined elements from both sorts of conspiracies: to crash airplanes

---

† *(cont.)*
terrorists," he complained in a formal paper. Pakistan officials also complained that the Afghan con-sulate in Peshawar had "decided to give dual nationality to a large number of illegal Arabs to facilitate their free movement across the Pakistan-Afghan border" and to ensure that they were not arrested by Pakistan authorities and turned over to their home countries. On practice of Iranian border guards, *9/11 Commission Report* 169, 240; eight hijackers transit Iran, *9/11 Commission Report,* 241; Pakistani complaints about "free crossing" from Judah, "Taliban Papers," 74; and complaint about Afghan con-sulate, Judah, 77.

into the World Trade Center and other American landmarks. Muhammad was not the only conspirator thinking in this direction. Bin Laden and his aides were determined to inflict mass casualties, but the question was by what method. His military commander (Muhammed Atef, also known as Abu Hafs al Misri) had reportedly done a study while in Sudan that concluded that conventional hijackings would not serve, as they were used to negotiate the release of prisoners rather than to inflict mass casualties. Muhammad's plan, conceived in 1995, was to hijack ten aircraft simultaneously and fly them into buildings in New York, Washington, D.C., California, and Washington State. Bin Laden listened without comment but invited him to join al Qaeda and move his family to Afghanistan, an invitation he declined. Throughout 1997 and the first half of 1998, Muhammad was a frequent caller on bin Laden; late in 1998 or early in 1999, he agreed to join al Qaeda.

In the spring of 1999, bin Laden summoned him to Kandahar and told him, apparently on Atef's recommendation, that he would support what came to be known as the "planes operation." Intense planning began. Muhammad submitted a scaled-down plan, but bin Laden told him to think big: "Why do you use an axe when you can use a bulldozer?" So the plan was to blow up a total of ten aircraft. At al Matar complex outside Kandahar, bin Laden, Atef, and Muhammad developed an initial target list that included the World Trade Center, the White House, the U.S. Capitol, and the Pentagon.[19]

By April 1999, bin Laden had chosen four men to serve in the operation; late that year, he dispatched two Saudis and two Yemenis to the United States for pilot training. Organizing the deployments turned into a learning experience for Muhammad. Khalid al Mihdhar and Nawaf al Hazmi, Mecca-born Saudis who had fought in Bosnia in 1995, secured their visas readily, but Yemenis Tawfiq bin Attash (aka Khallad) and Abu Bara al Yemeni were turned down. It was one of the quirks of U.S. immigration practice to turn down male Yemeni applicants, not out of concern about terrorism but because they might overstay their visas and take on illegal work. Muhammad later said, "Because individuals with Saudi passports could travel much more easily than Yemenis, particularly to the U.S., there were fewer martyrdom opportunities for Yemenis." So Muhammad split the operation in two: Saudis and other nationalities with ready access to U.S. visas would conduct the American operations, and Yemenis would staff the East Asian planes operation, because they were able to enter South Korea, Thailand, Hong Kong, and Malaysia without visas. By this time, the target set had been broadened to include CIA and FBI headquarters, nuclear power plants, and the tallest buildings in California and Washington State. (Muhammad had hoped to hijack the tenth plane himself and, upon landing, make a statement denouncing U.S. policies in the Middle East, but bin Laden rejected the idea.)[20]

With so many operations planned to occur simultaneously and operatives going to different corners of the Earth to carry them out, good travel arrangements became a priority. Bin Laden's top aides—Muhammad, Abu Zubaydah, and Atef—constituted a security committee that planned operations and, as an adjunct, set up an office of passports and host country issues at Kandahar Airport. Atef was in charge of the office, which altered passports, visas, and identification cards, and held onto passports of those who were sent to the front in the internal conflict against Massoud; if they died in combat, their papers would be recycled for the use of others. The security committee also relied on outside facilitators to obtain fraudulent documents, arrange visas (whether real or fake), and make airline reservations. For those who needed fake documents and could not make it to Kandahar, there was at least one safe house in Kabul that had a stock of forged official stamps of the United Nations and the city councils of Turin and Milan, Italy, as well as for travel in Pakistan and Malaysia.

In autumn 1999, bin Laden opened a new camp at Mes Aynak, an abandoned Russian copper mine near Kabul, where the focus of training was on physical fitness, firearms, close-quarters combat, shooting from motorcycles, and night operations. Muhammad organized a follow-on course at a safe house in Karachi, where he would train operatives in basic English words and phrases, how to read airline timetables and use the Internet, and code words in communications. He also offered flight simulator training, computer games, and films featuring hijackings. Operatives were trained to alter passports by substituting photos and erasing and adding travel stamps. A critical skill to master was "cleaning off" Pakistani visas for operatives who were applying for American visas or for Saudis returning to their home country. Drawing on the time he had spent in the United States, Muhammad also offered a course on adapting to American culture.*[21]

Bin Laden's choice of operatives was not always on target, but he did not like to give up on them. Muhammad complained that both al Hazmi and al Mihdhar lacked motivation to learn English and graduate from flight school, but bin Laden insisted on retaining them, while taking note of the criticism.

His recruitment and training apparatus came to the rescue when four Arab volunteers from Hamburg, Germany, turned up in Kandahar as new recruits at the end of November 1999. The volunteers—Muhammad Atta of Egypt, Ramzi Binalshibh of Yemen, Marwan al Shehhi of the United Arab Emirates, and Ziad Jarrah of Lebanon— had intended to volunteer to fight in Chechnya, but a chance meeting on a German train with an al Qaeda sympathizer led them to travel first to Pakistan and then

---

*After attending secondary school in Kuwait, Muhammad had enrolled in Chowan College, a small Baptist school in Murfreesboro, North Carolina. He later transferred to North Carolina A&T in Greensboro, a historically black state university, where he received a degree in mechanical engineering in December 1986.

to Kandahar. There they pledged *bayat* to bin Laden. Thousands of recruits had passed through his training camps, and some of them no doubt were highly capable, but bin Laden had supreme confidence that he could intuit who was best suited for his operations. Though he had just met them and not yet trained them in demolition or other operations, bin Laden picked the four to lead the assault on the World Trade Center. He chose Atta as his "emir" or tactical commander, then gave each of the four $5,000 to pay for their return to Germany. Atta, Jarrah, and Binalshibh departed for Karachi to attend Khalid Sheikh Muhammad's training course on living in the United States. Back in Germany, they shaved their beards, donned Western clothes, cut off all contact with Islamic radicals, and researched flight schools. They left for the United States by June 2000; within a few months, they were studying flying in Florida. Binalshibh, the Yemeni, was unable to obtain a visa and served as the Germany-based liaison with bin Laden.[22]

The camps were the centerpiece of the al Qaeda infrastructure, drawing recruits from around the world and graduating trained and determined mass killers. They featured multifaceted training, coordinated curriculum, and ideological and religious indoctrination, built around a portrayal of the United States and Israel as evil, and Arab rulers as illegitimate. Most of the recruits went through boot camp for conventional combat, and the best and most zealous went on to the advanced courses. The Al-Farouq camp near Khost was "tantamount to a military college," according to bin Laden's bodyguard, Abu Jandal, who said he spent months on training courses there in 1996 and 1997. Cadets passed through a series of courses until they graduated "as military commanders capable of leading any jihadist action anywhere." * Bin Laden was active as overseer and guest lecturer, preaching hatred against his stated enemies and the virtues of martyrdom. The result was a climate "in which trainees and other personnel were free to think creatively about ways to commit mass murder," U.S. investigators later concluded.[23]

Selection of future martyrs was not left to chance. Every recruit for training in the camps filled out a questionnaire. The questions included "What brought you to Afghanistan? How did you travel here? How did you hear about us? What attracted you to the cause? What is your educational background?"

It was through such a questionnaire that bin Laden discovered Hani Hanjour, a Saudi who had already had pilot training in the United States and had come to Afghanistan as a volunteer. Bin Laden enrolled him straight out of the al-Farouk camp. This was a fortuitous recruitment, for

---

* The three-stage training consisted of boot camp, an exhausting fifteen-day test of stamina; a military preparation and drilling stage, which lasted forty-five days and included extensive weapons training; and finally, training in guerrilla tactics and irregular warfare, which lasted another forty-five days.

it became clear in the course of 2000 that al Hazmi and al Mihdhar would be flight school dropouts.[24]

The USS *Cole*

The plan to blow up a U.S. warship in the Persian Gulf came from a free-lance jihadi looking for a new target. Abd al Rahim al Nashiri (like bin Laden, a Saudi of Yemeni origin) had been fighting a doomed jihad against the government of Tajikistan in 1996 when he heard of bin Laden's arrival in Afghanistan and traveled with a group to meet him in Jalalabad. He heard the lectures and watched the videos but declined bin Laden's invitation to swear *bayat*. Instead, he returned to Yemen, where he conceived the idea of blowing up an American vessel. In 1997, Nashiri was back in Afghanistan, this time as a Taliban volunteer fighting Massoud. He traveled several times to Kandahar, saw bin Laden, and joined al Qaeda. Late in 1998 he presented his plan; bin Laden agreed to it and directed him to start the planning and send militants to Yemen. Nashiri later told investigators that throughout the planning phase, he reported directly to bin Laden, who was the only other person who knew all details of the operation. The original plan—to attack a vessel along Yemen's western coast—proved unworkable; bin Laden instructed him to check out the port of Aden in the south.[25]

To support Nashiri, bin Laden in early 1999 sent a personal acquaintance from his days in Jeddah who had followed his own path to militant Islam. Tawfiq bin Attash (Khallad) was another Saudi of Yemeni origin. Khallad's father had been expelled from Yemen for religious extremism, and Khallad grew up in Jeddah, Saudi Arabia. As a child he met bin Laden, who was twenty-two years his senior. In 1994, at the age of fifteen, Khallad traveled to Afghanistan. After the Taliban took power, he joined the fight against Massoud, where he lost his lower right leg in a training accident. (His own version was that he lost it in battle.) After losing a brother in 1997, he pledged *bayat* to bin Laden and volunteered to become a suicide bomber. Bin Laden must have had great trust in Khallad, for he assigned him to practically every project—he is the Zelig of the story, but he often stumbled. Bin Laden wanted to send him to the United States on a suicide mission, but his visa application was rejected, not because of his links with bin Laden but because he failed to provide enough documentation to support the application. Next, he was arrested in Yemen in a case of mistaken identity: he was driving the car of another member of the ship-bombing conspiracy who was wanted by police. Fearing that Khallad would reveal the operation, bin Laden personally intervened with Yemeni officials to secure his release. At this point, Khallad returned to Afghanistan, where bin Laden sent him to commando training at Mes Aynak and to Khalid Sheikh Muhammad's finishing school in Karachi. A number of members of the 1999 graduating class at Mes Aynak were destined for major suicide operations.[26]

The plotters in Aden settled down to wait (without Khallad) for a U.S. warship. The first to arrive was the USS *The Sullivans*, a destroyer named for five brothers from Waterloo, Iowa, who lost their lives on the same ship during the battle of Guadalcanal in World War II. The plotters loaded the explosives on board a thirty-five-foot fiberglass boat. The suicide pilots were Ibrahim al Thawar ("Nibras"), who had attended the Mes Aynak commando training, and Hassan al Khamri. But the boat, overloaded with explosives, sank "like a rock" upon launch, according to Yemeni officials. Nibras, al Khamri, and a third operative, Fahd Muhammad Ahmed al Quso, fled the scene, and others went into hiding.[27]

Nibras and al Quso flew from Yemen to Bangkok with the leftover funds. They delivered the money to Khallad, who had been assigned to the Pacific section of what would become the 9/11 attacks. Khallad traveled to Kuala Lumpur, ostensibly to have a prosthesis fitted for his right leg, but bin Laden asked him to case Western airlines for hijacking possibilities. Also arriving in Kuala Lumpur at the time were Hazmi and Mihdhar, both destined for the United States, and Abu Bara, who was assigned to the Pacific aircraft bombings. All bunked at the apartment of Yazid Sufaat, a Malaysian member of the al Qaeda affiliate Jemaah Islamiya. The four then moved to Bangkok, where Khallad was to meet Nibras and al Quso. The two plots almost intersected, as both groups of suicide bombers slept in the same hotel at one time, but Khallad said he never introduced the different plotters to one another.[28]

The Kuala Lumpur stopover provided intelligence and law enforcement officials with a first glimpse of those who would be responsible for the calamities in store. Sufaat's apartment was under surveillance, and both Malaysian intelligence and the CIA noted the comings and goings of the visiting Arabs and took photographs.

Bin Laden rebounded from the setback in Aden by tightening the reins. In April or May 2000, he called off the East Asian part of the planes operation directed at the U.S. West Coast, on the grounds that it would be too difficult to synchronize the hijacking and crashing of these flights with those against East Coast targets. He reassigned Khallad once again. Originally appointed as a pilot for the East Coast attacks, he had become coordinator of the West Coast attacks; now he was reassigned to the warship account. Meanwhile, bin Laden had learned an important lesson from the Jordan disaster: to avoid open communications. According to al Nashiri, throughout the operation to destroy a U.S. warship, he had neither telephone nor e-mail contact. Whenever bin Laden wanted to communicate with him, he would send an al Qaeda member to Pakistan to summon Nashiri.[29]

The conspirators returned to Yemen with more funds—$5,000 to $10,000, according to one source—and instructions to try again. Incredibly, when they returned to the launch point, they found their skiff underwater, still packed with explosives, where they had abandoned it seven months earlier. The vessel was salvageable, although the engine was missing. But Aden is a small town, and they recovered the engine for what was described as "a ransom." Using lighter, more powerful explosives, they built a new bomb into the same boat. After the abortive first attempt, bin Laden turned micromanager. Worrying that the team would fail again, he told Nashiri in September to replace the two suicide bombers, al Khamri and Nibras. But in another example of the decentralized power structure bin Laden fostered, Nashiri disagreed and left for Afghanistan to make his case. Before departing Yemen, he instructed al Khamri and Nibras to attack the next U.S. warship that entered the port.[30]

It was the USS *Cole*, a guided missile destroyer. Fresh from duty in the Red Sea, the *Cole* steamed into port for a four-hour refueling call on October 12, 2000. Shortly after 11:00 a.m., the skiff headed toward the $1 billion warship at a high speed. The two Arab men on board were dressed in white. One, of medium height, had a foot on the gunwale. The second, farther forward, crouched slightly. A witness aboard the destroyer recalled seeing a five-foot covered storage well in the bow of the skiff. The small boat circled toward the left side of the *Cole*, cut its engines, and drifted into the warship. The two men smiled and waved, and thirty feet above, some of the sailors on the deck, expecting a garbage skiff, waved back.

At that moment, some six hundred pounds of plastic explosives detonated with a force that lifted the 8,300-ton warship out of the water and cut a twenty- by forty-foot gash into its side. When it dropped back, the ship was listing four degrees. Only the skill of the crew saved the destroyer from sinking, but seventeen sailors were killed and thirty-nine were injured.[31]

The assault occurred less than a month before U.S. presidential elections, but neither outgoing vice president Al Gore nor Texas governor George W. Bush made an issue of it. "If, as it now appears, this was an act of terrorism, it was a despicable and cowardly act," Clinton said, adding, "We will find out who was responsible and hold them accountable." Bush spoke in a similar vein: "Let's hope we can gather enough intelligence to figure out who did the act and take the necessary action. . . . There must be a consequence." Gore said if it was a terrorist attack, "This is a situation that will bring a response."[32]

Bin Laden did not claim credit, but when a Kuwaiti newspaper reported him as disavowing any link with the attack, he sent word within twenty-four hours to journalist Rahimullah Yusufzai that his 1998 fatwa declaring jihad against the United States and Israel "remained valid and binding on Muslims." Bin Laden anticipated military retaliation and ordered the evacuation of the Kandahar Airport compound. With his entourage, he fled to a desert area near Kabul, then moved to Khost and Jalalabad before returning to Kandahar, where he rotated among five or six residences. To preserve the leadership in the event of his death, he sent Zawahiri to

Kabul and Atef to a different part of Afghanistan. The Taliban leadership was less worried. Foreign Minister Muttawakil told a visiting CNN crew that he did not foresee "any U.S. attack."[33]

In most quarters of Washington, it was obvious who had bombed the *Cole*. "All of us who saw that attack said, of course, where would this have come from?" recalled Inderfurth. John O'Neill, the senior FBI counterterrorism expert dispatched to Yemen to lead the investigation, "knew before he even got there that it was al Qaeda" and said as much, recalled an associate in the business world. A top official said the Defense Intelligence Agency (DIA) felt "pretty confident" that it was al Qaeda. "We had a very solid indication that it was al Qaeda. We presumed. Within a couple of weeks it was clear," he said. Was this conclusive? "I don't know what you would call conclusive," the official said. "100 percent sure? 98 percent sure?"[34]

Massoud's intelligence network picked up strong circumstantial evidence of bin Laden's involvement. According to a senior Massoud aide who had many contacts in the U.S. government, there were celebrations and prayers for the "martyrs" at Darunta camp and at the Kunduz military camp, where al Qaeda units were stationed. In addition, Massoud's network received intelligence that an operative named Abu Hidal had been involved in the planning in Afghanistan. This information was transmitted to the CIA within a week at a location in Central Asia, but officials at the CIA, the State Department, Richard Clarke's office at the White House, and the Senate Intelligence Committee later said they never heard of the information—it appears that the message never circulated within the U.S. government.[35]

Clinton had set an almost impossible standard of proof before undertaking any military operation against al Qaeda. He demanded that the CIA and FBI have enough evidence to "be willing to stand up in public and say, 'We believe that he did this.'" But everyone knew that direct evidence of the sort obtained after the 1998 bombings would be hard to come by, for bin Laden had stopped using a satellite telephone. The only hope was that an arrested suspect would directly link an attack to bin Laden, but those who were in contact with bin Laden could be presumed to have fled the scene. This meant that a conclusion could be reached only by assembling a mosaic of data from multiple sources. It was very difficult for anyone to do this at the top of the administration. For one thing, soon after the *Cole* attack, intelligence analysts (presumably at White House orders), stopped circulating written reports on who was responsible for the bombing and distributed all information only in informal briefings.

One month after the attack, on November 11, Yemeni authorities established the link to al Qaeda. Interrogations of Quso and Jamal al Badawi had helped identify the men who provided operational direction. They were Khallad and al Nashiri, both already known to have strong links to al Qaeda and the 1998 embassy bombings. A day later, Berger told Clinton that it was becoming increasingly clear that al Qaeda had "planned and directed the bombing." On November 25, he and Clarke told Clinton in writing that the investigations would soon conclude that a cell headed by senior al Qaeda members had carried out the attack. Most of those involved had been trained in bin Laden's camps, and two intelligence reports pointed to his involvement. But Berger said al Qaeda responsibility was an "unproven assumption."[36]

In late December 2000, the CIA informed a small group of cabinet members of its preliminary judgment that bin Laden had "supported the attack" on the *Cole,* based on strong circumstantial evidence linking al Nashiri and Khallad to al Qaeda. The CIA also said it did not have "definitive" proof bin Laden had directed the attack, and Clinton decided this was an insufficient basis for going to war. In January 2001, the CIA established that Khallad had been in Kuala Lumpur a year earlier with several other Arabs and that he was a senior security officer for bin Laden who had helped direct the *Cole* bombing. But the information was not widely shared.

It was obvious that Clinton, as a lame duck president, simply did not want to use force. While the U.S. Central Command prepared contingency plans for wide-ranging bombing in Afghanistan, cabinet-level agencies never held a discussion about the use of force.[37]

Those responsible for the attack on the *Cole* went unpunished, and so did the officers responsible for lax security on the destroyer. A Navy inquiry into preparations aboard the destroyer determined that the commander had failed to apply the most basic security procedures. No one was on the bridge, and those on watch had not been briefed on their responsibilities. According to Vice Admiral C. W. Moore, Jr., commander of naval forces in the Middle East, the destroyer's captain had failed to plan and implement a force protection plan, including how to fend off unauthorized vessels. No one was court-martialed, and no one resigned. As he left office, Defense Secretary William Cohen said everyone in the chain of command was responsible, starting with himself. The ship's captain, Commander Kirk Lippold, retained his command.[38]

"The Navy was myopic," General Anthony Zinni said later. "In the Gulf, security was really intense. Outside the Gulf, it may not have been as focused," especially for a ship arriving in the region for the first time. He said he personally took responsibility for the calamity. His successor as commander in chief of the Central Command, General Tommy Franks, was in place by early 2001; Franks had no doubts about what had occurred. "This is an act of war, and it needs a response," he told an audience at the National Defense University. Franks did not hesitate to confirm this quote later: "The quote reflected my view in 2001—still reflects my view of what should have been done post-*Cole.*" But the momentum had been lost. The new administration felt it was too late for a tit-for-tat response. Defense

Secretary Donald Rumsfeld thought too much time had passed, and Deputy Defense Secretary Paul Wolfowitz said the attack was "stale."[39]

Bin Laden was disappointed, it was later learned, and frequently complained to his associates in Afghanistan that the United States had failed to strike. In the absence of American retaliation, he told them he "would launch something bigger." The swagger in his complaint suggests anger that he was not being taken seriously by successive U.S. administrations. But what sort of retaliation was he expecting? Another U.S. attack of any sort would enhance his worldwide image—a failed attack all the more so. But the outcome could just as easily be his death (in his eyes, martyrdom). If U.S. leaders carried out the threats Inderfurth and Sheehan continually voiced to the Taliban, the result also would have been the end of the regime that gave him sanctuary. That, it can be presumed, he was not seeking. What is certain is that bin Laden did not want to be ignored.

Early in 2001, bin Laden used the *Cole* attack as the basis for a suicide bomber recruitment video that began circulating in the Arab world. *Destroying the Destroyer Cole* showed scenes of the damaged ship, scenes of Islamic suffering in Palestine and other places, and a parade of villains, including Bill Clinton and even Yasir Arafat, who was criticized for denouncing suicide bombings in Israel. Bin Laden then appeared for a lecture on how the "subservience and humiliation" of Muslims the world over was due to "the love of the present life and the hatred of death." Glory awaited the fighter who did not fear death, he proclaimed.[40]

In place of direct action of any sort, the United States pressed successfully for a new round of UN sanctions against the Taliban. The sanctions did not achieve their goal of forcing the Taliban to expel bin Laden, but they caused collateral damage, putting an end to UN–led diplomacy. Since January 2000, Francesc Vendrell—a veteran UN troubleshooter with expertise in Central America, Timor, Haiti, the Caucasus, and East Asia—had been in charge of the UN Special Mission to Afghanistan (UNSMA), with the rank of assistant secretary-general. In his quest to revive negotiations for a political solution, he met with Mullah Omar in the autumn of 2000, making him perhaps only the third non-Muslim to be received by the mullah. Omar agreed to UN–mediated dialogue with the armed opposition, and he agreed to let the United Nations set up civil affairs units in five major cities. But the arms embargo—imposed only on the Taliban—made a process of dialogue "virtually impossible."[41]

Massoud Loses Taloqan

Bin Laden's success in Yemen was paralleled by a major military breakthrough in Afghanistan, in which foreign fighters played an instrumental role.

The year 2000 began with a contest for control over outlying districts in the north-central highlands. After opposition forces recaptured the market town of Darra Souf in Samangan province in late 1999, under Hazara leader Ustad Mohammad Mohaqiq, the Taliban retook the territory in late January. Pashtuns and Tajiks displaced to Mazar-i-Sharif by the United Front (UF) advance charged the UF troops with summary executions, burning of houses, and widespread looting during the four months they were in control. Taliban cavalry recaptured the nearby crossroads town of Sangcharak and the Gosfandi Valley, and Mohaqiq charged they had made 20,000 people homeless in the bitter winter weather. From January to March 2000, the Taliban massacred civilians in five separate incidents in the Gosfandi district, killing ninety-six people by firing squad. The UF regained control over the district in mid-March, and the Taliban reclaimed it by early April. An independent survey of war crimes concluded that the abuses by the Taliban were "systematic, repeated, and part of a general campaign of collective punishment on civilians in areas that had surrendered to the Taliban but which continued to provide a base for resistance activity."[42]

Roughly at the same time as the Gosfandi massacres, Taliban forces seized more than thirty men from a number of hamlets in neighboring Baghlan province; first they beat the men, then they imprisoned them in a textile factory in Pul-i-Khumri, the main town in Baghlan, at the rear base of Mullah Shahzad Qandahari, a senior Taliban commander. Around May 8, the men (all Shia of the Ismaeli sect) were loaded onto a Toyota pickup truck and driven to the Robotak Pass in Samangan province, about 100 miles south of Mazar-i-Sharif on the main road to Kabul. Their hands were bound behind their backs, and they were tied together in groups of two or three by their turbans and headscarves as primitive ropes; they were shot in the back. Shepherds found them in shallow graves.*[43]

The fighting that summer had every appearance of the familiar back-and-forth, with control swinging back and forth in Kunduz province and on the Shamali plains north of Kabul. The Taliban launched two major offensives in July; they took heavy losses but gained no ground.

The U.S. government was not watching very carefully. On the eve of disaster, Rick Inderfurth painted a rosy picture: "We believe the Taliban now have little prospect of completing their goal of gaining control over the 15 percent of the country held by the opposition," he told the Senate Foreign Relations committee on July 20. "We believe the Taliban have reached their high-water mark." He spoke of "erosion in Taliban authority and effectiveness" and asserted that many Afghans were "giving up whatever hope they had for Taliban rule." But he was winging it, spinning a scenario

---

* UN officials appealed to Mary Robinson, the UN high commissioner for human rights, to denounce the massacre. A UN official said that, as after the 1997 Mazar-i-Sharif massacre, she responded coolly, asking, "Does this fall within my mandate to look into this 'massacre?'" Kamal Hossain, the special rapporteur, agreed to look into it; an investigator arrived in April 2001, a full year after the event. UNHCHR official, interview by author, Geneva, February 2003.

in the absence of good intelligence—"a little effort at psychological mess-
ing with Taliban minds," he later conceded. "We wanted them to think we
were convinced they would never take the country. By our saying that, perhaps they would think that it is so." In fact, he may have sent precisely the
opposite signal by declaring there would be no arms for Massoud: "I think
where we draw the line is offering the Northern Alliance military assistance. I think that that would be a mistake in terms of our becoming actively
involved militarily once again in Afghanistan."[44]

The big offensive was about to unfold. The target was Taloqan, the
capital of Takhar province, a vital city in northeast Afghanistan for the UF:
its main supply gateway, major base, and unofficial capital. Unlike practically every previous Taliban assault, this one was a well-planned conventional offensive that took advantage of the militia's strength in numbers,
basic logistics, and doggedness, as well as foreign support. It also used tactics
that might have originated in the guerrilla force's own training manual.

It began with two strategic moves: the capture of Nahrin and Ishkamish on August 1, cutting off Massoud's key supply line between the Tajikistan border and the Panjshir Valley; and the capture of Bangi a week
later, which opened a road to Kunduz for Taliban resupply. This time the
Taliban mounted repeated and, according to Massoud, "very fierce"
attacks with "huge forces," often starting in the middle of the night, on
August 9, 13, 14, and 19. The defenders destroyed about one hundred
small bridges, flooded the rice fields, and set up minefields around all their
positions, and caused heavy losses, Massoud said. On September 4, reinforced by new units and supported by an increased number of tanks, artillery
fire, and air assaults, the Taliban launched a powerful attack on Taloqan
from four directions. The militia announced that it had broken through
Massoud's front lines. His own spokesman said the Taliban had advanced
"a bit . . . but we have stopped it." After midnight on September 6, the Taliban force captured Taloqan, and Massoud ordered a tactical withdrawal.[45]

This was Massoud's biggest loss since Kabul, but the cause has never
been fully explained. Massoud's forces fought hard. The United Nations
estimated that the Taliban deployed up to 15,000 fighters, while Massoud
had less than half that number; of the 6,000–9,000 casualties, two-thirds
were Taliban. The Taliban undoubtedly drew on a strong foreign contingent. Anthony Davis reported that up to a third of the Taliban force—
which he estimated at 20,000 troops—was foreign, most of them Pakistani volunteers, as well as 1,000–1,500 Arab fighters. Davis quoted a
Western military analyst saying that 300–400 Punjabi-speaking infantry
displaying "extraordinary collective skills" (possibly commando elements
from the Pakistan Army Special Services Group or special forces) took
part in the offensive, embedded among the Pakistani volunteers. Massoud's
close aide, Masoud Khalili, then serving as ambassador to India, told
reporters that three senior Pakistani officers had commanded the offensive

and 3,000 "mercenaries"—including Arabs, Chechens, and Chinese Uighurs—had joined the fighting. Massoud himself said a Pakistani captain named Jamal was in charge of the fighting until August 20, when he was replaced by Allah Nawaz. But the assertions about a Pakistan command role have never been confirmed.*

And what was bin Laden's role? In Kabul business circles, the story circulated that bin Laden was contributing some $200,000 a day to the offensive, which would total as much as $7 million over five weeks. The funds not only would have sustained the Arab contingent but would also have helped persuade Massoud commanders to defect during and after the offensive. The offensive showed a far higher level of advance planning and strategic thinking, which the Taliban consistently lacked but which were characteristic of bin Laden's involvement; however, his exact contribution remains unclear.[46]

The other explanation, from a UN observer who spent considerable time in the Panjshir valley, was that Massoud simply ran out of ammunition. After five weeks of fending off Taliban offensives, and with his resupply cut since the previous month, this is highly plausible.

The Taliban held onto Taloqan with uncharacteristic tenacity, and Massoud never recovered it. The militia had as many as 1,000 dead and 1,500 wounded in the fighting, but when they moved into the city, it was nearly empty. Between 80,000 and 100,000 Taloqan residents had fled east and north, fearing the kind of Taliban wrath that had occurred in Mazar-i-Sharif. This mass evacuation generated yet another humanitarian nightmare, and both Pakistan and Tajikistan subsequently closed their borders. The fall of Taloqan had an immediate negative impact on the strange American plan for a Russian intervention: Uzbekistan was the logical jump-off point, but its leader, Islam Karimov, chose this moment to switch horses.

---

*HRW, in an apparent overstatement, said the U.S. government issued a démarche to Pakistan in late 2000, asking for assurances that Pakistan had not been involved in the conquest of Taloqan. But both Assistant Secretary Rick Inderfurth and Ambassador William Milam said they never sent any such démarche. "Every once in a while, it was as if General Patton descended on the battlefield," Milam commented, "but you'll never find evidence" of direct Pakistani involvement. Under Secretary of State Thomas Pickering, the lead U.S. official addressing Pakistan in 2000, said it was "hard" to determine that Pakistan played a key role "on the basis of the intelligence I saw . . . and I saw a lot." A top DIA official at the time said there were "linkages and sponsorships," and probably some "rogue elements" of ISI were more involved than official elements; otherwise, he said, "I would not put them that much in bed together. I saw nothing that would have come to the conclusion that [Pakistanis] were acting like battlefield strategists."

For its part, HRW said the démarche was the subject of a report by journalist Ahmed Rashid and added that U.S. diplomatic sources confirmed the report; however, an HRW staffer, who asked not to be identified by name but was directly involved in the drafting, said in 2006 that he was "puzzled by the use of the term 'démarche.'" He added, "I don't recall the U.S. ever issuing a démarche to Pakistan about anything that happened in Afghanistan." HRW, *Crisis of Impunity*, 26fns105 and 106; Milam, interview; Pickering, interview; and telephone interviews with former top DIA official, who spoke on condition of anonymity, July 2003 and March 2004; and e-mail message to author from HRW writer, February 2006.

"It had a huge impact on the Uzbeks," Vendrell recalled. In October, Karimov turned down Russia's proposal to sign a collective security agreement with the other "stans." Instead, he opened direct talks with the Taliban aimed at reconciliation.

Outside the region, Massoud's defeat drew almost no notice. The *New York Times* devoted one paragraph to the fall of Taloqan, more space than practically any other U.S. newspaper.[47]

9

Human Rights under Massoud and the Taliban

If ever there was a moment Massoud needed help, it was after the fall of his headquarters in Taloqan. A determined opponent had dealt him a devastating setback, and the death blow might not be far behind.

Massoud had backers in some quarters of the CIA and the White House, but they were more than offset by his critics. So long as there was no ambassador or special envoy to Afghanistan, or a respected voice from outside the executive branch calling for a policy review, Washington was in stalemate. The people who carried the day were State Department and National Security Council officials who remained deeply ambivalent about the guerrilla commander and routinely disparaged him as a "heroin trafficker" and "human rights abuser." As Madeleine Albright put it, "He killed a few people along the way. . . . There were questions about drugs and thugs and various aspects of the way that they operated." The accumulated charges bear examination.*

There is no question that opium was a major crop in Badakhshan, the last province under Massoud's control. Anyone driving from the airport to see Burhanuddin Rabbani in Faizabad would have noted poppy on both sides of the road, and there were at least three heroin refineries within sight of his remote capital. But was Massoud, the pious Muslim, involved in the trade?

The Taliban, which *did* profit from the opium trade, ordered a ban in July 2000; a year later, opium poppy cultivation was down 90 percent (to 7,606 hectares from 82,172). But in Badakhshan, it tripled from 2,458 hectares to 6,342 by mid-2001.

---

*Their disparaging views are reported in Steve Coll's *Ghost Wars* and in the *9/11 Commission Report*. In 1998 and 1999, diplomats argued that Massoud was tainted by "his reliance on heroin trafficking for income" (*Ghost Wars*, 430). His budget was "cobbled together from heroin smuggling deals" (458). State Department officials cited "persistent reports" that Massoud was engaged in drug trafficking. In 2000, Clinton referred to Massoud's "record of brutality" (466), and Albright and Berger felt that Massoud's forces were "too discredited to ever overthrow the Taliban" (490). Clarke is quoted saying of the United Front, "They're not a very good group of people to begin with; they're drug runners. They're human rights abusers. It's just not something you're going to build a government around" (516). The *9/11 Commission Report*, in a section reporting the views of CIA director George Tenet, described Massoud as "reflective and charismatic" and added, "but his bands have been charged with more than one massacre, and the Northern Alliance was widely thought to finance itself in part through trade in heroin." Massoud had not "shown much aptitude for governing except as a ruthless warlord," it added (139).

Still, the case against Massoud turns out to be very thin. "We are against the trade and our position is clear," Massoud told journalist Anthony Davis in mid-2001. By that time, however, the northeastern enclave was an important passage for narcotics exported to Central Asia and Europe, and opium traders who had been operating in the south of the country stimulated the production and developed it as a primary export route. UF helicopters were used to smuggle narcotics to Tajikistan, but with the Taliban at the gates promising gold to would-be defectors, Davis pointed out that an antinarcotics crackdown against well-entrenched local commanders "would have been tantamount to suicide." Davis doubted the allegation against Massoud. "I don't believe for a moment Massoud was personally involved in the narcotics trade," he said. And Vendrell, the UN special envoy, said in his talks with American officials in 2000–2001, "None of them ever said we're not talking to [Massoud] because of drugs. We all knew a lot of opium was cultivated in Badakhshan, in Faizabad. I never heard from the Americans that he was profiting from it."[1]

The major criticism of Massoud's human rights record centers on the 1993 killings of Hazara civilians in the Afshar neighborhood of Kabul. This was Massoud's operation, while defense minister, to capture the military and political headquarters of the Shia Hezbi Wahdat in west Kabul after Wahdat leader Abdul Ali Mazari withdrew from the government and began secret talks with Hekmatyar's Hezbi Islami. Massoud's Jamiat forces and Abdul Rasul Sayyaf's Ittihad-i-Islami sent in troops at five o' clock in the morning on February 11, 1993. Mazari and his commanders fled the University Social Science Institute, where they had their headquarters, by about one o' clock in the afternoon. Troops of both Jamiat and Ittihad undertook a search operation that investigators later described as "a mass exercise in abuse and looting." But according to witnesses located by the Afghanistan Justice Project, the force that entered Afshar and committed summary executions, disappearances, and rape was Sayyaf's Ittihad, which was not under Massoud's command. Massoud ordered a halt to the massacres and looting on February 12, but they continued (see chapter 3).

Was Massoud a "human rights abuser" with a "record of brutality?" In the seesaw fighting in northern Shamali in 1999, "there was a tendency in the heat of battle not to take prisoners," said Davis, who spent several months each year with Massoud's forces from 1981 to 2001. "But," he added, "atrocities in the real sense of that term I'm not aware of." There was "no pattern of repeated killings of enemy civilians or military prisoners" by Massoud's forces, according to Davis.

The United Nations's Francesc Vendrell doubted that Massoud's human rights record was the basis for U.S. policy. "That doesn't wash. I don't believe for one single minute that this was the reason," he said. He said the U.S. government had a lot of contact with other leaders who had much worse records. In addition, "I don't think the situation of human rights was terrible in the north." The reason the Americans disparaged Massoud, he said, was because "they probably thought he had no chance. It was very difficult to supply him."[2]

Atrocities and Abandonment

The more relevant human rights record for determining the American compass in South Asia was that of the Taliban. Here, the most notable pattern was the absence of an international outcry in the face of widespread, systematic, and repeated crimes. These included the random execution of noncombatants, organized massacres and other terror tactics, abduction of women, forced marriage, destruction of the agricultural infrastructure, and complete disregard for the plight of the populations displaced by their conquest.

The Taliban and the United Front were structured very differently. UF forces were said to "understand modern warfare"; they had "relatively organized forces with recognizable chains of command." Their rivalries weakened their military efficiency, wrote Andreas Schiess, chief investigator for the UN Office of the High Commissioner for Human Rights in September 1999, in the long-delayed investigation of the 1997 Mazar-i-Sharif massacre.

> The ability of the Northern Alliance to apply the law of war to a certain extent exists. Some commanders are aware of this and have the necessary background training to be in a position to implement it. Their problem lies in the shifting system of alliances and in the committee structure of their command arrangements. In addition, they have difficulty in taking disciplinary measures. This weakens the position of field commanders and certainly allows them to shift responsibility and blame for wrongdoing to others.

The Taliban were a very different story. Men were grouped in units of roughly one hundred, training was rudimentary, and commanders had the right of life or death over any soldier without the need for evidence or a fair trial. Taliban military operations appeared to have three fundamental characteristics, Schiess said: "a seemingly pathological desire for revenge, which clouds military judgment"; "an apparent inability to compromise on anything"; and "jealousy—if they can't have it, then why should anyone else have it either?" These attitudes "tended to influence the whole of their military behavior." Schiess added:

> Although professing a strong regard for Islam and its principles of warfare, they hardly apply them in battle. The strong command arrangements described above make it possible to enforce strict rules. The problem appears to be that they regard their enemies as beneath contempt. To murder or torture enemy soldiers or civilians who do not profess the same religious belief is not only condoned but encouraged.[3]

There is no question that Malik and his Jumbesh fighters were responsible for the mass killing of captured Taliban after the uprising when the movement failed to conquer Mazar-i-Sharif in 1997, or that Jamiat's shelling of Kabul Airport often hit civilian districts. By comparison, the abductions, torture, and systematic killing ascribed to the Taliban were not spontaneous occurrences but were ordered by senior officials in a pattern of collective punishment. In March 2001, the United Nations issued a list of the fourteen worst massacres in Afghanistan between May 1997 and February 2001—thirteen were ascribed to the Taliban. According to a UN observer at that time, the abuses were systematic and repeated, and each followed Taliban attempts to consolidate control over northern and central Afghanistan. The victims were members of the ethnic minorities: the Hazaras, Uzbeks, and Tajiks. The pattern was this: on their first attempt to conquer, the Taliban would use limited violence against civilians; where there was resistance to Taliban control and the militia had to reconquer an area, they would "hold the whole of the civilian population responsible and punish them indiscriminately." Every war crime on the United Nation's list of summary executions and massacres occurred in central or northern Afghanistan during the Taliban's attempted conquest of the region.[4]

Following is the list (with best information available about the death toll or displacement in parentheses):

Mazar-i-Sharif and Dasht-i-Leili, May 1997 (at least 2,000 Taliban killed)[5]

Mazar-i-Sharif Airport (Qezelabad), September 1997 (53 Hazara killed)[6]

Qaysar, December 1997 (at least 600 unarmed villagers killed)[7]

Mazar-i-Sharif, August 1998 (at least 2,000 killed)[8]

Kayan Valley, August 1998 (up to 40,000 civilians displaced)[9]

Bamiyan, May 1999 (120 killed, at least 20,000 civilians displaced)[10]

Shamali plains, August 1999 (140,000 civilians displaced)[11]

Khwaja Ghar, September 1999 (70 killed, 23,000 rooms destroyed)[12]

Gosfandi, January 2000 (50 men killed in mosque)[13]

Robotak, May 2000 (31 men executed)[14]

Taloqan, September 2000 (more than 300,000 civilians displaced)[15]

Yakawlang, January 2001 (at least 176 killed, 30,000 civilians displaced)[16]

Khwaja Ghar, January 2001 (34–50 civilians killed)[17]

Bamiyan, February 2001 (no detail in UN reports)[18]

Every entry on the list marks an atrocity. Take the massacre at Qezelebad in September 1997. Choong-Hyun Paik, the OHCHR's indefatigable special rapporteur for Afghanistan, traveled there in December 1997. He reported that the Taliban had made an attempt to capture Mazar-i-Sharif and, on withdrawing, had moved into the mostly Hazara village of Qeze-labad, near the airport. On the pretext of disarming civilians, they went door to door, shooting at whomever answered their knock. Paik reported, "If a person who had opened the door said that they did not have any [weapons], they were shot on the spot, in front of their family. If a person provided a weapon, the Taliban allegedly shot them on the spot with that same weapon. A number of farmers from the village were killed in the fields, some report-edly with their own agricultural implements." According to a report from the Office of the UN High Commissioner for Refugees (UNHCR), the Taliban captured a group of fourteen young men, whom they then tortured by gouging out their eyes and pouring boiling water on them before killing them. Fifty-three villagers were killed and twenty houses burned down. Another fourteen or fifteen young men were taken to the airport, where "they were subsequently tortured and executed," Paik reported.

Abdul Ali, the financial officer at Lepco, an NGO devoted to helping leprosy patients, was in the village during the four days the Taliban occu-pied it. He said the dead included a five-year-old boy, an elderly woman, and other people ages fifteen to sixty. "One had his neck cut from behind," he recalled. He said the total killed was seventy-one, plus forty-three Jum-besh soldiers who had surrendered at the junction of the airport road and had been executed.[19]

Human rights experts documented each of the cases on the United Nation's list. But the list is incomplete. Take the example of Sheikhabad, near Mazar-i-Sharif, where village elders told Paik that all the inhabitants had fled in fear of the Taliban except the oldest among them. The Taliban were reported to have "entered the village, tortured and killed the old men, and mutilated and dismembered some of the bodies," Paik reported. Thirty elderly people were reported to have been killed there.[20]

Mutilating and desecrating the dead was no aberration. Another mass execution of men from Mazar-i-Sharif not on the UN list occurred in the northeast Afghan city of Kunduz at about the same time as Qezelabad and Sheikhabad.

> I think it was October 1997 when a Taliban offensive into Mazar-i-Sharif had been turned back again. My friends told me later that while some di-visions were preparing for a retreat, others went from house to house and grabbed whatever men they could find from their homes and took the frightened men with them. Hundreds of men who were blindfolded and whose hands were tied behind their backs were stuffed into trucks like ani-mals and taken on the ten-hour trip between Mazar-i-Sharif and Kunduz. The trucks, filled with men ranging in age from teenagers to old men, were taken up the high hill where the Kunduz Airport is situated. I happened to be taking part in some training operations there. . . .

I was ordered to unload one of the trucks and then to escort the prisoners in a line toward a large field near the runway. . . . The prisoners,
around 240 men, were all lined up in a field. Ten at a time, they were led
forward with their blindfolds on, and shot in the head by the Taliban soldiers. In order to save bullets and minimize the chances of missing their
targets, the executioners stood within one meter of their victims. The soldiers
were standing in such close proximity to their targets that they themselves
were soon covered in blood. Their long scraggly beards became red and
sticky with blood. . . .

After all the men had been massacred, they ordered the truck drivers
to drive their heavy vehicles over the corpses. After many trips over the
bodies, they had been pushed down until they were even with the surface
of the earth.

The teller of the story was Gulbudin, son of Salim Khan, from Qarai
Yatim, Chahardara district in Kunduz province, a Pashtun who had become a Taliban official, going from village to village enforcing sharia laws.
He told an American humanitarian aid worker that he heard from friends
that wild dogs and vultures had devoured the flesh of the dead, and that
the dogs became mad because of all the human flesh they had consumed.[21]

One of the most frequent targets for the Taliban was the Bamiyan
Valley, which they discovered was easy to capture but hard to hold. Afghanistan's most impoverished region was desperately poor in the best of times;
over three years of fighting, the Taliban destroyed what there was of an
economy. Yakaolang, a small market town at the western end of the valley,
changed hands six times between 1998 and 2001, as did Bamiyan itself.
Both sides found it easier to capture the towns than to hold them; each time
the Taliban returned, the retribution against Hazaras grew harsher. At one
stage, human rights observers believe the Taliban decided to implement
what was essentially an ethnic cleansing of Hazaras (who are Shia), replacing them with Kuchi nomads (who are Sunni Pashtuns). By mid-2001,
every other tactic having failed, the Taliban settled on a scorched-earth
policy to render the land uninhabitable.

In September 1998, when the Taliban first captured Yakawlang, twenty
people were killed, according to the acting governor. Wahdat recaptured
the town later that year and the Bamiyan district in April 1999; in May
1999, the Taliban returned. Some 70,000 people (most of the population)
fled; about 500 died in the mountains of cold and exposure. The residents
who stayed behind were targets of systematic killings. About two-thirds of
the locals returned by August. After recapturing Bamiyan, the Taliban
force fanned out. In Fuladi, a prosperous farm town in a well-irrigated valley southwest of Bamiyan, more than 300 Taliban arrived around May 10,
after the fall of Bamiyan town, in pickups equipped with submachine guns
and rocket-propelled grenades. They arrested men in the town and in outlying villages, and shot 120 men, according to village records. For three days,

no one was allowed to bury the dead. Then the soldiers withdrew, replaced by so-called "police," who burned down more than 2,000 houses and at least one Shia mosque, and looted the cattle and sheep, which are the major source of income. Their intention was an ethnic cleansing. Said Ali, a religious student, was in a delegation of eight who traveled to Bamiyan to call on the Taliban commander, Mullah Fazil, to ask for assurances for the summer harvest. It was late May, almost three weeks after the Taliban takeover. "What is more important, your life or your harvest?" Fazil asked. "You should go." Pakistanis and Arabs who accompanied the Taliban also told locals, "You should leave. The land does not belong to you." One farmer recounted that Taliban leaders clearly stated their plan to bring in a new population. "They chose this place to remove the Shia and bring in the Sunnis," said Mohamed Riza. He lost three cows and two donkeys, and six of the sixteen rooms of his house were burned. He recalled Mullah Fazil saying at the time of the attack that the land should go to the Kuchis —nomadic Pashtuns who owned land closer to Yakawlang. "He gave the order to Kuchis to fight and conquer and keep the land."[22]

Wahdat recaptured the entire valley at the end of December 2000, but the following month the Taliban returned with a vengeance. It was snowing, the roads were blocked, and Wahdat was caught unprepared. Arriving in at least 250 pickup trucks, the Taliban quickly took control of the town and its public buildings, then sent out search parties to the villages in a six-mile radius. Males ages thirteen to fifty were rounded up and either killed in front of their families or taken to the Oxfam relief agency office in the center of town. The Taliban held onto the old men for one or two days, then executed the younger men by firing squad. Some victims were tortured with bayonets or knives before execution; at least one victim of the firing squad was mutilated by skinning.[23]

Most of the killings were conducted on January 8. Ibrahim, an illiterate farmer in the village of Gunbadi, recalls the return of the Taliban. "They arrived in cars, on horseback, and on foot," he said. "They shouted, 'You are part of the Northern Alliance. Hand over your weapons!'" Ibrahim said he replied that he was not in any military force but was just a farmer. "They took thirty-three people from our village—all the men. They tied our hands. They put us in a jail." Then they ordered them to walk, beating them with rifle butts as they went. At Qala Arbab Hassan Khan, a hamlet about 500 yards from the district center, a firing squad of three lined up thirteen people in front of a ditch and started to shoot. Among those who died were Ibrahim's father and another villager named Reza. Ibrahim was tied to Reza and could not recall what happened next. "I probably fell with him. I couldn't believe that I was alive." When he regained consciousness, "There was a dead body on me." Another man, Anwar, had also survived the execution; together they escaped to the mountains.

At least 178 people were executed, 175 of them noncombatants and the other three captured combatants, according to a UN paper. The executions were centrally planned, coordinated, and controlled by the operational command under Mullah Shahzad, the Taliban strike force commander, the paper said. One witness reported to this author seeing victims skinned alive with a scalpel, a claim a UN investigator also heard at the time. Several who saw the execution said that after the killing, the Taliban danced the Pashtun national dance.[24]

In Bamiyan, Fuladi, and Yakawlang, the killings followed the pattern from the Taliban conquest of Mazar-i-Sharif in August 1998. When Bamiyan was first captured in September 1998, people, livestock, and even dogs were killed. "Several of us went to see Mullah Brader and asked him what was going on," said a witness. Brader replied, "For the first three days, we had a free hand to do anything. But after three days, no one will touch you."[25] The initial order from Omar, monitored by the Hazara resistance, went to his chief of intelligence in the January 2001 massacres at Yakawlang: "Tell the commanders—Mullah Fazil, Dadullah, and Mullah Brader—that in Yakawlang, they rose up against the emirate. And Yakawlang should be recaptured. And the people should be taught a lesson, so that they couldn't repeat this. They are not real Muslims." The initial operational order was to "kill every living being." The killing lasted generally three days and was followed by an amnesty; the orders to destroy property came straight from Mullah Omar through his commander. "We found a written order of Mullah Shazdulah," recalled one witness. "In the first phase of reprisals, people should be killed. In the second phase, this place should be emptied of residents." The latter instruction translated into burning down houses and the market. The order originated with Mullah Omar after Taliban leaders informed him that they could capture Yakawlang but could not hold it. "Do something so the Northern Alliance cannot use it," he instructed.[26]

On May 5, 2001, the Taliban returned to Yakawlang for four weeks; with the participation of Mullah Abdul Razzaq, the minister of the interior, they executed at least thirty civilians. In June, Taliban commander Mullah Dadullah carried out what appeared to be a new strategy of scorched earth. He arrived on June 10, leading a column of 150–200 pickup trucks with a force the United Nations described as "mainly non-Afghan personnel" into the town. Before his arrival, Taliban aircraft bombed the old bazaar, the district hospital, and the Oxfam office; ground forces under his control burned down 800 shops in Nayak, the district center of Yakawlang, and reportedly 500 houses in the Darra Ali Valley and nearby villages. Another 150 people were brought for execution to central Bamiyan. But the United Front recaptured the town, and on June 15, Dadullah announced that Yakawlang was now a "war zone" and no longer a "district."

The abuses, Kamal Hossain concluded in a special UN report, were widespread and systematic. The recurrent pattern of massacres constituted gross human rights violations and breaches of international humanitarian law, in some cases amounting to crimes against humanity.[27]

The other pattern was unique to the Bamiyan Valley. Kuchi nomads, some of whom had been landowners in Panjab district, went in with the army behind them to claim lands inhabited by Hazaras. It was on the second attack on the valley in May 1999 that the plan became apparent. A UN official recalled the Taliban announcing, "We will let the Kuchis come." According to the head of the Afghan Independent Human Rights Commission, "Kuchis were coming to the area, with a military back-up." They began to arrive "by the thousands. . . . It probably was their plan to bring in Kuchis and take over all the grazing lands of the Hazarajat."[28]

Other cases were never recorded. Thousands of Afghans fled to Iran and Pakistan in the course of 2000–2001, and it was only by surveying them to discover what drove them from their homes that Médecins Sans Frontières (MSF) learned of a massacre of villagers in mid-April 2000 at a mosque in Abkhor, a key crossroads in Sar-i-Pol province. According to two families—one Hazara and the other Tajik—whom MSF interviewed separately, as many as fifty men were gathered at a village mosque; they were killed and then the mosque was burned down. This massacre was never reported in the news media or by the United Nations. Presumably, there are countless others.

What seems baffling in retrospect is that much of this record was available at the time it occurred—certainly by polling refugees abroad and collating information from humanitarian agencies inside the country—but neither the news media nor the U.S. government took it very seriously. "I honestly think it is now very easy for you or other people to go back and say ex post facto that the Taliban were terrible," Albright told this author when informed of the Taliban's record of crimes on the battlefield. "Whatever is clear now was not clear at the time," she said. "And . . . as people who were responsible for decisions, I feel that we did the right thing."[29]

"A Humanitarian Disaster of Enormous Proportions"

Taliban offensives in northwest and central Afghanistan, visiting terror and collective punishment on the vanquished non-Pashtun population, coupled with the worst drought for three decades, led to an enormous population displacement—some 1,150,000 people by mid-2001. Some 800,000 people were displaced internally, and 350,000 crossed into neighboring countries. Kofi Annan called it a "humanitarian disaster of enormous proportions." Driven by their single-minded quest for military victory, the Taliban did little for the victims of war but harassed the displaced and added ever-more restrictions on humanitarian aid agencies in 2000 and 2001. In July 2000, they banned foreign agencies from employing any Afghan women outside the health sector. In August, they ordered the

United Nations to close down the Kabul bakeries that were providing sub-sidized bread to the capital's poorest women (later revoked) and issued a new statute severely restricting the activities of the United Nations and its specialized aid agencies. In mid-May 2001, the Taliban closed all UN offices outside Kabul in retaliation for the formal closure of the Taliban office in New York. In July, they issued a decree requiring female foreign workers for international agencies to be chaperoned by a male escort, which would prevent them from meeting Afghan women.

As the human suffering grew, neighboring countries shut their doors, and the rest of the world turned away.[30]

After the fall of Taloqan and smaller towns in September 2000, some ten thousand people (including six thousand children) were marooned in subhuman conditions on two small islands in the Pyanj River along Af-ghanistan's northern border with Tajikistan. Many lived in mud huts cov-ered with flimsy roofs made of reeds. The Taliban controlled the river and the riverbank, preventing escape to the south; they periodically shelled the no-man's land, while Tajikistan closed its borders to the north. "Not a sin-gle refugee from Afghan territory will be allowed into Tajik territory," President Emomali Rahmonov declared. He stated that several hundred men were "armed to the teeth." Fleeing United Front fighters were indeed on the two islands, but the Afghan embassy in Dushanbe said they were armed only to protect their families. At first, refugees had only river water to drink and were totally dependent on humanitarian aid to survive.* Besides dysentery, typhoid, hepatitis, cholera, and chronic colds due to the damp and freezing conditions, they faced the risk of death from Taliban shelling, which occurred regularly.[31]*

More than sixty thousand new Afghan refugees fled to Pakistan before that country closed its borders in November 2000. Only Afghans with documents proving previous refugee status in Pakistan or documents from the Taliban were admitted, but refugees from northern Afghanistan had neither. Taliban authorities reportedly beat back thousands of would-be refugees from the border, and those who made it to the border area had to run a half-dozen gauntlets of guards who demanded money. Still, the number of refugees grew to 170,000 by April 1, 2001.

Children were dying daily at an internally displaced person (IDP) camp near Mazar-i-Sharif. One hundred fifty IDP families were crowded into Building No. 1 of IDP Camp No. 65, a freezing cold concrete build-ing with no light, no heat, and no sanitary facilities. "Five children sit near the wall with their hands on their chests. They are shaking and look very strange," wrote Maysoon Melek, a UN visitor. "For seconds, I cannot tell

---

*The Taliban allowed the United Nations to cross the front line with 750 tons of food to serve sixty thousand displaced persons in the Panjshir Valley in early December, but they then blocked all but one small convoy in early March.

why they look so strange. Then gradually it dawns on me. This is the very first time in my life I see NAVY BLUE CHILDREN. I have seen black children, white children, yellow children, coffee-colored children, but never navy blue children." At Building No. 2, "I get out of the car and as I look at them, face after face, I realize that the children, who wear cotton clothes but no shoes or socks, DO have navy blue faces, navy blue hands, and navy blue feet. A strong wind is blowing and everybody, including the members of our convoy, is shivering."[32]

Possibly the worst place in Afghanistan was the cluster of IDP camps near Herat. On one night at the end of January 2001, when the temperature dipped to 13°F below zero, 110 displaced persons died at those camps, the United Nations said. Ninety percent of them were children. Within a few days, Taliban officials said the number of deaths climbed to more than 500. In early February, the United States mounted an emergency airlift and sent in tens of thousands of blankets. The flow of IDPs turned into a flood. Some 80 families were arriving daily at the end of 2000, and the number quadrupled to 340 daily in April 2001; the number in the camps rose from 80,000 at the start of the year to 180,000 by autumn.[33]

Exacerbating the crisis was Iran's decision in 1999 to expel Afghan refugees by the tens of thousands. The UNHCR estimated that between 80,000 and 100,000 Afghans were deported to their homeland that year, among them persons holding documents that identified them as refugees. This was in breach of the principle of *nonrefoulement* under the 1951 International Refugee Convention, which forbade the repatriation of refugees into disaster or war zones. To halt these deportations, the UNHCR introduced a more orderly process in 2000, offering Afghans the option of being screened to determine who had valid grounds to remain as refugees and who would return home voluntarily. The upshot was that 180,000 Afghans returned to their war-torn, drought-stricken, and impoverished homeland, 133,000 of them with the aid of UNHCR. No international organization at the time had lead responsibility for monitoring the situation of IDPs, and according to a knowledgeable aid official, no one kept close tabs on what happened to deportees on their return to Afghanistan. How many became victims of the drought in their home villages? How many drifted into IDP camps? How many died? No one has a definitive answer.[34]

Circumstances in Pakistan were no better. The biggest of the new camps was Jalozai, a dust-choked patch of treeless land south of Peshawar, with open sewers and no fresh water supply. UN officials called it "a living graveyard." Pakistan authorities, eager to be rid of the eighty thousand refugees, blocked UNHCR from registering and feeding the inhabitants or even providing proper tents; the refugees survived in squalid tents made of discarded plastic bags held up by bamboo sticks, exposed to all the elements. Aid workers called it the worst refugee camp in the world, the London *Sunday Telegraph* reported. But these workers were probably not aware of conditions at Pyanj or Herat. Pakistani authorities prevented Kamal Hossain, the UN human rights rapporteur, and even Kofi Annan, the secretary-general, from visiting in March 2001.[35]

There is no question that the worst drought in living memory was responsible for a large part of the despair. Half or more of the livestock was killed in southern Afghanistan, and crop loss was estimated at 90 percent; by the middle of 2001, a quarter of the population was in need of outside assistance to survive, the United Nations said. At least some of the crisis was the doing of the Taliban regime, according to the United Nations. "A worrying feature of the current humanitarian crisis is the lack of significant action by the authorities in Afghanistan to provide assistance for their own people," Annan reported to the Security Council. The Taliban budget of $80 million was only a third of the amount the United Nations hoped to raise for humanitarian aid to Afghanistan.*

The international community also deserved some of the blame—through early August 2000, the world's wealthier countries donated only 60 percent of the $67 million sought to alleviate the effects of the drought. A year later, the United Nations asked the nations of the world for $250 million and received only $85 million.[36]

In statistics alone—the number of refugees and IDPs, and the plight of everyone else inside the country—it was Earth's biggest humanitarian disaster. If that was not enough reason to focus attention, the pattern of crimes by the government in the internal conflict and its negligence toward the civilians displaced by that conflict should have been. But the United States and other governments adopted an ambivalent attitude toward the two sides in the conflict, based on dubious and unexamined premises of moral equivalence. With few exceptions, among them the UN secretary-general and some intrepid UN and other aid workers in the field, the international community and the international media deserted the people of Afghanistan in their hour of need.

---

* A World Food Program paper on Afghanistan stated that "the absence of a well-functioning, development-oriented government in Afghanistan aggravates these problems, since some of the instruments normally used to promote food security—such as government-run safety nets, pricing policies, large irrigation and other infrastructure investments, and agricultural research and extension—are not available." Quoted in UN report #E/CN.4/2001/43, March 9, 2001, paragraph 54.

10

Radicalization
without Response

The catastrophic plight of refugees and IDPs was not the only story in Afghanistan that went largely unreported at the time. With almost no one abroad noticing, a cultural transformation was under way that Afghan scholar Rasul Amin called "Arabization." From the country's cemeteries to its greatest works of antiquity, from its schools to its libraries, and from the battlefield to the national calendar, the Taliban made a series of decisions to diminish the role of national history and tradition in culture and social practice in favor of Arab tradition and mores. This never-colonized country, with a proud history as a receptive crossroads of Asia, was now a magnet for Islamist militants from around the world, a center for intolerance, and a hub for revolution. Bin Laden did not start the process of Arabization, but he certainly spurred it on in 2001.

One of the first visible signs was the Taliban decision to drop the Persian solar calendar in March 1998 and adopt the Arab lunar calendar, the system used in Saudi Arabia and across the Arab world. This meant an end to Nawroz, the New Year's Day that had been celebrated at the spring equinox for a thousand years. In 1999, the Taliban banned this favorite holiday as an "ignorant" anti-Islamic practice and sent out baton-wielding militiamen to block families who thronged to pay an annual graveside visit to a hillside cemetery.[1]

School curriculum also changed. The trend had begun during the jihad, when any number of militia leaders—among them Sayyaf, Yunus Khalis, and Hekmatyar—had set up madrassas. They did this "because it was an efficient way to get cash from the Arabs," said Amin, director of the Afghan Study Center of the University of Peshawar.* The inner circle of the Taliban received their education under the mullahs of the Deobandi School, which is closely related to Wahhabi Islam. According to Amin, "That is why the Taliban were real instruments in the hands of al Qaeda and the Arabs." In March 2001, the process took off. Omar announced a new curriculum for primary, secondary, and higher education, emphasizing Islamic and Arabic-language subjects at the expense of secular arts and sciences. He said he would start up 2,500 madrassas throughout Afghanistan, supplanting

---

*Amin later became post-Taliban Afghanistan's first education minister, serving six months in the interim government of Hamid Karzai.

public education. Boys would wear turbans, and the language of the Koran would supplant English as the primary language. "As a matter of fact, the curriculum and medium of instruction would be Arabic," wrote Amin. "The question is which source will finance such a great network of madrassas? Definitely, the wealthy Arabs rich enough to afford huge expenses."[2]

Even the dead were not exempt from Arabization. Also banned was the Sufi tradition, both Shia and Sunni, of bringing a verse of the Koran to place at the tomb of the dead. After the ban took effect around the start of 2000, Hazrat Ahmad Amin Ismael al Mujadiddi, one of Afghanistan's Sufi leaders, said, "I called up Mullah Omar and told him, 'If you do this, people will never understand.' [But they did it] to the graveyards of all the great Sufis in Afghanistan." The Taliban posted signs banning the verses —"No Tarwiz. No ceremony for the dead. No women"—at the entrance to one of the major cemeteries in Kabul and in Sufi graveyards all over the country, he said. Al Mujadiddi was able to travel into Afghanistan during the Taliban period. He said, "The influence of bin Laden became more powerful by the day. Everyone saw it."

Arabization of Afghanistan's libraries translated into burning books and the buildings. Of the seventy-two libraries around the country, only two were left standing with books—one in Kabul and one in Herat— according to Nilab Rahimi, director of the Kabul public library. "They burned the libraries and saved only the Koranic books and *hadiths*," he said. In Faryab, Mazar-i-Sharif, Saipur, Maimon, and Andkhoi, they burned the libraries down. Nangahar province had seven libraries. "Now we have none," Rahimi said. "They were looted. They took the books, the chairs, and the tables to Pakistan." In Kabul, they did not burn books but destroyed pictures and removed hundreds of books, many of them rare, from the Afghan studies section of the main library. According to Rahimi (who was himself jailed at Pol-i-Charki prison from 1999 until 2001), the Taliban were assisted in the destruction by an unidentified Arab using a computer.[*3]

The population balance also changed, at least in Kabul and Kandahar. In the course of 2000–2001, observers noted a great many more Arabs settling into entire districts of cities; witnesses said the Arabs and other foreigners became a law unto themselves. Among the areas given to Arabs were compounds in Kandahar, large parts of Wazir Akbar Khan in Kabul, and portions of the Kayan Valley in north-central Afghanistan. According to a senior Massoud aide, there was pressure to give them large parts of

---

* At the author's request, Rahim compiled an inventory of lost books. All totals are by district unless otherwise indicated: Karta-e-char (Kabul) 13,349; Mikrorayon (Kabul) 8,336; Pul-i-Charki Prison (Kabul) 1,589; Ghor 1,400; Faryab 1,200; Sar-e-pul l27; Wardak 284; Nimroz 2,447; Jowzjan 2,671; Andkhoi 456; Balkh 1,598; Kapisa 323; Kohistan 656; City Library 755; Jalalabad Ada Farm 195; Zabul 1,106; Baghlan 311; Ghazni 4,970; Paktia 1,400; Kunduz 330; Samangan 711; Laghman 1,430; Khost 909; Uruzgan 1,179; Kandahar 1,612; Mazar-i-Sharif 377; Mirwais in Maidan district 3,000; Qahsabz district 2,000; Mirbachakot district 3,500; Bagram district 3,000; Charasyab district 2,500.

Herat, as well as Bagram, north of the Kabul Airport. By late 2001, there were two thousand or more Arabs in Kabul, and they were taking more and more houses, said a senior international humanitarian aid official who remained in Kabul during the entire Taliban era.* When the United Nations was forced out of its compound in Kabul in mid-2001, Arabs moved in.[4]

The sphere of life that most visibly revealed the impact of Arabization —and Mullah Omar's loss of control to his Arab and Pakistani "friends"— was Afghan culture. The destructive spree that cost humanity some of the greatest works of antiquity in this historic crossroads, culminating in the destruction of the gigantic Buddhas of Bamiyan, seems to have begun with an exhibition at the Kabul Museum in the summer of 2000. During the battle for Kabul, Darul Aman Palace had been the front line, and every shift in the war left it more battered and looted. After 1995, with help from UNESCO and the Pakistan-based Society for the Preservation of Afghanistan's Cultural Heritage (SPACH), foreign volunteers and local museum staff had been cataloging the priceless collection. In mid-August 2000, at the behest of Deputy Minister of Culture Abdurrahim Hotak and in the presence of Nancy Hatch Dupree, a renowned American friend of Afghanistan and cofounder of SPACH—the Taliban opened Darul Aman to the public for six days. The shrapnel craters from shells and rockets and bullet damage on the front of the museum had been caulked and the façade repainted. Much was missing from the collections, but on this occasion, a remarkable recent find was displayed: an inscription engraved in stone from the Kushan empire of the second century A.D., which frontline troops digging a trench in Baghlan province had unwittingly unearthed in 1993. The extraordinary find was the Robotak stone—a one-and-a-half-meter-wide block of white limestone inscribed with King Kanishka's order to his builders to create a shrine for a variety of Buddhist, Hindu, and Zoroastrian gods. It was evidence, Kate Clark of the BBC reported, of religious tolerance at a time when Afghanistan was at the crossroads of the known world. Also on display was a small statue of Buddha. The Taliban, a strict Islamic movement not famous for its tolerance, believed that any depiction of the human being is blasphemous, "but they seem to be making an exception for the museum," Clark said. A brief moment it was.

The Voice of Sharia radio quoted Hotak saying it was "necessary for us and all officials of the Islamic Emirate of Afghanistan to protect these valuable artifacts, which express the high and the low points of our country

---

*Anthony Davis quoted an Afghan student who lived opposite an important al Qaeda communications and command post on Karte Parwan Street in Kabul, not far from the Intercontinental Hotel. The student described constant activity: "From one window, I could look down at the Arab house. There was coming and going the whole time—hundreds of them, mostly Arabs, but also Chechens. They'd keep some heavy weapons in the forecourt and sometimes trucks with multibarreled rocket launchers would be parked there, which they'd assemble before leaving for the front line." Davis, "The Afghan Files," Jane's Intelligence Review, February 14–19, 2002.

at various stages of its history." Education Minister Amir Khan Muttaqi told those assembled that thieves and robbers might have been able to steal historical artifacts and treasures, "but they cannot loot the history of the country and our national treasures, because each stone, each mountain, each plain are historical and nobody can loot them." But no one could top Qudratullah Jamal, the culture minister, who said before the museum even reopened that "Afghanistan is an ancient country with an ancient history. It has preserved its national and international status in the course of many centuries. It has produced excellent cultural masterpieces" and was working jointly with UNESCO "to retrieve our ancient heritage."* Nancy Hatch Dupree said the opening of the exhibition showed that the Islamic Emirate of Afghanistan was making all-around efforts to protect historical monuments.[5] They would regret their words.

On November 1, the phone rang in a modest bungalow in Bubendorf, a village near Basel, Switzerland. Paul Bucherer-Dietschi, a Swiss architect, answered. Bucherer-Dietschi had been so taken by Afghanistan during visits as a youth and later while living there with his wife that he had established an Afghanistan institute and built a small museum of Afghan antiquities adjoining his home. "Please come immediately and help us," was the plea. He flew to Kabul, where he saw Qudratullah Jamal, then to Kandahar, where Abdul Jalil (the toenail-picking deputy minister of foreign affairs and a close aide to Omar) received him. Both men said they were "under constant pressure" from al Qaeda. "Our foreign friends have found out that we are hiding materials from them," Jalil said. "We have managed to put it off from month to month. We have moved this material from one corner to another to hide it from our friends. We can't continue." Both Jalil and Jamal had visited him in Bubendorf and discussed a noble but unlikely scheme to rescue a large quantity of Afghan antiquities and display them in Bucherer-Dietschi's tiny museum adjoining his home.

From the time of the exhibit at Darul Aman, bin Laden and others in his inner circle had tried to convince Omar to withdraw his protection of the Afghan cultural heritage, starting with the Kabul National Museum. Jalil, in Bucherer-Dietschi's view, was one of a group of Taliban who were "Afghans in their hearts and were ready to take a great risk," but that group was losing influence. The continuing drought had brought "great problems," he recalled Jalil saying. The Taliban had banned growing opium in the hopes that the U.S. embargo would be lifted, but they were being slapped with a second embargo. "It all drives us more and more into the arms of our friends," he said.

This was the scheme: if a Western country would send a Hercules transport aircraft filled with humanitarian aid, Jalil and others would manage to

---

* It was not his first foray into support of the arts. In February, Jamal was present with Hotak, reopening the National Gallery of Art. The aim of the gallery, he said, was to preserve the work of Afghan masters and "promote the new talent." AP Kabul, February 17, 2000.

stock it for the return trip with the holdings of the Kabul National Museum. "This would have included the most important holdings from prehistoric times," Bucherer said. Jalil never said exactly what would be exported, nor did the director of the museum, with whom Bucherer subsequently met. At the museum, staff started taking everything they could move and placed it in vaults or inside rooms, the entrances to which they covered with paper seals. Bucherer won the support of officials at UNESCO in Paris, on the condition that the Swiss government would pay the 200,000 Swiss francs for the charter. A UNESCO official, Christian Manhart, said Germany was willing to send an aircraft on a humanitarian mission but wanted sufficient security guarantees from the Taliban regime. But those guarantees were not forthcoming. "This offer of a deputy minister was not backed up by his hierarchy," Manhart said. Germany withdrew its offer, and the scheme died.[6]

Behind the scenes, the iconoclasts had been gaining influence during 2000. In July, Dupree reported that Omar, on the advice of his Supreme Court and Council of Ministers, had begun steps to place members of the Ministry for the Promotion of Virtue and Suppression of Vice (a religious police modeled after Saudi Arabia's *Muttawi* and on which bin Laden was reported to have influence) on the committee overseeing museums to determine whether the holdings were appropriate under Sharia law. The iconoclasts were led by Mullah Mohammad Hassan Akhund (the ultra-hard-line governor of Kandahar province and Rabbani's first deputy) and Mullah Nooruddin Turabi (the minister of justice), both of whom had strong influence among the vice and virtue police. According to Vahid Mojdeh, Jamal played into their hands in the Council of Ministers. Instead of defending the reopening of the museum, he blamed the decision on his deputy, Hotak. Hassan and Turabi kicked the dispute up the chain to Mullah Omar himself, who ordered the ancient relics, including the statue of Buddha, to be sent to Kandahar. But Hotak resisted. In the final months of 2000, the role of the religious police in the oversight over all museums tightened. In February 2001, they disclosed the content of a secret edict by Omar ordering the destruction of all statues that represented living beings, including all museum statues. Mojdeh informed Dupree and the Iranian government, and asked his contact there to inform UNESCO, but the reaction everywhere was muted.

The turning point was the removal of Hotak for insubordination in early February. At a meeting of the Council of Ministers, he protested the policy change. "If there is a new policy, why haven't I been informed?" he asked. He was sent home in disgrace. Replacing him as deputy minister of information and culture was Maulana Abdul Baqi Haqqani, an "extremely fanatic and narrow-minded" opportunist, according to Mojdeh. Haqqani invited Turabi and officials from the vice and virtue police to meet him at the museum. "The museum door opened and the group, each armed with a stout club of some kind for breaking things, entered and hammered the statues, while uttering 'God is great,'" Mojdeh reported. The first blow fell on the limestone statue of the feet and torso of King Kanishka.[7]

A few days later, on February 12, the BBC's Kabul correspondent, Kate Clark, reported that government officials had smashed at least a dozen objects, including a priceless meter-high clay bodhisattva or follower of Buddha. Reporters were barred from the museum, and Clark, who constantly held the Taliban to account, was expelled from the country.[8]

On February 26, an aide to Omar released to the international press the edict mandating the destruction of all non-Islamic statues in Afghanistan, including the Bamiyan Buddhas:

> On the basis of consultations between the religious leaders of the Islamic Emirate of Afghanistan, the religious judgments of the Ulema and the rulings of the Supreme Court of the Islamic Emirate of Afghanistan, all statues and non-Islamic shrines located in the different parts of the Islamic Emirate of Afghanistan must be destroyed. These statues have been and remain shrines of infidels, and these infidels continue to worship and respect these shrines. Allah almighty is the only real shrine and all false shrines should be smashed.

Omar instructed the religious police and the Ministry of Culture to carry out the order.

The titular head of government, Mullah Rabbani, learned of the plan to destroy the Buddhas while on hajj to Mecca. In the presence of other ministers, he telephoned Omar and tried to talk him out of it. "I am not the sculpture seller. I am the sculpture destroyer," Omar responded. "Don't destroy them," Rabbani pleaded. But Omar replied, "Friends are advising me." And who were they?* Arabs and two mullahs from Karachi, responded Omar.[9]

UNESCO scrambled to head off the decision but was much too late. At UNESCO's behest, a special delegation of eleven Islamic clergymen headed by the prominent Qatar-based scholar Sheikh Youssef al Qaradawi and Egypt's highest Muslim authority, Mufti Nasr Farid Wasel, traveled to Kandahar to call on Omar. But the destruction was already under way, and the Taliban went out of their way to humiliate the visitors. En route to Omar's residence, young men from the vice and virtue police stopped their car and told them to disembark and pray in the road. "We told them we were Muslim authorities and knew when and where to pray," Qaradawi later told a UNESCO official. After prostrating themselves in the mud, they were permitted to continue their journey, but they arrived "completely dirty" at Omar's residence. The meeting lasted four hours and was in vain. Omar's final argument was the most telling: "Allah came to him in his dreams at

---

* The identity of the two Pakistanis was not clear, but journalists in Peshawar believe that one was Mufti Rashid Ahmad, founder of the al Rashid trust and publisher of *Zarb-i-Momen (Muslim Power)*.

night and gave him this order. He didn't want to disappoint Allah," Qaradawi recounted. It was a wasted trip. "These Taliban had absolutely no knowledge about Islam," Qaradawi later said. "They are so naïve, they really can be influenced."[10]

Pakistan sent its interior minister to dissuade Omar, as well as Colonel Imam, who knew better than to even try. "I had lunch with them," he recalled. "They asked me 'Why are you here? Is there something we can do for you?'" Knowing that he could not change their decision, he said, "I just came to have a meal." When Mullah Omar left the room, "I told the other people sitting with us that actually I was asked to convey the message of Pakistan that we don't want the Buddhas to be destroyed." But he did not deliver this message directly to Mullah Omar.[11]

Taking advantage of the tensions with the West and the growing isolation, Arab extremists had deftly manipulated the discontent, strengthening their hold over like-minded Taliban in the higher echelons of power, particularly within the Supreme Court and the religious police. Dupree wrote, "Mullah Omar lost control."

According to journalist Hamid Mir, bin Laden's close aides did everything in their power to radicalize the credulous Omar—when it suited their purpose, they even played on the occult. Nature cooperated in their endeavor. Other than the lack of total authority over the country, one of Omar's biggest frustrations was the drought. Mir said Taliban officials were receiving advice from noted clerics, who told them, "You must destroy the statues. God will give you rain." Mir said he asked which cleric was dispensing the advice. It was Ayman al Zawahiri, bin Laden's number two, who readily admitted to Mir that he was manipulating the Taliban. "I know astrology. I know anatomy. I know numerology. I can influence the illiterate Taliban," Mir quoted Zawahiri as saying. "This star is moving north to east, when it moves farther, you need some suggestions." In Mir's assessment, "They were fooling the Taliban."[12] The Buddhas of Bamiyan had been carved out of the sandstone cliffs in the third and fourth centuries; they were possibly the most spectacular images of Buddha ever devised. The sandstone was covered with mud and wheat straw and then with a layer of plaster that was painted. For centuries, travelers on the Silk Road would stop at Bamiyan to admire the colossi, one 125 feet high and the other 180 feet high, and to stay in the caravanserai below. The two statues were not built at this spot by happenstance; they were the expression of a new school of Mahayana Buddhism that King Kanishka had helped found in the second century, with the aim of humanizing Buddha.[13]

When the Taliban originally conquered Bamiyan in 1998, Mullah Omar had explicitly ordered protection for the historic monuments. Under the influence of the Islamists, he now reversed course.

It took the Taliban two full weeks to demolish the two 1,500-year-old statues. Photographers were banned from the valley, but Taysir Alony of

Al Jazeera disguised himself as a Taliban and filmed the process. "It took them several attempts, dozens of explosions," he said. "They ran out of explosives, dynamite, and TNT. Then they discovered an ammunition depot and used that material." Sayyed Miraz Hussain, whose family lived in a cave near one of the Buddhas and witnessed the destruction, said the Taliban "had no idea how to blow up things properly." He alleged that Pakistan and Saudi engineers conducted the final explosions, a claim that has yet to be documented. "The Taliban were happy. They had destroyed something that could never be rebuilt. It was gone forever. They clapped their hands, and jumped around for joy," he told filmmaker Christian Frey.

As the demolition advanced, Qudratullah Jamal took on the role of hard-charging Taliban spokesman. "The edict will be implemented," he said. "There is no question of changing the decision." He disparaged the visit of Qaradawi and the other visiting clerics, saying they had come to the wrong place; they should have gone to India when Hindu fanatics destroyed the historic Babri Masjid mosque in 1991, or to Jerusalem to challenge Israel's occupation.[14]

On March 17, Jamal took the lead role during a second destructive visit to Kabul Museum. Dupree later wrote, "Jamal, goaded by his hard-line cohorts, personally continued the iconoclastic campaign by smashing to bits with a sledgehammer some of the museum's most popular sculptures." This time they smashed about forty statues and afterward invited the international news media to see that the museum was sculpture-free. The pile of rubble—stone, stucco, and wood—amounted to several cubic yards, according to Bucherer-Dietschi, who visited in December 2001. The question remains whether Jamal was an eager participant. Museum caretakers later told Bucherer-Dietschi that although Jamal led the destruction, he called a "time out" after about forty-five minutes. "It's time to have tea and to pray," he told his fellow vandals. They did not return. "If he had wanted, they could have destroyed much more," Bucherer-Dietschi said. But Dupree believed that Jamal was "one of the worst offenders."[15]

Religious extremists from the Islamic world heaped praise on Omar, questioning only why he had not acted sooner. In atonement for the delay, Omar ordered the slaughter of one hundred cows and distribution of the meat among the needy (not an usual Islamic ritual), thus managing to offend not only Buddhists but also Hindus. According to Mojdeh, the al Rashid trust—whose magazine *Zarb-i-Momen* celebrated the destruction of the Buddhas with the headline "Afghanistan, the Land of Idol-Breakers" —paid for the animals. *Zarb-i-Momen* also distributed a calendar with photographs showing the demolition process.[16]

The destruction of the Buddhas cost the Taliban what little support they had among the general public and with governments in Western countries, most of Asia, throughout the Islamic world, and in much of the Middle East. For national-minded Afghans in and outside the government, it was a deeply offensive move, and the Taliban's own military structure in key locations began to unravel. The evidence is anecdotal but compelling. In Jalrez, near Maidanek, on the road to Bamiyan, Gulam Mohamed Hotak, a senior intelligence commander who had played a key role in the takeover of central Afghanistan, became disenchanted with Taliban rule. Their power grab in 1996, their inability to govern competently, and their hostile relations with the international community were the prelude, and now they had crossed a line. "It was the destruction of the Bamiyan Buddhas and the issue of the destruction of statues of animals in the museum," he said.

Within the Council of Ministers, there was a wide feeling of disgust and depression. "The destruction of the Bamiyan statutes inspired feelings of hatred and disgust worldwide toward the Taliban," wrote Mojdeh. "For those who witnessed the events from outside, Mullah Omar's actions seemed pure madness. . . . Even among the Taliban, many were also opposed to the deeds. The majority of ministers, deputies, and other notables were individually unhappy with the situation and believed that the Taliban had to revise their conduct."[17]

For the world at large, Dupree put it most forcefully: "It is absolutely sickening. I can't believe what I'm hearing. You could not enter the Bamiyan Valley without being in awe of the creative dynamism of these figures. They belong to the whole world; they don't belong only to Afghanistan." As for the museum, "Why spend money on an old building when the people need so much? These old buildings are Afghanistan's identity. And when you lose your identity, you've lost your soul."

For Islamic militants, on the other hand, blowing up the Buddhas was the quintessential jihadi move, and it proved to be a recruiting tool for bin Laden. Taliban and Arab fighters reported that the number of Arab volunteers joining al Qaeda and Taliban troops in Afghanistan shot up tenfold in the following month.[18] The central fact of Arabization was that militant foreigners were becoming a dominant influence in Taliban Afghanistan. This was nowhere more striking than on the battlefield. Massoud forces attempting to reconquer Taloqan found themselves in repeated clashes with a new fighting force: a 300-strong unit of the Islamic Movement of Uzbekistan, under the command of Juma Namangani, a former Soviet paratrooper and now militant Islamist. It was no longer Arabs but the IMU, founded in Kandahar, that was defending the town of Koh-e-Siah Boz (Black Goat Mountain) for the Taliban. Increasingly, wrote Anthony Davis in 2001, the civil war was becoming a "transnational conflict." Foreign fighters were closely integrated into the Afghan fighting machine, having become an indispensable element of the Taliban order of battle. By August 2001, there were 8,000–12,000 foreign combatants, and they constituted between one-fifth and one-quarter of the Taliban combat strength of 40,000–45,000. They included 5,000–7,000 Pakistanis, most recruited from Deobandi madrassas in Pakistan, and a significant number of volunteers from militant jihadi organizations. There were 2,000–3,000 Arab combatants in the field; Chechen units probably in the hundreds;* and 1,500–2,000 IMU forces, consisting of Uzbeks, Kyrgyz, Tajikistanis, Uighurs, and some Pakistanis.[19]

Their impact spilled over to Kabul, where foreign militant leaders even sought a role in government. Mullah Omar had a phenomenon on his hands and decided to try to bring it under control. The phenomenon was that as foreign fighters became the vital spearhead of Taliban military and recruits flocked to the country, Afghanistan was becoming a center for revolution throughout Asia. Omar's appetite for leading that revolution had grown, and early in early 2001, he called together the leaders of all groups active in Afghanistan and gave them formal commands. Bin Laden would lead all Arab groups in Afghanistan. Qari Taher Jan (aka Taher Yoldash), an Uzbek leader, was given command over fighters in Central Asia, east Turkey, and China. Maulana Muhammad Masood Azhar —the leader of Jaish-e-Muhammad who was freed during the Indian Airlines hijacking—would be in charge for Pakistan, Kashmir, Bangladesh, and Burma. Namangani would serve as military commander of foreign mujahideen in Afghanistan. The quid pro quo was that these leaders wanted a role in Taliban decision making. Yoldash's headquarters in the Taymani district of Kabul was a gathering place for Uzbeks, Tajiks, Chechens, Kyrghiz, Cossacks, and even Uighurs from Sinkiang, China, and he demanded a voice in Afghan foreign policy. Since Mullah Omar had designated him commander for Central Asia and the Caucasus, the Foreign Affairs Ministry had to consult with him on any actions involving those regions. Yoldash (who, according to Mojdeh, fancied himself the "Emir of Transoxiana"—the region beyond the Oxus River) also assumed the power to arrest rivals and alleged criminals in Afghanistan and to coordinate the arrival and departure of fighters in the IMU.[20]

Although the U.S. government was paying little attention to internal developments and American reporters were rarely on the scene, some observers noted Omar's growing dependence on bin Laden. In a July 2001 cable from the U.S. embassy in Pakistan, the political officer said that Omar relied on "only a small circle of advisers, including a few Arabs, and does not have a wider intelligence net informing him, nor does he have even a rudimentary understanding of what the Afghan people are thinking." The officer said that bin Laden had a "direct line" to Omar and that Afghan politicians, journalists, and aid workers saw the increasingly visible Arab presence in Kabul as a source of growing concern. Arabs were issued special license plates indicating that their cars should not be stopped, the cable said. "Even six months ago you didn't see that," said the embassy's source. [21]

---

* Russian sources claimed that some 2,500 Chechens were operating in Afghanistan, but Anthony Davis said the figure likely included families and other civilians.

Buried deep inside Francesc Vendrell's routine UN report in mid-August 2001 was a warning of the true state of affairs: "It is a matter of particular concern that the number of foreigners fighting alongside the Taliban has not declined, but rather to the contrary, the presence of so-called 'guests' is increasingly noticeable in the major urban centers. This adds to the suspicion that certain foreigners play a growing decision-making role within the Taliban leadership to the detriment of those Afghan elements within the Taliban who are considered more pragmatic or moderate."[22]

By the middle of 2001, the regime had come to depend on foreign fighters to defend its own territory, under strong and growing influence from bin Laden, and—linked with these two developments—increasingly was becoming a jihadi state. The more Omar outraged the rest of the world, the more Islamic jihadis flocked to the cause. The vicissitudes of war, Taliban terror tactics, and drought had uprooted more than a million of his countrymen; they were dying of starvation and exposure, and desperately beating on the locked gates of neighboring states to escape Afghanistan. But Omar's vision was fixed on global jihad.

One of the big losers in the process was Pakistan, which had thrown its backing to the Taliban. Musharraf had declared, "We cannot alienate the Taleban, as we want the Pushtoons on our side." But in supporting the Taliban, Pakistan gave up much of its residual influence. For strong national security reasons, Musharraf, like his predecessor, demanded the closure of eighteen training camps in Afghanistan and the handover of suspected terrorists who had attacked civilians in Pakistan: Mullah Omar gave him the brushoff; instead, he demanded that Pakistan hand over Taliban opponents and threatened unrest in Pakistan. In fact, Omar had appointed as commander for jihad in Pakistan and parts east Masood Azar, who was on the U.S. terrorism list and whom Musharraf's government had allowed to flee into Pakistan and make public speeches.

The broader threat was to established governments everywhere, and this suited the patron of the process. "I have invited Muslim youth from all over the world to come to Afghanistan and live in this land for a while," bin Laden said. "By living in Afghanistan, one feels closer to his nature." Actually, young Muslim men were coming for military training and ideological education, often sent by underground militias in their home countries. The network of al Qaeda camps provided instruction in explosives, poisons, and, apparently, chemical weapons; after completing basic training, graduates were sent to Taliban encampments throughout the country.* Viewed

---

* By mid-2001, Arab military camps, some of which were used for training, were located at Ghaziabad and Darunta (both near Jalalabad), the Naghloo Dam near Sarobi, Kunduz, and Kandahar Airport, and there were reports that one or more training facilities had been opened in Herat province as well, according to Anthony Davis. Rishkhor was the biggest camp, with as many as 1,500 trainees. It was closed in June 2000, and journalists were permitted to visit, but it was put off-limits again in 2001 and appeared to be in use for training. Davis, "Foreign Fighters Step up Activity in Afghan Civil War," *Jane's Intelligence Review*, August 1, 20001.

from inside the regime, the entire country had become a training camp, and training for jihad had taken on a life of its own. "Afghanistan had thus become a place where individuals had come to be tried, tested, and approved. After training they were fully prepared for action [in Afghanistan] or they would return to their own or any other country where they had to carry out a mission," Mojdeh wrote.[23]

Downplaying the Threat

The threat to regional peace was growing rapidly, and bin Laden's continuing operations within his Afghan sanctuary challenged the United States. But Bill Clinton and his aides had little interest in internal developments in Afghanistan, preferring to focus on bin Laden. Had he set up a dedicated apparatus of listening posts to debrief refugees and other open sources or named a troubleshooter like Peter Tomsen to develop a new policy, Clinton might have acquired the information he needed to forge a new path in his final year. Outside the public eye, he could have tasked the U.S. intelligence community to throw significant resources into data collection or developed a far closer relationship with Massoud. None of this occurred, according to intelligence experts. At key moments, the administration was unaware of significant changes—for example, the shift in the internal military balance in September 2000—and failed to react in a meaningful way, other than to dispatch humanitarian aid for IDPs. One of the big fears was that intervention would lead to a massive post-conflict responsibility. "Nobody wanted to assume the liability for taking on a train wreck like Afghanistan and trying to bring it right," was the summary of Thomas Pickering, under secretary of state for political affairs. Avoidance was the watchword. After the devastating attack on the USS *Cole*, Clinton all but ruled out retaliation. In effect, he kicked the can down the road.

Moving into the White House on January 20, 2001, George W. Bush had come from a very different world, one that favored military muscle, self-reliance, and decisive action instead of patient multilateralist diplomacy, working within international institutions, and observing the confines of treaties and international law. His primary national security aim in the first eight months of office was to establish a missile defense system to protect the United States from a nuclear missile attack by a rogue state (presumably North Korea), despite the immense cost, uncertain technology, and the disturbance to traditional U.S. alliances that would result from abrogating the U.S.-Russia antiballistic missile (ABM) treaty. Richard Clarke and Sandy Berger both informed the new administration of their deep concern over the threat of future terror attacks from bin Laden; Clarke and others felt strongly that if and when the intelligence analysis was complete, there should be retaliation for the attack on the *Cole*.

But the question before the new administration was, with what goal in mind? An armed attack on the Taliban (over the vigorous protests of Pakistan) that fell short of an invasion to bring regime change could boomerang. Decapitating al Qaeda by killing bin Laden, if it could be accomplished, would be a tactical step that fell well short of destroying al Qaeda. That was the dilemma facing the Bush administration. Clinton had bequeathed tactics but no strategy to his successor, a burning concern but no well-thought-out policy for dealing with it. The new administration took eight months to craft a policy (not an inordinate period at the start of a new term) that would have taken several years to implement. Plainly, it came too late.

As soon as Bush took office, Clarke urged Condoleezza Rice, the national security adviser, to organize a meeting of cabinet officers to discuss the bin Laden threat. Clarke and his staff had drafted a memo titled "Eliminating the Threat from the Jihadi Networks of al Qaeda." It built on a CIA plan known as the "Blue Sky memo" that had been produced without reference to financial or policy constraints. CIA counterterrorism experts had proposed major new funding for the United Front to help it stave off the Taliban army and tie down al Qaeda fighters, to increase support to Uzbekistan, and to help other anti-Taliban groups. Clarke added a few more proposals: renewed flights over Afghanistan by Predator drone aircraft in March 2001 and military action to destroy al Qaeda command and control targets and infrastructure, as well as Taliban military and command assets. He set the goal of rolling back al Qaeda over a period of three to five years.[24]

The plan received a cool reception, and Rice decided to reduce the profile of Clarke's office to become, like the rest of the National Security Council (NSC), a coordinating bureau for the major departments of government rather than an office that crafted and implemented domestic security decisions. In early March, her deputy, Steve Hadley, organized a comprehensive policy review, looking at Afghanistan, Pakistan, and the region, as well as the threat from al Qaeda. In the same month, CIA briefers told Rice that a "strong circumstantial case could be made against al Qaeda" for the bombing of the *Cole*, but they admitted that they lacked conclusive information on the external command and control for the attack.

Deputies to the cabinet officers met in April and May; in June, they produced a draft presidential directive on terrorism. They approved covert aid to Uzbekistan (which may have benefited Dostum, who had returned to Afghanistan in early April), but they could not agree on bolstering Massoud without first assembling a broader group, including Pashtuns, to receive covert U.S. military aid. Clarke and CIA representative Cofer Black urged agreement on sending enough aid to keep Massoud in the fight and to tie down al Qaeda terrorists "without aiming to overthrow the Taliban," but Rice, Hadley, and NSC expert on Afghanistan Zalmay Khalilzad all opposed sending aid only to Massoud. Clarke warned that delay risked Massoud's "final defeat at the hands of the Taliban."

Three months passed between the deputies' meeting on June 7 and the meeting of cabinet officers on September 4, at which a three-phase policy was adopted with little discussion. The strategy was to offer the Taliban one last chance and then destroy the regime. There would be covert action to encourage anti-Taliban Afghans to stalemate the Taliban in the civil war and attack al Qaeda bases, an international coalition to undermine the regime, and covert action to topple the Taliban leadership from within. It was a thoughtful and solid approach, probably inadequate for dealing with the infrastructure already in place but still a plan that could be adapted. But it was months, if not years, too late.[25]

Amidst the furor over the Taliban destruction of the Bamiyan Buddhas, Ahmed Shah Massoud flew to Moscow for talks with Russian officials in late March; in April, he made his first trip to Europe—a one-week tour of Paris, Strasbourg, and Brussels—to raise his profile. His brother Walid in London had organized the trip; at the last minute, the Aga Khan provided his personal plane for transportation. Gary Schroen flew in from Washington and asked Massoud once again what he could do to help the United States capture bin Laden. "Why do you guys keep asking me about bin Laden?" Massoud replied. "I can't. If I could, I would. What I need is helicopters. Military equipment. I have to pay cash for terrible helicopters." Schroen noted that only the CIA traveled to see Massoud; the State Department was not represented. The tour was a public relations success but did not resolve Massoud's desperate need for military support, and Europeans were as reluctant as the Americans to forge a new policy in Afghanistan. President Jacques Chirac of France snubbed Massoud, and European Union commissioners also stood him up, fearing Taliban retaliation against European relief groups operating in Afghanistan. Hubert Védrine, the French foreign minister, offered a little less than $4 million in drought relief for Taliban- and United–Front controlled areas, and his Belgian counterpart, Louis Michel, also promised humanitarian aid.

In Strasbourg, Massoud was blocked from addressing the full European parliament; instead, he met a group of legislators and reporters. He used the occasion to denounce Pakistani "interference in Afghanistan in terms of training, soldiers, funding, and logistics," and called for "strong pressure on Pakistan." But he also had the opportunity to put across his claim to moderation. "We are in favor of a moderate Islamic state, which would be the only one that could confront the Taliban's extremism, could bring people together, and permit men and women to take part in free elections," he said. Nicole Fontaine, president of the European parliament (which plays almost no role in setting foreign policy), said she was sending a solemn message to Pakistan: "Stop providing assistance to the fanatic and obscurantist" regime in Kabul. Responding to a question from reporters, Massoud had a strong message for the United States. "If President Bush doesn't help us, then these terrorists will damage the United States and Europe very soon —and it will be too late."[26]

Later that month, Elie Krakowski, an Afghanistan specialist with strong Republican ties, traveled to Faizabad to ask Massoud's input for developing a comprehensive strategy by the United States. Massoud responded with a laundry list that revealed a near-desperate situation. "It is extremely important for us to have a radio station," he said. Second, he needed help marketing lapis lazuli and emeralds. "Quality-wise, our emeralds are competing with the Columbians. We are not finding good markets for this. If we are helped in this sector, it covers part of our expenses." In the political sphere, he asked the United States to reopen the Afghan embassy in Washington and to supply humanitarian assistance through NGOs rather than using Pakistan as a distribution center. Krakowski asked him if he could help the United States get rid of terrorist bases in Afghanistan. "If we are assisted, we do not see any problem to work directly against the terrorists," he replied. "But we have very, very limited resources. You can see how difficult it is here from a financial point of view."

However strapped he was financially, Massoud was in the thick of developing a multiethnic resistance movement. He described the creation of a new military council for the United Front, including Haji Qadir, the Pashtun leader from Jalalabad; Ismail Khan, who had escaped Taliban imprisonment and was about to return to the Herat region; Karim Khalili, the Shia leader; Abdul Rashid Dostum, who had just returned to northern Afghanistan; and Mohamed Arif, a Kandahar Pashtun. "We have agreed on certain principles," Massoud said. The principles included fighting the Taliban to compel them to join negotiations, establishing a broad-based interim government, drafting a new constitution, and holding multiparty elections.[27]

But on returning to Washington, Krakowski had no traction. "I had a very hard time in Washington," he said. The atmosphere "was very negative toward Massoud and toward the [United Front]." He briefed Khalilzad and other senior administration officials. "They listened. And I don't think it went very much further." He thought this was because U.S. policy toward Afghanistan was "a derivative of Pakistani policy. Pakistan always bad-mouthed the United Front. And since the State Department thought the Pakistanis knew the region, this has been a catastrophic approach."[28]

Massoud was used to operating on the slenderest reed of support. With the encouragement of Krakowski, Peter Tomsen, and Otilie English (sister of Republican congressman Phil English of Pennsylvania and a lobbyist for the United Front), he began rebuilding his military and political alliance. Dostum had returned from exile in Turkey and was waiting for Massoud when he got back from Europe. In a matter of weeks, the former

Communist militia leader and some 200 Uzbek horsemen were back in the field, but they suffered a serious setback in Balkh province when the Taliban mounted air attacks. Rebasing in Sar-e Pul province in north-central Afghanistan, they mounted a series of unsuccessful assaults in Badghis and Faryab. By the beginning of September, Dostum had some 1,000 mounted cavalry. Ismail Khan had rebased himself in Ghor province in the west of the country and had successfully mounted operations cutting main roads to the provincial capital of Chaghcharan.[29]

Having chosen the pilots for the hijack air attacks in the United States and sent them off for pilot training in early summer 2000 (Hani Hanjour, who had already had a pilot's certificate, arrived early in 2001), bin Laden spent the summer and autumn of 2000 selecting the "muscle" hijackers— the men who would take control of the passenger cabins of the four hijacked aircraft. Twelve of the fourteen men were Saudi, all were 20–28 years of age, and none had fought in the anti-Soviet jihad. A number of them had originally intended to fight in Chechnya but were rebuffed because of their lack of training and instead were diverted to Afghanistan. Seven of the men received their basic training at al-Farouk camp near Kandahar and two at Khaldan, near Kabul. The boot camp featured training in firearms, heavy weapons, explosives, and topography. The emphasis was on discipline and military life; they were subjected to psychological stress testing. Bin Laden would deliver lectures and personally meet the trainees. Once selected, the trainees were asked to swear *bayat* to bin Laden. Khalid Sheikh Muhammad put them through his own training program, filmed each for a martyrdom video, and paid them $2,000 for expenses.

To obtain a U.S. visa, each was to apply from his home country, taking care first to obtain a new passport without a Pakistani visa on it. Then they were to return to Afghanistan overland via Iran for final training in conducting a hijacking, this time at the al Matar complex. The instruction included disarming air marshals, handling explosives, storming a cockpit door, bodybuilding, and some elementary English. The instructor, a Jordanian named Abu Turab, had them butcher a sheep and a camel with a knife for practice. They went from there to Karachi and thence, via Dubai, to the United States. Between late April and early June, fourteen of the fifteen had arrived. Most of them settled in south Florida, where they opened bank accounts, rented apartments, and spent their time learning English and working out in gyms.

Late in May 2001, Ramzi Binalshibh reported to bin Laden near Kandahar. Bin Laden asked him to inform Atta of his own preferred targets: the World Trade Center, the Pentagon, the White House, and the Capitol. Early in August, Binalshibh met Atta in Spain for a final meeting on targeting and timing. Atta agreed to include the White House in the target list but said they should keep the Capitol as the alternative in case the

White House proved too difficult. He specified that the attacks should not be before the first week of September, when Congress was back in session.[30]

Red Alert

In spring and summer 2001, intelligence tips about bin Laden's planned terror attacks poured into the CIA and the FBI. Some came from walk-in informants, others from electronic eavesdropping or anonymous telephone calls to U.S. embassies. In April, the CIA circulated a warning that bin Laden was preparing multiple operations; in May the warning was of attacks on London, Boston, and New York; and in June of a high probability of near-term "spectacular" terrorist attacks. The terms of the official internal warnings were not understated but spoke of "calamitous" impact or damage of "catastrophic" proportions. The Bush administration gave no hint to the pubic of its internal state of alarm until late June, when it ordered the U.S. Fifth Fleet out of port in Bahrain, citing terrorist threats. Once again, few American reporters were on the case, and America's intelligence agencies seemed unaware of those that were. [31]

One exception was veteran American journalist Arnaud de Borch-grave, who used contacts in Saudi Arabia to arrange a meeting with bin Laden in early June. Something went awry, and he instead wound up interviewing Mullah Omar at his quarters in Kandahar in mid-June. If Mullah Omar's words were to be believed, he had no inkling of what was under way. Responding to a question about bin Laden's threats to the United States, Omar explained that theologically this was impossible. "Bin Laden is not entitled to issue fatwas as he did not complete the mandatory twelve years of Koranic studies to qualify for the position of *mufti*," he told de Borchgrave. "Only *muftis* can issue fatwas. . . . [Bin Laden] is not a *mufti* and, therefore, any fatwa he may have issued are illegal and null and void." He used similar reasoning to explain why he would not expel bin Laden: Afghan and Muslim hospitality, and bin Laden's written pledge not to attack any other country from his Afghan base. In addition, Omar stated without further elaboration that if the government and people of Afghanistan were to change their position on bin Laden, "many problems would result."

This may have been the first interview the "emir" gave to an American reporter, perhaps his fourth meeting with any non-Muslim. (Vendrell believes he was the third.) The soft-spoken "one-eyed, 6-foot-6–inches, five-times-wounded" veteran of the war against the Soviet occupation sat "cross-legged on the carpeted mud floor of his Spartan adobe house on the west end of town," de Borchgrave wrote. "Omar's shrapnel-scarred face, topped by a black turban, shows no emotion as he answers in quick succession a military field telephone, walkie-talkies, and a sideband radio." A

2,500-word story ran on the UPI wire on June 14, 2001, and de Borchgrave got front-page play in the June 18 *Washington Times*. But the CIA, despite its preoccupation with bin Laden, was unaware.*

Tenet learned of the interview in early July during a dinner party at de Borchgrave's home. "George arrived late and seemed puzzled by the conversation," de Borchgrave recounted. "What were you doing there? Are you going to publish it?" Tenet asked. De Borchgrave said the story had been in print for three weeks.[34]

In the spring of 2001, with the media unable to beat a path to his door and the U.S. government seemingly determined to play down his role as U.S. enemy number one, bin Laden decided to drop broad hints of his plans.† His cohorts circulated a 100-minute recruitment video throughout Kuwait and other countries, in which he read a poem celebrating the attack on the USS *Cole*. "In Aden, they charged and destroyed a destroyer that fearsome people fear, one that evokes horror when it docks and when it sails," he intoned, dressed in traditional Yemeni white robe with dagger. "We give you the good news that the forces of Islam are coming and the forces of Yemen will continue in the name of God." The tape showed his masked followers training in the al-Farouk desert camp—jumping hurdles, handling explosives, and target-shooting at images of President Clinton and King Hussein of Jordan over a soundtrack of a song about the attack. "We thank God for granting us victory the day we destroyed the *Cole* in the sea," it said. Bin Laden urged recruits to come to his secret training camp in Afghanistan and to be prepared for a violent struggle against non-Muslims.[33]

At the same time, bin Laden invited Baker Atyani, a reporter for the Saudi-owned satellite channel MBC (Middle East Broadcasting Centre), to see him at a secret location outside Kandahar. It was a three-hour journey from Kandahar in a car with blackened windows, and bin Laden specified in his invitation that he would discuss his latest pledge of loyalty to Mullah Omar. When Atyani arrived, the script changed. "In the next few weeks we will carry out a big surprise, and we will strike or attack American and Israeli interests," Abu Hafs told Atyani. When Atyani asked bin Laden to confirm the plan, he smiled but did not speak. Atyani spent three hours

---

* De Borchgrave had traveled to the region in hopes of seeing bin Laden, but when he got to Islamabad, the interview fell through despite three previous messages of confirmation. So he went to the Afghan embassy and concocted a note for Mullah Omar. "I got your message in Washington. So sorry, I had the flu. I hope I'm not too late to see you." The flustered Afghans gave him a visa on the spot; he flew to Quetta and took a taxi to Kandahar, getting directions to Omar's house from local policemen. De Borchgrave, telephone interview by author, January 2004.

† In an article on April 3, 2001, the *Wall Street Journal* reported that the administration had deliberately decided to play down bin Laden's role by not mentioning him in public: "U.S. counterterrorism officials believe they inflated Mr. bin Laden's power and prestige in recent years by portraying him as the ultimate terrorist mastermind and the top threat to America's security." Indeed, the State Department's annual *Patterns of Global Terrorism* report, which had devoted an entire page to bin Laden's life history and ambitions in 2000, omitted that page in the 2001 edition.

interviewing the top al Qaeda leadership. None would be quoted on film, but the camera panned over to bin Laden, Zawahiri, and Abu Hafs sitting together on a couch as irrefutable proof that the reporter had been with them. Atyani saw only Arabs during his visit. "It felt like bin Laden had his own Arab kingdom in southern Afghanistan," he said. He also reported that bin Laden had moved out of Kandahar the previous week and that al Qaeda forces were in a "major state of mobilization." Atyani had spent more time with bin Laden than any reporter since early 1999, and his report was about as timely as news could get; but it drew no direct attention from the U.S. government. No official ever contacted Atyani for more details, and, to his knowledge, no one ever asked MBC for the rushes of his tape.[34]

Atyani's June 23 report added to the alarm in Washington, but with no strategy in place, the Bush administration took the path of least resistance that Bill Clinton had trodden so often. Milam delivered yet another pro forma warning to Abdul Salam Zaeef, the Taliban representative in Islamabad: the United States would hold the Taliban responsible if bin Laden launched any attacks against the United States. The FBI and the CIA, completely unaware that most of the nineteen hijackers were already in the United States, were doing everything they could abroad, coordinating disruption operations against al Qaeda–affiliated cells in twenty countries. Other than tactical defensive measures, the administration took no action against the Taliban and made no effort to link up with Massoud.

By mid-July, the CIA reported indications that bin Laden had delayed his plans for up to two months. Later that month, the warnings spiked again. "The system was blinking red," Tenet later said. It could not "get any worse." But other officials were skeptical. Paul Wolfowitz, the deputy secretary of defense, questioned the reporting and asked whether bin Laden was just trying to study U.S. reactions. Tenet responded that the intelligence reporting was convincing.[35]

Taliban officials were less skeptical about Atyani's report and demanded that bin Laden disavow it. Abu Hafs himself declared the report "baseless and false." The Taliban Foreign Ministry issued the familiar disclaimer that bin Laden's activities "are under control" and said there was "no possibility of using Afghan territory against any other country." But Mullah Omar was less troubled. "What Ayman and Osama did was not correct. But the harm has been done, and there is no point in arguing about it now," he told his aides, according to Vahid Mojdeh. Clearly, Omar was no longer in control.

But Foreign Minister Muttawakil was furious that Afghanistan would be blamed for bin Laden's activities. His thinking was that the Taliban had accepted bin Laden and his followers as guests, but now they wanted to destroy the entire domicile. Mullah Amir Khan Muttaqi and Muttawakil went to see bin Laden in Kandahar to give him a dressing down. The Taliban, Muttaqi told bin Laden, "have already faced hundreds of problems.

We have problems with internal enemies and external pressure. You can help us by not creating more issues for us."

Bin Laden responded cryptically, "Very well. I will solve your internal problems. I will get rid of your internal enemies so you don't tell me I'm nothing but trouble for you."[36]

The target was Massoud, and the planning had been under way apparently since April, following Massoud's trip to Europe. Two Tunisian men had received training in bin Laden's camps starting in late 2000, and sometime in spring or early summer of the following year, they were selected for the suicide mission. Abdelsattar Dahmane, a Tunisian living in Belgium, would play the role of journalist, and Rachid Bourawi Alwaer, an illegal immigrant to Belgium, would act as his cameraman. Equipped with stolen Moroccan passports, false Pakistani visas, phony letters of introduction from the Islamic center in London, and an old television camera shipped to Kabul via Pakistan, they crossed the front lines in mid-August, claiming to be Arab journalists in search of an interview with Massoud. The trip was facilitated by Abdul Rasul Sayyaf, a senior resistance leader, who received a phone call from Abu Hani, an old Egyptian friend from the anti-Soviet jihad. Hani claimed to be phoning from Bosnia (he was actually in Kandahar) and asked Massoud to take care of two reporter friends. Sayyaf later said he was unaware that Hani was working with bin Laden.

For three weeks, the assassins waited for an interview. In the meantime, as many as sixteen thousand Taliban and Arab fighters had massed in Takhar province for what was certainly intended to be the final offensive against Massoud. They were awaiting the signal to attack and, they hoped, capture Panjshir. Omar had told de Borchgrave that it was the final offensive. Massoud and his fighters "will soon get their just deserts," he said, calling for a "total victory."[37] As the assassins waited, bin Laden approached the Taliban *shura* and gave formal notice that an attack would take place in the coming weeks. Some members objected, but bin Laden countered that Mullah Omar had no authority to prevent al Qaeda from conducting jihad outside Afghanistan.[38]

On September 8, 2001, Massoud met with twenty-five of his local commanders to warn them of the coming assault. "Be brave," he said. "It's a big offensive. The goal is to get Badakshan, and get us out." One of his commanders asked whether Pakistanis would take part. "Naturally, from the madrassas," he replied. "But this is the war of al Qaeda."

Massoud stayed up much of the night, and his former spokesman, Masoud Khalili, read Persian poetry aloud. Massoud mused about the cost of defeat. "If we are out of Afghanistan, the next [to fall] will be Central Asia. Bokhara [Uzbekistan] will be the capital of the Islamic movement of al Qaeda." Khalili said he doubted this was possible. "I believe what I told you," Massoud said.

"Do we lose Afghanistan?" Khalili asked.

"The Pakistanis never succeed in anything. Do you ever see Arabs suc-
ceeding in anything? The defeated ones become heroes," Massoud replied.

Khalili read from Hafiz, the fourteenth-century Persian Sufi poet:
"You two who are talking together tonight, value it. Because tomorrow you
will not be able to see it again."

Massoud interrupted: "What are they talking about?"

Khalili continued. "This dark night is pregnant with tomorrow. You
two do not know what will be the child. The world is a clear story, full of
deception. You do not know what will be the trick of tomorrow morning."

Massoud called a halt. It was 4:00 a.m. and time to sleep.[39]

Seven hours later, Massoud invited "Karim Touzani" and "Kacem
Bakkali," as they had renamed themselves, for the interview they had so long
sought. Some of Massoud's aides urged him not to see the two Arabs, but
he was desperate for a foreign audience to convince the Arab world that
the Taliban was oppressing Afghans with the help of Pakistan and foreign
Arabs. Times had changed from the days when he had instructed his aides
not to allow journalists to call on him.

Massoud asked for the questions and then declared, "You can start
filming now." A "blue thick fire" rushed out of the camera with a "poof."
The bomb in the battery pack had exploded. "Pick me up," Massoud whis-
pered to his bodyguard. The guerrilla leader was covered with blood. He
was taken to Tajikistan by helicopter but died of loss of blood en route.
Two pieces of shrapnel had pierced his heart. Massoud's aides gathered at
the clinic and agreed to tell the world that he was injured but still alive.
Only the CIA was told that Massoud was dead.[40]

On September 10, the Taliban broke through Massoud's front lines.
But they faltered; Massoud's own fighters threw themselves into the breach,
and Dostum—who, according to a UN official, had "armed everything
taller than a Kalashnikov"—fought for his life.[41]

One day later, bin Laden's nineteen hijackers seized four commercial
aircraft and attacked the twin towers of the World Trade Center in New
York City and the Pentagon in Washington, D.C. They would have flown
the fourth plane into the U.S. Capitol, but for a passenger mutiny that
crashed the aircraft into a Pennsylvania farm field.

Epilogue
Clemenceau Revisited

Two months after Osama bin Laden's operatives blew up the U.S. embassies in Nairobi, Kenya, and Dar es Salaam, Tanzania, in August 1998, Congress invited ten leading military, intelligence, and law enforcement experts to recommend changes in policy for preventing and punishing terrorism. After consulting the country's top terrorism specialists, the National Commission on Terrorism published its report in June 2000. The only advice offered on Afghanistan was to designate it a sponsor of terrorism and impose economic sanctions.

More than two hundred innocent civilians were killed in the August 1998 attacks, but Afghanistan, where the plot had been hatched and the operatives trained, was ranked fourth behind Iran, Syria, and Sudan among the countries allegedly supporting terrorists or using terrorism as an element of state policy.

U.S. government officials concluded in the first half of 1999 that the Taliban regime had effectively become captive to bin Laden. But the commission, chaired by Paul Bremer, former head of counterterrorism at the State Department (and later chief civilian administrator in Iraq), seemed unaware of this and underestimated the threat of the man and his movement.

"Neither al Qaeda's extremist politico-religious beliefs nor its leader, Osama bin Laden, is unique," the report said. "If al Qaeda and Osama bin Laden were to disappear tomorrow, the United States would still face potential terrorist threats from a growing number of groups opposed to perceived American hegemony."

"We were seeing with one eye," commented James Woolsey, a former CIA director who served on the commission. "Most other folks had very dark glasses on both eyes." The view among universities, think tanks, and government was that terrorism "was a nuisance." The same view held sway among the news media.[1]

The Bremer Commission produced many proposals for intelligence gathering and contingency planning that provided the basis for policy changes after 9/11. But at the time, its members failed to ring the right alarm bell.*

---

* According to cochairman Maurice Sonnenberg, of the twenty-five recommendations the commission made, twenty were incorporated into the USA PATRIOT Act passed after 9/11. Members included Bremer, then managing director of Kissinger Associates and a former ambassador-at-large for counterterrorism; Fred Ikle, an under secretary of defense in the Reagan administration; James Woolsey, Clinton's first CIA director; Richard Betts of Columbia University; Gen. (ret.) Wayne Downey; Rep. Jane Harman (D-CA); Juliette Kayyem of the Kennedy School of Government, Harvard University; John Lewis, former senior FBI official; and Gardner Peckham, one-time senior aide to former house speaker Newt Gingrich. Maurice Sonnenberg, cochairman of the National Commission on Terrorism, telephone interview by author, February 2006.

Yet it was into the hands of counterterrorism experts that Bill Clinton and Madeleine Albright entrusted much of U.S. policy on Afghanistan and bin Laden. Counterterrorism experts advocated and drafted the U.S. and UN sanctions in 1999 that drove bin Laden and the Taliban into each other's arms, an outcome that damaged U.S. interests; and then they drafted a second set of sanctions in 2000. They also proposed policies against Pakistan so tough that other aides feared a government collapse.

Putting U.S. policy in the hands of "so-called experts on terrorism" was analogous to "putting the U.S. Navy and Marine Corps in World War II in the hands of those whose job it was to stop kamikazes," commented Woolsey. Just as Georges Clemenceau warned that war is "much too serious a matter to be left to military men," counterterrorism is much too serious a matter to be left to counterterrorism experts. The experts in this field carry a mystique that strikes awe in the hearts of laymen, and demystification is long overdue.

Terrorism—violence directed against noncombatants to intimidate for a political or social purpose—is a tactic that states often use in conflict. There cannot be a war on terrorism, that is, a war against a tactic. More precisely, there cannot be a *successful* war on terrorism. Law enforcement, covert action, or the military can use force to disrupt plans to commit violence. But counterterrorist tactics will not defeat a movement that is grounded in a totalitarian or millenarian ideology and that relies on terror. Without a political counterstrategy, terrorists will rebound and revive the tactic.

Terror tactics do not spring out of thin air but emerge from a domestic political context, or from civil or regional war. In the post–Cold War era, local conflicts have shown great potential for disturbing world order. Osama bin Laden, a nearly powerless outsider with larger-than-life political ambitions, seems to have had a better grasp of the inherent opportunity in such conflicts than a succession of U.S. presidents. Before 9/11, three administrations—those of George H. W. Bush, Bill Clinton, and George W. Bush—started from the premise that after the collapse of the Soviet empire, the United States could withdraw from parts of the world where it had no obvious material or strategic interest, such as the Balkans. But when an empire collapses, power and security vacuums form where they are least expected. Power vacuums may lead to civil war, and when no outside power can guarantee security, it is a short path to regional conflict.

In this new world, the gravest threats to American security and international stability may come from places that were on the periphery of superpower competition. The wars that develop in such power and security vacuums turn out to be highly relevant to U.S. security, for they provide a cover for those who would launch bigger wars, commit genocide, or organize acts of terror.

Afghanistan was the venue for the bloodiest and longest battle of the Cold War, as well as the place where Soviet military power went down to defeat, and it became the bridge to a more dangerous world. Washington viewed the internal struggle between Ahmed Shah Massoud and Gulbuddin Hekmatyar as a contest between warlords, but it was, in fact, a conflict between two national visions—one based on home-grown nationalism, moderate Islamism, and successful insurrection against an occupying power, and the other on a radical anti-American Islamist vision, a record of ruthlessness, and a pattern of short-sighted manipulation by an outside backer, Pakistan. James Baker famously said on the eve of Yugoslavia's devastating wars that the United States had "no dog in that fight." U.S. officials wore the same blinders with Afghanistan after 1992.

Nowadays, there is no such thing as a faraway war where the United States has no interest. Whether the American public wants the role or not, the sole remaining superpower has to be the major player in every region —or find an ally to step in for it. Americans may not like acting as world policemen, but the opponents of American power will search out safe havens in the least inviting places on Earth, starting with obscure conflict zones, to establish a base against a U.S.-dominated world order. Being world policemen does not mean resorting to force everywhere. In Afghanistan, simply sending a special envoy at a time of instability stabilized the situation in the early 1990s, at least temporarily.

The Taliban were already radical Islamists when they took power, but bin Laden brought to their regime an extremist global vision, calling for war through terror tactics against U.S. interests as well as all Christians and Jews. He drew on Koranic text and hadith and the writings of medieval philosophers to stake out his claim to a divine mission. But what allowed him to become a magnet for jihadis the world over was his articulation of the grievances of Muslims, whose political rights are minimal or nonexistent in most Muslim-led countries and whose coreligionists in Israeli-occupied territories lack sovereignty or independence. In Bosnia, Kosovo, and Chechnya, Muslims had been the target of massive crimes against humanity, even genocide. Muslim grievances were real, as was bin Laden's manipulation of them to advance his own political aims.

When groups abroad employ terror outside their borders to voice their grievances, the only lasting response can come from the realm of politics: the domestic politics of the country in which they are operating and the foreign policy of the United States and other powers. If a local government does not observe international norms, a way must be found through internal and external allies to convince it to conform.

Devising the political counterstrategy is the task of diplomats, as well as politicians who are prepared to use force to back up their threats. That is the essence of effective foreign policy. Diplomacy that is not backed by a credible threat of the use of force will miscarry; so will the use of force without a clear diplomatic purpose. Relating force to political objectives lies at the heart of strategy. Karl von Clausewitz, the great Prussian military thinker, said, "No one starts a war—or rather, no one in his senses ought to do so—without first being clear in his mind what he intends to achieve by that war and how he intends to conduct it."

The measures for changing behavior cover the spectrum from friendly persuasion to supporting one side in an internal armed conflict, with armed invasion the last resort. A surgical military strike, America's weapon of choice, is a temporary fix at best.

The Clinton administration developed counterterrorism tactics but not a political strategy. It viewed Afghanistan in the context of Osama bin Laden, as a counterterrorism expert might, instead of seeing bin Laden in the context of Afghanistan. Great effort went into intelligence gathering, but in the form of "actionable intelligence" that would guide a surgical strike or the assassination of bin Laden rather than in the form of political cues that would provide the key to his power and resilience.

A closed country under the control of extremists, like Afghanistan under the Taliban, presents a special challenge for developing an effective strategy. The workaround begins by naming a competent envoy to gather the facts and develop a concept. If the door is closed or it is unsafe to work inside, the next step is to construct a diplomatic operation abroad and redouble efforts to obtain intelligence. Peter Tomsen, a skilled diplomat who had never visited Afghanistan until the end of his tour as special envoy, got results in the early 1990s by figuring out the internal politics and working with forces that were already on the U.S. side. The next step in developing a political strategy is to put the concept through a rigorous process to determine goals and means. In the Clinton administration, counterterrorism specialists were given charge of the principal policy review after the 1998 embassy bombings, and their major recommendation was to apply economic sanctions.

Bill Clinton's failure to set up a bureaucratic structure to cope with the threats coming from Afghanistan, and his disinclination to support opposition forces inside the country or to use force, led to a reliance on proxies—mainly Pakistan, at one point Russia, and for several years Iran. But Pakistan had its own agenda and would not play the U.S.-assigned role. A schizophrenic U.S. government attitude over how to deal with Pakistan—with Clinton supporting congressionally mandated sanctions for its nuclear weapons program and the U.S. military blocking any policy shift that would upset the Pakistan military—ruled out a get-tough policy for Afghanistan.

This left the United States with no option but to tolerate the Taliban. Long after bin Laden's blood-curdling call for attacks on American civilians in February 1998, and after Mullah Omar pledged to protect him, the administration went out of its way to declare its neutrality in Afghan politics and to meet the Taliban halfway.

Afghanistan has long been a never-never land in the modern world, where perception often trumps reality and where internal alliances are in constant flux. Figuring out the functioning of local politics takes study, but the beginning of wisdom is to work with the forces that are already on your side.

An astute policymaker would have known when to switch sides, as everyone else does in Afghanistan. But switching required a sophisticated understanding of the political facts on the ground. Bin Laden was an expert on Afghanistan and knew how to cultivate a local constituency that would protect him. Arriving at the end of the mujahideen regime, he quickly shifted allegiance to the Taliban. The United States, lacking a special envoy devoted exclusively to Afghanistan, did not have the political intelligence essential for knowing when to switch sides.

There was an alternative: Ahmed Shah Massoud. The CIA visited him and paid him cash for handing over Stinger missile systems, but the State Department never accorded him top-level attention, never invited him to Washington, and treated his rump regime as just one more faction. However flawed the mujahideen government was in the 1992–1996 time frame, Massoud was the world's foremost guerrilla leader, with a strong following, at least in the north of the country, and the capability to learn from his mistakes. But Bill Clinton and George W. Bush both failed to seek his counsel, use his talents, harness his resources, or provide sufficient support to his forces to shift the balance until after he was assassinated.

What was the right moment for the shift? It was probably after the August 1998 attack on the U.S. embassies in East Africa, when it became clear that Mullah Omar had an unshakable commitment to grant sanctuary to bin Laden. By acting as if war could be avoided and the problem could be managed with sanctions, the United States emboldened the other side.

In dealing with bin Laden the political figure, any strategy would begin with a serious assessment of the man, his charisma, his hold over others, and his influence in the Islamic world. The challenge was not to kill him but to undercut his reputation, weaken his charisma, and raise doubts among current and future followers about the moral character of a zealot who was responsible for the deaths of thousands of innocent civilians. Intelligence, law enforcement, and military policy should defer to these aims and support them instead of the other way around. At the same time, the grievances that allowed bin Laden to rally would-be martyrs from around the globe had to be examined seriously and addressed.

To the extent that they have reflected on their management of the Afghanistan and bin Laden issues (not much, if their memoirs are any indication), those at the top of the Clinton administration disagree with the foregoing analysis. Former Secretary of State Madeleine Albright, for one, has no regrets over policy decisions. "While everybody wishes that life had turned out differently, if you look at everything we did, I'm pretty satisfied that we did everything we could, given what we knew and given the pre-9/11 situation," she said in an interview. "I really think we did an awful lot. I don't have the sense that we failed in any way. . . . We did the right thing."

Albright does not see the value of appointing a special envoy in a country where there is no ambassador because of an ongoing conflict. "Bureaucratically, it undercuts the system," she said. It is "not something I considered." She does not recall giving a lead role in combating bin Laden to her counterterrorism adviser, Michael Sheehan. "I don't remember that Mike was in charge of the policy," she said. "It was not as if counterterrorism was running things." Albright's own autobiography indicates otherwise, as do former top State Department aides.*

The thesis underlying this book is that the 9/11 attack was not so much an intelligence or military failure as a strategic foreign policy failure, which can be understood only by examining where things went wrong. Albright disagrees. "You have a thesis that you want proved, and you'll prove it. But that's not the way it was. . . . Given what we knew and what we were doing, we did the best we could with the intelligence we had and with the atmosphere that we had."

It is possible that there was nothing the Clinton administration could have done differently. The Bush administration certainly did no better, and the news media also failed to sound the alarm. What is staggering is that officials from neither administration seem to have searched their souls for lessons learned or, if they have, shared them for the benefit of the country and the general public.

The question is one for future administrations: how will anyone in office master the challenges of a complex world and get it right without first examining past failures in depth, acknowledging errors, and making the needed course corrections?

To the extent the national debate on 9/11 has not been overwhelmed by the war in Iraq, it has focused on ways to improve surveillance and tighten security—that is, on the symptoms, not the causes, of the cancer.

The debate should center on how the sole superpower is to relate to the rest of the world in the post–Cold War era, and how it can ensure its own security and international security as well. For bin Laden, the aim is to provoke a clash of civilizations; by emphasizing military tactics over political strategy, the United States has stepped into the trap he so cunningly set.

---

* Albright wrote in her autobiography that she named Sheehan to the post of counterterrorism adviser in late 1998, and with input from colleagues such as Inderfurth, Sheehan "soon developed a strategy for increasing pressure on the Taliban." The strategy called for sending "a message" that they would be held accountable for anything bin Laden did, reserving the right to use military force and impose bilateral and UN economic sanctions. She noted that "the plan did not work." According to Albright's under secretary of state, Thomas Pickering, Sheehan led a policy review in late 1999 that would have imposed "very tough" sanctions on Pakistan. Pickering helped shoot it down. "It was like taking a chance of playing with an open vat of gasoline in hopes that they would be more frightened than we," he said. Albright, Madame Secretary, 369–70; and Pickering, interview.

An additional problem in devising an effective strategy was the shift in ideology when George Bush succeeded Bill Clinton. The Bush administration reacted to the multilateralism of Bill Clinton by embarking on a unilateralist approach to foreign affairs from its first day in office. One of the ironies of domestic politics is that the 9/11 attacks gave the president the political clout to pursue this controversial path when it made even less sense.

What is needed to counter bin Ladenism is a foreign policy worthy of the name.

The history of U.S. relations with Afghanistan offers a lesson, chiefly on what foreign policy is *not*. The United States poured in weapons and funds to support a population that was trying to overthrow Soviet invaders but failed to establish relations with the local forces or to involve them in political talks leading to a political outcome. In fact, successive administrations, with the advice of specialists in both parties, focused exclusively on the damage that could be done to the Soviet Union while overlooking the need to try to achieve a stable political end-state in Afghanistan. Successive administrations treated Afghanistan as a theater for CIA operations instead of a real country. But the often-preferred tools of American foreign policy—assassinations, weapons running, surgical military strikes, and engineered coups—cannot work unless they are embedded in a long-term foreign policy that is aimed at achieving a stable end-state. A quick fix is not a lasting solution.

Relying on an unstable neighbor (in this case, Pakistan) to play the lead role was fated to fail, but the Clinton administration compounded the error by not appointing an envoy for Afghanistan. Cutting U.S. aid when it was most needed, treating the weak mujahideen government with disdain, then looking to the Taliban to put things right were the logical consequences. The administration's failure to put the spotlight on the Taliban after the 1998 Mazar-i-Sharif massacre may seem a minor omission, but viewed in the context of vigorous efforts to rally allies to join an intervention in Kosovo, it signaled the Taliban that no one abroad cared what they did. Pursuing patient diplomacy with the Taliban in 1999—even after top U.S. officials knew that bin Laden had effectively hijacked the regime—not only lulled the American public into a false sense of security but also sent a signal of indecision and weakness to both Mullah Omar and bin Laden, as did Bill Clinton's passivity following the bombing of the USS *Cole*. The Bush administration's inaction during its first eight months in office, despite all the briefings and warnings from its predecessor, was a further signal of American indecisiveness.

The news media's absence from the scene before 9/11 is one of the great lapses in the modern history of the profession. The gates to Afghanistan were often locked to the media, and those who managed to get in had their movements circumscribed. Still, the principle of watchdog journalism is that if the door is closed or a government restricts the media, "That's where I need to be." Even without freedom to enter the country, the media could have reported widespread and systematic war crimes by interviewing even a tiny portion of the refugees who fled the country. Within twenty-four hours of the destruction of the two U.S. embassies in East Africa in August 1998, a Taliban force (which bin Laden claims to have helped organize and train, and which he supported with his own Arab fighters) captured a major city in northern Afghanistan and executed thousands of civilians. The American press, with one or two exceptions, missed the story. Through close monitoring of the conflict, reporters might have discovered that bin Laden's Arab fighters had become the backbone of the Taliban fighting force. A closer focus on the secretive Taliban might have uncovered the Arabization of Afghanistan. The religious terror campaign that accompanied the capture of Mazar-i-Sharif in 1998, the takeover of areas of Kabul by Arabs, and the plans to shut all public schools and replace them with madrassas where the language would be Arabic were among the clues.

"The worst thing that happened to Afghanistan is that the media were not there," says Afghan Sufi religious leader Hazrat Ahmad Amin Ismael al Mojadiddi. "They didn't try hard enough. They didn't speak to refugees." American policymakers share that judgment. Former U.S. ambassador to Pakistan William Milam puts it this way: "If you guys had sort of been keeping the heat on the administration for stuff like this, it might not have turned out the same way." In the view of Rick Inderfurth, former assistant secretary of state for South Asian Affairs and a former television reporter, "Had you guys focused your attention more, we wouldn't have missed the story. I think everyone missed the story. No one got it right." Thoughtful reporters agree. In the view of *New York Times* reporter John Burns, who won a Pulitzer prize for his reporting on the Taliban takeover, the media largely stopped covering Afghanistan after the Soviet withdrawal. For international reporters, based mostly in New Delhi, he said, "Unless you had an abiding interest in Afghanistan, it was always the last place to be attended to." He added, "If the press fails to do its job, the intelligentsia have nothing; then the government and Pentagon are way out on a storm-tossed sea without a compass. In Afghanistan, we did fail to do our job."[2]

The lesson for the media is the continuing need for in-depth reporting from far-flung places where the United States does not have an active policy, as well as from those places where it does. Obscure, faraway conflicts have given rise to the evils of this era, providing cover for criminals, terrorists, drug production, and war crimes, as well as the seeds for far bigger wars. Too often, governments try to ignore small wars. The media—and the general public—should keep the government's feet to the fire and constantly check its judgment. Too often, it is deeply flawed.

Chronology

DECEMBER 24, 1979—Soviet troops invade Afghanistan, install Babrak Karmal as president, and overthrow Hafizullah Amin, who had seized power by murdering his predecessor.

JANUARY 1980—Afghan army revolts in Kandahar, there is street fighting in Herat and Kabul, and mullahs throughout the country declare a jihad against Soviet occupiers.

JUNE 1982—UN undersecretary Diego Cordovez opens "proximity" talks between the Soviet Union and Pakistan on ways of ending the Afghan war.

SEPTEMBER 1984—Osama bin Laden and Abdullah Azzam launch the Services Office in Peshawar, Pakistan, to support Arabs seeking to join the jihad against Soviet occupation of Afghanistan.

MARCH 1985—Mikhail Gorbachev is named general secretary of the Soviet Communist Party.

FEBRUARY 1986—Gorbachev tells the Politburo Afghanistan is a "bleeding wound" and says there will be a phased troop withdrawal.

FEBRUARY 1986—The Reagan administration decides to ship Stinger missiles to the mujahideen.

MAY 1986—The Soviets install Najibullah Ahmedzai, head of the Khad secret police, to replace Babrak Karmal as president of Afghanistan.

APRIL 1987—Bin Laden comes under Soviet attack at his Jaji training base.

FEBRUARY 1988—The United Nations' Cordovez has his first meeting with mujahideen external-based leadership in Peshawar.

APRIL 14, 1988—The final accord on Soviet withdrawal is signed in Geneva.

AUGUST 1988—Bin Laden founds al Qaeda.

FEBRUARY 15, 1989—The last Soviet troops depart Afghanistan.

MARCH 1989—At Pakistani urging, the mujahideen launch a disastrous offensive to capture Jalalabad.

AUTUMN 1989—Al Qaeda's first recruitment meeting is held in Khost, Afghanistan; bin Laden returns to Saudi Arabia.

NOVEMBER 11, 1989—The Berlin Wall opens, leading to the collapse of the East German regime, the Soviet presence in East Europe, and Communist parties throughout East Europe.

NOVEMBER 1989—Bin Laden returns to Saudi Arabia.

SEPTEMBER 11, 1991—Boris Yeltsin demands that Gorbachev halt arms shipments to Afghanistan effective January 1, 1992.

JANUARY 1992—Bin Laden moves to Sudan.

MARCH 18, 1992—Najibullah, in a speech drafted by the UN mediator, announces he will step down.

APRIL 29, 1992—Ahmed Shah Massoud and ten thousand troops take control of Kabul; his Pakistan-backed rival Gulbuddin Hekmatyar begins bombardment of the capital.

MAY–OCTOBER 1993—Period of relative calm in Kabul.

JANUARY 1, 1994—Former communist army commander Abdul Rashid Dostum links up with Hekmatyar in abortive Pakistan-backed coup attempt against Massoud.

NOVEMBER 1994—Taliban take control of Kandahar.

JANUARY 1995—Taliban capture Ghazni from Hekmatyar with aid from Rabbani and Massoud.

FEBRUARY 1995—Taliban capture Hekmatyar stronghold of Charasyab with government help.

March 1995—Massoud forces oust Taliban from Charasyab, and Kabul enjoys a relative calm until October 1995.

September 1995—Taliban capture Heart; rioters sack Pakistan embassy in Kabul.

OCTOBER 1995—Taliban recapture Charasyab, begin a new siege of Kabul.

MAY 18, 1996—Osama bin Laden and retinue arrive in Jalalabad from Sudan.

JUNE 26, 1996—Hekmatyar takes up prime minister's post; Taliban bombard Kabul.

SEPTEMBER 1996—Bin Laden, in a newspaper interview and eight thousand word statement, declares jihad against the United States and promises to topple Saudi Arabian leadership.

SEPTEMBER 26, 1996—Massoud stages nighttime retreat from Kabul; a day later, the Taliban capture Kabul, impose sharia law, and execute Najibullah.

OCTOBER 10, 1996—Dostum renews alliance with Massoud; Taliban declare jihad.

FEBRUARY 22, 1997—Bin Laden issues fatwa calling for jihad against Jews, "Crusaders," and Americans.

MAY 19-28, 1997— Gen. Abdul Malik Pahlawan ousts Dostum and invites Taliban into Mazar-i-Sharif; Pakistan recognizes Taliban government, but other armed forces rebel, blocking Taliban's exit.

JULY 1997—UN Secretary General Kofi Annan names Lakhdar Brahami special envoy to Afghanistan.

NOVEMBER 1997—Dostum returns to power, discovers mass graves in which usurper Malik Pahlawan reputedly buried thousands of captured Taliban.

FEBRUARY 12, 1998—Bin Laden and Ayman Zawahiri issue "legal fatwa" approving the killing of American civilians.

APRIL 17, 1998—Bill Richardson, U.S. ambassador to the United Nations, sent on one-day peace mission to Afghanistan.

MAY 11-13, 1998—India conducts a series of nuclear tests.

MAY 28-30, 1998—Pakistan conducts its own tests.

AUGUST 7, 1998—Islamic extremists blow up U.S. embassies in Kenya and Tanzania, in plot traced back to bin Laden.

AUGUST 8, 1998—Taliban capture Mazar-i-Sharif, execute eight Iranians and thousands of Hazara civilians.

AUGUST 20, 1998—The United States fires seventy-five cruise missiles at training camps near Khost.

JANUARY 1999—U.S. officials conclude bin Laden has "hijacked" the Taliban state.

JULY 1999—The United States imposes economic, trade, and travel sanctions against Afghanistan.

OCTOBER 1999—Pakistan prime minister Nawaz Sharif, after allying with Bill Clinton to crack down on the Taliban, is ousted by Gen. Pervez Musharraf, an open Taliban backer.

OCTOBER 1999—The United Nations announces wide-ranging sanctions against Afghanistan.

NOVEMBER 1999—Four Arab volunteers from Hamburg, Germany, turn up in Kandahar.

JANUARY 2000—Militants trained in bin Laden camps attempt to blow up a U.S. warship in Yemen, hotels in Jordan, and a terminal at Los Angeles airport, but all attacks fail.

JANUARY 2000—Taliban and Chechnya open diplomatic relations, establish embassies.

MARCH 25, 2000—Clinton visits Pakistan for five hours.

SEPTEMBER 6, 2000—The Taliban capture Taloqan, Massoud's headquarters, his biggest defeat since abandoning Kabul.

OCTOBER 12, 2000—Islamic militants suicide-bomb the USS Cole, killing seventeen.

JANUARY 21, 2001—George W. Bush sworn in as forty-third president.

FEBRUARY 2001—Mullah Omar's edict calling for the destruction of statues that represent living beings is published; Taliban begin the destruction of two giant Buddhas in Bamiyan.

APRIL 2001—Massoud makes his first trip to Europe, visiting Paris, Strasbourg, and Brussels.

JUNE 23, 2001—A bin Laden deputy tells Saudi television "in the next few weeks we will carry out a big surprise . . . and strike . . . American or Israeli interests."

SEPTEMBER 9, 2001—Two Arab "journalists" equipped by bin Laden suicide-bomb Ahmed Shah Massoud.

SEPTEMBER 11, 2001—Bin Laden's chosen air hijackers fly planes into the World Trade Center and the Pentagon.

Dramatis Personae

MADELEINE ALBRIGHT—U.S. ambassador to the United Nations, 1993–1996; secretary of state, 1997–2000

ABDULLAH AZZAM—charismatic Palestinian, who cofounded with bin Laden the Services Office in Peshawar to support Arab volunteers in the anti-Soviet jihad

MUHAMMED ATEF (ABU HAFS AL MISRI)—former Egyptian police officer who became bin Laden's military commander and helped reorganize Taliban military

MAHMOUD AHMED—Gen. Pervez Musharraf's director-general, Inter-Services Intelligence Directorate, 1999–2001

MAJ. GEN. NASEERULLAH BABAR—Pakistani interior minister under Prime Minister Benazir Bhutto, 1993–1996, who played a major support role in supporting the Taliban takeover

BENAZIR BHUTTO—prime minister of Pakistan, 1988–1990 and 1993–1996

LAKHDAR BRAHIMI—Algerian foreign minister, later UN special representative in Afghanistan, 1997–1999 and 2001–2004

DIEGO CORDOVEZ—UN undersecretary-general, 1981–1989; in charge of 1988 Geneva Accords that ended the Soviet occupation

ABDUL RASHID DOSTUM—led ethnic Uzbek militia under communist rule, backed Massoud's takeover in Kabul, joined Hekmatyar in abortive coup attempt, and then allied with Massoud after Taliban takeover

PRINCE TURKI AL FAISAL—head of Saudi Intelligence Service, 1977–2001

LT. GEN. HAMID GUL—director-general, Pakistan Inter-Services Intelligence Directorate, 1987–1989

ABDUL HAQ—moderate Pashtun Islamist resistance leader during Soviet occupation and Massoud ally who was killed by Taliban in October 2001

JALALUDIN HAQQANI—Pashtun Islamist guerrilla leader against Soviets who joined Taliban as minister of tribes and frontiers and oversaw military training camps

GULBUDDIN HEKMATYAR—Pashtun Islamist guerrilla leader, founder of radical Hezb-I Islami party, and lifelong rival of Massoud who bombarded Kabul; briefly joined mujahideen government as prime minister

KARL (RICK) INDERFURTH—assistant secretary of state, South Asia, 1997–2000

HAMID KARZAI—Kandahar-born Pashtun who joined the mujahideen government (1992–1994) and promoted the Taliban; briefly served as UN envoy then helped lead opposition to them, later serving as Afghan president

KARIM KHALILI—leader of the Shia Hazara Hezbi Wahdat party, ally of Massoud

ISMAIL KHAN—military and political leader in Herat of mixed Pashtun and Tajik ancestry during mujahideen regime, ally of Massoud

YUNIS KHALIS—Pashtun religious leader who created his own resistance faction, Hezb-I Islami

OSAMA BIN LADEN—Saudi-born leader of al Qaeda

ROBERT OAKLEY—U.S. ambassador to Pakistan, 1988–1991

GENERAL ABDUL MALIK PAHLAWAN—Uzbek militia leader and second in command to Dostum who invited Taliban to take control of northern Afghanistan in May 1997

AHMED SHAH MASSOUD—charismatic Tajik resistance leader who took control of Kabul and became defense minister in mujahideen government (1992–1996), then led anti-Taliban armed resistance until his assassination on September 9, 2001

EDMUND MCWILLIAMS—special envoy to the Afghan resistance 1988–1989

MAHMOUD MESTIRI—former Tunisian foreign minister, UN special representative for Afghanistan, 1994–1996

GEN. PERVEZ MUSHARRAF—Pakistan army chief of staff 1998, ousted Nawaz Sharif as prime minister in 1999 to become Pakistan military ruler

WILLIAM MILAM—U.S. ambassador to Pakistan, 1998–2001

NAJIBULLAH AHMADZAI—head of Khad secret police during Soviet occupation who became last president of Communist Afghanistan and was executed by Taliban

MULLAH MANON NIAZI—Pashtun governor of Mazar-i-Sharif after the Taliban conquest in August 1998; personally oversaw the executions of thousands of Hazara civilians

CHOONG-HYUN PAIK—UN special rapporteur for human rights in Afghanistan, 1995–1998

THOMAS PICKERING—undersecretary of state, 1997–2000

MULLAH MOHAMMED OMAR AKHUND—Pashtun supreme leader of Taliban and "Emir" of Afghanistan

HAJI QADIR—Pashtun ally of Massoud, leader of the Eastern shura at the time bin Laden arrived

ARNOLD RAPHEL—U.S. ambassador to Pakistan, 1987–1988

ROBIN RAPHEL—assistant secretary of state for South Asia, 1993–1996

BURHANUDDIN RABBANI—Tajik theologian, moderate Islamist, Afghan president, 1992–1996

MULLAH MOHAMMAD RABBANI—Pashtun head of Kabul-based Taliban governing council, deputy to Omar, and relative moderate

BILL RICHARDSON—U.S. ambassador to United Nations, 1997–1998

ABDUL RASUL SAYYAF—Saudi-backed Pashtun leader who joined Rabbani-Massoud government

GARY SCHROEN—CIA officer in Islamabad, 1978–1980, 1988–1990, and 1996–1999

BENON SEVAN—Cypriot-born UN representative for Afghanistan, 1991–1992

NAWAZ SHARIF—prime minister of Pakistan, 1990–1993; 1997–1999

THOMAS SIMONS—U.S. ambassador to Pakistan 1996–1998

RICHARD SMYTH—U.S. consul in Peshawar, Pakistan, 1992–1996

SHAHNAWAZ TANAI—Najibullah defense minister who failed in coup attempt; later backed the Taliban

AMIR SULTAN TARAR (AKA COLONEL IMAM)—Pakistan Special Forces officer, trained thousands of guerrillas during anti-Soviet jihad, returned to Afghanistan 1994 as Pakistan envoy to the Taliban

PETER TOMSEN—special envoy to Afghan resistance, 1989–1992

FRANCESC VENDRELL—personal representative of UN secretary general in Afghanistan, 2000–2001

ZAHIR SHAH—Afghan king from 1933 to 1973 who was exiled in Rome and returned to Kabul in 2002, renouncing his throne

DR. AYMAN AL ZAWAHIRI—Egyptian doctor and head of Islamic Jihad who was closely allied with bin Laden from 1998

ZIA UL-HAQ—military ruler of Pakistan, 1977–1988

ZULFIKAR ALI BHUTTO—president of Pakistan, 1971–1973, and prime
  minister, 1973–1977; overthrown and executed by the military

Notes

Introduction

1. Joint Inquiry of the Senate and House Select Committees on Intelligence, December 2002, 123.

2. Peter Bergen provides an excellent analysis of bin Laden in *Holy War, Inc.* (New York: Simon and Schuster, 2001). Steve Coll gives a blow-by-blow account of the CIA's secret wars in Afghanistan in *Ghost Wars* (New York: Penguin Press, 2004). Ahmed Rashid provides a gripping account of the Taliban rule in Afghanistan in *Taliban* (New Haven: Yale University Press, 2001). Jonathan Randal takes a close look at bin Laden in *Osama* (New York: Knopf, 2004). Lawrence Wright provides a thoroughly researched history of al Qaeda in *The Looming Tower* (New York: Knopf, 2006).

1. Comrades

1. The 40th Army's final depredations are detailed in Henry Bradsher, *Afghan Communism and Soviet Intervention* (New York: Oxford Pakistan Paperbacks, 2001), 308–309. On January 27, 1989, State Department spokesman Charles Redman quoted eyewitness reports that Soviet and Afghan forces had killed hundreds of civilians and obliterated all the houses in villages near the Salang Tunnel. *St. Petersburg Times,* January 27, 1989.

2. George Crile, *Charlie Wilson's War* (New York: Atlantic Monthly Press, 2003), 504–05; and Milt Bearden and James Risen, *The Main Enemy* (New York: Random House, 2003), 354–55.

3. Testimony by Jamal Ahmed al Fadl, witness for prosecution, USA vs. Usama bin Laden, Southern District Court, New York, February 6, 2001; on the camp and some of those present, Jason Burke, *Al Qaeda: Casting a Shadow of Terror* (London: I. B. Taurus, 2003); and on the first formal meeting of al Qaeda, Lawrence Wright, *The Looming Tower,* 131–34. Gilles Keppel maintains that bin Laden's database of all the jihadis who had passed through his training camps gave birth to an organization built around a computer file; thus the organization's name—*al Qaeda,* or "the base." Keppel, *Jihad: The Trail of Political Islam* (Cambridge, Mass.: Belknap Press, 2002), 321.

4. Gary Schroen, interview by author, Herndon, Virginia, December 10, 2003; and John Burns, "Afghans: Now They Blame America," *New York Times Magazine,* February 4, 1990, 22.

5. *Special National Intelligence Estimate: USSR, Withdrawal from Afghanistan,* National Security Archive (CIA, March 1988), 1–2; and *Lessons from the War on Afghanistan,* National Security Archive (CIA, 1989), 5.

6. Bergen, *Holy War, Inc.,* 50–51.

7. Ibid., 53–56.

8. Ibid., 56, 58.

9. Ibid., 59; Burke, *Shadow of Terror,* 73–74; and Steve Coll, *Ghost Wars,* 157–58.

10. Osama bin Laden, interview by Hamid Mir, *Pakistan,* March 18, 1997, in Urdu, translated by Foreign Broadcast Information Service (FBIS).

11. Coll, *Ghost Wars,* 163.

12. Toryali Hemat, interview by author, Peshawar, April 20, 2003.

13. Bergen, *Holy War, Inc.,* 61.

14. On Mohamed Sadeek Odeh's training at camps, testimony of FBI special agent John Anticev, USA vs. Usama bin Laden, February 27, 2001.

2. A Half Solution

1. Presidential press conference, January 27, 1989; confirmation hearing for James A. Baker as secretary of state, Federal News Service, January 17, 1989; and explanation for embassy closure by Ed McWilliams, a former embassy official, telephone interview by author, December 2005.

2. Crile, *Charlie Wilson's War,* 104; and Coll, *Ghost Wars,* 62–64.

3. Ahmed Rashid, *Taliban* (New Haven: Yale University Press, 2000), 89, quoted in Coll, *Ghost Wars,* 180

4. Crile, *Charlie Wilson's War,* 238.

5. Stephen Tanner, *Afghanistan: A Military History from Alexander the Great to the Fall of the Taliban* (New York: Da Capo Press, 2002), 253–54; and on Pakistan's selection of the Mujahidin parties, Henry Bradsher, communication with author, July 2007.

6. Diego Cordovez and Selig Harrison, *Out of Afghanistan: The Inside Story of the Soviet Withdrawal* (New York: Oxford University Press, 2002), 85.

7. Cordovez and Harrison, *Out of Afghanistan,* 111, 123–24.

8. Ibid., 175.

9. Ibid., 187–88.

10. National Security Decision Directive (NSDD) in David Ottaway, "What Is 'Afghan Lesson' for Superpowers?" *Washington Post,* February 12, 1989; and Coll, *Ghost Wars,* 125–28; details of aid to the rebels in Alan J. Kuperman, "The Stinger Missile and U.S. Intervention in Afghanistan," *Political Science Quarterly* 114, no. 2 (1999): 227–30; Coll, *Ghost Wars,* 127, and Abramowitz trip described in Cordovez and Harrison, *Out of Afghanistan,* 196.

11. Cordovez and Harrison, *Out of Afghanistan,* 197–98.

12. William Maley, *The Afghanistan Wars* (New York: Palgrave Macmillan, 2002), 142.

13. Cordovez and Harrison, *Out of Afghanistan,* 82; also Diego Cordovez, telephone interview by author, January 2004.

14. Michael Armacost, telephone interview by author, April 2004; and Cordovez, telephone interview.

15. Masoud Khalili, interview by author, New Delhi, June 2004.

16. Cordovez and Harrison, *Out of Afghanistan,* 254; and Cordovez, interview.

17. Description of ceremony drawn from accounts published on April 15, 1988, by Hella Pick *(Guardian)*, Paul Vallely *(Times),* Richard Weintraub and David Ottawa *(Washington Post),* Alan McGregor *(Christian Science Monitor),* and Norman Kempster *(Los Angeles Times).*

18. David Isby, unpublished paper, cited in James Phillips, *Consolidating Victory in Afghanistan* (Washington, D.C.: Heritage Foundation, February 2, 1990).

19. Kissinger remarks quoted in Cordovez and Harrison, *Out of Afghanistan,* 285; Brzezinski remark from *Washington Post,* February 19, 1988, and quoted in Cordovez and Harrison, *Out of Afghanistan,* 338; and *Washington Post* editorial from April 10, 1988, cited in Cordovez and Harrison, *Out of Afghanistan,* 362.

20. Zia ul-Haq, interview by Selig Harrison, *Le Monde,* quoted in Coll, *Ghost Wars,* 175.

21. Robert Oakley, telephone interview by author, March 30, 2004.

22. Coll, *Ghost Wars,* 196; and Oakley, interview.

23. On the State Department announcement of McWilliams's appointment, Associated Press (AP), Washington, D.C., September 26, 1988; and on the McWilliams-Oakley clash, Steve Coll, "U.S. Envoy Reassigned in Policy Clash," *Washington Post,* August 10, 1989. Coll's account indicates that McWilliams was appointed in July 1988, but McWilliams said he took up his new post in September, after Oakley, who arrived in August. See also Coll, *Ghost Wars,* 170–72.

24. Maley, *Afghanistan Wars,* 149–51; Barnett Rubin, "The Fragmentation of Afghanistan," *Foreign Affairs* 68, no. 5: 249–51; Burns, "Afghans: Now They Blame America," 22; U.S. intelligence assessment from Coll, "U.S. Envoy"; and Edmund McWilliams, e-mail to author, December 16, 2005.

25. Dennis Kux, *The United States and Pakistan 1947–2000* (Washington, D.C.: Woodrow Wilson Center Press, 2001) 298; Coll, *Ghost Wars,* 192; and Oakley, interview.

26. Rubin, "Fragmentation," 150.

27. Rubin, "Fragmentation," 150; Eqbal Ahmad, "Stalemate at Jalalabad," *Nation,* October 9, 1989, 384; Maley, *Afghanistan Wars,* 175; on Massoud and Haq, Phillips, "Consolidating Victory," 8; Haq comment in McWilliams, e-mail to author; and Bradsher quoted in Maley, *Afghanistan Wars,* 176.

28. Maley, *Afghanistan Wars,* 171, 174, 175; McWilliams, e-mail to author, December 15, 2005.

29. Richard Smyth, interview by author, Reston, Virginia, December 14, 2003.

30. Richard Mackenzie, "30 Key Afghan Rebels Killed," *Washington Times,* July 17, 1989; and Maley, *Afghanistan Wars,* 176.

31. McWilliams, e-mail to author, December 16, 2005.

32. Robin Raphel, interview by author, Washington, D.C., April 9, 2004.

33. Coll, *Ghost Wars,* 205–10; and Peter Tomsen, interviews by author, McLean, Virginia, March 11 and April 23, 2004.

34. Rubin, "Fragmentation," 252–53.

35. Steve Coll, "Afghan Plot Leader Flies to Pakistan," *Washington Post,* March 7, 1990; and Gen. Mohamed Payenda, interview by author, Afghanistan embassy, Washington, D.C., January 16, 2003.

36. Sandy Gall, "An Interview with Commander Ahmed Shah Massoud, Former Minister of Defense, at His Base in Jebal Seraj, North of Kabul, on June 28, 1993," *Asian Affairs* 25 (June 1994): 139–55; Tomsen, interview; Coll, *Ghost Wars,* 210–11; and Rubin, "Fragmentation," 151, 253t.

37. Rashid, *Independent,* October 2, 1990; Rubin, "Fragmentation," 253, 339n15; and Coll, *Ghost Wars,* 218–19.

38. Rubin, "Fragmentation," 254; Coll, *Ghost Wars,* 218; and Tomsen, interview, April 23, 2004.

39. Rubin, "Fragmentation," 254–55; on CIA payments, Coll, *Ghost Wars,* 190, 198, 211, 219, 220; Tomsen, interview; and Rubin, "Fragmentation," 255.

40. Burns, "Afghans: Now They Blame America," 22; and Tomsen, interview.

41. Tomsen, interview.

42. James A. Baker, *The Politics of Diplomacy* (New York: Putnam, 1995), 528.

43. Maley, *Afghanistan Wars,* 179, 187.

44. On Massoud's gains, see Warren Strobel, "Rebels Make Major Gains in Northern Afghanistan," *Washington Times,* August 5, 1991; on the unraveling of the Najibullah government, Rubin, "Fragmentation," 268; Maley, *Afghanistan Wars,* 188; and Gall, "An Interview with Massoud."

45. Tom Post, with Steve Levine, "A Showdown in the Capital," *Newsweek,* May 4, 1992, 41; and Coll, *Ghost Wars,* 236–37.

46. On bin Laden at Jalalabad, Burke, *Shadow of Terror,* 77, and Peter Bergen, *The Osama bin Laden I Know* (New York: Free Press, 2006), 85–92; on bin Laden in Saudi Arabia, Bergen, *Osama,* 81; on Bin Laden searching for a cause and volunteering to lead the resistance to Saddam Hussein, Coll, *Ghost Wars,* 222; and on bin Laden interview in Eastern Afghanistan, Peter Arnett, CNN, March 1997.

47. "Interview with Prince Turki al-Faisal," Part 4, *Arab News* (Jeddah), November 1, 2001.

48. On explanation for his departure from Afghanistan, see Osama bin Laden, interviews by Hamid Mir, Islamabad, May 2, 2003, and April 23, 2004; Rabbani version from Burhanuddin Rabbani, interview by author, Kabul, April 29, 2003; "Interview with Prince Turki," *Arab News;* and Saudi-CIA version from Coll, *Ghost Wars,* 231, 601–02 (fn 13). Bergen has bin Laden arriving in Pakistan in April 1991. See Bergen, *Holy War, Inc.,* 82.

49. Hemat, interview by author, Peshawar, Pakistan, April 2003; and Coll, *Ghost Wars,* 236.

50. Tomsen, interviews.

3. With Massoud

1. Lakhdar Brahimi, interview by author, Kabul, April 2003.

2. Mohammad Eshaq, *Some Letters from Ahmad Shah Masoud,* trans. Eshaq and Julie Sirrs (Kabul: Maywand Press, 2003), Letter 24 (September 1, 1984).

3. Eshaq, Letter 11a (February 21, 1984).

4. Eshaq, Letter 23 (August 1, 1984).

5. Anthony Davis, e-mail messages to author, April 25 and May 29, 2004.

6. Anthony Davis, *Jane's Intelligence Review*, April 1, 1996; and Michael Griffin, *Reaping the Whirlwind* (Sterling, Virginia: Pluto Press, 2003), xvii.

7. Davis, *Jane's Intelligence Review*, April 1, 1996; and Griffin, *Reaping the Whirlwind*, 16–19.

8. Eshaq, *Letters from Ahmad Shah Masoud*.

9. Eshaq, Letter 5 (September 14, 1982).

10. Eshaq, Letter 10 (December 23, 1982).

11. Anthony Davis, e-mail message, May 29, 2004; and Davis, *Jane's Intelligence Review*, April 1, 1996.

12. Anthony Davis, e-mail message, May 29, 2004.

13. Eshaq, Letter 9 (October 10, 1982).

14. Eshaq, Letters 10 and 11 (both dated December 23, 1982).

15. Edward Girardet, "With the Resistance in Afghanistan," *Christian Science Monitor*, October 2, 1984.

16. Eshaq, Letter 15 (June 5, 1982).

17. Eshaq, Letter 17 (September 6, 1983).

18. Eshaq, Letter 20 (June 24, 1984).

19. Eshaq, Letter 16 (September 1, 1983).

20. Masoud Khalili, interview by author, New Delhi, June 2004.

21. Eshaq, Letters 20 and 21 (June 24 and 25, 1984).

22. Eshaq, Letter 24 (September 1, 1984).

23. Eshaq, Letter 29 (October 6, 1984).

24. Eshaq, Letter 30 (November 20, 1984).

25. Eshaq, Letter 30.

26. Eshaq, Letter 32 (March 20, 1985).

27. Amir Sultan Tarar (Colonel Imam), interview by author, Rawalpindi, June 2004.

28. Eshaq, Letter 35 (April 22, 1986).

29. Eshaq, Letter 37 (September 15, 1986).

30. Eshaq, Letter 39 (June 1, 1988).

31. Gall, "Interview with Massoud."

32. Oakley, interview; and Raphel, interview.

33. Zahid Hussein, a journalist, interview by author, Islamabad, June 5, 2004.

34. "U.S. Ties Reopening Embassy in Kabul to Improved Security," AFP, June 14, 1992.

35. Smyth, interview.

36. Ibid.

37. Gall, "Interview with Massoud"; Raphel, interview; and "Bastards" quotation from John Jennings, former AP correspondent in Kabul, telephone interview by author, December 23, 2003.

38. Reuters, July 6 1992.

39. Nancy Hatch Dupree, interview by author, Peshawar, April 2003.

40. Gall, "Interview with Massoud"; Rubin, "Fragmentation," 272; and estimate of gold reserves and account of Pakistan weapons deliveries from Jennings, interview.

41. Gall, "Interview with Massoud"; Rubin, "Fragmentation," 273; Maley, *Afghanistan Wars,* 199; and Smyth interviews.

42. Gall, "Interview with Massoud"; Kathy Gannon, interview by author, Islamabad, April 1, 2003; Jennings, December 23, 2003; *Blood-Stained Hands* (New York: Human Rights Watch, 2005), 107–8, 122; Khalili, interview; and Maley, *Afghanistan Wars,* 205.

43. Gall, "Interview with Massoud"; "Country Fact Sheet: Afghanistan," U.S. Department of State, June 6, 1994; Crile, *Charlie Wilson's War,* 362–73; and Tomsen, interview.

44. Smyth, interview, December 14, 2003.

45. Confirmation hearing for Warren Christopher as secretary of state, Federal News Service, January 13, 1993; Brian Atwood, telephone interview by author, February 10, 2004; Raphel, interview; Smyth, interviews; Margaret Carpenter, telephone interview by author, February 16, 2004; and Thomas Gouttierre, interview by author, April 7, 2004.

46. Gall, "Interview with Massoud."

47. *New York Times,* August 11, 1994; and interview with senior U.S. government analyst who spoke on condition of anonymity, February 10, 2004.

48. Gall, "Interview with Massoud."

49. On the ISI, Edward Girardet and Jonathan Walter, *Afghanistan* (Geneva: Media Action International, 2004), 252–53; Neamatollah Nojumi, *The Rise of the Taliban in Afghanistan* (New York: Palgrave, 2002); on Dostum's background, Richard Ehrlich, "Afghanistan's Man at the Top," *Toronto Star,* June 4, 1992; and assessment of Dostum, e-mail message, Whitney Azoy, April 29, 2004.

50. Anthony Davis, *Jane's Defense Weekly,* July 1, 1994. Davis's exhaustive account of this offensive and his careful, detailed reporting on the rest of the civil war is a unique resource for reconstructing Afghanistan's history in the 1990s.

4. "A Very Exciting Development"

1. This account is based largely on an Afghan informant who approached the U.S. embassy in Islamabad. It also includes elements of stories related by two Taliban diplomats and by Colonel Imam. The informant's account is contained in "Finally, a Talkative Talib," cable, U.S. embassy Islamabad, February 2, 1995, released by the NSA. Colonel Imam's account and the material from the Taliban diplomats is contained in Kamal Matinuddin, *The Taliban Phenomenon* (New York: Oxford University Press, 2001), 26. There are at least three versions of the rape story. John Burns and Steve Levine reported in the *New York Times* (December 31, 1996) that a local mujahideen commander kidnapped two girls from the village of Singesar and raped them repeatedly. Omar, who was the mullah at the local madrassa, gathered a group of thirty students and sixteen AK-47s, and descended on the checkpoint, killed the commander, and freed the girls. A second version, told by Ashraf Qazi, then director of the ISI, in an April 2003 interview with the author in Rawalpindi, is that two boys from Omar's own madrassa were abducted by a local commander and sodomized. The students raided the commander's house, the guards changed sides, and the movement was born. A third version, recounted by Colonel Imam and quoted by Matinuddin, is that a family traveling to Kandahar from Herat was stopped sixty miles from Kandahar by local bandits; the boys were taken away and molested; the girls were raped. All were killed and their bodies burned. Omar was the first to arrive on the scene; he gathered some Talibs, collected the bodies, washed them, and gave them a decent burial.

2. "Who Knows What the Movement Means?" cable, U.S. consulate, Peshawar, Pakistan, November 28, 1994, released by the NSA; Anthony Davis, "How the Taliban Became a Fighting Force," in *Fundamentalism Reborn,* ed. William Maley (New York: University Press, 1998), 44; Nojumi, *Rise of the Taliban,* 117; and "New Fighting and New Forces in Kandahar," cable, U.S. consulate, Peshawar, Pakistan, November 3, 1994, released by NSA.

3. Ahmed Muslem Hayat, military attaché, embassy of Afghanistan, interview by author, London, November 1993. Details of the transaction from Nina Hjelmgren, a Swedish journalist who was in Afghanistan at the time (interview by author, Vasteras, Sweden, January 2004); Ismail Khan material from "Who Knows What the Movement Means?"; on Rabbani and Naqibullah, Colonel Imam, interview by author, Rawalpindi, June 2004.

4. BBC World Service Report, October 9, 1994; on Mullah Naqib, "The Long and Winding Road Gets Rockier," cable, U.S. consulate, Peshawar, Pakistan, March 11, 1994, released by NSA; and Colonel Imam, interview.

5. Colonel Imam, interview; Nojumi, *Rise of the Taliban,* 130–31; and Davis, "How the Taliban Became a Fighting Force," 44–47.

6. Smyth, interview; and on the Taliban commanders accompanying the trip, Davis, "How the Taliban Became a Fighting Force," 48.

7. Qazi, interview; Gen. Naseerullah Babar, interview by author, Peshawar, May 2003; Colonel Imam, interview; and on Imam's arrival, Matinuddin, *The Taliban Phenomenon,* 62.

8. "Government: We supported the Taliban," cable, U.S. consulate, Peshawar, February 2, 1995; Gen. Ahmed Muslem Hayat, interview by author, London, February 2004; and Colonel Imam, interview.

9. Advanced weapons and fuel reported in "The Taliban: What We've Heard," cable, U.S. embassy Islamabad, January 26, 1995, released by NSA; training camps in this cable and in Davis, "How the Taliban Became a Fighting Force," 55; and Pakistan aid from report by Xinhua (Chinese news agency), datelined Islamabad, December 2, 1994.

10. On Uruzgan, Anthony Davis, *Jane's Intelligence Review,* July 1, 1995; on Ghazni, Hekmatyar warning in Radio Message of Freedom, December 13, 1994, BBC Summary of World Broadcasts; on the bombings, Nasratullah Mir, former Massoud aide, interview by author, New York, May 2003; Muslem, interview; and briefing by Amrullah Saleh to Smyth in "Government: We Supported the Taliban," cable; on Charasyab, "Rabbani Emissary States," cable, U.S. embassy Dushanbe, February 21, 1995, released by NSA.

11. On aid to Taliban, Muslem, interview; and "Rabbani Emissary States…" cable; "Government: We Supported the Taliban," cable.

12. Muslem, interview; Tanner, *Afghanistan: A Military History*, 222–23; and Nancy Hatch Dupree, *An Historical Guide to Afghanistan* (Kabul: Afghan Air Authority, 1977), 68–69.

13. Muslem, interview; on U.S. contact, "Government: We supported the Taliban," cable; on subsequent military developments, Anthony Davis, *Jane's Defense Weekly,* April 22, 1995, 19; and Davis, *Jane's Intelligence Review,* July 1, 1995. Massoud associate was Abdal Hai Elahi, interview by author, Kabul, July 2003.

14. Davis, *Jane's Intelligence Review,* July 1, 1995; "Meeting with the Taliban in Kandahar," cable, U.S. embassy, Islamabad, February 15, 1995, released by NSA; and "Foreign Assistance in Afghanistan: An Informal Survey," cable, U.S. embassy, Islamabad, April 17, 1995, released by NSA.

15. On Amir's briefing, President Burhanuddin Rabbani, interview by author, April 29, 2003; Babar, interview by author, May 2003; Qazi, interview; and Colonel Imam, interview.

16. "The High Road to Central Asia," cable, U.S. embassy, Tashkent, Uzbekistan, December 5, 1994, released by NSA; "Dostum Meets Taliban…," cable, U.S. embassy, Islamabad, January 29, 1995, released by NSA; on Morghab, Davis, "Capturing Kabul," *Jane's Defense Weekly,* April 22, 1995; and on Pakistan's assistance to Dostum, "Foreign Assistance in Afghanistan," cable, U.S. embassy, Islamabad, April 17, 1995, released by NSA.

17. Davis, *Jane's Intelligence Review,* July 1, 1995, 315; on the fall of Herat, "Eyewitness to the Fall of Heart," cable, U.S. embassy, Islamabad, September 18, 1995, released by NSA; "Afghanistan: Taliban Take Shindand," cable, U.S. embassy Islamabad, September 4, 1995, released by NSA; and Mir interview, May 2003.

18. Griffin, *Reaping the Whirlwind,* 46.

19. Davis in Maley, *Fundamentalism Reborn,* 64–65.

20. AFP, April 20, 1996; Raphel, interview; Lee Coldren, former State Department official, interview by author, February 2004; "Looking for a Way Out," cable, U.S. embassy, Islamabad April 22, 1996, released by NSA; and "Chernyshev Fails to Take the Bait," cable, U.S. embassy, Moscow, May 13, 1996, released by NSA.

21. Hamid Gul, interview by author, Rawalpindi, April 2004; and Nina Hjelmgren, *No Problem* (Stockholm: Cisco Vision, 1999), 105–06.

22. Davis in Maley, *Fundamentalism Reborn,* 68; and Hjelmgren, 108–09.

23. Hjelmgren, *No Problem,* 61–64; and Muhammad Riaz, "Ex-Afghanistan Leader Remembered," AP, Peshawar, Pakistan, September 27, 1997.

24. On Tanai, Stefan Smith, AFP reporter in Kabul, e-mail message to author, February 2004; and Hjelmgren, "Strong Rumors" and Griffin, *Reaping the Whirlwind,* 4.

25. Griffin, *Reaping the Whirlwind,* 7–9.

26. State Department briefing, Federal News Service, September 27, 1994.

27. "Dealing with the Taliban in Kabul," cable, State Department, September 28, 1996, released by NSA; and Coldren, interview.

28. Theresa Loar, interview by author, March 2003; State Department briefing, Federal News Service, September 30, 1996; and Tom Simons, former U.S. ambassador to Pakistan, interview by author, January 2004.

29. Raphel, interview.

5. "An Endless Tragedy of Epic Proportions"

1. Interview with former Clinton aide, Washington, D.C., January 2004; UN assessment in quarterly *Report of the Secretary-General*, November 14, 1997, A/52/682; and Ahmed Shah Massoud, interview, *Le Figaro*, October 21, 1996.

2. Peter Arnett, "Terror Nation? U.S. Creation?" (part 4), January 16, 1994, CNN transcript, 273–74.

3. Training of Kashmiris from Anthony Davis, "Foreign Combatants in Afghanistan," *Jane's Intelligence Review*, July 1, 1993; Haqqani quote from Mike Winchester (the byline sometimes used by journalist Anthony Davis), "Terrorist U," *Soldier of Fortune*, April 1991, 64; Gary Schroen, interview by author, Herndon, Va., December 10, 2003; on redistribution of control of camps, Burke, *Shadow of Terror*, 96, 151–53; and on Haqqani role, Vahid Mojdeh, interview by author, Kabul, April 2003.

4. On number of al Qaeda members, Bergen, *Holy War, Inc.*, 86; on Sudan emissaries, Burke, *Shadow of Terror*, 130–31; on bin Laden, his fatwas, and his time in Sudan, Jamal Al Fadl, testimony, USA vs. Usama bin Laden, U.S. District Court, Southern District of New York, February 6, 2001.

5. Yemen explosives in al Fadl testimony; al Qaeda deployment into Somalia, from testimony about the questioning of Mohamed Sadeek Odeh, USA vs. Usama bin Laden, testimony of FBI special agent John Anticev, February 28, 2001; Nairobi in Bergen, *Holy War, Inc.*, 89; Chechnya and chemical weapons in al Fadl testimony; nuclear weapons in al Fadl testimony, February 7, 2001; and other activities described in Burke, *Shadow of Terror*, 133.

6. Bin Laden's business and construction activities detailed in al Fadl testimony; al Fadl cross-examination, February 20, 2001; Daniel Benjamin and Steven Simon, *The Age of Sacred Terror* (New York: Random House, 2002) 110–14; Bergen, *Holy War, Inc.*, 82–83; and Scott McLeod, "The Paladin of Jihad," *Time*, May 6, 1996, 51.

7. Benjamin and Simon, *Sacred Terror*, 223; on assassination attempt, Burke, *Shadow of Terror*, 139, 268fn31; al Zawahiri's expulsion detailed in "Knights under the Prophet's Banner: Al Zawahiri's Secret Papers," *Al Sharq al Awsat*, December 18, 2002, translated by FBIS; and bin Laden on notice, Burke, *Shadow of Terror*, 141.

8. On the stripping of citizenship and the assassination attempt, Prince Turki al Faisal, interview (part 5), *Arab News*, November 8, 2001; Nasir Abdallah al-Bahri (Abu Jandal), interview by Khaled Al-Hammadi (part 3), *Al Quds al Araby*, March 18, 2005, translated by FBIS, June 1, 2005; return home in dignity —bin Laden interview with *Al Quds al Araby*, reported in *Mideast Mirror*, November 27, 1996; $500 million from Osama bin Laden, interview by Robert Fisk, *The*

Independent, March 22, 1997; Yemen hotel, Burke, *Shadow of Terror,* 129; Benjamin and Simon, *Sacred Terror,* 234; and Saudi National Guard in Bill Gertz, *Breakdown* (New York: Regnery, 2003), 7–8. Lawrence Wright reported that although bin Laden's men had fled the scene when U.S. helicopters were shot down in Mogadishu, he attributed both the downing of the choppers and the desecration of the dead American servicemen's bodies to al Qaeda volunteers. Wright, *The Looming Tower,* 188–89.

  9. Barton Gellman, "U.S. Was Foiled Multiple Times in Efforts to Capture Bin Laden or Have Him Killed," *Washington Post,* October 3, 2001; Richard Miniter, *Losing Bin Laden,* (Washington, D.C.: Regnery, 1993), 99–102.

  10. "Insane to force him out"—the view of Lee Coldren, diplomat in charge of Afghan affairs at the State Department, telephone interview by author, June 2004; al Fadl cross-examination, U.S. District Court, February 20, 2001, 103; and Benjamin and Simon, *Sacred Terror,* 238.

  11. Sandy Berger in Gellman, "U.S. Was Foiled"; and Nancy Soderberg, telephone interview by author, December 2003.

  12. Turki interview (part 3), *Jeddah Arab News,* November 6, 2001.

  13. Turki interview (part 5), *Jeddah Arab News,* November 8, 2001; copilot Jahid Azimi, interview by author, Kabul, April 2003; President Rabbani, interview; Col. Ad Sharzai, interview by author, Seven Towns, New York, March 2003.

  14. On the attractiveness of the location, Paul Bucherer-Dietschi, interview by author, Bubendorf, Switzerland, March 2003; Alain de Bures, interview by author, Jalalabad, March 2003; on Hadda Farms, Stefan Smith, e-mail message to author, February 2004; on Hekmatyar connection with Hadda Farms, Lee Coldren, interview by author, June 2006; and Kabul safe houses, Schroen, interview.

  15. On the invitation to bin Laden, Mojdeh, interview; Vahid Mojdeh, "Afghanistan Under Five Years of Taliban Sovereignty," unpublished English translation of original in Dari language (manuscript in author's possession), 20; Burke, *Shadow of Terror,* 73,145–46; guesthouse and airport reception, Kathy Gannon, AP bureau chief, interview by author, Islamabad, April 2003; on the welcome, Din Muhammad, interview by author, Jalalabad, April 2004; Qadir's nonwelcome, Smith, e-mail message; and other welcomers, Schroen, interview.

  16. Smyth, interview.

  17. Robert Fisk interviewed bin Laden in Afghanistan and produced a series of articles in the *Independent:* "Arab Rebel Leader Warns the British: 'Get out of the Gulf'," July 10, 1996; "Why We Reject the West," July 10, 1996; and "Small Comfort in Saudi Rebel's Dangerous Exile," July 11, 1996.

  18. Bergen, *Holy War, Inc.,* 95–97; Burke, *Shadow of Terror,* 146–50; and Robert Fisk, "Saudi Calls for Jihad against US 'Crusader'," *Independent,* September 2, 1996.

  19. Din Muhammad, interview; Rahimullah Yusufzai, interview by author, Peshawar, April 2003; and Mullah Sadiq as quoted in *Time,* December 16, 1996, 22.

  20. Steve Levine in *Newsweek International,* October 13, 1997, 22; $250 million estimate in *Time,* December 16, 1996, 22; Turki interview (part 5), *Jeddah Arab News,* November 8, 2001.

21. Schroen, interviews, March and December 2003; Coldren, interview.

22. Nojumi, *Rise of the Taliban*, 155–57; Anthony Davis, *Asiaweek*, October 25, 1996, 24; Davis, *Jane's Intelligence Review*, December 1, 1996; Tom Simons, telephone interview by author, January 2004.

23. Davis, *Jane's Defense Weekly*, October 9, 1996, and *Jane's Intelligence Review*, December 1, 1996.

24. Babar, interview, May 2003; Colonel Imam, interview on behalf of author by Pakistani journalist Ahmed Muktar, Rawalpindi, May 2003; Sartaj Aziz, former foreign minister, interview by author, Islamabad, May 2003; and Norbert Heinrich Holl, *Mission Afghanistan* (Munich: Herbig, 2002), 123–44.

25. *Al Quds al Araby* interview recounted in *Mideast Mirror* 10, no. 232 (December 6, 1996); bin Laden, interview by Hamid Mir, *Pakistan*, March 1, 1997, translated from Urdu by FBIS.

26. Bergen, *Holy War, Inc.*, 98–99; Burke, *Shadow of Terror*, 158–59; and State Department response by spokesman Jamie Rubin, Federal News Service, February 25, 1997. Only the *Washington Post* wrote about bin Laden's threat, according to a Nexis search.

27. On ban against anti-Saudi propaganda, Amir Shah Muttaqi, the acting minister of culture, quoted by AFP, March 6, 1997; bin Laden's move to Kandahar in testimony by Charles Santos, former UN political adviser, then resident in Kandahar, House International Relations Committee, October 3, 2001; Burke, *Shadow of Terror*, 164; AP, quoting the London-based *Al Hayat*, April 8, 1997; on the United States in Saudi Arabia, AFP, March 26, 1997; and on the bin Laden construction work, Bergen, *Holy War, Inc.*, 47–48.

28. Abu Jandal, interview by Al-Hammadi, *Al Quds al Araby;* Prof. Nasrullah Stanikzai, Kabul law faculty, interview by author, Kabul, April 2003; Schroen, interview, December 2003.

29. "Ambassador Meets Taliban: We Are the People," cable, U.S. embassy, Islamabad, November 12, 1996, released by NSA; "Afghanistan: Mullah Ghaus Says Taliban Want Peace, but Keeps Military Options Open," cable, U.S. embassy, Islamabad, December 8, 1996, released by NSA; "Taliban Rep Won't Seek UN Seat for Now," State Department cable, December 13, 1996, released by NSA (Karzai's name is redacted from this cable, but another internal memorandum identifies him as calling on Raphel that same day); "U.S. Engagement with the Taliban on Osama bin Laden," secret State Department memorandum, distributed approximately July 1, 2001, and released September 8, 2003, by NSA; and on Karzai's motives, from a source close to him.

30. On bin Laden's access to Omar, Information Minister Muttaqi, quoted in the *Washington Post*, April 11, 1997, 34; and Schroen, interview, December 2003.

31. Rashid, *Taliban*, 185.

32. Colonel Imam, interview by author, Rawalpindi, June 2004; Colonel Imam, interview by Muktar; Mir, interview, Islamabad, May 2003; Col. Mohammad Effendi, former ISI analyst, interview by author, Rawalpindi, April 2003; and Khan, interview. Details about the attack over the Shibar Pass are from Stefan Smith, e-mail message to author.

33. Anthony Davis, *Jane's Intelligence Review*, April 1, 1997; and Choong-Hyun Paik, special rapporteur, UN Commission on Human Rights, final report on human rights in Afghanistan, February 20, 1997, E/CN.4/1997/59, paragraph 96.

34. Anthony Davis, *Jane's Intelligence Review*, February 1, 1997; Roger Howard, *Jane's Defense Weekly*, April 9, 1997; and Davis, *Jane's Defense Weekly*, May 7, 1997. Stefan Smith and Davis witnessed the airlift of Ismail Khan and his troops into Maimana in October 1996 in transport planes from Mashhad, Iran. Smith, e-mail message to author, March 2006.

35. This account of the military moves is drawn from Davis, *Jane's Defense Weekly*, August 1, 1997, 359. The ISI's facilitation of contacts between Malik and the Taliban is from Mojdeh manuscript, 20.

36. On the Taliban secret deal, Mervyn Patterson, at the time chief UN representative in northern Afghanistan, in an e-mail communication to author, March 2004; Malik's story, Gen. Abdul Malik Pahlawan, interview by author, Mazar-i-Sharif, April 2003; military movements and arrests, dispatches by Phil Goodwin, David Loyn, and Carolyn Hawley, BBC World Service, May 25–26, 1997, courtesy of BBC; Davis, *Jane's Defense Weekly*, August 1, 1997; scene at Hazrat Ali mosque, Griffin, *Reaping the Whirlwind*, 98–99; full text of the Malik-Taliban agreement from United Nations Investigation Team for Afghanistan, "Confidential Report to the High Commissioner for Human Rights," September 30, 1999, paragraph 71.

37. Malik, interview; Khan, interview; and Holl, *Mission Afghanistan*, 227–28.

38. On destruction in the shops, Payenda, interview, Washington, D.C., May 2004; on Saidabad, Mervyn Patterson, e-mail message to author, March 2004, and Griffin, *Reaping the Whirlwind*, 99.

39. Smith, e-mail messages to author, February 2004 and March 2006; Davis, *Jane's Defense Weekly*, August 1, 1997; Paik, *Human Rights Questions . . . Situation of Human Rights in Afghanistan*, A/52/493, October 16, 1997; Malik, interview; and Jean-Paul Monod, International Committee of the Red Cross (ICRC), interview by author, March 2003.

40. On Pakistan role, Mojdeh unpublished manuscript; on Gohar's announcement, Holl, *Mission Afghanistan*, 217; and Hamid Gul, interview by author, Rawalpindi, April 2003.

41. Colonel Imam, interview by Muktar; Pakistani diplomat quoted in Griffin, *Reaping the Whirlwind*, 100; UN secretary-general report, #A52/682, November 14, 1997, paragraphs 43, 53; Smith, e-mail messages to author, February 2004; Gannon, interview; and on conscription, "Pakistani Supporters of the Taliban," cable, U.S. consulate, Peshawar, August 19, 1997, released by NSA.

42. The story of Bin Laden's role in advising Omar based on author interviews in April and May 2003 with Pakistani reporter Hamid Mir, bin Laden's offical biographer, who had several interviews with bin Laden at the time.

43. Abdullah statement on the death of Ghaforzai, Smith, e-mail message to author, March 2006; Massoud's conversation with Omar, Dr. Abdullah Abdullah, Afghan foreign minister, interview by author, Kabul, April 2003, and Jamshid, secretary to Massoud, interview by author, Kabul, July 2003.

44. Inderfurth testimony, Federal News Service, October 22, 1997; Madeleine Albright remarks in Pakistan, AP, November 18, 1997; Rick Inderfurth, interview by author, Washington, D.C., November 2004; and on Inderfurth remarks, Madeleine Albright, interview by author, Washington, D.C., April 2006. The visit by Jan, Acting Planning Minister Din Muhammad, and Acting Information Minister Amir Khan Muttaqi to the United States was announced on Kabul's Voice of Sharia radio on December 4, 1997 (BBC monitoring, December 8, 1997). Coll colorfully describes the visit to Houston but identifies the delegation leader as Mullah Wakil Ahmed, Mullah Omar's chief aide. *Ghost Wars*, 364–66. According to Voice of Sharia, however, it was Jan.

6. "Silence Cannot Be the Strategy"

1. *Financial Times*, November 17, 2001; and *Los Angeles Times*, November 25, 2001.

2. Senior ICRC officials, interview by author, Geneva, March 2003; Jamshid, interview, July 2003; and Massoud comments in Alan Eastham, untitled cable from U.S. embassy, Islamabad, October 30, 1997, released by NSA.

3. Lakhdar Brahimi, interview by author, Kabul, April 2003; Alan Johnston, BBC World Service report, November 25, 1997, courtesy of BBC; initial UN investigations detailed in *The Situation in Afghanistan and Its Implications for International Peace and Security, Report of the Secretary-General*, March 17, 1998, S/1998/222, paragraphs 36–39; Paik's depiction of the camp in UN report #A/52/493, October 16, 1997; Rashid, *Taliban*, 62; and BBC report on Malik role by Alan Johnston, December 11, 1997, courtesy of BBC.

4. "U.N. Tells How Taliban Were Killed by the 100's," *New York Times*, December 17, 1997; *Situation of Human Rights in Afghanistan, Report of the Secretary-General*, March 12, 1998, E/CN.4/1998/71, section on Sheberghan; Malik letter, copy in possession of author; Mark Skinner, "Human Remains from Alleged Mass Graves in Northern Afghanistan," Office of the UN High Commissioner for Human Rights, January 6, 1998, (copy obtained by author); UN report #S/1998/222, March 17, 1998, paragraphs 36–37, 46–49; and UN General Assembly Resolution A/RES/52/211, February 27, 1998.

5. William G. O'Neill and Stuart T. Groves, "Report into the Feasibility of an Investigative Mission, Afghanistan," Office of the High Commissioner for Human Rights May 20–29, 1998 (copy obtained by author); Paik report #E/CN.4/1998/71, March 12, 1998, recommendations in paragraphs 6 and 10; Albright's Peshawar remarks, released by Office of the Spokesman, Department of State; on Albright's appearance in Peshawar, Carol Giacomo, Reuters reporter on Albright's trip to Pakistan, telephone interview by author, July 2004; Albright explanation of her strong remarks, author interview; staff comments on Robinson from author interview, Geneva headquarters, March 2003; and Robinson quoted in Paul McGeough, "Too Slow: The UN Digs Its Own Grave in Mazar," *Sydney Morning Herald*, March 2, 2002.

6. Anthony Davis, *Jane's Defense Weekly*, January 21, 1998; Schroen, interview.

7. Smith, e-mails; and UN report # A/52/493, October 16, 1997.

8. The fatwa was submitted with its original date as evidence by the FBI in its November 1998 indictment of bin Laden; the judgment that planning had begun for the bombings of two U.S. embassies is from the *9/11 Commission Report*, 69; the U.S. embassy in Islamabad protest to the Taliban ambassador to Pakistan on March 2 and the response of the Taliban envoy to the UN are from "U.S. Engagement with Taliban on Osama bin Laden," State Department memorandum, ca. July 16, 2001, released by NSA; bin Laden's London spokesman, Khaled al-Fawwaz, is quoted in Bergen, *Holy War, Inc.*, 99; and bin Laden's message was published by AP Cairo, March 19, 1998. The forty Afghan clerics met March 12, 1998, and the Pakistani clerics, based in Karachi, met at the end of April; the Medina imam was Sheikh Ali al-Hudaifi. Bergen, *Holy War, Inc.*, 102.

9. UN report #S/1998/2222, March 17, 1998, annex.

10. Albright comments on "Common Ground," radio program produced by the Stanley Foundation, April 7, 1998, www.commongroundradio.org; Eleanor Smeal, interview by author, Arlington, Virginia, January 2004, repeated in cover essay of *In These Times*, April 24, 2004 (www.inthesetimes.com); the pledge was not stated in Clinton's prepared remarks published by the White House (see http://clinton6.nara.gov); and Inderfurth quotes from Rick Inderfurth, interview by author, Washington, D.C., November 2003.

11. Quotes are from an extraordinary interview with Omar conducted by Jamal Mahmud Ismail in the London-based Arabic daily *Al Sharq al Awsat*, May 10, 1998, translated by FBIS on July 2, 1998.

12. Inderfurth quoted in *Washington Post*, April 19, 1998; and U.S. letter cited on Pakistan state television, April 19, 1998, and Radio Pakistan, April 21, 1998.

13. Calvin Mitchell, telephone interview by author, February 2004; and Brahimi, interview.

14. Anthony Davis, "Fateful Victory," *Asiaweek*, August 28, 1998, 30; Davis, "Taliban Continue the Killing," *Jane's Intelligence Review*, November 1, 1998, 17; attack on Taloqan from *The Situation in Afghanistan, Report of the Secretary-General*, S/1998/532, June 19, 1998; Attack on Kabul Airport from *Report of the Secretary-General*, S/1998/913, October 2, 1998; "Afghanistan: _____ [name redacted] Describes Pakistan's Current Thinking," cable, U.S. embassy, Islamabad, March 9, 1998; UN report #S/1998/532; "Bad News on Pakistan Afghan Policy," cable, U.S. embassy, Islamabad, July 1, 1998; and "A Report of Pakistani Military Assistance to the Taliban," cable, U.S. consulate, Peshawar, March 24, 1998, released by NSA.

15. *9/11 Commission Report* (New York: W. W. Norton, 2004), 111–15.

16. Bin Laden quote from *Al Quds al Araby*, cited in *Mideast Mirror*, April 15, 1998; bin Laden, interview by Hamid Mir, *Daily Aushaf*, May 13, 1998, translated by writer Kashi Zaman; Rahimullah Yusufzai, interview by author, Peshawar, April 2002; bin Laden's first group media event was on April 26, 1998; BBC News carried the first reports on May 27 and 28, 1998; on May 27, 1998, AFP quoted the Afghan Islamic Press on the threat to the Saudi regime; Miller's May 28, 1998, interview at www.abcnews.com; and reference to "time cap" in ABC's *Nightline*, June 10, 1998.

17. U.S. security measures in AP Washington dispatch, June 5, 1998; "_____ [name redacted] Defends Discriminatory Edicts on Women and Girls," confidential cable, U.S. embassy Islamabad, July 2, 1998, released by NSA.

18. Turki interview with MBC, carried in *Jeddah Arab News* in English, November 3, 2001; and *9/11 Commission Report*, 115. The most detailed account is in Coll, *Ghost Wars*, 397–402.

19. U.S. embassy protest in classified cable, "_____ defends"; UN report #A/52/493, October 16, 1997; UN report #E/CN.4/1998/71, March 17, 1998; UN report #A/53/539, October 26, 1998; and UN report #E/CN.4/1999/40, March 24, 1999; on videorecorders, AP, Kabul, July 12, 1998.

20. Massoud remarks in Davis, "Fateful Victory"; United Nations on Pakistanis, UN report #S/1998/532. June 19, 1998; Massoud intelligence on Pakistanis in Davis, "Fateful Victory" and "Taliban Continue the Killing," *Jane's Intelligence Review,* November 1, 1998; United Nations on Pakistanis, UN report #S/1998/913, October 2, 1998; ICRC official on Arab fighters, senior ICRC official in Afghanistan at the time, interview by author, Geneva, February 2003; pickup trucks, Davis, "Taliban Continue the Killing"; Massoud calculation of cost, Amrullah Saleh, interview by author, Kabul, April 2003; Schroen quotes from a 1997 conversation with Massoud, Schroen, interview; and bin Laden and al Qaeda income estimates from *9/11 Commission Report*, 170–71.

21. Time of explosions and casualty count from *9/11 Commission Report*, 70; Bergen, *Holy War, Inc.*, 109–16; and the driver, commonly called Azzam, was identified in the *9/11 Commission Report* as Jihad Mohammad Ali al Makki (p. 152); "Our Target Was Terror," *Newsweek,* August 31, 1998, 24.

22. Details of Owhali activities in *Washington Post*, August 28, 1998; Khalfan Khamis Mohamed story from Jerrold Post, interview by author, Bethesda, Md., October 2001; and USA vs. Usama bin Laden, Southern District Court, testimony of FBI special agent Abigail Perkins, March 19, 2001.

23. Balkh betrayal, testimony of Witness 6, a Tajik, interviewed by UNHCR in Islamabad on September 16, 1998, and Witness 9, a half-Pashtun, interviewed on September 25, 1998 (copies in author's files); antiaircraft mounted, from Kenneth Cooper, "Taliban Massacre Based on Ethnicity," *Washington Post*, November 28, 1998; on ICRC, UNHCR interview reports, refugees who fled Mazar-i-Sharif to Pakistan (author's papers); and "Intimidation of Aid Agency Staff in Mazar-i-Sharif," undated UNHCR memo (author's papers).

24. Sipah-e-Sahaba's "premeditated plan" from Mojdeh, unpublished manuscript, 40–41; and Shahsavan from Iran Network I in Persian, September 16, 1998, BBC worldwide monitoring.

25. Tajik witness, interviewed by Dutch journalist, Interview 2 provided to UNHCR and contained in memo by Rupert Colville, December 8, 1998; and Tajik witness, Mazar-i-Sharif/Taliban Case 12, interviewed by UNHCR on October 14, 1998;

26. Hazara street trader, UNHCR Witness 2, interviewed by UNHCR on September 26, 1998.

27. Tajik-Pashtun witness, UNHCR Witness 9, interviewed September 25, 1998.

28. Human Rights Watch (HRW), *The Massacre in Mazar-i-Sharif* (November 1998): 16.

29. Not a sin to kill Hazaras, "Ethnic Cleansing in Mazar-i-Sharif," Cooperation Centre for Afghanistan, September 1998; "When Wahdat was killing. . . ," interview, Witness 3, Hazara, interviewed by UNHCR on September 26, 1998; Griffin, *Reaping the Whirlwind*, 191; "We are here to govern. . . ," female Hazara witness, interviewed by Dutch journalist and provided to UNHCR, Interview 1, Colville memo, December 8, 1998; "So far we have done. . .," Hazara witness, UNHCR interview, September 26, 1998; Tajik Witness 12; and "Hazaras can live . . .," Paik, UN report #A/53/539, October 26, 1998.

30. "Niazi turned . . . ," female Hazara witness, interviewed by Dutch journalist as Witness 1 and provided to UNHCR; "Trucks were brought . . . ," UNHCR overview, undated, author's files; "One way of trapping . . . ," Tajik Witness 12; "In a short time . . . ," half-Tajik Witness 9; "Governor Niazi . . . ," HRW, *Massacre in Mazar-i-Sharif*, 10; and "If they couldn't . . . ," Eckhard Schiewek, interview by author, Kabul, July 2003.

31. "There one witness . . . ," Paik, UN report #A/53/539, October 26, 1998; "I said I . . . ," male Tajik witness, interviewed by Dutch journalist, provided to UNHCR as Witness 2; "This year we . . . ," female Hazara, Witness 1; and "Shias are like . . . ," Hamid Safwet, Cooperation Centre for Afghanistan, interview by author, Mazar-i-Sharif, April 2003.

32. "One Talib told . . . ," HRW, *Massacre in Mazar-i-Sharif*, 13–14; "He told them that shops . . . ," Tajik male witness, UNHCR, interviewed September 15, 1998; "But this was not . . . ," Tajik Witness 12; "They can go all . . . ," from article by Zaheeruddin Abdullah; "Hundreds of minorities being held in Afghanistan detention camp," AP, Jalalabad, Afghanistan, September 18, 1998; Paik, #A/53/ 539, October 26, 1998; and "As of early . . . ," Hazara Witness 11, UNHCR interview, November 6, 1998.

33. "One conservative . . . ," HRW, *Massacre in Mazar-i-Sharif;* "The total . . . ," former U.N. official Mervyn Patterson, e-mail message to author, April 7, 2004; and "The Taliban had cut...," AP Kabul, August 20, 1998, on news blackout.

34. AP Kabul/Teheran, August 8, 1998; AP Kabul, August 10; AP Teheran, August 14; AP Teheran August 19; on the fall of Taloqan, Anthony Davis, *Asiaweek*, August 28, 1998; and AP Kabul, August 11, 12, 14.

35. Coll, *Ghost Wars*, 409–15; on missing bin Laden, Mushahid Hussain, interview by author, Islamabad, May 2003; and Abu Jandal, interview by Al-Hammadi (part 9), *Al Quds al Araby*.

36. Rahimullah Yusufzai, "Somewhere in Afghanistan," *The News* (Islamabad), August 22, 1998; "Bin Laden's 'Right Hand' on U.S. Attack" *The News*, August 27, 1998; "Myth and Man" and "Exporting Jihad?" *Karachi Newsline*, September 1, 1998; "New Muslim Hero," *The News*, September 1, 1998; and on actual destruction, Yusufzai, interview, April 2002.

37. Clinton's doubts recounted in Benjamin and Simon, *Sacred Terror*, 360; memo on al Shifa and conclusion of 9/11 Commission in *9/11 Commission Report*, 117–18; "A Question of Evidence," *New York Times*, October 27, 1999; and confirmed to author by former State Department officials.

38. Shootings in Kabul, Smith, e-mail to author, March 2006; Schroen, interview; Omar quoted on BBC, August 20, 1998; Hatch and Gingrich on

CNN "Breaking News," August 20, 1999; and Helms in *Chicago Tribune,* August 21, 1998.

39. "To reduce the . . . ," from chronology provided to author by former White House national security adviser Sandy Berger, February 2004.

40. Massacre in Mazar-i-Sharif in "Afghanistan: Possible Massacres in the North, Report of Refugees Being Detained," cable, U.S. consulate, Peshawar, August 20, 1998, released by NSA; Omar phone call in "Taliban's Mullah Omar's 8/22 Contact with State Department," cable from secretary of state, August 23, 1998, released by NSA; Inderfurth talking points in "Message to the Taliban on Bin Laden," cable from secretary of state, August 23, 1998, released by NSA; Taliban refusal to receive U.S. message, "U.S. Offers . . . ," by Aimal Khan, *Frontier Post* (Peshawar), August 26, 1998; "Taliban Formally Receive U.S. Offer . . . ," Khan, *Frontier Post,* September 4, 1998; Omar on U.S. desire for talks and account of the fatwa in "Security Situation," cable, U.S. embassy, Islamabad, August 25, 1998, released by NSA; and Yusufzai, "Myth and Man."

41. State Department briefing by James Rubin, September 15, 1998; senior aide to Albright, who spoke on condition of anonymity in telephone interview, May 2003; and Albright comment from Albright, interview.

42. Mashhad meeting, Davis, *Jane's Intelligence Review,* November 1, 1998; Omar order, AFP Kabul, September 14, 1998; Bamiyan, UN report, *Situation of Human Rights in Afghanistan,* A/54/422, September 30, 1999; only old men still alive, *Middle East International,* November 13, 1998, quoted in Griffin, *Reaping the Whirlwind,* 192; Babar, interview; Massoud rocketing, Davis, *Jane's Intelligence Review,* November 1, 1998; and death toll, HRW, *Crisis of Impunity,* July 2001.

43. Reconstruction of the Omar-Turki exchange is based mostly on Pakistani sources and Turki; "I have never . . . Osama" from Aziz Ahmed Khan, then ambassador to Kabul, who was in Kandahar at the time, interview by author, Islamabad, April 2003; "He's our guest . . . those troops" from former foreign minister Sartaj Aziz, who was at the meeting, interview by author, Islamabad, May 2003; "Turki . . . checkbook" from Hamid Mir, interview by author, Islamabad, April 2003; "He called an attendant . . . to you" from senior Pakistan diplomat, interview by author, Islamabad, April 2003; "American pimp," Hamid Mir quoting Omar, interview; "I wished," Turki account from interview on MBC and with *Jeddah Arab News,* November 3, 2001; "High price," from AP interview, November 23, 2001, quoted in Coll, *Ghost Wars,* 629fn34; and "Fanatics," from former top White House aide, who spoke on condition of anonymity, interview by author, Washington, D.C., January 2004.

44. Clinton speech before United Nations, September 21, 1998, Federal Document Clearing House (FDCH) transcripts; on Jalil, Yusufzai, "Taliban Let bin Laden Break His Silence," *The News,* January 6, 1999; Milam, telephone interview by author, September 2005; "Usama bin Laden: Coordinating Our Efforts and Sharpening Our Message on Bin Laden," cable U.S. embassy, Islamabad, October 19, 1998, released by NSA; and on Pickering, AFP, October 21, 1998.

45. "The people . . . ," untitled cable, U.S. embassy, Islamabad, November 28, 1998, released by NSA; and Abdol Hayy Mutma'in, spokesman for Omar, in interview with London Arab newspaper *Al Majallah,* November 1, 1998.

46. Paik, UN report #A/53/539, October 26, 1998; and BBC report by Rob Watson, November 5, 1998 (transcript courtesy BBC).

47. Sarah Horner, telephone interview by author, September 2005; Colville, author interview by telephone, February 2003, and interview by author, Geneva, March 2003; "As with all . . . ," report by William Reeve, BBC, October 31, 1998 (transcript courtesy of BBC); "There were certainly . . . ," Reeve, BBC, November 8, 1998; " . . . peaceful, calm, but . . . ," Reeve, BBC, December 11, 1998; " . . . used 'brutal' tactics . . . ," Reeve, BBC, December13, 1998; and Gannon, interview, Islamabad, April 2003.

48. Abdol Hayy Mutma'in, interview in *Al Majallah*; Omar on the "false-hood" of the charges, *Al-Wasat* (London), December 17, 1998; written assurances, untitled cable, U.S. embassy, Islamabad, December 30, 1998, released by NSA; and on bin Laden's relationship with his "minder," Yusufzai, "Taliban Let Bin Laden Break His Silence," *The News,* January 6, 1999.

49. Bin Laden remarks to Afghan Islamic Press, reported by AFP, December 24, 1998; Yusufzai interview in *Time,* January 3, 1999; " . . . warmongers . . . ," in *Al Sharq al Awsat*, quoted in AFP Beirut, December 25, 1998; "It would be a sin . . . ," in *Time,* January 3, 1999; Eastham, "Bin Laden Hoodwinked Them," cable, U.S. embassy, Islamabad, December 30, 1998, released by NSA.

7. Hijacking a Regime

1. Inderfurth testimony, House International Affairs Committee, March 3, 1999.

2. Omar quoted in *Al Hayat* (London), February 16, 1999, translated by FBIS; Omar on defending bin Laden, in *Le Monde,* May 3, 1999, translated by FBIS; and Yusufzai, e-mail message to author, October 2005.

3. Milam, interview; Inderfurth, interviews by author, Washington, November 2003 and March 2004; and former senior White House aide, who spoke with author on condition of anonymity, December 2003.

4. Inderfurth, interview, November 2004; U.S. demands from State Department briefing, February 3, 1999, the day of the meeting; Taliban response, AFP Islamabad, February 9, 1998; State Department intelligence analysis from Inderfurth; CIA analysis from author interview with U.S. government official, who spoke on condition of anonymity, Langley, Va., February 2004; Berger view from author interview with former top official, who spoke on condition of anonymity, Washington, D.C., January 2004; author telephone interview with another senior official, who spoke on condition of anonymity, December 2003; Oakley, telephone interview, October 2005; Sheehan, interview by author, January 2004; Albright, interview.

5. Tenet remarks on December 4, 1998, reported in "Tenet Leaves Legacy," *Washington Post,* June 4, 2004.

6. Albright, interview; and Inderfurth, interview.

7. P. J. Crowley, telephone interview by author, October 2005.

8. See Roy Gutman, "Nuclear Policy Straitjacket," *Newsday*, June 11, 1998, 21.

9. Karamat, interview by author, Lahore, April 2003; author interview with former member of the Joint Chiefs of Staff, who spoke on condition of anonymity, Washington, D.C., March 2003; and on CIA failure to brief on its conclusion about a "terrorist-sponsored state," Sen. Robert Graham (D-FL), telephone interview by author, April 2004.

10. On Albright, Phyllis Oakley, telephone interview by author, October 2005; on distrust for Pakistanis, author interviews with Alan Eastham, Washington, D.C., December 2003; Strobe Talbott, Washington, D.C., July 2003; Inderfurth, March 2003; Furth, December 2002; and Albright senior aide, who spoke on condition of anonymity, December 2002; and Madeleine K. Albright, *Madame Secretary* (New York: Hyperion, 2003), 369–70.

11. Roger Cressey, interview by author, Arlington, Va., December 2003; and Gen. Anthony Zinni, telephone interview by author, January 2004.

12. Thomas Pickering, telephone interview by author, December 2003.

13. *9/11 Commission Report*, 118, 137–40.

14. Massoud on his own strength in *Rossiskaya Gazeta*, September 18, 1999, translated by FBIS; Davis reported on the Iranian trainers in *Jane's Defense Weekly*, July 21, 1999; confirmed by HRW, *Crisis of Impunity*, July 2001, 39; and details of the rail shipment in HRW, *Crisis of Impunity*, 37 and appendix I.

15. Walid Massoud, interview by author, London, January 2004; and former top White House aide, who spoke on condition of anonymity, January 2004.

16. Haron Amin, interview by author, Washington, D.C., April 2003; and former top White House aide, who spoke with author on condition of anonymity, January 2004.

17. Interviews with U.S. government officials, who spoke on condition of anonymity, January 2004; interview with senior U.S. official, who spoke on condition of anonymity, Kabul, April 2003; Walid Massoud, interview; Senate Foreign Relations Subcommittee on Asia, October 8, 1998; Massoud on "the terrorists" from diary of Massoud's spokesman, Massood Khalili, in e-mail message to author, January 2004; Massoud quotes to the CIA, *9/11 Commission Report*, 139, 142; statements to Schroen, Schroen, interview, December 2003; and Walid Massoud, interview.

18. Interviews: Milam, August 2005; Eastham, Washington, D.C., December 2003; Abdullah, Kabul, April 2003; Sheehan, January 2004; and former senior White House official, who spoke on conditon of anonymity, January 2004.

19. On Wilson, see Richard Whittle, "Former Congressman Under Investigation," *Dallas Morning News*, October 20, 1997; Khalilzad testimony at Senate Foreign Relations Committee hearing, October 8, 1998; and white paper published by the Afghanistan Foundation, July 12,1999, www.rebuildingafghanistan.org/.

20. Inderfurth testimony, House International Relations Committee (HIRC), Subcommittee on Asia and the Pacific, October 20, 1999; Crowley, interview, October 2005, and Milam, interview, December 2005.

21. Smeal, interview by author, January 2004; Mavis Leno, telephone interview by author, February 2004; for a critical account of the campaign, see Sharon

Waxman, "A Cause Unveiled," *Washington Post*, March 30, 1999; and memorandum summing up March 19, 1999, meeting drafted by Theresa Loar, State Department adviser on women's issues, March 25, 1999 (in author's possession).

22. On deal-breaker, National Public Radio (NPR) *Morning Edition*, March 15, 1999; on sequence of talks, UN secretary-general reports #A/53/889, March 31, 1999, and #A/53/1002, June 21, 1999; and AFP Kabul, April 10, 1999.

23. Analysis of early fighting, unpublished report by UN official Michael Semple, November 1999 (in author's papers); Kamal Hossain account in UN reports #A/53/1002, June 21, 1999, and #A/54/536, November 16, 1999; situation of human rights in Afghanistan, UN reports #A/54/422, September 30, 1999, and #E/CN.4/2000/33, January 10, 2000; and Web site of Islamic Emirate of Afghanistan, reconstructed at www.geocities.com.

24. Inderfurth, interview; Muttaqi quote on Americans from AP Tashkent, July 20, 1999; Muttaqi on the talks from Uzbek Television, July 19, 1999 (BBC monitoring, July 22, 1999); Inderfurth statement to Muttaqi from "U.S. Engagement with the Taliban on Osama bin Laden," secret State Department memo, July 1, 2001, released by NSA; Taliban quote on war beginning in *Straits Times*, July 23, 1999; and Abdullah, interview by author, July 2003; Inderfurth, interview; and Walid Massoud, interview.

25. Massoud on the Shamali offensive, in *Rossiskaya Gazeta*, August 8, 1999, translated by FBIS; on Taliban tactics, Ali Jalali, *Parameters* (Spring 2001), a publication of Army War College, Carlisle Barracks, Pa.; on summoning students to return, Rahimullah Yusufzai in *The News International* (Islamabad), August 9 and 10, 1999; level of destruction in Semple, unpublished report, 1999; eyewitness account from Bazarak, Barry Bearak, "Onslaught by the Taliban Leaves Afghans Dead or Homeless," *New York Times*, October 18, 1999; UN criticism in report #E/CN.4/2000/33, January, 10, 2000, paragraphs 39–40; and number displaced from UN report #A/54/536, November 16, 1999.

26. UN reporting on the mistreatment of women in #E/CN.4/2000/33, January 10, 2000; Ali Jalili, interview by author, Kabul, July 2003; and discussion of phony war in Semple, unpublished report.

27. Pickering, interview.

28. Kargil account from Bruce Riedel, *American Diplomacy and the 1999 Kargil Summit at Blair House* (Philadelphia: Center for the Advanced Study of India, University of Pennsylvania, 2002); Burke, *Shadow of Terror*, 170; Dennis Kux, *The United States and Pakistan 1947–2000* (Washington, D.C.: Woodrow Wilson Center Press, 2001), 352–54; Bill Clinton, *My Life* (New York: Vintage Books, 2004), 864–66; Riedel, telephone interview by author, January 2004; and A. G. Noorani, "The Truth about Kargil," *Frontline* (India), December 3, 2003.

29. Author interviews with Gohar Ayub Khan, Sartaj Aziz, and Mushahid Hussain, Islamabad, May 2003.

30. Musharraf speech discussed in commentary by Gen. (ret.) A. R. Siddiqi, *Nation* (Islamabad; Internet edition), August 25, 1999, carried by FBIS; Ziauddin commandos, Schroen, interview; Clinton view in *My Life*, 866; Berger view from author interview with former senior official who spoke on condition of anonymity, January 2004; Pickering view from Pickering, interview; CIA view in *9/11*

Commission Report, 142; Inderfurth on Musharraf in Inderfurth, interview; Ziauddin trip reported by Shakil Shaikh in News (Internet edition), October 6, 1999, and *Nation,* October 7, 1999, both carried by FBIS; discussion on the flight from Owen Bennett Jones, *Pakistan, Eye of the Storm* (New Haven: Yale University Press, 2002), 42; Dubai account of Sharif trip in Reuters Dubai, *Al Quds al Araby,* October 14, 1999; description of Ahmed from Coll, *Ghost Wars,* 504–05; and Mir Aziz Khan from Anthony Davis, *Jane's Defense Weekly,* December 1, 1999.

31. Schroen, interview, December 2003; Berger view from author interview with aide who asked not to be identified, July 2003; and Inderfurth view of Musharraf in *9/11 Commission Report,* 183.

32. Nic Robertson, telephone interview by author, October, 2005; Mojdeh on gas pipeline, unpublished manuscript, 52, 31; and Mir, interview.

33. On the Arab contingent deployment, Mojdeh, unpublished manuscript, 54; Burke, *Casting a Shadow,* 171; Arabs in Ghorband Valley, Burke, *Shadow of Terror,* 171; Abdullah, interview; and Gul Haidar, interview by author, Kabul, July 2003.

34. On Namangani and Yoldashov, Mojdeh, unpublished manuscript, 24, 48; Burke, *Casting a Shadow,* 171–72; Rashid, *Jihad,* 147-48, 167, 172–73, 209; Muttaqi quoted in Ahmed Rashid, "The Taliban: Exporting Extremism," *Foreign Affairs* 78, no. 6 (November/December 1999): 31.

35. *9/11 Commission Report,* 174–80.

36. Bergen, *Holy War, Inc.,* 215.

37. Riedel, interview; on Azhar speech, AP Karachi, January 5, 2000; on recognition, AFP and AP Kabul, January 16, 2000; on troops going to Chechnya, AP Islamabad, January 31, 2000; on Yandarbiyev's speeches, AP Peshawar, February 5, 2000; on Yandarbiyev's departure from Pakistan, Anwar Iqbal, UPI Islamabad, February 25, 2000.

8. Coasting toward Catastrophe

1. *ABC News,* November 9, 2000.

2. Milam quoted in *9/11 Commission Report,* 176; on Ressam, see *Seattle Times* series "The Terrorist Within: The Story Behind One Man's Holy War against America," June 23–July 7, 2002; Jordan arrests in *New York Times,* February 2, 2000; Zinni trip in *9/11 Commission Report,* 176; and U.S. embassy, Islamabad, cable, February 1, 2000, released by NSA.

3. Inderfurth, interview; *9/11 Commission Report,* 183.

4. U.S. embassy, Islamabad, cable, February 1, 2000, released by NSA; and Sheehan quoted in State Department briefing, May 1, 2000, FDCH transcripts.

5. *9/11 Commission Report,* 183, 503fn64.

6. On transiting Iran, *9/11 Commission Report,* 240; Vendrell, interview by author, December 2005; and on reopening the border, Griffin, *Reaping the Whirlwind,* 207.

7. Ahmed talks with Taliban from Tim Judah, "The Taliban Papers," *Survival* 44 (Spring 2002): 70–71; Pickering, interview; Inderfurth, interview; Milam, interview; and Albright, interview.

8. Asif Farooqi, "Pakistan Chief Executive Outlines Policies, Strategies, Goals," *Business Recorder*, May 26, 2000, 1.

9. Pakistan ambassador quoted in Judah, "Taliban Papers," 74; camps list handover from UN report #A/55/393, paragraph 21, September 18, 2000.

10. Judah, "Taliban Papers," 73.

11. Papers recovered from Pakistan embassy after Taliban ouster were made available to author by senior Afghan government official in Kabul, July 2003.

12. UN report #A/55/633, November 20, 2000, paragraph 81; Vendrell, interview; and HRW, *Crisis of Impunity*, 23.

13. Strobe Talbott, interview by author, July 2003; Judah, "Taliban Papers," 70; author telephone interviews with Inderfurth, Milam, and Pickering, February 2006; and UN reports #A/54/918, June 16, 2000; #A/55/393, September 18, 2000; #A/55/633, November 20, 2000; and #A/55/907, April 19, 2001.

14. *9/11 Commission Report*, 66.

15. Estimate of wealth from *9/11 Commission Report*, 169–70; on training camps, *9/11 Commission Report*, 67; and 9/11 Commission Staff statement 15, www.9-11commission.gov/staff_statements/, 10.

16. Joint Inquiry of the Senate and House Select Intelligence Committees, December 12, 2002, 123.

17. Iran as transit route from Mojdeh, interview.

18. Ramzi's links with bin Laden, *9/11 Staff Statement 15*, 6; Muhammad's meeting with bin Laden, *9/11 Commission Report*, 146; and plan to crash airplanes, *9/11 Commission Report*, 153.

19. *9/11 Commission Report*, 149, 155.

20. *9/11 Commission Report*, 156.

21. On Mes Aynak, *9/11 Commission Report*, 157; "cleaning" visas, *9/11 Commission Report*, 169; and on Muhammad's schooling, *9/11 Commission Report*, 146.

22. Details of Hazmi and al Mihdhar's failure to prepare, *9/11 Staff Statement 16*, www.9-11commission.gov/staff_statements/; the story of the four men, *9/11 Staff Statement 16*, 11; and *9/11 Commission Report*, 159, 168.

23. *9/11 Staff Statement 15*, 9; Abu Jandal, interview by Al-Hammadi (parts 4 and 5), *Al Quds al Araby*.

24. *9/11 Commission Report*, 234; and *9/11 Staff Statement 16*, 6.

25. *9/11 Commission Report*, 152–53.

26. *9/11 Commission Report*, 155–56, 492fn44.

27. Details of boat in Patrick Sloyan, *Newsday*, March 4, 2001, 7; and description of the launch is from *ABC Prime Time*, January 18, 2001.

28. *9/11 Commission Report*, 159.

29. *9/11 Staff Statement 16*, 14; *9/11 Commission Report*, 491fn30.

30. Recovering the engine, *Prime Time*, January 18, 2001; and attempt to fire Nibras, *9/11 Commission Report*, 191.

31. Sloyan, *Newsday*.

32. Benjamin and Simon, *Sacred Terror*, 327–28.

33. Bin Laden disavowing disavowal, article in *Al Rai al Aam*, reported by AFP, November 13, 2000; response by a bin Laden associate in Islamabad, *News*, November 15, 2000, 18; and dispatch of bin Laden aides to other points, *9/11 Commission Report*, 191. The confidential letter from Pakistan ambassador in Kabul to Foreign Ministry (undated but approximately October 20, 2000) is based on a message sent by the CNN team to their Atlanta base; it is not clear how the Pakistani official gained access to the message. The letter is in the possession of the current Afghan government and was made available to author, Kabul, July 2003.

34. Inderfurth, interview; on O'Neill, investment banker Maurice Sonnenberg, vice chairman of the National Commission on Terrorism, telephone interview by author, November 13, 2006; and telephone interviews with former top Defense Intelligence Agency (DIA) official, who spoke on condition of anonymity, July 2003 and March 2004.

35. Author interviews with senior Afghan intelligence official, who spoke on condition of anonymity, Kabul, April and July 2003.

36. *9/11 Commission Report*, 192–94.

37. *9/11 Commission Report*, 196, 266.

38. www.navysite.de

39. Zinni, interview, January 2004; Franks's remark from Gen. Jehangir Karamat, interview by author, Lahore, Pakistan, April 2003; Franks's confirmation, Franks, e-mail message to author, February 2006; and Wolfowitz's view, *9/11 Commission Report*, 202.

40. Bin Laden disappointment, *9/11 Commission Report*, 191; content of video in Benjamin and Simon, *Sacred Terror*, 154–55.

41. Vendrell, interview.

42. Attacks on Darra Souf in HRW, *Crisis of Impunity*, 21. Sangcharak homeless in BBC report, January 29, 2000; other massacres in Gosfandi district from Afghanistan Justice Project, *Casting Shadows;* and *War Crimes and Crimes against Humanity 1978–2001*, www.afghanistanjusticeproject.org, 123. Patricia Gossman, a chief researcher for Human Rights Watch, was principal researcher for this report.

43. UN report #E/CN.4/2001/43, March 9, 2001, paragraph 43; Semple, interview, Islamabad, April 2003; and Eckhard Schiewek, interview by author, Kabul, July 2003. Mary Robinson declined repeated requests to be interviewed for this book.

44. Inderfurth, interview, January 2006; and congressional testimony in AFP Washington, July 20, 2000.

45. Anthony Davis, *Jane's Defense Weekly*, October 4, 2000; Griffin, *Reaping the Whirlwind*, 215; Massoud description of fighting from Payam-e Mojahed Web site in the Dari language, www.payamemujahid.com/radio/index.htm, August 24, 2000 (BBC summary); and details of final capture from UN report #A55/393, September 18, 2000, paragraph 29.

46. Casualties from UN report #A/55/633, November 20, 2000, paragraph 25; estimates of foreign fighter involvement from Davis, *Jane's Defense Weekly*, October 4, 2000, *Jane's Intelligence Review*, August 1, 2001, and e-mail message to author, January 2006; Khalili quote from "What the Papers Say," Moscow, Agency WPS, September 29, 2000; Massoud on foreigners from Payam-e Mojahed Web site; bin Laden role from author interview with Kabul businessman who asked not to be identified, July 2003.

47. HRW, *Crisis of Impunity*, 26fns105 and 106; UN observer's explanation from Schiewek, e-mail message to author, March 2004; and newspaper coverage of the fall of Taloqan from Nexis search, September 1–November 1, 2000.

9. Human Rights under Massoud and the Taliban

1. Albright on Massoud, Albright, interview; UN reports #A/55/633, November 20, 2000, and #A/56/681, December 6, 2001; Anthony Davis, *Jane's Intelligence Review*, October 1, 2001; and Davis e-mail to author, January 2006.

2. Afghanistan Justice Project, *War Crimes*, 82–88; Davis, e-mail message to author, January 2006; Vendrell, interview.

3. *UN Investigation Team for Afghanistan, Confidential Report to the High Commissioner for Human Rights,* September 30, 1999.

4. Kamal Hossain, *Report on the Situation of Human Rights in Afghanistan,* March 27, 2001, paragraph 7; former UN official Michael Semple, e-mail message to author, March 2003.

5. According to Schiess, the estimates of those killed ranged from 800 to 4,050. He cited the figure 2,000. *UN Investigation Team*, paragraph 73. The UN's special rapporteur for extrajudicial executions, Asma Jehangir, said, "Hundreds of Taliban were killed. It is reported that hundreds were taken into custody and executed in batches. Some bodies were bound together and hundreds thrown down the wells, possibly after being shot." *Report on Mission to Afghanistan, 13 to 23 October 2002*, E/CN.4/2003/3/Add.4 3, February 2003.

6. Paik, UN report #E/CN.4/1998/71, March 12, 1998; and O'Neill and Groves, OHCHR report, May 20–29, 1998, 11. A BBC report by Sadeq Saba on September 19, 1997, put the death toll at 70.

7. Schiess, *UN Investigation Team,* paragraph 91; and O'Neill and Groves, OHCHR report, May 20–29, 1998, 13.

8. Schiess, *in UN Investigation Team,* paragraph 94, quotes an interim report by the special rapporteur estimating that approximately three thousand Hazara were executed summarily, in their homes or in the street, during the first six days after the Taliban takeover of Mazar-i-Sharif. Also see chapter 6.

9. OHCHR report, E/CN.4/2001/43/Add.1, March 27, 2001.

10. Author interviews with Said Ali, religious student, Mohamed Riza, farmer, Nazer Hussein, pharmacist, all in Fuladi, Afghanistan, July 2003.

11. UN report #S1999/994, September 21, 1999, paragraphs 21 and 23, states that one hundred thousand civilians were displaced into the Panjshir Valley, and forty thousand more were displaced to Kabul.

12. "Civil War and Massacres, 2001," United Nations Assistance Mission in Afghanistan (UNAMA) map obtained by author; and destruction of dwellings from confidential UN report, cited by Mervyn Patterson, a former UN official, in e-mail message to author, March 2003.

13. Witness testimony cited in Médecins Sans Frontières (MSF), "Report on New Afghan Refugees' Situation in Gulshar Town, October 2000-January 2001," MSF, Paris, late 2001; also, Francois Calas, MSF Paris, e-mail messages to author, February and March 2003.

14. Afghanistan Justice Project, *War Crimes,* 120.

15. Norwegian Refugee Council, *Profile of Internal Displacement: Afghanistan,* (Geneva, April 2001), 8; Kamal Hossain (UN report #E/CN.4/2001/43, March 9, 2001, paragraph 25) estimated that at least five hundred thousand were displaced in the second half of 2000.

16. Afghanistan Justice Project, *War Crimes,* 120; UN report # E/CN.4/2001/43, March 9, 2001, paragraph 23; Amnesty International's March 2001 report estimated the number at three hundred, a total also cited by Pamela Constable (*Washington Post,* February 19, 2001) based on an HRW report and the *Post*'s own interviews in Pakistan.

17. "Summary Execution and Detention of Civilians, Khwagaghar, Takhar, January 2001," draft report by UN observers (in author's possession); also, Patterson, e-mail message.

18. No specific massacre was detailed in UN reports.

19. Paik in UN report #E/CN.4/1998/71, March 12, 1998; on the tortures at Qezelebad, see Rupert Colville, "Note for the File," December 15, 1997, in "Mass Killings and Atrocities in Northern Afghanistan," unpublished report; and Ali, interview by author, Kabul, March 2003.

20. Paik in UN report #E/CN.4/1998/71, March 12, 1998.

21. Reproduced with permission, Alex Klaits and Gulchin Gulmamadova-Klaits, *Love and War in Afghanistan* (New York: Seven Stories Press, 2005), 49–68.

22. Acting Governor Saed Tahir, interview by author, July 2003; on movement of the displaced, Norwegian Refugee Council, *Profile of Internal Displacement,* 40–41. Other quotes from author interviews with Said Ali and Mohamed Riza in Yakawlang and Bamiyan, July 2003.

23. *Interim Report of the Special Rapporteur . . . on the Situation of Human Rights in Afghanistan,* A/56/409, September 26, 2001, paragraphs 37–47.

24. Author interviews with painter Fata Sayed, Yakawlang, July 2003; Ibrahim, survivor of massacre, Bandi Amir, Afghanistan, July 2003; and Sayad Kazim, hospital nurse, witness to skinning alive and Pashtun dancing, Yakawlang, July 2003; HRW report, *Massacres of Hazaras in Afghanistan,* February 2001, contains a number of details of Ibrahim's account, including the date; and analysis of operational command contained in unpublished 2001 paper by then-UN official Michael Semple, quoted in Afghanistan Justice Project, *War Crimes,* 141.

25. Author interview with witness Allahdot, Bamiyan, July 2003.

26. Author interviews with Daoud Salaqat, Bamiyan, July 2003, on Omar's order, which was intercepted by the resistance; Saed Tahir, Yakawlang, July 2003, on "kill every living being"; Sayed Awaz Hashemi Nijad, a teacher, Yakawlang, July 2003, on Shazdula's instruction; and Ahmed Bahran, office of Wahdat leader Masoud Khalili, Kabul, July 2003, on Omar's order.

27. Afghanistance Justice Project, *War Crimes,* 150; UN report #A/56/409, September 26, 2001, paragraphs 54–57.

28. Faiq Abdul Samad, interview by author, Bamian, Afghannistan, July 2003.

29. Cases 121 and 123, December 23, 2000, MSF survey of families arriving at Mashad, Iran, made available to author by François Calas and Pierre Salingon of MSF, Paris; and Albright remarks, Albright, interview.

30. Displaced estimate from UN report #A/56/409, September 26, 2001, paragraph 63; Annan statement in UN report #A/56/681, December 6, 2001, paragraph 59; restrictions in UN report #A/55/346, August 30, 2000, paragraphs 56–57; and UN report #A/55/1028, August 17, 2001, paragraph 44.

31. BBC, December 8, 2000; January 6, 2001; and January 22, 2001; Institute for War and Peace reporting, May 1, 2001; situation report on emergency at the Tajik-Afghan border by UNHCR, February 5, 2001; report by Ravshan Kasimov, *Transitions Online,* March 8, 2001; shipment to Panjshir in UN Report # A/54/791, March 10, 2000, paragraph 29.

32. UN report #E/CN.4/2001/43, March 9, 2001, paragraphs 36–37 and appendix.

33. UN report #E/CN.4/2001/43, March 9, 2001, paragraph 24; also Rahimullah Yusufzai, *News,* February 2, 2001; and UN report # A/55/907, paragraph 34.

34. The deportations from Iran, even when they became more orderly, remain a source of embarrassment to UNHCR officials. Source for this data is a knowledgeable aid official, who was familiar with the situation in Afghanistan at the time but asked not to be identified by name, e-mail messages to author, February 2006.

35. Kathy Gannon, AP Jalozai, March 11, 2001, and April 28, 2001; Jemima Khan, *Sunday Telegraph,* April 8, 2001; and statement by Kamal Hossain, 57th Session of the Commission on Human Rights, Geneva, March 29, 2001.

36. On the drought, UN report #A/54/918, June 16, 2000, paragraphs 46–47; UN report #A/56/681, December 6, 2001, paragraph 59; on the Taliban failure to cope with its internal crisis, UN report #A/55/1028, August 17, 2001, paragraph 42; and on the international community response, UN report #A/55/346, August 30, 2000, paragraph 32, and *Report of the Secretary-General,* April 19, 2001.

10. Radicalization without Response

1. BBC, March 5, 1998; AFP Kabul, March 16, 1999; AFP Kabul, March 21, 1999; and BBC, February 5, 2002.

2. Amin, interview by author, Kabul, April 2003; Amin article, *Frontier Post,* August 11, 2001; Eckerd Schiewek, interview by author, Kabul, July 2003; and UN report #A/55/1028, August 17, 2001, paragraph 17.

3. Author interviews with Saeed Makhdoon Rahim, minister of culture, Kabul, April 2003; Hazrat Ahmad Amin Ismael Mujadiddi, Islamabad, April 2003; and Nilab Rahimi, Kabul, April 2003 and July 2003.

4. Author interviews with senior government official, who spoke on condition of anonymity, Kabul, April 2003; and Davis, "The Afghan Files," *Jane's Intelligence Review,* February 14–19, 2002.

5. BBC, August 17, 2000; Society for the Preservation of Afghanistan's Cultural Heritage (SPACH) bulletin, July 2001; Voice of Sharia radio, August 17, 2000, monitored by BBC; and Jamal quoted in Hewad, Afghan Taliban newspaper, May 11, 2000, monitored by BBC.

6. Bucherer-Dietschi, interview by author, Bubendorf, Switzerland, March 2003; Bucherer-Dietschi, telephone interview by author, February 2006; and Christian Manhart, telephone interview by author, December 2005.

7. On Hotak, Dupree interview, April 2003; Mojdeh, unpublished manuscript, 27.

8. Nancy Hatch Dupree, "Assaults on the Afghan Cultural Heritage" in *La Tutela del Matrimonio Culturale in Caso di Conflitto* (Naples: Massa Editore, University of Naples, 2003); and role of Turabi and Hassan, Mojdeh, unpublished manuscript, 26–27.

9. Author interview with Kabul businessman who was with Rabbani but spoke on condition of anonymity, April 2003.

10. Author telephone interviews with Manhart, December 2005, and French special envoy Pierre La France, January 2006.

11. Colonel Imam, interview conducted for author, March 2003.

12. Dupree, *La Tutela,* 300; Dupree, interview, April 2003; Hamid Mir, interview.

13. Dupree, *An Historical Guide to Afghanistan,* 2nd ed. (Kabul: Afghan Tourist Organization, 1977), 155–66.

14. Alony and Frey quotes from the film *The Giant Buddhas,* an excellent recounting of the demolition process (see www.giant-buddhas.com); and Jamal quote from AP Kabul, March 10, 2001.

15. Nancy Dupree, "Cultural Heritage and National Identity in Afghanistan," *Third World Quarterly* 23, no. 5 (2002): 986; and Bucherer-Dietschi, interview, February 2006.

16. Mojdeh, unpublished manuscript, 29.

17. Gulam Mohamed Hotak, interview by author, Jalrez, Afghanistan, March 2003.

18. Dupree quoted on Archeology Online News, March 2, 2001; and Arab recruiting from Mojdeh, unpublished manuscript, 30.

19. Anthony Davis, *Jane's Defense Weekly,* July 18, 2001, and *Jane's Intelligence Review,* August 1, 2001.

20. Mojdeh, unpublished manuscript, 22–24.

21. "Postcard from Peshawar," confidential cable, U.S. consulate, Peshawar, Pakistan, July 30, 2001, released by NSA.

22. UN report #A/55/1028, August 17, 2001, paragraph 53.

23. Mojdeh, unpublished manuscript, 22–23.

24. *9/11 Commission Report,* 197.

25. *9/11 Commission Report,* 201–14.

26. Wali Massoud, interview by author, London, January 2004; Schroen, interview; AFP Paris, Strasbourg and Brussels, April 3–7, 2001; and Massoud warning in Craig Pyes and William C. Rempel, "Report of the Global Terror Network behind 9/11" (*Los Angeles Times,* December 16, 2001).

27. Massoud remarks were taped by Otilie English, a Washington-based lobbyist for Massoud, who helped arrange Krakowski's trip.

28. Krakowski, telephone interview by author, November 2003.

29. UN report #A/55/1028, August 17, 2001, paragraphs 35–36; Eckert Schiewek, UN official in northern Afghanistan at the time, interview by author, March 2003.

30. *9/11 Commission Report,* 225–46.

31. *9/11 Commission Report,* 254–58. Assessment of lack of disclosure based on Nexis search of all publications for references to bin Laden from April through June 2001.

32. de Borchgrave, telephone interview by author, January 2004; and UPI Kandahar, June 14, 2001.

33. Niles Latham and Andy Soltis, "War Chant: Bin Laden Urges 'Blood, Blood, and Destruction,'" *New York Post,* June 20, 2001; "Bin Laden Terror Video," *Scotsman,* June 21, 2001; and AP Sana'a, Yemen, June 19, 2001.

34. AP Cairo, June 24, 2001; Bergen, *Osama,* 284–85; Pamela Constable, "U.S. refuses to Confirm Taliban Warning, but Says bin Laden Must Be Ejected," *Washington Post,* July 10, 2001; Atyani, e-mail message to author, February 2006.

35. *9/11 Commission Report,* 257–59.

36. Mojdeh, unpublished manuscript, 52–53.

37. Pyes and Rempel, "Global Terror Network," *Los Angeles Times;* and de Borchgrave, interview.

38. *9/11 Commission Report,* 252.

39. Masoud Khalili, interview by author, New Delhi, June 2004.

40. Pyes and Rempel, "Global Terror Network," *Los Angeles Times.*

41. Schiewek, interview.

Epilogue

1. James Woolsey, telephone interview by author, March 2006.

2. Albright, interview; Albright, *Madame Secretary,* 369–70; Pickering, interview; Mujaddidi, interview by author, Islamabad, April 2003; Inderfurth, interview; Milam, interview; and Burns, telephone interview by author, July 2003.

Index

women's rights, suppression of *(cont.)*
  extension to foreign aid workers,
    230
  Feminist Majority's protest
    against, 174–176, 176*n,* 187
  news focus on, 131
  U.S. denunciation of, 113–114,
    149
Woolsey, James, 255, 255*n,* 256
World Food Program, 232*n*
World Islamic Front for Jihad against
  the Jews and Crusaders, 97
World Trade Center bombing, 88,
  91, 209

Yakowlang, 177, 177*n,* 224, 226, 228
Yandarbiyev, Zelimkhan, 193
Yeltsin, Boris, 33, 193, 199
Yemen, 35, 85
  terrorist attacks in, 87, 192, 196–
    197, 206, 211 (*See also* USS
    Cole attack)

Yoldash, Taher (Qari Taher Jan), 242
Yoldashov, Taher, 190–191
Yousef, Ramzi, 91, 206
Yugoslavia, 13, 81, 119, 162, 257
Yusufzai, Rahimullah, 92, 129, 144,
  148, 157, 160, 198*n,* 212

Zaeef, Abdul Salam, 251
Zahir Shah, King, 20, 41
Zakiri, Amir Maulana Abdullah,
  148*n*
zarbati, 42
Zarb-i-Momen (Muslim Power),
  238*n,* 240
Zargar, Mushtaq Ahmad, 192
Zawahiri, Ayman al, 84, 86, 122,
  144, 239
Zhawar complex, 144
Ziauddin, Khwaja, 184–185
Zia-ul-Haq, Muhammad, 11, 20, 26
Zinni, Anthony, 165, 183, 197, 214
Zubaydah, Abu, 191, 196, 20

About the Author

ROY GUTMAN has been a foreign affairs journalist for nearly four decades. Currently the foreign editor for McClatchy newspapers, he spent more than twenty years at *Newsday,* twelve at Reuters, and had briefer stints at *Newsweek* and UPI. While *Newsday* Europe correspondent, his reports on "ethnic cleansing" in Bosnia-Herzegovina, including the first documented accounts of Serb-run concentration camps, won the Pulitzer Prize for international reporting in 1993, the George Polk Award for foreign reporting, the Selden Ring Award for investigative reporting, the Hal Boyle award of the Overseas Press Club, the Heywood Broun Award of the Newspaper Guild, a special Human Rights in Media award of the International League for Human Rights, and other honors. While at Newsweek, he was a cowinner of the Edgar Allan Poe award of the White House Correspondents' Association in 2002 and the National Headliners First Prize for Magazines and the Society of Publishers in Asia awards for excellence in magazines and reporting in 2003. He is the author of *Banana Diplomacy* (1988) and *A Witness to Genocide* (1993) and coeditor, with David Rieff and Anthony Dworkin, of *Crimes of War: What the Public Should Know* (second edition, 2007). He lives with his wife and daughter in McLean, Virginia.

About the Institute

The United States Institute of Peace is an independent, nonpartisan, national institution established and funded by Congress. Its goals are to help prevent and resolve violent conflicts, promote post-conflict stability and development, and increase peacebuilding capacity, tools, and intellectual capital worldwide. The Institute does this by empowering others with knowledge, skills, and resources, as well as by directly engaging in peacebuilding efforts around the globe.

Chairman of the Board: J. Robinson West
Vice Chairman: María Otero
President: Richard H. Solomon
Executive Vice President: Patricia Powers Thomson
Vice President: Charles E. Nelson

Board of Directors

J. Robinson West (Chair), Chairman, PFC Energy, Washington, D.C.

María Otero (Vice Chairman), President, ACCION International, Boston, Mass.

Holly J. Burkhalter, Vice President, Government Affairs, International Justice Mission, Washington, D.C.

Anne H. Cahn, Former Scholar in Residence, American University, Washington, D.C.

Chester A. Crocker, James R. Schlesinger Professor of Strategic Studies, School of Foreign Service, Georgetown University, Washington, D.C.

Laurie S. Fulton, Partner, Williams and Connolly, Washington, D.C.

Charles Horner, Senior Fellow, Hudson Institute, Washington, D.C.

Kathleen Martinez, Executive Director, World Institute on Disability, Oakland, CA

George E. Moose, Adjunct Professor of Practice, The George Washington University, Washington, D.C.

Jeremy A. Rabkin, Professor of Law, George Mason University, Fairfax, Va.

Ron Silver, Actor, Producer, Director, Primparous Productions, Inc., New York, NY

Judy Van Rest, Executive Vice President, International Republican Institute, Washington, D.C.

Members ex officio

Robert M. Gates, Secretary of Defense

Condoleezza Rice, Secretary of State

Richard H. Solomon, President, United States Institute of Peace (nonvoting)

Frances C. Wilson, Lieutenant General, U.S. Marine Corps; President, National Defense University

How We Missed the Story

This book is set in Adobe Caslon; the display type is Clearface Gothic. Katharine Moore designed the book's cover and the interior. Helene Y. Redmond made up the pages. The text was copyedited and proofread by EEI Communications. The index was prepared by Mary Coe. The book's editor was Kurt Volkan.